TEACHING
IN THE EARLY YEARS

PRENTICE-HALL SERIES IN EARLY CHILDHOOD

Bernard Spodek, *editor*

SECOND EDITION

TEACHING IN THE EARLY YEARS

BERNARD SPODEK

Professor of Early Childhood Education
University of Illinois

PRENTICE-HALL, INC., ENGLEWOOD CLIFFS, NEW JERSEY 07632

Library of Congress Cataloging in Publication Data

SPODEK, BERNARD.
   Teaching in the early years.

   (Prentice-Hall series in early childhood)
   Bibliography: p.
   Includes index.
   1. Education, Primary. I. Title.
LB1523.S66 1978   372.21   77-14036
ISBN 0-13-892562-3

*To Esther Yin-ling and Jonathan Chou and to their teachers,
past, present, and future.*

10 9 8 7 6 5 4 3 2 1

PRENTICE-HALL INTERNATIONAL, INC., *London*
PRENTICE-HALL OF AUSTRALIA PTY. LIMITED, *Sydney*
PRENTICE-HALL OF CANADA, LTD., *Toronto*
PRENTICE-HALL OF INDIA PRIVATE LIMITED, *New Delhi*
PRENTICE-HALL OF JAPAN, INC., *Tokyo*
PRENTICE-HALL OF SOUTHEAST ASIA PTE. LTD., *Singapore*
WHITEHALL BOOKS LIMITED, *Wellington, New Zealand*

CONTENTS

PREFACE

It is heartening in many ways to be able to write a preface to the second edition of this book. That the first edition was well enough received by the field to warrant a revision is satisfying. That the field of early childhood education is vital and dynamic enough to warrant a revision is equally satisfying. This edition does not present a basic change in point of view from the first edition. Additions were made to bring the material up to date and to make it more understandable and more useful. New ideas, new evidence, and new concerns are addressed here. Material that is less relevant or less current now than at the time of first writing has been deleted.

This book is addressed to teachers and to those who are preparing to be teachers of young children. Although eclectic in its foundation, the approach suggested here is not a conglomerate of all the approaches available in early childhood education today. Rather it is based upon a judgment of what can be done with children, selecting from educational points of view that fit within a consistent framework.

Early childhood education is a unified field, encompassing the nursery, kindergarten, and primary years. Although levels may be separated administratively, children do not change from year to year to fit the expectations of educational grade levels. Change that does occur is gradual and developmental, with differences in rates of change among individual children. This change is one of the assumptions upon which this book is based. Other assumptions relate to the nature of early childhood curriculum and the role of the teacher.

Curriculum comes from many sources. Values are an important base of curriculum, as is understanding how children grow and learn.

The various subject areas provide yet another source. The state of the art of education must also be recognized as an important source, determining both possibilities for and limitations of education for young children. Finally, the tradition of the field becomes an important source of classroom practice. The teacher is viewed here as more than just a participant in classroom activities. She is a decision maker whose actions— even prior to her entrance into the classroom—help determine what her students will learn.

This book is divided into three parts. The first three chapters provide the foundation for a look at curriculum and teaching in the early years. The second section, chapters 4 through 10, deals with the specific subject areas that make up the school program. Each chapter is divided into two sections, one reviewing what we know about the particular area of the curriculum and one suggesting the content for school programs and the ways this might be approached. Play is treated as a legitimate part of the school program.

The final portion of the book deals with the teacher's other educational concerns: classroom organization, techniques of working with parents and children, and the evaluation of education.

Two chapters relate to children with special educational needs. The concern for identifying and educating children with handicapping conditions as early as possible, and for providing this education in the least restrictive environment, has motivated the inclusion of the first of these chapters. The second chapter addresses the needs of culturally diverse young children who, like the handicapped, may not fit in the educational "mainstream."

An apology is in order to all my male colleagues in the field. Throughout the text, the pronoun *she* is used when referring to the teacher. The decision to use this pronoun is based upon the observation that most teachers of young children are women. No slight is intended to the increasing number of men who, like myself, have found their way into the field of early childhood education.[1] Nor is any slight intended by the use of the pronoun *he* when referring to children. Both boys and girls make up the population of children in their early years with whom this book is concerned. The single male pronoun is used to avoid confusion with references to teachers.

---

[1] In 1976 D. Bruce Gardner, then president of the National Association for the Education of Young Children, surveyed the group's membership. Of the members sampled, 92.1 percent were female, 6.3 percent were male, and 1.8 percent failed to note their sex. This association is the largest one representing the field of early childhood education. Thus, the survey confirms the observation that the field continues to be staffed predominantly by females.

A number of acknowledgments are also in order. I want to thank the editors of *Young Children* for permission to use, in modified form, material that previously appeared in that journal. I also wish to acknowledge my debt to the many teachers and children with whom I have worked over the past two decades. The ideas expressed here have grown out of interaction with many people who have influenced me as I hope that I have been an influence upon them. I should like to thank a number of my colleagues, friends, and students, especially Rhoda Becher, Betty Rowen, Olivia Saracho, Ann Sartin, Jeanne Morris, and James Hoot. Nancy Perkins and Peggy Harrison helped with the final preparation of the revision.

Finally, and most important, I want to acknowledge the encouragement, love, and support I have received and continue to receive from my wife, Prudence.

James L. Hoot

CHAPTER ONE

TEACHING

A roomful of children in the early years of school presents an exciting picture. Children may be involved in a number of activities that are all available at the same time. Many different materials may be in use and activities will continually shift as children move through the daily program. Groups of children will form and reform and individuals may continually vie for the attention of the teacher.

Whether standing in front of the classroom commanding the attention of all the children or sitting quietly in a corner working with a small group, the teacher is central to all activity. Directly or indirectly, she controls much of the activity and is responsible for all that occurs to these children during school. She must respond to their many needs as they become apparent during the day. She must assure purposeful activities that produce educational benefit for the children.

The teacher must perform many different tasks. She functions as lecturer, storyteller, group discussion leader, traffic director, mediator of conflicts, psychological diagnostician, custodian, assigner of academic work, and file clerk as she operates in her multifaceted role. Most important are the times when she directly interacts with children. The interactions may be verbal, as in a discussion, or behavioral, as when she places her arm around a child's shoulders or puts a child on her knee. The interactions may be gross, like redirecting a child from one part of the room to another, or subtle, such as giving a child a "knowing look."

Many things determine what teachers do in a classroom. Even with the limited age range of early childhood education—between three and eight years as defined in this book—different ages demand different responses from the teacher. Teaching in a day care center may require a greater degree of concern for the physical well-being of a child than teaching in a half-day nursery school. In addition, institutional requirements may often involve teachers in a range of teaching activities that have nothing directly to do with the children's learning. Thus, a teacher's duties vary according to place and time, because of the nature of the educational institution and its educational program. More will be said about these in the next two chapters.

READINESS FOR TEACHING

What does it take to become a teacher of children in their early years? Few people are born with a desire to teach young children or with the necessary competencies. Yet both desire and competencies are requirements for successful teaching. The motives that cause people to teach young children may vary greatly and are often personal. But there are other important requisites to teaching.

Over the years early childhood educators have stressed different requirements for teachers of young children. Millie Almy and Agnes Snyder suggested that early childhood teachers need physical stamina, world-mindedness, an understanding of human development, a respect for personality, and a scientific spirit.[1] Others, like Sarah Lou Leeper, have focused on personal qualities such as patience, warmth, kindness, security, and a love of children.[2]

More recently, educators have attempted to specify requirements for early childhood personnel in terms of observable behaviors. The Child Development Associate program was designed to credential early childhood workers based upon an assessment of classroom performance. Rather than specify particular observable behaviors, the Child Development Associate Consortium has developed a set of six general areas of competence in which assessors make judgments. These areas are defined as follows:

1. Establishes and maintains a safe and healthy learning environment
2. Advances physical and intellectual competence
3. Builds positive self-concept and individual strength

[1] Millie Almy and Agnes Snyder, "The Staff and Its Preparation," *Early Childhood Education.* 46th Yearbook of the National Society for the Study of Education, Part II (Chicago: University of Chicago Press, 1947), pp. 224–46.

[2] Sarah Lou Leeper, *Nursery Schools and Kindergarten* (Washington, D.C.: National Education Association, 1968).

4. Promotes positive functioning of children and adults in a group
5. Brings about optimal coordination of home and center child-rearing practices and expectations
6. Carries out supplementary responsibilities related to children's programs.[3]

The Child Development Associate Credential is not a teaching certificate. States certify teachers, each using its own criteria. All states certify primary teachers, often with an elementary school teaching certificate. Forty-nine states offer certificates for kindergarten teachers, while fewer states certify teachers of three- and four-year-olds.[4] In many states certification is required only for teachers who work within public school systems. Since the majority of nursery schools and day care centers are not within these systems, other criteria for assessing teacher competence might prevail. In most states, an agency other than the Office of Education licenses nursery schools and day care centers. Presently, a great range of requirements exists from state to state. A state agency might require a college degree in early childhood education and a teaching certificate, only graduation from high school, or some limited amount of post high school education and early childhood teacher training.

Many teachers of young children are prepared in colleges and universities, in either early childhood education or child development programs. Many junior colleges also offer associate degrees or one-year programs in child development or early childhood education for persons who wish to work in nursery schools, day care centers, or child development centers.

While such programs vary in depth and breadth, the majority meet a general set of requirements for content. Course work is generally required in human growth and development, in methods and curriculum, and in the history, theory, and philosophy of early childhood education. A general education background is also a normal expectation, although this might be constituted differently in different programs. Courses in health, nutrition, parent education, or family relations might also be required. Each program has a requirement for direct experience with children, either in a student teaching experience, a practicum, or an internship.

---

[3] Evangeline H. Ward and the CDA staff, "The Child Development Associate Consortium's Assessment System," *Young Children,* 31, no. 4 (May 1976), 244–54.

[4] Elaine Goldsmith, "Certification for Teachers of Young Children," *NAEYC Affiliate,* 2, no. 2 (December 1975), 2–3.

While official descriptions vary, they generally expect the person preparing to teach young children to have a knowledge of how young children develop and how they learn, and of the families and culture in which they are reared. Knowledge of educational programs and methods of teaching young children is important. Future teachers should be prepared to relate theory to practice and they should be able to perform well in a classroom setting. Persons preparing to teach special populations of young children will be expected to master additional skills and knowledge.

We still do not know whether one program of education is better for young children than the others. Similarly, we do not know if one way of preparing teachers to work with young children is better than the others. This variety in programs should allow for a range of styles and preferences in emphases and in sequencing of experiences.

TEACHING INTERACTIONS

While there are many functions in the role of the early childhood teacher, persons considering the role often focus almost entirely on the teacher interacting with young children. Teacher-child interactions serve many purposes. They are used to further instruction and to provide information about the child as well as to communicate emotional support and assurance.

The classroom behavior of teachers, however, is not all there is to teaching—it may represent the least rational aspects. Much of the activity of teaching occurs away from children. This activity includes the determination of what to teach; the selection, procurement, and organization of materials and equipment for teaching; the evaluation of learning; and the recording and reporting of children's progress.

Philip Jackson has differentiated between two modes of teaching behavior—*preactive* teaching and *interactive* teaching:

> Preactive behavior is more or less deliberate. Teachers, when grading exams, planning a lesson, or deciding what to do about a particularly difficult student, tend to ponder the matter, to weigh evidence, to hypothesize about the possible outcomes of a certain action. During these moments teachers often resemble, albeit crudely, the stereotype of the problem solver, the decision maker, the hypothesis tester, the inquirer. At such times teaching looks like a highly rational process.
>
> . . . In the interactive setting the teacher's behavior is more or less spontaneous. When students are in front of him, and the fat

James L. Hoot

is in the fire, so to speak, the teacher tends to do what he *feels*, or *knows*, rather than what he *thinks*, is right.[5]

Jackson identifies two cognitive styles, a feeling and an inquiring style. He suggests that the differences in teachers' cognitive styles that are evident in preactive and interactive teaching behavior stem from two conditions of the interactive phase of teaching: the fact that the students place controls on what the teacher does, and the rapid pace of events that occur in the classroom. The teacher is to a great extent reacting to the children in her class. The children control the behavior of the teacher by forcing certain responses which are required by their initial action. The control is not necessarily conscious. Jackson suggests that there are approximately one thousand changes in the teacher's focus of concern that take place during the day—far too many to be able to handle individually in a rational, problem-solving manner. The teacher is responding to the flow of events all during the school day, without time to think through each response, and the style of behavior required is more often intuitive than analytic.

[5] Philip W. Jackson, "The Way Teaching Is," in *The Way Teaching Is* (Washington, D.C.: Association for Supervision and Curriculum Development, 1966), p. 13.

Understanding the intuitive nature of interactive teaching helps to explain why this form of teaching is so resistant to change, especially through the tactics used in most teacher-education programs. Courses, conferences, and workshops are verbally oriented activities that focus primarily on the language of teaching. These activities can help set the rational basis for the profession, but do not extend the repertoire of behaviors. It is the more practice-oriented teacher education activities such as classroom participation, microteaching, or student teaching that seem to have a better chance of changing the interactive behavior of teaching.

The behavior of teachers, however, does have a rational basis. How one behaves is a function of how one feels he ought to behave, and what one feels is right cannot be fully separated from what one thinks is right. Teachers' behaviors go hand in hand with teachers' beliefs. Perhaps the process of teacher education needs to include, to some extent, the training of intuition based upon rational thought.

A book such as this must address itself to the more rational aspects of teaching behavior, assuming that a discussion about teaching will affect not only the thoughts of teachers but ultimately their behavior as well. It is based upon the assumption that the professional actions of teachers are manifest primarily in the decision-making process during the time children are in the presence of teachers as well as when teachers are operating alone. It is, as a matter of fact, the decision-making process that is at the heart of the professional behavior of teachers.

THE ROLE OF THE TEACHER

The teacher of young children plays a complex role of many dimensions. These facets of the teaching role and the way in which they are acted out are responses to the school situation and its expectations, the expectation of the profession, and the expectations of the teacher herself. Different schools set their own expectations for teachers. Teachers may be involved in all the major decisions relating to children and what they learn, or be told what to do. In some schools great stress is placed upon *caring* for children; in others, only *instruction* is considered important. Whether a range of teaching styles is encouraged varies among schools.

In all situations, to a greater or lesser extent, teachers seem to serve a nurturant role, an instructional role, a relational role, and a decision-making role. Sometimes the teacher must clearly separate the professional role from all other roles she plays as a person. In other situations, the personal qualities of the individual are allowed to transcend the role dimensions. In every case, what a teacher does is a function both of what she wishes to do and of what the setting requires of her. A teacher should be aware of these many role dimensions.

TEACHING AS NURTURANCE

Young children are relatively dependent upon the adults in their environment for their health care and safety. Teaching in the early years requires one to accept the nurturant role of the early childhood educator. It has long been evident that a child cannot learn if he is hungry, ill, frightened, or uncomfortable. The teacher and the school need to be concerned with the noninstructional elements that lead to these conditions. From its inception, the nursery school provided for the care of children. Day care centers were specifically designed to provide this care. Kindergartens and elementary schools are accepting responsibility for caring elements as well, as they include feeding breakfast and lunch to children and providing various screening tests to identify physical problems. Often the responsibility for this care falls on the classroom teacher.

Teachers of young children have to go beyond these basic nurturing responsibilities. They need to provide love and comfort. They may,

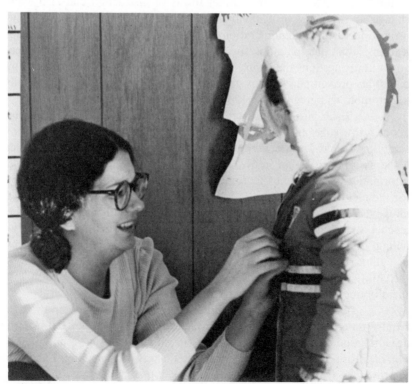

James L. Hoot

in a limited sense, serve as a parent substitute. They may even be called upon to toilet train a child. All these are important and reasonable educational requirements.

However, a problem is evident when the nurturing acts become the only interests of the teacher. It is easy to become aware of the children's needs for nurturing, and in some circumstances they cry out for response. They should never be ignored. Some of the other educational needs of children are less apparent and thus more easily overlooked. When the teacher's nurturant role becomes the only role dimension that is manifest, the program is apt to be more a child-minding operation than an educational endeavor. This shortchanges children.

TEACHING AS INSTRUCTION

When we think of teaching, what usually comes to mind is the instructional role of the teacher. The conventional view of a teacher is of a person who transmits knowledge to others by talking. The use of books, displays, or audio-visual devices is another way of telling something to children. Telling and demonstrating comprise one form of instruction— a direct form. Other, more indirect forms of instruction can also elicit changes in responses or behavior without giving specific directions in the form of lectures or demonstrations. Indirect instruction includes creating learning situations, planning for encounters with instructional resources, and asking questions that cause the child to think through his conclusions or test his present perceptions of reality. These techniques cause the child to act upon his perceived world to create his own knowledge.

Each view of instruction is based upon a set of assumptions about knowledge and schools that often remain unexamined. One assumption is that knowledge consists of a body of facts and information to be assimilated by an individual who has read or heard the facts and information. The teacher must determine what knowledge is important for the children in her class. (That decision may have been made for her already; this is one of the policy decisions discussed later.) Then the teacher "tells" the children what they must know through lectures, storytelling, or demonstrations, as well as through more sophisticated forms of telling such as films, sound recordings, or television. Over the years the child attends school, he accumulates more facts and information and therefore becomes more knowledgeable.

Other views of education and the development of knowledge require different forms of instruction. Knowledge is not the result of an accumulation of facts and information but rather the result of an integration of information within some structure that gives it meaning. Facts are the raw data from which knowledge is developed, and as raw data, they may be easily discarded, once used. To create knowledge, a person, whether adult or young child, must do something to these facts; he must become an active seeker and creator of knowledge. Passively receiving information is not enough to make the child a true learner.

The concept of the teacher as instructor is adequate for an understanding of only one of her roles. It represents part of the whole picture.

TEACHING AS RELATING

While some educators view the instructional role of the teacher as crucial, others view the relational aspect of teaching as being of primary importance. The teacher is continually interacting with children during the school day, and the quality of these interactions may be more important than the specific instructional practices.

Arthur Combs defines the effective teacher as "a unique human being who has learned to use himself effectively and efficiently to carry out his own and society's purposes in the education of others."[6] The use of oneself in carrying out the purposes of education includes professional competency, but it goes beyond that. It requires that the teacher's total self, the personal side as well as the professional side, be involved in the educational process. Developing ways of relating to and interacting with people is an important part of becoming a teacher.

In addition to providing instruction, the teacher serves as a guide and a helper to the children. She must create an atmosphere in the classroom in which children gain a sense of trust. The teacher helps the child feel secure as a learner and a person, guides him in making decisions, and provides a rich environment for learning.

Each teacher brings a set of values to a classroom. These values help determine what she considers important and how she deals with individual children. They even determine her selection and use of material and classroom arrangement. Ultimately, they will influence the values of the children. The value aspects of the program are often described as "caught rather than taught" because of the personal way in which they are expressed and transmitted.

Above all, the teacher provides warmth and support for the children. The relationship established in the classroom is not based on achievement alone. Children are accepted as they are—total human beings with strengths and weaknesses. Through her personal relationship with the child, the teacher helps him to grow.

[6] Arthur W. Combs, *The Professional Education of Teachers* (Boston: Allyn & Bacon, 1965), p. 9.

Although teachers can be taught appropriate behaviors for classroom settings, the relational aspects of teaching are not based upon any set of teacher actions; what is important is that the teacher manifest her personality in an authentic way. Teacher-training programs concerned with the teacher as a person must go beyond conventional courses in methods and foundations of education; they must help students explore the meaning that education and teaching have for them and help them understand the nature of their relationships with others.

TEACHING AS DECISION MAKING

With the increased use of teacher aides and assistants, educators have been hard-pressed to differentiate the role of the professional from that of the paraprofessional. An analogy can be drawn between the roles of teacher and doctor. Years back, if one went to a physician's office for an examination, the doctor performed the entire examination. Today, a number of technicians and paraprofessionals help a physician in an examination. They may draw blood for tests, administer electrocardiograms, take case histories, and do other tasks that were formerly the responsibility of the doctor. But they are not doctors. The doctor reserves for himself the diagnostic function, often basing his diagnosis

Bernard Spodek

upon the information supplied by others. He maintains a prescriptive function, although the prescription of drugs or treatment may be administered by others. He also performs some highly skilled technical functions, such as surgery.

In many cases teacher aides and assistants act almost as surrogate teachers. The major difference between professional and paraprofessional lies not in the kinds of interactions that take place between the adult and the children, but rather in the responsibility taken for these actions. The paraprofessional acts, in many ways, as an extension of the teacher, who has ultimate responsibility for the class and who must make the major decisions about classroom activity. Teachers, as decision makers, continue in the other described roles. The decision-making role, however, becomes central to the professional act. Some of these decisions are made outside the class; many, however, must be made on the spot, in reaction to specific situations.

How does the teacher respond to immediate situations? She may, for example, decide that a group reading situation is appropriate at a particular time. A host of decisions follow. She may ask herself the following questions:

Should I read or tell a story?

Which book should I select?

Should the story precede or follow the cleanup from the prior period of activity?

Should all the children be expected to attend to the story, or only a few, with alternative activities available?

Should the children sit on chairs, on the floor in a semicircle, or simply informally grouped around me?

Should I show the pictures from the book as I read?

If a child is disruptive, should I interrupt the reading to focus on him, or ignore him until I have finished?

If the class seems restless, should I stop reading momentarily, lead the class in a few finger-plays, and then continue? Should I stop the activity and move on to something else, or ignore their behavior?

Should I ask the children questions about the content of the story upon its completion to test what they have learned, or should I simply let the story "sink in"?

Should I relate the story to other activities of the day, or allow the experience to remain isolated?

How should I move the children on to the next activity?

Within a simple five-minute segment of the school day the teacher may have had to make a dozen decisions. Multiply this by the sixty or more five-minute periods that might confront the teacher during the day to realize the complexity of the process of any teaching decision.

Because teachers make multiple decisions does not mean that they all are actively and consciously involved in a rational decision-making process. Roger Farr and Virginia Brown suggest that most instructional decisions are made by forfeit. The teacher does not recognize that a decision can be made or is not aware of possible alternatives and hence gives up the decision by default, often leading to a continuation of existing practice.[7]

A FRAMEWORK FOR ANALYZING
DECISION MAKING

What are the legitimate bases for teacher decision making? Unfortunately, little study has been done on the decision-making process in education. What few studies there are of the teaching process have focused on the *behavior* of teachers, the *reasons* for the behavior often being assumed. Teachers are not robots, however. Their behavior must be seen as a selection of possible alternative behaviors from a range of options.

The decisions that teachers make can be roughly organized into three categories: policy decisions, institutional decisions, and technical decisions. Policy decisions relate generally to the setting of goals for education. Institutional decisions concern the maintenance of the school. Technical decisions relate to the "nuts and bolts" activities of the teacher as she carries out educational policies.

POLICY DECISIONS

Policy decisions, relating to the goals and purposes of education, may be highly abstract or may be more specific in nature. Goals of instruction are usually derived from statements of *values* as well as from *educational ideologies*. Values are statements about the worth of things and their desirability, often in societal terms. These may relate to concepts of the "good life" that a community holds.

An ideology refers to a belief. It is possible to hold specific beliefs about the nature of childhood, the role of the teacher, and the purposes of schools that are independent of values but are basic to the

---

[7] Roger Farr and Virginia Brown, "Evaluation and Decision-making," *Reading Teacher,* 24 (January 1971), 341–42.

policy decisions made about education. Although a particular goal might be considered worthy in its own right, it may be viewed as inappropriate for the school or for a specific level of childhood. Teachers might consider it appropriate to support autonomous learning in children, but their ideology could lead them to believe that young children are necessarily dependent on adults and that opportunities for autonomous behavior should therefore be postponed until later in the child's life.

Historically, teachers in American schools have had little involvement in policy decisions. While for decades educational philosophers debated the purposes of school and the goals of education, the classroom teacher was always well-removed from the establishment of policy for a particular school or school system. Policy was made "downtown" to be adhered to by teachers. Educational policy was viewed as being outside the "professional" sphere.

In school systems, policy is the domain of the board of education, a group of knowledgeable laypeople who speak for the community. Even community nursery schools, outside the body of public education, often have governing boards independent of teacher or administrator to set policy. The Head Start program, noted for its parent and community involvement, also requires the establishment of local policy advisory boards.

The relationship of the professional to policy decision making is tenuous. The professional educator has knowledge of educational alternatives and is often in the position to weigh the possible outcomes of policy decisions. His role, however, is usually considered advisory—helping lay people see possible consequences of their decisions. However, by controlling the lay person's access to information he can significantly influence policy decisions.

Although policy decisions in school have been considered outside the teacher's domain, teachers have nevertheless become involved. In many school systems, they have been involved with curriculum committees that recommend educational policy for the school, determining the goals of instruction in each program area, and formulating the general strategies by which these goals are to be achieved. These committees are also charged with recommending the materials to be used in helping the children achieve these goals. Although the work of such committees must have the approval of lay authorities, such approval is often more ceremonial than real.

Teachers have also involved themselves in policy decisions on a less organized basis. They have a major influence in seeing that policies are carried out. Policy may be changed by the nature of its administration. A school may have a specific policy for promotion and retention, but this remains valid only as long as the teachers adhere to it. If, for example, specific criteria for promotion are stated but teachers refuse to use them, the actual school policy may be quite different from the stated one.

INSTITUTIONAL DECISIONS

Institutional decisions have no direct bearing on the achievement of educational goals, but rather are concerned with the maintenance of the school itself. Many decisions about staffing and grouping are institutional ones, for they cannot be considered in terms of the achievement of educational goals.

Similarly, classroom teachers make decisions about children that have little to do with the achievement of educational goals directly but are directed toward the maintenance of the school as an institution. The teacher may demand that children remain quiet in classrooms, stay in their own seats, and speak only when spoken to. Such demands can only be related to policy if the policy of the school is the establishment of conformity in children. This is seldom the case. These decisions, however, can be understood in terms of the maintenance of order, which is deemed necessary for the operation of even the school in which conformity is not valued. Many classroom decisions that teachers make are institutional in nature. Harry Gracey has suggested that many of the activities of the kindergarten are designed primarily to teach children appropriate student responses rather than to prepare them for academic or intellectual pursuits.[8]

The need to make institutional decisions is not good or bad in itself. When the institutional decisions conflict with the instructional goals of a program, however, these goals may be distorted or completely subverted. Educational institutions need to be maintained as vehicles for the achievement of educational goals. Too often, however, institutions develop a life of their own and care must be taken that the institutional decisions are not in conflict with the policy decisions of the school.

TECHNICAL DECISIONS

Technical decisions relate to the translation of policy into classroom activity and to the development of educational experiences that will help achieve goals determined in educational policy. Long- and short-range classroom planning belongs at this level of decision making, as does the selection and use of educational resources.

---

[8] Harry L. Gracey, "Learning the Student Role: Kindergarten as Academic Boot Camp," in *Readings in Introductory Sociology,* eds. Dennis W. Wrong and Harry L. Gracey (New York: Macmillan, 1967), pp. 288–99.

Technical decisions have to do with matching educational resources and tasks to the educational needs of children. This suggests a diagnostic model of teaching. The teacher uses her knowledge and skill to elicit information about children. She must be able to match methods and materials to children in order to achieve goals. This requires that she have a range of techniques and materials available so she may effect the match. She may find she can be more effective with some methods than others, and depend heavily on a few that reflect her style. Flexibility and sensitivity are still needed.

The teacher must know each child as a person and be aware of his learning abilities and style of behavior. She is then in a position to make differentiated educational decisions concerning individuals, such as the educational activities in which they should be involved, the social interactions that should be supported, or the amount of structure in which activities should be framed.

A knowledge of alternative ways of achieving policy goals is important if the teacher is to operate in a diagnostic fashion. While all children may ultimately be expected to achieve the same goals, they may be starting from different positions based upon levels of maturity or varied background experiences. One approach to learning might be more appropriate for one child than another because of these reasons, or even because of different personal styles.

Finally, the teacher must develop means of assessing the consequences of school activities for individuals. Judgments made about earlier experiences should be used as the basis for providing later experiences. Such decisions require not only a knowledge of the child and the curriculum but also a knowledge of the teaching field. The teacher must be skilled personally and aware of the results of research, development, and practice activities in the field.

Decision making of this nature is crucial to teaching young children. What children can learn in these years is more a function of developmental level than in any other period of schooling. In addition, the greater dependency of young children on the teacher requires different kinds of behaviors and organization. Similarly, the relational and nurturing aspects of teaching are of prime importance while the instructional aspects are unique in these early years.

A BASIS FOR DECISION MAKING

What are the bases for the teacher's decision making? Most teachers make decisions based upon some sort of explicit or implicit theory. Sometimes the theory is elaborated and formal, such as might be derived from the field of child development. Another theory might be simple, rather restricted, based upon the teacher's prior experience of what "has worked." A theory allows a person to make a decision based upon a set of expectations. Some sources of teacher's theories are found in the history and traditions of the field, and others in the statements of accepted goals of early childhood education. Additional sources include the bodies of knowledge from which academic subjects have been derived, and those related to teaching children—curriculum and method. Special consideration needs to be given to play as an educational method in the early years, and the way that play can be used to help children approach, abstract information from, and generate knowledge about the world.

Other sources of decision making need to be identified as well. Institutional decisions are often related to the organization of the classroom and the deployment of resources and persons in school. Ultimately, the consequences of teachers' decisions are judged and results of earlier decisions become the basis for making future decisions.

The organization of the rest of this book is as follows. The next two chapters deal with the models of schools and the curriculum of early childhood education. These relate to teachers' policy decisions. The chapters that follow address themselves to content and method in the instructional area of reading, language arts, mathematics, science, social studies, and the expressive arts. A chapter is also provided on play as a tool of learning. These chapters relate to the technical decisions of teaching. Chapters on classroom organization and ways of working with children are related to institutional teaching decisions. Special consideration is given to programs for parents, since they, as well as children, are the clients of early childhood education.

Two chapters on educating children with special needs are presented in the latter part of the book. Whenever children differ from the norm or average, their programs need to be modified. Many of the assumptions upon which early childhood programs are based do not hold for a broad range of children.

The final chapter concerns evaluation, which can help teachers judge their goals and their effectiveness in achieving these goals; adequate judgments of teachers' decisions can result only from adequate evaluation.

SUGGESTED READING

ALMY, MILLIE, *The Early Childhood Educator at Work.* New York: McGraw-Hill, 1975.

FRAZIER, ALEXANDER, ed., *Early Childhood Education Today.* Washington, D.C.: Association for Supervision and Curriculum Development, 1968.

GORDON, IRA J., ed., *Early Childhood Education*. 71st Yearbook of the National Society for the Study of Education. Chicago: University of Chicago Press, 1972.

HYMES, JAMES L., JR., *Early Childhood Education: An Introduction to the Profession* (2nd ed.). Washington, D.C.: National Association for the Education of Young Children, 1975.

SPODEK, BERNARD, and HERBERT J. WALBERG, eds., *Early Childhood Education, Issues and Insights*. Berkeley, Ca.: McCutchan Publishing Corp., 1977.

Bernard Spodek

CHAPTER TWO

SCHOOLS FOR YOUNG CHILDREN

Early childhood education in the United States is practiced in nursery schools, day care centers, Head Start programs, kindergartens, and primary classes. Although there are many common elements among these institutions, there are differences as well—differences in institutional setting, age of children served, traditions from which the programs developed, goals set for programs, and psychological theories subscribed to. A look at the traditions of early childhood education and contemporary schools should help in understanding the field as it is organized.

Early childhood education programs have been available in the United States for over a century, but they have served only a minority of young children (until recently, a very small minority) below the primary level. The situation may be changing, however. The estimates of enrollment in preprimary education for three-, four-, and five-year-olds for the year 1974, the most recent figures available at this writing, show a continuation of a trend toward dramatically increased enrollments of children at the nursery-kindergarten level. This increase of enrollment contrasts with a decline in the size of the population in that age range, a decline that began in 1966 and has continued. The graph of these trends is presented in figure 2-1.

In October 1974, 2,693,000 five-year-olds (78.6 percent), 1,322,000 four-year-olds (37.6 percent), and 685,000 three-year-olds were enrolled in schools. This represented an enrollment increase of 11 percent for the group from the previous year.[1] These figures become in-

---

[1] Irene A. King, *Preprimary Enrollment, October, 1974* (Washington, D.C.: Government Printing Office, 1975).

creasingly significant when one realizes that during the same period enrollments at the elementary and secondary levels have been decreasing. One cannot be certain that the trend of increased enrollments will continue, or for how long, if it does. The trend does suggest, however, that schools for young children may finally be coming into their own.

Figure 2-1 Total Children 3 to 5 Years Old and Percent Enrolled in Preprimary Programs: United States, 1966–1974

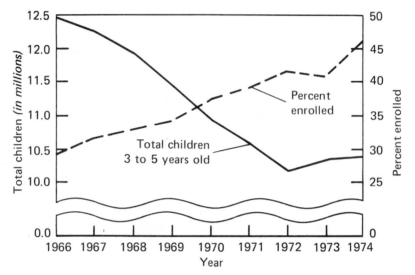

Irene A. King, *Preprimary Enrollment, October, 1974* (Washington, D.C.: Government Printing Office, 1975), p. 2.

Schools for young children include programs at the primary level, as well as kindergartens, nursery schools, day care centers, Head Start Child Development Centers, and centers with a range of other names. The schools may be sponsored by local education authorities, private groups, or service groups; they can be run by individuals, governing boards, or cooperators; and they may be supported by tuition and fees, private donations, tax funds, or some combination of these sources. The field has grown in so many ways during its history that schools for young children can best be characterized by their diversity.

THE ROOTS OF EARLY CHILDHOOD EDUCATION

Some of the differences in schools for young children stem from the distinct traditions and backgrounds that helped develop the separate institutions of the nursery, kindergarten, and primary grades. Each institution was developed and influenced by educators and philosophers with different points of view and from different cultures. As the years have passed the institutions have been modified, influenced by varied schools of educational thought and assorted cultural contexts.

THE PRIMARY SCHOOL

The primary grades were conceived to provide instruction in the basic skills subjects. Reading, writing, and computational skills are the core of learning and teaching at this level. Although other areas of study may be included in the primary grades, these are never afforded the status of the skill areas, and they may be removed, limited, or shifted around. A teacher would not have the same freedom to eliminate or even limit instruction in reading as she might in science or art.

The goal of contemporary primary education descends directly from the goal of colonial primary education. Especially in the New England colonies, the pressure of religious belief required that persons be able to read the scriptures in the vernacular. This led to the establishment of primary schools under the supervision of the community church. The content of the schools was the teaching of reading, with instruction in spelling, grammar, and arithmetic added later.

The preamble to the Puritan School Law of 1647 gives evidence of the religious roots of colonial primary education:

> It being one chief point of that old deluder, Satan, to keep men from the knowledge of the Scriptures, as in former times, by keeping them in an unknown tongue, so in these latter times, by persuading from the use of tongues, that so at last the true sense and meaning of the original might be clouded by false glosses of saint-seeming deceivers, that learning might not be buried in the grave of our fathers in church and commonwealth, the Lord assisting our endeavors,—It is therefore ordered that every township in this jurisdiction, after the Lord has increased them to the number of fifty householders, shall then forthwith appoint one within their own town to teach all such children as shall resort to him to write and read.[2]

As the American colonies became a nation, the content of school learning lost some of its religious flavor as concern for developing

---

[2] E. Nohle, in *Report of the United States Commissioner of Education* (1897–98), I, 24–25, as reported in C. S. Parker and Alice Temple, *Unified Kindergarten and First-Grade Teaching* (Chicago: Department of Education, University of Chicago, 1924), p. 6.

patriotism in children grew. The content of primers used for reading instruction in the late eighteenth century shifted from excerpts from or about the Bible to tales of patriotism and morality. Now the school was viewed as a unifying force for the New America. In the nineteenth century the education of children became a public concern, and schools began to receive financial support from the states. At this time the concept of universal education began to take hold, and children of all backgrounds were admitted into the publicly supported schools.

While the primary school of the early nineteenth century was basically concerned with teaching the "Three R's," new elements of instruction were slowly added to the curriculum: arts and crafts, nature study (later to be supplanted by science), geography (later to be incorporated into the social studies), music, and physical education.

Teachers in the colonial primary schools were hired with little regard for professional qualifications or credentials. Indentured servants and widowed women often served as teachers. The method of instruction consisted mainly of recitation and rote memorization, with the limited number of textbooks available providing the core of the instructional program.

New educational methodologies developing in Europe during the nineteenth century were to have their impact on the American primary school. Interpretations of the Pestallozzian system of education, with its emphasis on education through objects, were leading to new developments in German primary education. Reports about these schools influenced American educators to modify their verbal methods of teaching and to enrich their curricula. The establishment of normal schools for the preparation of teachers helped to increase the concern of American educators about teaching methodology.

During the latter half of the nineteenth century, the educational philosophy of the German educator Johann Friedrich Herbart greatly influenced the American primary school. Educational lessons were organized into five steps of the Herbartian system: preparation, presentation, association, generalization, and application. All lessons were to start with preparation of the class and all learnings were to culminate in the child's demonstration of his ability to apply new learning. Remnants of the Herbartian method still remain in the organization of lesson plans, which may begin with "motivating the children" and end in a "culminating activity."

The American Progressive Education movement had a great impact upon the organization of instruction in the primary grades during the first half of the twentieth century. In many cases the Herbartian lessons gave way to the more organic *project* method, which in turn led to the *unit* approach that one may find in some science and social studies programs.

The move toward urbanization and the development of large schools and school systems in the nineteenth century also led to a change in the organizational patterns of primary education. The nongraded structure of the one-room country school was supplanted by the multiroom school organized by grade, with instructional objectives determined and all children of like age being grouped together in a single class.

The Infant School, a form of primary education in Britain, was founded in 1816 in New Lanark, Scotland, by Robert Owen, the social reformer. The original principles of infant education were

> that the children were to be out of doors as much as possible and to learn "when their curiosity induced them to ask questions," to dance and sing and not to be "annoyed with books." They were to be educated and trained without punishment or the fear of it, no unnecessary restraint was to be imposed on them and they were to be taught only "what they could understand." The teachers were told to think about such matters as forming good habits and helping the children to treat each other kindly.[3]

Owen's school, designed for the children of workers in his mill, was conceived as a part of a broader program of social reform. Owen's conception of the Infant School foreshadowed the concerns of many contemporary educators. As the Infant School developed in England, however, it took on characteristics similar to those of the American primary school with its stress on book learning and the immobility of the children. Some of the English concepts of infant education of the last decade are closely related to the original ideas of Owen.

THE FROEBELIAN KINDERGARTEN

The kindergarten was developed in Germany in the first half of the nineteenth century. Based upon a mystical religious philosophy relating to the unity of the individual and nature, God, and other people, Friedrich Froebel designed a series of activities for children aged three to six to symbolize these relationships. The Froebelian kindergarten was composed, in essence, of the use of the *Gifts,* the *Occupations,* and the *Mother's Plays,* as well as the care of plants and animals.

The *Gifts* were sets of small manipulative materials to be used by children in prescribed ways. The first was a series of six yarn balls, each a different color. The single surface of the ball, a sphere, symbolized the unity and wholeness of the universe. The next set—a wooden sphere,

---

[3] D. E. M. Gardner, *Education Under Eight* (London: Longmans, Green and Co., n.d.), p. 6.

a cylinder, and a cube—represented unity and diversity, as well as the mediation of opposites—the sphere and cube representing opposites, the cylinder representing a mediating shape. Other *Gifts,* including a cube broken up into smaller cubes, followed by square and triangular tablets, were presented to children in a prescribed sequence. At each presentation, children were supposed to build specific forms, each representing some deeper meaning. Throughout the manipulations, little attention was paid to the physical properties of the objects, for sensation and perception of the real world were not considered important.

The *Occupations,* consisting of weaving, paper-folding, cutting, sewing, drawing, painting, and clay modeling, reflected the activities of primitive people. They also provided the children with opportunities for artistic expression. The *Mother's Plays,* specifically designed songs and games, were derived from the play of peasant women with their young children and from the activities of the social and natural world.

In time, the Froebelian kindergarten began to expand as an educational movement, and kindergartens were established in many German communities. With the extension of kindergarten education came a need for training *kindergarteners,* as kindergarten teachers were then called. Soon kindergarten training institutions began to attract a number of young German women as their students. It is interesting to note that the original kindergarten teachers were men. Froebel approved of women kindergarteners later in life, after his marriage.

Matilda H. Kreige, *The Child* (New York: E. Steiger, 1877)

With the wave of German migration in the mid-nineteenth century, many German women with kindergarten training came to the United States. The desire to apply the principles of the Froebelian kindergarten to their own children led many of these women to establish kindergartens in their homes. Margarette Schurz, who was trained as a kindergartener in Germany, invited the children of relatives into her home to join her children in what became the first American kindergarten, in Watertown, Wisconsin in 1855. Other kindergartens were established in the homes of German-American women and in German-American academies in various communities in the United States in the 1850s and 1860s.

Elizabeth Peabody became interested in kindergarten education through her reading and through contact with Margarette Schurz. She established the first English-speaking kindergarten in Boston in 1860. The philosophy of Froebel was compatible with that of New England Transcendentalism, a philosophic movement that provided intellectual support for the establishment of kindergarten programs in America. Although kindergartens were introduced into the public schools of St. Louis by 1873, the inclusion of kindergarten in public education did not become common for at least two more decades. Kindergartens were being established in many cities during this time, however, by various associations and mothers' clubs and by philanthropic agencies.

The kindergarten was seen as especially useful to the children of the poor in these early days. With the rapid rise of urban centers, the immigration of Europeans to America, and the growth of large city slums, philanthropic kindergartens were established in many areas. Arguments, not unlike those heard today in support of the Head Start program, were used to support kindergarten education for the poor:

> Centering among, and concerning itself with, the children of the poor, and having for its aim the elevation of the home, it was natural that the kindergarten as a philanthropic movement should win great and early favor. The mere fact that the children of the slums were kept off the streets, and that they were made clean and happy by kind and motherly young women; that the child thus being cared for enabled the mother to go about her work in or outside the home—all this appealed to the heart of America, and America gave freely to make these kindergartens possible. Churches established kindergartens, individuals endowed kindergartens, and associations were organized for the spread and support of kindergartens in nearly every large city.[4]

---

[4] Laura Fisher, "Report of the Commissioner of Education" as quoted in Vanderwalker, *The Kindergarten in American Education* (New York: The Macmillan Co., 1908), pp. 19–20.

By the beginning of the twentieth century a significant rift had developed in American kindergarten education. Traditional kindergarten educators felt that Froebel had discovered the significant elements of education for young children that were relevant to all children at all times. A more liberal group saw greater meaning in Froebel's educational philosophy than in the specific educational activities and methods derived from it. This liberal group felt that although the original kindergarten program was a step in the right direction, specific activities ought to be discarded when inappropriate. The emergence of the Child Study Movement, which was then establishing an empirical base of knowledge about childhood through the study and observation of children, and the progressive education movement, with its emphasis on freedom and activity in the classroom, lent support to the liberal kindergarteners.

The emerging philosophy of the reform kindergarten movement was probably best stated by Patty Smith Hill in the *Second Report of the Committee of Twelve of the International Kindergarten Union,* presented in 1913. According to her, the content of the kindergarten program should be related to the present life of the child rather than to the life of children of another culture and another generation. The child should be helped to acquire the knowledge of the civilization, which is best done by using the child's personal experiences as a means of achieving insight into knowledge. Hill proposed concrete child-oriented experiences and classroom play that was based more upon the natural activities of childhood, in which the child was free to reconstruct his own reality. The reform movement tried to retain the philosophy of Froebel while doing away with the unnecessary formalism of kindergarten method.[5]

Some of the elements of Froebelian philosophy supported by these educators included the following:

1. THE CONCEPT OF DEVELOPMENT IN CHILDHOOD. Froebel's basic concept that the young child is not a miniature adult suggested that education for young children ought to differ in form and content from that offered to older children. While Froebel's conception of child development is incompatible with present knowledge, the educational implications of the assumption that education ought to be developmentally oriented remains sound.

2. EDUCATION AS SELF-ACTIVITY. Education takes place as the human organism unfolds. The child's involvement in educational ac-

[5] For an interesting narrative of the lives of Margarette Schurz, Elizabeth Peabody, and Patty Smith Hill, among other women educational pioneers, see Agnes Snyder, *Dauntless Women in Childhood Education* (Washington, D.C.: Association for Childhood Education, 1972).

tivity supports this unfolding process. Here, too, we find that while child development has moved from an acceptance of an "unfolding" process, the concept of education as self-activity is still supported in education.

3. THE EDUCATIONAL VALUE OF PLAY. Froebel saw play as an important activity in helping the child mature and learn. In play, Froebel observed the child's symbolic reproductions of adult activity. He attempted to abstract the significant elements of these and provide them in a meaningful order in his educational program. This idea of the use of play in the education of young children is still supported by educators.

The kindergarten reformers felt that many of the Froebelian occupations were too tedious and required hand movements too small to be appropriate for young children. They also felt that other arts and crafts activities could be profitably included in the kindergarten program. Since the play of the American child was different from that of the German child, different kinds of play activities should also be encouraged. In addition, the reformers felt that the child's current life should provide a source of learning. School play became freer and more reflective of the child's life. Large blocks replaced the *Gifts* for constructions, and dolls and miniature housekeeping materials were included in the program.

The reform of kindergarten education continued through the 1920s and 1930s, leading to the creation of the modern American kindergarten we find in many schools today. A number of factors have influenced the development of kindergarten education since the 1920s. The changing economy of the 1930s and 1940s saw a lessening in the number of public school kindergartens as shortages in funds and building space led to the exclusion of this level of education from the public schools. The influence of the mental health movement led to an increase in concern for social-emotional learnings and a deemphasizing of the "habit-training" of the 1920s. In the late 1950s and 1960s kindergarten education began to receive more positive attention. A concern for intellectual development in children led to a reexamination of kindergarten curricula. In addition, psychological theory pointing up the importance of early education gave support to increased public aid for kindergartens and the extension of kindergarten education to large numbers of children in many states.

THE NURSERY SCHOOL

The nursery school movement developed from a different culture context than did the kindergarten. Out of their experience in English health clinics for children of the poor, Rachel and Margaret Macmillan conceived of the nursery school as a preventive for children's illnesses, both mental and physical, that were so prevalent in the slums. The basic philosophy of nursery education was one of *nurturance.*

Nurturance was conceived of as dealing with the whole child, including the social, physical, emotional, and intellectual aspects of the human being. The responsibilities of the original nursery school included bathing the children, clothing them in clean outfits, resting them, and seeing that they got plenty of fresh air—all at the same time they were being educated. The original nursery schools established in the slums of London were single-story buildings with large doorways or French windows that opened into gardens and large play spaces. Children's play flowed freely between indoors and outdoors.

The educational program developed by the Macmillans was social rather than religious in origin, concerning itself with helping the child learn the observable rather than the symbolic. The Macmillans were influenced more by Edward Seguin than by Froebel in their educational approach. This French educator had developed many activities to improve the sensory education of retarded children. His influence can be seen in current programs for "special" children as well as in the Montessori method.

For the three- and four-year-olds, the program of the nursery school included learning the skills involved in caring for oneself (washing, tying shoelaces, and so forth) and taking care of special responsibilities having to do with plants, keeping animals, or cleaning the school. In addition, specific activities were included to develop the "senses," such as music and rhythmic activities, language activities, and activities that

Mary Dabney Davis and Rowna Hansen, *Nursery Schools* (Washington, D.C.: Government Printing Office, 1932)

taught form and color. Activities leading to reading and writing as well as number work and science work were recommended by Margaret Macmillan, while Grace Owen, another nursery school pioneer, objected to the introduction of the "Three R's" and object lessons in the curriculum. Free play activities were included in the program, with opportunities for art construction and work with water, sand, and other nonstructured materials.

The work of the Macmillans with children was so successful that nursery schools were given an official stamp of approval by the Fisher Act of 1918, which allowed for the establishment of nursery schools in local school systems throughout England. Unfortunately, the funds needed to establish these programs were not forthcoming and the expansion of opportunities for nursery education was and is today a slow process.

In about 1920 a number of teachers who had worked with Margaret Macmillan and Grace Owen came to the United States to demonstrate the English nursery school. Nursery schools were started at Teachers College, Columbia University, the Merrill Palmer School of Motherhood and Home Training, and several other agencies in the United States. Many of these schools enrolled children younger than the presently accepted beginning age of three.

During the next decade the idea of the nursery school spread slowly throughout the United States. A survey of nursery schools in 1931 listed 203 in existence. About half these schools were related to colleges and universities, a third were privately controlled schools, and a fifth were related to child welfare agencies. This diversity of sponsorship, a continuing characteristic of nursery schools, paralleled their diversity of function. All nursery schools were concerned with educating children. Additional purposes varied with the sponsorship of the school:

> A large number of colleges and universities use the nursery school as a laboratory for the preparation of teachers and for research. The schools sponsored by departments of home economics in colleges and universities act as laboratories and demonstration centers for preparental education and instruction on home management. Relief of parents from daytime care of their children is chiefly supported by nursery schools connected with day nurseries and conducted by family welfare or philanthropic organizations.[6]

---

[6] Mary Dabney Davis, *Nursery Schools: Their Development and Current Practices in the United States,* Bulletin 1932, No. 9, U.S. Office of Education (Washington, D.C.: Government Printing Office, 1933), p. 31.

In the 1930s the Great Depression overshadowed all other elements of American culture. The depression had its impact on the development of nursery education. With incomes low and the collection of taxes down, many school systems found that they had to curtail educational services and release teachers whose salaries they could no longer pay. These unemployed teachers became an additional burden to the economy. In 1933 the federal government, first under the Federal Emergency Relief Act (FERA) and then under the Works Projects Administration (WPA), provided money to establish nursery schools that would hire unemployed teachers. These nursery schools operated through normal public school channels. Emergency teacher training programs were instituted to provide teachers with the necessary skills for working with young children.

Many communities took advantage of the opportunity provided by the WPA nursery schools, which not only provided relief to unemployed teachers but provided a valuable educational experience to children as well. Federally sponsored schools were operated in most states in the United States. The number of schools established ran into the thousands, far outstripping the number of nursery schools that had been in existence in this country up to that time.

The end of the depression and the beginning of World War II brought an end to the WPA nursery school as teachers ceased to be an unemployed group. The burgeoning economy, along with the manpower needs of the armed services and the defense industry, required additions to the labor force. The labor problem was answered by hiring women for war work. Agencies were needed to care for the children of those women workers who were mothers. Under the Lanham Act, the federal government again became involved in servicing the needs of young children. Child care centers were established in most centers of war industry to provide care and education to the children of working mothers.

Shortly after the end of the war, federal support for these programs was withdrawn. In many cases, however, since the need for the day care centers remained, they continued to operate under the sponsorship of local governments or philanthropic agencies. Even when operated by the local government, these centers seldom became a part of the public school system.

The decade of the 1950s saw the expansion of the parent-cooperative nursery school movement. While cooperatives had been established as far back as the 1920s, their greatest growth was in the 1950s. The desire for high quality nursery education at a reasonable cost, as well as for increased parent education, supported this development. In a parent-cooperative nursery school, the parents own the school and may serve as participants in the children's program as well. Adult classes or parent meetings relating to child development, child rearing practices, or other topics are often included as part of the program.

Nursery school education continued to develop slowly under its varied sponsorship until the mid-1960s, when the federal government again became involved in providing preschool education for disadvantaged children under the Economic Opportunity Act and the Elementary and Secondary Education Act.

While nursery school education went through a series of organizational metamorphoses, its development did not elicit the deep theoretical conflict that characterized the development of the kindergarten. Nursery programs did change, but the original eclectic approach to nursery education was broad enough to encompass modification and diversity without serious conflict.

Among the important changes that took place in nursery school thought are the following:

1. THE CHANGE FROM NURSERY EDUCATION AS A PROGRAM FOR THE POOR TO ONE FOR THE AFFLUENT. The originators of nursery school conceived of their programs as an antidote for many of the problems of poverty.

In the United States, the nursery school became a source of information about children, a place for young women to practice for motherhood and home management, a place to "keep" children, or a place to educate middle-class children. One of the first nursery schools in the United States was operated by faculty wives of the University of Chicago, a very different socio-economic group from the wives of the workers in the London slums.

This change came about as a consequence of the sponsorship of nursery schools in the United States. Without government support, most nursery schools outside of philanthropic agencies were supported by individual tuition payments, thereby limiting opportunities for nursery education primarily to the children of the affluent.

2. A DEEMPHASIS OF THE HEALTH ASPECTS OF NURSERY EDUCATION. Because the children served by American nursery schools had less need for the total care provided by the English nursery schools, programs were shortened to half-days or school hours, and the responsibility for nutrition, health, and hygiene was omitted. Only in day care centers and the Head Start programs of today, both concerned with providing nursery education to the poor, do we see a manifestation of the original concept of nurturance.

3. A SHIFT FROM THE EMPHASIS ON "TRAINING THE SENSES" TO A MORE BROADLY BASED EDUCATION. The same conditions that led to the reform movement in the kindergarten led to the shift in emphasis in nursery education. There was less concern for cognitive learning and more

for emotional and social learning in the kindergarten. With the current return to a concern for intellectual learning in young children, nursery educators have generally supported broad cognitive skills and strategies rather than the too-specific learning tasks of the original nursery school.

THE MONTESSORI SCHOOL

Paralleling the development of the nursery school in England, a similar institution developed in Italy, the *casa dei bambini*. Dr. Maria Montessori, the originator of this new educational institution, attempted to break from traditional Italian education just as Macmillan had broken from the rigid formalism of the British primary schools. While Montessori education has developed separately from nursery and kindergarten education, interesting parallels exist between the systems as well as an evident intertwining of ideas, especially in their early years of development.

Montessori began her work as a physician dealing primarily with retarded children. Impressed by her knowledge of the work of educators of retarded children, such as Seguin, she began to use and modify some of their methods and materials. Soon she moved from working with retarded children to creating an educational program for normal children in the slums of Rome. The target population and the root methods of the nursery school and Montessori school were basically the same. They both

Florence E. Ward, *The Montessori Method and the American School* (New York: Macmillan, 1913)

worked with children of the poor, they were both influenced by the work of Seguin, and they both saw sensory education as an important development in the education of children. The British nursery school was more broadly conceived, however, and took responsibility for aspects of development and work with parents that was absent to a great degree in the Montessori system. The freedom of nursery educators from a specific dogma also allowed them to develop programs more fully and more flexibly, utilizing new knowledge that became available and responding to new social situations. The Montessori method, however, strongly influenced the content and method of nursery schools.

An investigation of Montessori philosophy also shows some interesting parallels with Froebelian educational thought. Montessori saw the development of the young child as a process of unfolding, a concept found in Froebelian writing. Montessori perceived education as self-activity, again an idea found in Froebel's work, as was the idea of self-discipline, independence, and self-direction. A significant difference in philosophy was the Montessori emphasis on sensory education, less important to Froebel than symbolic education and the identification of sensitive periods of instruction in the development of the child.

Montessori education caught the imagination of many persons concerned with the welfare of children. The movement expanded, first in Italy and then throughout the world, with Montessori schools being established in several communities in the United States in the 1920s. While Montessori schools remained well-established in Europe, most of them disappeared in the United States during the 1930s and 1940s, either when they closed down or when the schools watered down the Montessori elements in their programs and became nursery schools not unlike others around them.

At the beginning of the 1960s, a resurgence of Montessori education occurred in the United States. An American Montessori movement was reestablished and Montessori schools for children as well as training programs for teachers were founded in many communities. Some of these schools show a wide range of activity in the name of Montessori education. Some adhere exactly to the regimen of activity set down by Montessori in her original writings; others modify these activities or include additional activities found in non-Montessori nursery schools, such as block-building and dramatic play activities.

The revival of the Montessori method has had its impact on the continued thinking about educational activities for young children. Currently, Montessori programs are again being suggested for children of the poor.

The genius of American early childhood education has been in its eclectic nature. Rather than reject new or foreign methods and theories, American educators and the public to which they are ultimately responsible have been willing to accept them at least in some limited form. Seldom, however, did any "pure" form of early childhood education remain uncontaminated. As a result of the interaction of often opposing ideologies and the pragmatic approach of many American educators, an American form of early childhood education emerged, consistent yet flexibly developed, taking the best from Froebel, Montessori, Macmillan, and other European theorists and incorporating American theories and techniques. Just as the above-mentioned European educators influenced the emergence of early childhood education, so did Americans such as John Dewey, Patty Smith Hill, Caroline Pratt, and a host of others.

Today many educators view the kindergarten and the nursery school as a downward extension of the primary school. The goals for the nursery school and kindergarten are exactly those goals set for all schooling. The differences in activities found at these earlier levels stem from developmental differences in the clientele rather than from philosophic differences or differences of purpose. The form and content of early childhood schools must be related to how we define the goals of the school and how we conceive of schooling.

THE CHILD CARE CENTER

Unlike the institutions previously discussed, child care centers—or day care centers or day nurseries, as they have alternatively been called—were originally designed to serve a custodial rather than an educational need. The American day nursery was fashioned after the French crèche, which literally translates as "crib." The first crèche was established in Paris in 1844 to help working mothers, fight infant mortality, and teach hygiene. The first American day nursery was established in New York City in 1854 by the New York Nursery and Child's Hospital.[7]

Child care centers are a product of the Industrial Revolution. Prior to that period, women's work, even for pay, was done in a home— theirs or someone else's—where children could be kept near at hand. With the establishment of the factory system and the subsequent hiring of large numbers of women and children, who provided cheap labor to oversee the machines, a need arose to care for very young children who were separated from their mothers during the long work day. The day nurseries served the working class during this period, for the middle and upper classes had access to servants to care for their young.

---

[7] Ilse Forest, *Preschool Education: A Historical and Critical Study* (New York: Macmillan, 1927), pp. 310–12.

During the latter half of the nineteenth century a number of day nurseries were established in the United States, often by settlement houses or philanthropic groups wishing to help the children of immigrant and poor working women. Sometimes Froebelian activities were provided to the children. Often the only responsibility of the caregiver was to keep the children fed, clean, and safe. Descriptions of day nurseries picture rows of iron beds, sometimes so crowded together that little space remained for play or educational activities. Matrons cleaned and prepared meals, in addition to caring for the children. A broad range was enrolled, including infants and toddlers along with nursery-age children.

Not until the 1920s, with the introduction of the nursery school into the United States, did day nurseries begin to implement educational programs for their charges. During the period that followed, child care centers structured their age groups much as the nursery schools did, limiting the age range to children already toilet-trained. Staff members prepared as nursery school teachers began to work with more informally trained caregivers.

During World War II the number of child care centers in the United States dramatically increased. The Lanham Act of 1941 provided federal funds for child care on a matching basis to war-impacted communities. The increase in child care facilities, it was felt, would lead to an increase in the number of women in war work. Many of these Lanham

Day Nurseries Bulletin, 1, no. 2 (Oct. 1925), p. 1

Act centers were high-quality, even though created by an emergency program. They provided staff training and adequate support for materials and equipment. Some centers operated as many as twenty-four hours daily to match the three shifts on which mothers worked.[8]

In 1946, shortly after the end of the war, the Lanham Act was terminated and with it federal support for child care services. Some centers continued, serving local needs and supported by state or local tax funds, or funds provided by community agencies. Many centers simply ceased to operate. Where day care continued to be provided, it was much more limited. Often it was considered a child welfare service, a temporary aid to a family in difficulty that could not assume traditional child-rearing responsibilities.

In the past decade the demand has heightened for child care as a normal service to working women. Women from the middle and lower classes were seeking greater equality and finding that the lack of child care interfered with continual employment and promotion to positions of greater responsibility. Possible baby-sitting arrangements using family or friends, family day care, or existing group day care were considered unsatisfactory or too expensive. People desired good quality child care services, subsidized by the government. Too often, however, some calling for these services were willing to compromise quality for quantity of service.

The history of child care centers includes several periods of growth and reconceptualization. Margaret O'Brien Steinfels has identified three periods in the history of the field. In the first, prior to 1920, child care centers were seen as an essential service to poor working mothers. The availability of such a service often allowed both father and mother to work, thus hastening their social movement upward. From about 1920 to 1940 child care services were curtailed and limited, to be provided only in cases of special need. A stigma was attached to them and their availability was limited. This perception of day care was held by some professionals through the 1960s. Since the mid-'60s we have entered the third phase. Child care services are again being seen as essential to working women, poor or not. The feeling has increased that this service should be available to mothers who want to work as well as those who need to work.[9]

The change in attitude toward child care centers is the result

---

[8] James L. Hymes, Jr., "The Kaiser Answer: Child Services Centers," in *History and Theory of Early Childhood Education,* eds. Samuel J. Braun and Esther P. Edwards (Worthington, Ohio: Charles A. Jones Publishing Co., 1972), pp. 169–75.

[9] Margaret O'Brien Steinfels, *Who's Minding the Children? The History and Politics of Day Care in America* (New York: Simon & Schuster, 1973), pp. 13–88.

of many diverse factors. Certainly the changing status of women in our society is one, as are the increase in urbanization and the shift to a nuclear family. Just as important is the developing body of knowledge that demonstrates that a good quality child care program does not have a negative effect on young children, and that daily separation of mother from child during working hours is not comparable to a total separation such as family break-up or death. Increased concern for the adequacy of child care services and the quality of facilities, program, and staff, needs to be exhibited by those who advocate and provide expanded child care services.

THE CONTEMPORARY SCENE

Just as different schools for young children have different traditions, they have various current forms. The nature of the schools is often determined by the age range served and the sponsorship of the program. Few primary-grade children attend private schools and the number of private kindergartens is dropping. These forms of early schooling are most often found in the public elementary school; unfortunately, the conceptual separation of kindergarten from the primary grades remains as much a problem today as it was at the turn of the century. Too often the kindergarten and primary grades differ not only in form, but also in the ways teachers define their goals and purposes.

The movement of kindergartens into the public schools is recent, however. In Illinois, for example, public schools were first required to provide kindergarten education in 1970, although permissive legislation had allowed many school systems to offer it long before that time. As of 1974 all states but Mississippi, North Dakota, and Idaho provided some form of state aid for kindergartens.[10] Where kindergartens are not a part of the public school system, private kindergartens are often available for those who wish to send their children and who can afford the fees.

The picture of education for children below age five is rather confusing. Montessori schools, an outgrowth of the original model, again became available in the late 1950s and early 1960s. These schools are generally privately operated and charge tuition. Teachers are trained specifically in Montessori methods and the schools are accredited by one of two Montessori accrediting associations. Adherence to Montessori methods and procedures may vary as individual schools have modified original prescriptions and added additional program elements.

---

[10] James L. Hymes, Jr., *Early Childhood Education: An Introduction to the Profession,* 2nd ed. (Washington, D.C.: National Association for the Education of Young Children, 1975), p. 13.

Nursery education for children below kindergarten age is generally offered on a half-day basis, although full-day nursery schools are a part of the tradition. Children might attend five days or part of a week. Few nursery schools or junior kindergartens are available within public schools, although some do exist. A large number of the nursery schools are operated on a private, often for-profit, basis. These may be run by a husband-and-wife team for whom the profit is little more than an adequate salary. They may be operated as a branch or franchise of large corporations, sometimes including all-day care and part-day education in the same program.

Some of the nursery schools in the United States operate as parent cooperatives. In this case a group of parents as cooperators owns and operates the school, administering and setting policy, while a hired teacher is responsible for the program. Parents may work with the children under the director's guidance and even be responsible for school maintenance. Parent cooperatives often emphasize parent as well as childhood education and the director must be responsible for all these educational activities. She will also act as consultant to the parent governing board. Teaching in a cooperative nursery school requires commitment and skill in working closely with adults and children.

Nursery school teachers work one or two half-day sessions that range from two to three hours in length. The teacher in a child care center, however, may work an eight-hour shift daily and be responsible for both caring for and teaching children. Lunch, rest, and toileting time become periods of intense work rather than times for a coffee break. Even with long shifts, a single teacher cannot cover the total day in a child care center, which may be open from 7:00 or 8:00 A.M. to 5:00 or 6:00 P.M. Overlapping staff work schedules become a requirement. This may mean that less qualified staff are responsible for the children part of the day, and teachers might not have aides available at other times. However, the full complement of children is not at the school at all times during this long day.

The child care center's extended day allows the inclusion of a nursery school program with the other time spent in eating, resting, and free play activities. Staff plan other activities to fill the daily schedule. Child care centers, like nursery schools, can operate under a variety of sponsorships. Private centers abound, but many operate under the auspices of community agencies or are tax supported. Often, however, when public funds are used to support child care services, they are a "purchase of service," paying fees for children in existing centers. Many times priority is given to children of parents in Aid for Dependent Children or Work Incentive programs.

The one major exception to the absence of governmental involvement in prekindergarten education is in what has been called *com-*

pensatory education. Since 1965 federal funds have supported preschool education for poor and minority children defined as "disadvantaged." Project Head Start began in the summer of 1965 and continues today, having served over five million children in its brief history. Additional early childhood programs have been made available under Title I of the Elementary and Secondary Education Act. Head Start continues even though its parent organization, the Office of Economic Opportunity, was dismantled. Its programs have influenced existing primary education, as Project Follow Through extended the models of the Planned Variations programs into kindergarten and the early grades. Although these program efforts seem large compared to what preceded them, many three- to five-year-old children are still not receiving an early education.

The number of schools for young children has steadily increased, but one cannot assess the impact of education in the early years without some information about the quality of schools serving children. The issue of what constitutes a good education for young children is still being debated, and the discussion about different program models in Chapter 3 will address that issue. But even with a minimum consensus of what constitutes a good early educational program, one must question the quality of schools that are available to young children.

There are nursery schools that teach only social behavior or conformity to rules, and there are child care centers that serve only a custodial function. Of course schools also exist at the other extreme that provide as good an education for young children as can be imagined. Unfortunately, studies suggest that more schools fall near the bottom— while plenty of room remains at the top of our scale. Few state agencies responsible for licensing nursery schools and day care centers set and supervise standards that demand a good educational experience. Too often, only physical facilities are evaluated for licensing. In public schools, too few kindergartens are staffed by teachers who are prepared in early childhood education. More often than not, a kindergarten teacher is required to have an elementary teaching certificate. In Illinois, for example, the elementary teaching certificate covers kindergarten through grade nine. Strangely, the recently created early childhood certificate in this state specifically excludes public school kindergarten.

Studies of programs for young children show a great range in the type and quality of service being provided. Elizabeth Prescott and Elizabeth Jones vividly describe the range of child care centers available to children in California; although some are quite good, unfortunately many are less than adequate.[11] John Goodlad, M. Frances Klein, and

11 Elizabeth Prescott and Elizabeth Jones, *The Politics of Day Care,* Vol. I, and *Day Care as a Child-Rearing Environment,* Vol. 2 (Washington, D.C.: National Association for the Education of Young Children, 1972).

Jerrold Novotney studied early schooling in a range of cities in the United States, with results that were less than heartening. Although the directors in their wide sample of schools were aware of newer trends in early education and supported the fostering of development and learning in many areas, the study's observations of program and program supports showed that these aims were not being addressed in the schools. The authors concluded:

> Most of the nursery schools in cities in the United States are, apparently, rather sublimely isolated educational enclaves, each following passively a relatively traditional and narrow set of activities which constitute both means and justification for ends. They operate quite apart from, though not entirely unaware of arenas of intense inquiry into the educational potentialities of young children. . . . Nursery school directors firmly believe that what they are doing is good for children and that those who attend have advantages over those who do not. We have a lot to learn.[12]

Some of the things we in the field have to learn relate to which educational activities are truly worthwhile in achieving our educational goals. We also have to learn how to help teachers involve children in these activities in schools. One answer is in more knowledgeable professionals. Another is in the lessening of the isolation of practitioners. Finally, we need to learn how to gain greater support for schools for young children. As long as schools must depend upon tuition for their existence, they will be limited in educational facilities, salaries they can pay, and materials and supplies they can provide. As long as nursery schools and day care centers pay teachers low salaries, they will be unable to compete for the best professionals.

In recent years there has been talk about providing greater public support for early education. Two bills supporting comprehensive day care services for children have passed Congress in recent years, only to be vetoed by presidents. Some states are advocating comprehensive early education programs for children four through eight years of age. California has such a program now and reports its success.[13] Other states may follow in supporting early education. With declining enrollments in elementary schools, space is often available although tax funds many

---

[12] John I. Goodlad, M. Frances Klein, and Jerrold M. Novotney, *Early Schooling in the United States* (New York: McGraw-Hill Book Co., 1973), pp. 142–43.

[13] Wilson C. Riles, "ECE in California Passes the First Test," *Phi Delta Kappan*, 57, no. 1 (September 1975), 3–7.

times are not for early educational services. The question of whether the public schools should supply all early childhood education services, including child care, is presently being debated. Whatever the outcome, the profession will have to deal with the isolation of these programs from one another and from the entire field.

The availability of a wide range of schools with a variety of programs requires a reexamination of the assumptions and goals of early childhood education, and of the methods used in achieving these goals. These goals and methods, and sources of early childhood curricula, are analyzed in the next chapter.

SUGGESTED READING

GOODLAD, JOHN I., M. FRANCES KLEIN, and JERROLD M. NOVOTNEY, *Early Schooling in the United States.* New York: McGraw-Hill Book Co., 1973.

GROTBERG, EDITH, ed., *Day Care: Resources for Decisions.* Washington, D.C.: Office of Economic Opportunity, 1971.

LILLEY, IRENE M., *Friedrich Froebel: A Selection from His Writings.* Cambridge: Cambridge University Press, 1967.

PRESCOTT, ELIZABETH, and ELIZABETH JONES, *The "Politics" of Day Care,* Vol. 1. Washington, D.C.: National Association for the Education of Young Children, 1972.

————, *Day Care as a Child-Rearing Environment,* Vol. 2. Washington, D.C.: National Association for the Education of Young Children, 1972.

STEINFELS, MARGARET O'BRIEN, *Who's Minding the Children? The History and Politics of Day Care in America.* New York: Simon & Schuster, 1973.

WEBER, EVELYN, *The Kindergarten: Its Encounter with Educational Thought in America.* New York: Teachers College Press, 1969.

Bernard Spodek

CHAPTER THREE

EARLY CHILDHOOD CURRICULUM

Schools for young children serve a purpose. They are expressly designed to achieve certain goals for children. Although different schools may have different goals, once a model is chosen, school personnel must fill the day with activities designed to achieve these goals—to develop a school curriculum. How does one derive a curriculum? The curriculum may be defined as the organized experiences designed to provide opportunities for learning to children in a school setting. It can be both formal and informal. In this chapter the sources of an early childhood curriculum and its appropriate goals are discussed.

THE SOURCES OF EARLY CHILDHOOD CURRICULA

During the past fifteen years, many innovative programs have been proposed for the education of young children. Each purports the *right* kind of educational experience, the best for young children. Many of the programs were originally designed for special subpopulations of children, such as poor or handicapped children, but the proponents of at least some of these programs have generalized the appropriateness of their curricula to all young children. Although some programs described as "new" are essentially modifications of existing practice, the difference between a

The material in the first part of this chapter appeared in an earlier version in Bernard Spodek, "What Are the Sources of Early Childhood Curriculum?" *Young Children,* 26, no. 1 (October 1970), 140–46.

number of innovative programs and traditional nursery school and kindergarten practice is great. The difference in the sources of these curricula
is even greater than the difference in practice.

CHILDREN AS A SOURCE OF CURRICULA

According to some theorists, early childhood curricula should
originate from children themselves. If you read the works of Friedrich
Froebel or Maria Montessori, you will quickly note that both these
pioneers of early childhood education used their observations of children
as the main source of their curricula.

The kindergarten of Friedrich Froebel consisted of the ordered
use of manipulative activities, or *Occupations,* and the use of songs and
finger plays, his *Mother's Plays and Songs.* Froebel conceived of these
activities as they were revealed to him by the children themselves.[1] Similarly, Montessori developed her educational approach by observing the
uses children made of didactic materials provided them, abstracting the
essential elements for learning and ordering them into her famous *Montessori Method.* The observation of children was for Montessori the essence of scientific pedagogy.[2] Froebel's analysis of child behavior was
more mystical than scientific.

The use of "natural" childhood activities as the source of curricula is a romantic ideal. Such educational arguments can be traced as
far back as Jean-Jacques Rousseau. The ideal of the unsocialized savage
whose best instincts are destroyed by the surrounding culture is echoed
by contemporary critics. Educators who use such arguments take comfort
in the feeling that they are not violating the child in any way but are
"doing what comes naturally."

Unfortunately these arguments do not hold up well. There is
nothing natural about any school, even a preschool. Nursery classes and
kindergartens cannot be directly derived from the natural activity of
children. Even the play activities provided children in these settings are
modified by teachers who allow certain activities to take place, disallow
other activities, and regularly intervene in the play directly and indirectly
to make these activities educational. Selecting a room's furniture, materials, and equipment can be seen as an act of intervention. The very
nature of the educational process requires, if it is effective, that the child
be modified as a result of his experiences within it. The child should exit

---

[1] Friedrich Froebel, "The Young Child," in *Friedrich Froebel: A Selection from His
Writings,* ed. Irene M. Lilley (Cambridge: Cambridge University Press,
1967), pp. 68–119.
[2] Maria Montessori, *The Montessori Method* (Cambridge, Mass.: Robert Bently,
Inc., 1964), pp. 47–88.

the program in a *less* natural state than the one in which he entered it. All schools, as a matter of fact, are cultural contrivances to *do* things *to* children—to change them.

Looking more closely at the curricula derived from natural observations of children, one becomes aware of the selectivity of the observations and the uses to which they have been put. When one observes an object, one must define certain attributes as critical. This definition provides a focus for the observation and the descriptions that follow. Other attributes besides those observed may exist, but they are overlooked because they are considered uncritical. The purpose for which one is observing determines what one is looking at and what one will see. For example, a young woman preparing for a date may consider the color and cut of a dress. Her mother may observe the fabric and stitching with which the dress has been assembled. Ralph Nader might be more concerned with the flammability and price of the garment, while a sociologist might consider the garment's effects on the wearer and on outside observers. Who has seen the real garment?

In analyzing the arguments about the natural activity of childhood as a source of the curriculum, one becomes similarly aware that the purposes of the observer or educational theorist often determine what is seen and the products of such observations are far from natural.

The same child may be seen by a variety of educators in many different ways. One educator may see a set of potentials while another sees only deficits; one may see only the intellectual behavior of the child, another only the emotional or social behavior. One educator may view a particular child as a problem solver, while another may see him as a respondent to external rewards. The natural child ceases to be natural and becomes a product of the theoretical scheme that helps to determine which observations should be attended to and which discarded in a complex organism.

Few contemporary educators can fail to see the contrived nature of both the Froebelian kindergarten and the Montessori school. If one is to understand the curricula determined by Montessori, Froebel, or any other educational developer, one must go beyond simple natural observation and identify the basis for selecting the observations and the conceptual framework used to give meaning to these observations in developing educational experiences for children.

DEVELOPMENTAL THEORY AS A SOURCE OF CURRICULA

A second source of curricula used by early childhood educators has been child development theory. One such theory, derived from Arnold Gesell's research, considers child development as primarily maturational. Children are studied to determine the process of the unfolding of childhood. The developmental norms produced by Gesell and his colleagues are based on many observations of children of various ages. As a result of this theory, children have been grouped by age in nursery and kindergarten classes and provided with experiences that are considered specifically appropriate for their age level.

Arguments derived from Gesellian theory have been used to exclude activities thought to be inappropriate and to insure inclusion of appropriate experiences in the school life of children. The argument that we must "protect the right of the child to be five" has often been heard in answer to the suggestion that reading instruction be included in the kindergarten program. However, the nature of "fiveness" is difficult to determine, for age norms do not adequately describe the range of heights, weights, skills, abilities, or other attributes of children at any age. Nor would these attributes remain constant at all times for all persons in all cultures if they could be identified. Average heights and weights of children have risen in the last fifty years and vary from one geographic area to another, not necessarily as the result of natural differences but rather of environmental differences. Other attributes of childhood also vary as a result of the environment—cultural as well as physical. What a child is at any level of development is to some extent a result of what a culture says he ought to be.

Psychoanalytic theory, concerned primarily with the personality, has also been used to formulate curricula for young children. Interpretations of the work of Sigmund Freud, Carl Jung, and Erik Erikson have led to emphasis on expressive activities, dramatic play, and group interactions. Sometimes as a result of psychoanalytic theory teachers were admonished not to interfere with the activities of children. In excesses such as this, educational practices based upon this theory resembled child therapy sessions as much as educational activities. With the increased emphasis on ego development, however, psychoanalytic thinkers became concerned less with catharsis and more with building an integrated self requiring personal competencies, and many of the excesses eventually disappeared.

More recently, the work of Jean Piaget has been used as a source of curricula. Gesell is no longer as fashionable, and Freud is considered suspect by some educators. Although Piaget is primarily a developmental epistemologist, his theories have been used by many American psychologists and educators.

A number of recent projects have used strategies to enhance intellectual development as the basis for creating specific curricula for disadvantaged children. Celia Lavatelli created a program to develop a number of intellectual schemata in children. These included one-to-one correspondence, classification, and seriation. Additional activities involved children in conservation of quantities.[3]

A Piaget-based curriculum developed in Ypsilanti, Michigan, uses a Piagetian scheme of analysis. Activities are designed to move children through levels of representation from the index level to the symbol level to the sign level.[4]

Is child development theory, Piagetian or otherwise, a legitimate source of educational curricula for young children? The "child development point of view" has been popular in early childhood education for many years. However, one may seriously question its appropriateness as the prime source of curricula.

Child development is a descriptive science. At its best it can tell us what *is*. Education by its very nature deals not with what is, but with what *ought* to be. Choices and preferences are involved in creating educational experiences that cannot be rationalized by recourse to child development theory. If anything, this theory can provide us with useful information, often negative, about what we cannot do to children at a particular point in their development if we want them to learn, and with information about readiness stages for learning.

Too often educators have analyzed developmental theory to determine the goals of education. In excess, this has led to teaching children the tasks used by the researcher to test his theory. Children in a Piaget-oriented nursery school, for example, might spend hours "learning" conservation tasks. This is as much a distortion of child development theory as is preparing children for specific items on the Stanford-Binet test of intelligence as a way of demonstrating that an educational program can boost intelligence.

Child development knowledge might be used most productively in education as an analytic tool. Educators could identify consistencies and inconsistencies in what they do, as well as develop ways of judging the consequences of their programs and the "match" of program activities to the developmental level of the children.

This role is not to be understated. In the last few years, increased recognition of Piaget's theories has had a significant impact on early childhood education. This recognition has been partly due to Piaget's framework of intellectual development, which provided educators with a broad concept of children's readiness for intellectual learning in the early years. Piaget identifies four broad stages in the development of

[3] Celia Stendler Lavatelli, *Piaget's Theory Applied to an Early Childhood Curriculum* (Boston: American Science and Engineering, 1971).
[4] David P. Weikart et al., *The Cognitively Oriented Curriculum* (Washington, D.C.: National Association for the Education of Young Children, 1971).

children's logico-mathematical knowledge, each with many identifiable substages. These broad stages are a sensorimotor, preverbal stage; a stage of preoper tional representation; a stage of concrete operations; and a stage of fo mal operations.

Piaget suggests that four main factors explain the development of new intellectual structures in the child: maturation, experience, social transmission, and equilibrium or self-regulation.

The third factor, social transmission, is the one about which educators are concerned. Piaget highlights the teacher's need to be aware of children's readiness for educational experiences:

> The third factor is social transmission—linguistic transmission or educational transmission. This factor, once again, is fundamental. I do not deny the role of any one of these factors; they all play a part. But this factor is insufficient because the child can receive valuable information via language or via education directed by an adult only if he is in a state where he can understand this information. That is, to receive the information he must have a structure which enables him to assimilate this information. This is why you cannot teach higher mathematics to a five-year-old. He does not yet have structures which enable him to understand.[5]

Although social transmission, part of which is formal education, is identified as having an important role in intellectual development, Piagetian theory provides no guidelines for improving its effectiveness.

LEARNING THEORY AS A SOURCE OF CURRICULA

Child development theory is only one form of psychological theory that has been identified by program developers as a source of curricula; learning theories and theories of intelligence have also been used. Developmental theory deals with change in the human being over long periods of time. Learning theory attempts to account for short-term change. The recourse to learning theory as a source of curricula has been manifest in several different ways.

The "conduct curriculum," developed in the early childhood program at Teachers College under the leadership of Patty Smith Hill, gives evidence of the influence of Edward L. Thorndike's school of be-

---

[5] Jean Piaget, "Development and Learning," in *Piaget Rediscovered,* eds. Richard E. Ripple and Verne N. Rockcastle (Ithaca, N.Y.: Cornell University Press, 1964), p. 13.

haviorism.[6] Kindergarten was seen as a place for habit training to take place. Lists of appropriate "habits" and recommended stimulus situations for five-year-olds were developed for kindergarten teachers at this time.

Today the theories of behaviorist B. F. Skinner are having similar influence. Skinner's learning theory contains six major concepts:

1. *Operant conditioning.* Skinner's conditioning consists of re-inforcing operations or responses that occur normally. Learn-ing increases at the rate at which they occur.

2. *Reinforcement.* A new stimulus that increases the rate at which an operation occurs is called a *reinforcer.* A wide variety of reinforcers can be used in education: food, toys, money, tokens, or praise. Knowledge of results (feedback) might also be considered a reinforcer.

3. *Immediate reinforcement.* There should be a minimum delay in time between the operant behavior and its reinforce-ment; otherwise some other response might be emitted and reinforced.

4. *Discriminated stimuli.* Behaviors that should be emitted un-der specific circumstances are reinforced only under those circumstances.

5. *Extinction.* Any response that has been increased by rein-forcement can be decreased by its failure to be reinforced.

6. *Shaping.* Complex behaviors can be analyzed into simple components. A sequence of reinforcement procedures can be designed to build up to the complex behavior.[7]

The technology of programmed instruction is rooted in this theory. Through a procedure that breaks down complex learning into a series of simple sequential steps, children can be taught a range of things. Programmed instruction might use a teaching machine, a book, a series of tasks with manipulative materials, or a set of human interactions as the context for learning procedures.

A number of psychologists have rejected behaviorism as the prime way of looking at psychological phenomena, including learning. Often referred to as "third force" psychologists or phenomenological psychologists, this group views behaviorism as too mechanistic and sim-plistic to provide an adequate framework for understanding complex

---

[6] Patty Smith Hill and others, *A Conduct Curriculum for Kindergarten and First Grade* (New York: Charles Scribner's Sons, 1923).

[7] B. R. Bugelski, *The Psychology of Learning Applied to Teaching* (Indianapolis: Bobbs-Merrill Co., 1964), pp. 208–12.

human processes. They suggest an alternate approach in dealing with human learning.

Donald Snygg and Arthur Combs, for example, view the process of education, and implicitly of learning, as a process of change in the phenomenological field. How a person behaves, they suggest, is a function of his understanding of a situation. Understanding, rather than responding, becomes the important goal of a learning setting. The meanings of behavior and of situations become the focal point of learning. Learning, therefore, requires not simply recall of words or actions, but developing organizing frameworks that give meaning to situations. Meanings are personal and therefore vary from individual to individual. (Meanings, by the way, cannot always be fully verbalized.) The goals of learning are also individual. What a person learns depends upon his goals and needs, which are not always externally manipulable.

Within phenomenological psychology, the *self* plays an important role. How a person views himself affects his behavior and what he learns. A child who views himself as competent will be more ready to learn and will learn more than one who thinks of himself as incompetent. The school, it is suggested, needs to concern itself with developing adequate selves in its pupils.[8]

Phenomenological psychology, when used in classrooms, leads to a different set of instructional strategies than does behavioral psychology. Complex learning situations are used intact, with children being helped to develop their own meanings of them; their behavior is not "shaped," nor are specific behavioral goals predetermined. Instead, the teacher is concerned with moving children in the direction of appropriate behavior—a wide range of behavior is acceptable. Such an approach allows a greater degree of freedom for children, enabling them to select alternatives and develop personal responsibility for their learning and their growth.

Another form of learning theory that has been addressed to early childhood education is social learning theory. Urie Bronfenbrenner has summarized the basic concepts of social learning theory and some of its applications to education.[9] He suggests that social psychologists have demonstrated that behavior is contagious—that children learn by watching others. This process is called modeling. In this process children acquire specific behaviors or patterns of response through observation; this is more than simple imitation because the behaviors learned are

---

[8] Donald Snygg and Arthur Combs, *Individual Behavior* (New York: Harper and Brothers, 1949), pp. 204–25.

[9] Urie Bronfenbrenner, *Two Worlds of Childhood: US and USSR* (New York: Russell Sage Foundation, 1970), pp. 120–51.

"symbolic equivalents" of the model's behavior rather than absolute mimicry. The modeling process can take place without external reinforcement, since the imitative behavior is its own reward. Modeling together with social reinforcement that gives approval or affection when the child manifests a desired behavior is an even more potent learning tool.

The school is an acculturating institution. Many of the behaviors we wish children to learn can be taught through modeling and social reinforcing. The issue of which behaviors we wish children to learn is outside the realm of this theory.

The use of behaviorist learning theory carries with it the admonition to develop behavioral objectives. Actually there is nothing psychological about the use of behavioral objectives, nor are objectives more profound because they are stated in behavioral terms. The translation of curricula goals into behavioral objectives, however, allows for an easy though often misleading evaluation of achievement.

Psychological processes are not directly observable; they must be inferred. Behaviors are observable, but psychologists sometimes forget that the *meanings* of behaviors must still be inferred. A psychologist may identify the ability to attend to auditory signals as a legitimate goal of nursery school or kindergarten education. This might be translated into the following criterion behavior: "The ability to sit still for ten minutes and listen to a story as part of a group." Whether a child is actually gaining meaning from the auditory environment is not directly observable. The relationship between sitting still and listening (certainly not a one-to-one relationship) has led psychologists to list as the goal a behavior that might better represent *conformity* than *attention*.

Psychological theory focusing on behavior and behavior modification has determined the structure of a number of curricula in early childhood education. While short-term change is easily observed and evaluated, there are seldom any attempts to study long-term effects of these curricula. In the final analysis, such programs may be based as much on ultimate faith as are any of the more traditional programs. The description of a program in psychological terminology and the great emphasis on the evaluation of effectiveness without analyzing ultimate goals may, in the long run, obscure the ultimate consequences of these programs.

Nor can phenomenological psychology or social learning theory help us to determine what should be taught to children, a problem often ignored by psychologists involved in educational programs. At best, learning theory can help us in developing new instructional methodologies and in analyzing and assessing established methodologies. This, in itself, is no small role.

TEST ITEMS AS A SOURCE OF CURRICULA

One other facet of psychology that is often used for formulating curricula is psychological testing and evaluation. This is used more in practice than in theory. Many of the programs in early childhood education, for example, are justified as ways of increasing intelligence, and one way of judging the intelligence of children is through the administration and scoring of intelligence tests. Such tests consist of items that purport to sample a broad range of intellectual behaviors in children. Each item achieves its validity from the fact that it represents many other kinds of behaviors that might have been elicited from the total number of intelligent behaviors.

Since the effectiveness of educational programs can be demonstrated by students' achievement of higher scores on intelligence tests, it is easy to use tasks taken from or related to intelligence tests as the actual content of the program. Justification for this approach to curriculum development is often an argument that suggests that since these items are samples of intelligent behavior, having children practice these behaviors is the same as having children practice behaving in an intelligent manner. Such logic is devastating—rote learning of responses to particular stimuli cannot be called intelligent behavior.

Such distortions of psychological testing and curriculum development are not limited to the area of intelligence testing. They may take place in the realm of language development or academic achievement, or in any other area where samples of behavior are mistaken for the total population of behaviors they represent. The small number of items that determine the difference in age or grade placement of a child make this form of justification all too attractive for persons who have developed short-term intervention techniques for young children.

ORGANIZED KNOWLEDGE AS A SOURCE OF CURRICULA

Almost two decades ago, Jerome Bruner suggested that the organized fields of knowledge should become the basis of educational curriculum for children at all levels. The "structure of the disciplines," it was argued, could provide a vehicle to insure that school learning would be intellectually significant.[10] Key ideas in each area of knowledge would be revisited in more sophisticated ways as children moved through their academic careers. These key ideas could be taught in an intellectually

---

[10] Jerome S. Bruner, *The Process of Education* (Cambridge, Mass.: Harvard University Press, 1960).

honest way at every level of development. *New Directions in the Kindergarten* provides examples of how this proposal could be translated into an early childhood program in the fields of science, social science, and mathematics.[11]

The proposal to develop school curricula based on the structure of knowledge was attractive. During the 1960s a large number of curriculum development projects were organized along these lines. A number of new elementary textbook series were also based upon this proposal, as were the curriculum guides of many school systems. As the work in these projects continued, a number of problems became evident.

Scholars had difficulty identifying the actual structure of the disciplines. They identified many different structures, but some disciplines, such as social science, did not seem unified. Another problem was that identifying intellectual structures did not help to determine what school experiences would help children attain significant understandings in a field.

The strategies for understanding the sciences did not seem to help in understanding the arts and the humanities. Fewer projects dealing with these areas and with the expressive elements of school learning were mounted, leading to a distorting thrust in curriculum development.

The relationship between the conceptual structures of mature disciplines and children's less mature understandings is more complicated than was originally thought. Issues dealing with relevance to children, individual learning rates and style, personal interests, and so forth complicated what had once seemed a simple task.

Although the content of the disciplines—the areas of knowledge—could help to determine the significance of school content, by itself it was inadequate for determining school curricula at any level, especially at the early childhood level.

SCHOOL CONTENT AS A SOURCE
OF CURRICULA

Although psychological theory represents one area used in justifying curricula proposals, it is by no means the only source; another in popular use is the content of later schooling. "Reading readiness," for example, is considered important because it prepares children for reading instruction. Though readiness skills have no importance in themselves, they and certain other kinds of learnings are considered good because they prepare children for later school expectations. Thus the pressures of

---

[11] Helen F. Robison and Bernard Spodek, *New Directions in the Kindergarten* (New York: Teachers College Press, 1965).

later life and schooling are heaped upon the child in anticipation of what is to come.

A caricature of such a justification is to be found in the Bereiter-Engelmann Program. Its content (reading, language, and mathematics) is considered important because it is required of children in primary grades. The organization also prepares the child for behaving appropriately for his school life ahead. The legitimacy of such a justification is questionable; whether such preparation will benefit students later is debatable.[12]

One of the few long-range studies of the effects of education, the *Eight-Year Study* of progressive high schools, demonstrated that children in open school situations did better than those from more restrictive school environments when they went to college.[13] Although extrapolation to a lower age level may not be appropriate, the study certainly raises some questions about the desirability of providing children with rigid early schooling as preparation for rigid later schooling.

Unfortunately, such preparation for later learning also obscures the concern for the sources of curricula. Later school learning is not a goal in and of itself, but a means to a goal. Using such a justification only delays decisions about curriculum content. As it is, too little concern is given to the proper source of curriculum.

THE PROPER SOURCE OF CURRICULA

The sources of curriculum theory used through the years have been reviewed and analyzed. A number of them must be rejected. Neither test items nor school content can be viewed as proper sources of any curriculum. Using either represents a circularity of thought that supports existing practice merely because it exists. School content is devised to achieve societal aims, no matter how ill-defined they might be. To support school content as an end in itself is to deny the purposes of schooling and to legitimize activity solely on the basis of tradition.

Test items themselves are part of evaluation procedures. The role of such procedures is to help in judging the educational experience, but to use them to determine curriculum content is to distort both the educational process and the process of evaluation. Rather, the reverse should occur—test items should be determined by educational practices.

[12] Carl Bereiter and Siegfried Engelmann, *Teaching Disadvantaged Children in the Preschool* (Englewood Cliffs, N.J.: Prentice-Hall, Inc., 1966).
[13] William M. Aiken, *The Story of the Eight Year Study* (New York: McGraw-Hill, 1942).

A third source of curriculum might also be questioned—using children themselves to determine educational programs. Since what we see in children is determined by prior conceptions, it might be more fruitful to legitimize these conceptions and make them explicit. This is done when we define the developmental theories and learning theories to which we adhere when we observe children's behavior. Learning theory, developmental theory, and conceptions of organized knowledge and ways of knowing are all sources of curricula that must be used in concert. But even together they are inadequate to determine a curriculum. Only within the context of human values can these sources function properly.

Schools at all levels serve two functions. On the one hand, schools help children learn those behaviors that will help them adjust to an effective role in society. This we might call socialization. They also help children develop sensitivities and competencies that will help them lead personally satisfying lives. This we might call self-fulfillment. To the extent that schools help to define the "good life" and the "good society," they are moral enterprises. The set of values growing out of this enterprise determines how we should use our knowledge of human development, human learning, or knowledge in determining educational experiences for young children.

This would suggest that school programs are derived from, in addition to child development or learning theory, statements about social purpose and different forms of knowledge. All schools, including those for young children, are designed to serve social purposes. These purposes can be identified by studying the cultural values, levels of technology, cultural organizational forms, and cultural symbol systems of the school's community.

Cultural values tell us what is important for an individual to know, and thus help us judge the worth of educational content. Our society is based upon such values as liberty, justice, equality, and the importance of the dignity of the individual. Our valuing of the individual's dignity causes us to consider the way we treat children in school and the nature of the materials we use. It is important, for instance, that individuals or groups are not demeaned in books used in classes. Our concern for equality leads us, under one interpretation, to treat all children alike and demand the same language learning for each; under another interpretation, we support diverse programs for different children, such as bilingual/bicultural education. Our valuing of cooperation, competition, or independence can also directly influence the kinds of materials we provide young children and the forms of behavior we reward or restrict.

A society's level of technology determines to a great extent what forms and levels of knowledge an individual must acquire to cope with community life and to be productive. The change from teaching "nature study" to teaching "natural science" during the twentieth century is an example of how changing school content responds to changing levels of technology.

Forms of social organization also have their impact on school programs. In the primary grades, for example, it is traditional to study families, communities, and community workers. Our social interrelation requires that we make children aware of roles and structures in their communities.

Cultural symbols allow us to share ideas and feelings. Consequently, language instruction is a basic part of all school programs. Other symbols are taught as well—music, art, and movement provide nondiscursive symbolic forms. Our flag is another type of symbol; even the clothes we wear can take on symbolic meanings.

These are but a few examples of how our culture sets requirements for what is taught in school. These cultural imperatives become so much a part of our thinking that we seldom identify them explicitly. Cultural options, sometimes referred to as "stylistic differences," also exist.

FORMS OF KNOWLEDGE

Human development theory can tell us what children can learn. The cultural context of schools can tell us what children ought to learn. The content of schools must be abstracted from existing forms of human knowledge. A number of attempts have been made over the years to identify the varying forms of knowledge that can be used as the basis for school curricula. One conception is based upon the work of Jean Piaget.

Constance Kamii has used a Piagetian framework to identify objectives of early childhood education that include five forms of cognitive knowledge. These are

1. *Physical knowledge*—the observable properties and physical actions of things
2. *Logico-mathematical knowledge*—the relation between and among objects, such as classifications, seriation, and number
3. *The structuring of time and space*—although these are observable in external reality, reasoning is required in the creation of these structures
4. *Social knowledge*—the social conventions that are structured from people's feedback

5. *Representation*—the development of symbols and signs that can stand for objects[14]

Kamii and Rheta DeVries have elaborated upon this scheme and designed activities to teach logico-mathematical knowledge and physical knowledge to children.[15] The activities were created to help children construct knowledge through interactions with their physical and social environment, knowledge that must be verified in ways consistent with each specific form of knowledge. Kamii and DeVries criticize existing programs for not doing this and for focusing instead on teaching specific content in subject matter areas.

Using the framework above, one may know many things about a table, for example. A child may determine if the table has a hard or soft, smooth or rough surface, if it is high or low, and if its top is round or rectangular. These are elements of physical knowledge directly accessible through the child's senses. The child can then place the table he has observed into a previously constructed category of objects called "table," containing similar objects that may actually look different in many ways. He can also distinguish this table from objects that are not tables. He can count the tables in the room, and order them by size, by height, or by some other attribute. These are forms of logico-mathematical knowledge. The child can identify where the table stands in relation to other objects in the room and recall whether the table was covered with a cloth last night, thus placing the table in a structure of time and space.

The child learns that it is permissible to place things on, write on, and eat from the table, but not to sit on it or jab a sharp knife into it. These learnings are not directly accessible through sensory experience, nor are they the result of logical processes. They are matters of social knowledge, common as they may seem, and must be communicated to the child, directly or indirectly. Finally, the child may represent the table by drawing a picture of it, creating a model of it, or writing the word *table*.

These various forms of knowledge deal with the same object,

---

[14] Constance Kamii, "A Sketch of the Piaget-Derived Preschool Curriculum Developed by the Ypsilanti Early Education Program," in *Early Childhood Education*, ed. Bernard Spodek (Englewood Cliffs, N.J.: Prentice-Hall, Inc., 1973), pp. 209–29.

[15] Constance Kamii and Rheta DeVries, *Piaget Children and Numbers* (Washington, D.C.: National Association for the Education of Young Children, 1976); Kamii and DeVries, *Physical Knowledge Using Piaget's Theory in Preschool Education* (Englewood Cliffs, N.J.: Prentice-Hall, Inc., in press).

but each is derived and verified in a particular way. This Piagetian framework is limited to cognitive knowledge; however, early childhood curriculum is not limited to the cognitive realm. The pioneers in nursery and kindergarten education embedded their concern for intellectual learning in a wider concern for supporting a broad base of learning and nurturing children. Recent interest in affective education and career education demonstrates that even today the intellectual realm alone is too narrow a focus for early childhood programs. A conception of knowledge upon which to base a program must go beyond cognitive knowledge.

Other conceptions of knowledge, developed by philosophers of education, should prove useful to early childhood educators.[16] Some of these have been elaborated elsewhere.[17]

Our views of the school's role, the relationship between the individual and his development, society's demands, and the sources of knowledge can be used to identify goals for education. R. F. Dearden, for example, has suggested that the goal of education is "personal autonomy based upon reason," which seems quite appropriate as *one* of the goals of early childhood education. He describes this autonomy as follows:

> There are two aspects to such an autonomy, the first of which is negative. This is independence of authorities, both of those who would dictate or prescribe what I am to believe and of those who would arbitrarily direct me in what I am to do. The complementary positive aspect is, first, that of testing the truth of things for myself, whether by experience or by a critical estimate of the testimony of others, and secondly, that of deliberating, forming intentions and choosing what I shall do according to a scale of values which I can myself appreciate. Both understanding and choice, or thought and action, are therefore to be independent of authority and based instead on reason. This is the ideal.[18]

This concept of autonomy is not alien to the education of young children. Erikson's framework for human development includes the stage of autonomy early in the scale, just after the development of

[16] For example, see Philip Phenix, *Realms of Meaning* (New York: McGraw-Hill Book Co., 1964); and P. H. Hirst and R. S. Peters, *The Logic of Education* (London: Routledge & Kegan Paul, 1970).

[17] Bernard Spodek, "What Are Worthwhile Educational Experiences for Young Children?" in *Teaching Practices—Reexamining Assumptions,* ed. Bernard Spodek (Washington, D.C.: National Association for the Education of Young Children, 1977).

[18] R. F. Dearden, *The Philosophy of Primary Education* (London: Routledge and Kegan Paul, 1968), p. 46.

trust.[19] The child's autonomy in these early years may not, however, be based upon reason since he is heavily influenced by the arational. As the child's intelligence continues to develop, the basis for personal autonomy becomes more rational.

Dearden's concept of autonomy is closely related to that of liberty, or freedom, a basic value of American society. Often freedom is thought of in its negative sense alone, that is, as the absence of external constraints, or a freedom *from* something. In this view, the fewer laws or external impositions that exist, the more free an individual is. A second concept of freedom is based upon the range of alternative possibilities available to a person. This suggests a freedom to act. Probably the most satisfying definitions of freedom include elements of both: that is, both a freedom *from* and a freedom *to,* embedded in Dearden's conception of autonomy.

If we accept the goal of "personal autonomy based upon reason" as legitimate for early childhood education, then of what use is psychological theory to the educator? For one thing, it helps us determine ways of testing the effectiveness of a program in achieving this ideal. We can test whether children in a program do, in fact, become more autonomous. Second, knowledge of developmental processes can help us order activities in terms of which ones can serve an educational purpose to a child at a particular level of development, and suggest which activities might precede or follow others. We can determine whether children can adequately cope with the degree of autonomy we provide them. Developmental theory becomes a tool for the analysis of curriculum rather than its source. The forms of knowledge also provide us with ways of analyzing curricula. They can help to determine whether the methods of teaching are consistent with the forms of knowledge being taught, and whether children can become not only independent learners, but independent verifiers of what they have come to know. The content of school programs must be recognized as a product of educators' imaginations, to be tested by psychological means rather than as natural consequences of children's behavior, adults' thinking, or institutional organization.

ESTABLISHING GOALS FOR EARLY CHILDHOOD EDUCATION

Building on the prior discussion, one can state that one of the prime goals of early childhood education, as of all education, is the develop-

[19] Erik H. Erikson, *Childhood and Society* (New York: W. W. Norton & Co., 1950).

ment of knowledge in children. Knowledge, however, must be broadly defined, and continually redefined as the socio-cultural context changes. We should provide children access to not only formal scholarly disciplines, but also self-knowledge, that is, knowledge of what one can do, feel, and communicate to others. Values, aesthetic appreciations, attitudes, and predispositions are communally shared forms of knowledge that children must also learn. These cannot be isolated by subject area. Knowledge of the culture's symbol system, both linguistic and otherwise, must be developed by children. Teachers need to judge which areas of knowledge should be given a high priority for young children and which levels we should expect children to attain—a judgment based upon the community's values and imperatives, and the teacher's knowledge of the children's developmental level.

The attainment of knowledge is a lifelong task. Although this can begin in the early years, the goals of education can never be fully attained in these years. Therefore, teachers must identify *instrumental* goals as well as *terminal* goals for our educational programs. Instrumental goals are those that must necessarily be attained if our terminal goals are to be achieved. They are limited in nature and often do not have any validity of their own. For example, children might be taught to discriminate among and to name different colors and shapes in kindergarten. The names of the colors and shapes are not significant in their own right. However, the processes of discrimination, categorization, and labeling are important cognitive processes. Once learned, these processes can be applied to many similar activities. Since they can be achieved through studying colors and shapes, the activity of sorting and naming has educational merit.

Sometimes we teach things to young children that they will have to unlearn later. This occurs when these early learnings are a necessary step to mature knowledge, even though they are inadequate for the mature scholar. Beginning reading instruction is a case in point. Much of what we teach young children in early reading instruction would be dysfunctional for the mature reader. A mature reader does not sound out words or use a large memorized sight vocabulary to gain meaning from the printed page. Such an approach to reading is discarded because it hinders the mature reader's progress in gaining meaning efficiently. But we can see no way for the young child to become a mature reader without learning a sight vocabulary and a set of letter–sound associations. These constitute a transitional stage, and the child must be helped to discard them later. Our instrumental goals, although they might not look like our terminal goals, must be directly related to them in a psychological if not a logical way.

MODELS OF EARLY CHILDHOOD CURRICULA

Within the last two decades a range of program alternatives have been developed for the education of young children. Many of the newer programs grew out of work done in the 1960s when a heightened concern for social justice led to the development of programs to aid children of the poor and of minority groups. Preschool programs were designed to "compensate" for differences found in the natural curricula of these children's early rearing as compared with that of children in the mainstream of American life. These differences, often considered deficits, were thought to be the causes of failure in school and in later life.

The field of early childhood education has had a tradition of responding to the needs of the poor. The original English nursery school and the *casa dei bambini* of Montessori were originally designed to serve poor children growing up in city slums. Just as these earlier programs have been generalized to serve all children, so program approaches originally labeled as "compensatory" are now being seen as alternative approaches for *all* children. Any number of individual new programs have been generated, but most have some essential elements in common with a number of other programs so that they can be grouped together and identified as a set of program models, with variations upon the basic themes of each model. Many of these programs can be found in the Planned Variations program of Head Start and Follow Through, a federally funded effort to evaluate and compare a range of program alternatives for young "disadvantaged" children.

It is beyond the scope of this chapter to present the content of each program. The various curriculum models can be found elsewhere in detailed description and comparison.[20] Rather, the discussion that follows will concern itself with ways of analyzing and comparing models.

Early childhood programs have been traditionally identified with various theories of child development, often to the point, as suggested earlier, that educators seem to believe these programs were directly derived from developmental theory. The Educational Products In-

---

[20] For example, see Ellis D. Evans, *Contemporary Influences in Early Childhood Education,* 2nd ed. (New York: Holt, Rinehart and Winston, Inc., 1975); Eleanor E. Maccoby and Miriam B. Zellner, *Experiments in Primary Education: Aspects of Project Follow-Through* (New York: Harcourt Brace Jovanovich, Inc., 1970); Mary Carol Day and Ronald K. Parker, eds., *The Preschool in Action: Exploring Early Childhood Programs,* 2nd ed. (Boston: Allyn & Bacon, Inc., 1977); and Bernard Spodek, *Early Childhood Education* (Englewood Cliffs, N.J.: Prentice-Hall, Inc., 1973).

formation Exchange (EPIE) report on early childhood education seems to take this point of view. This report is an attempt to help the reader determine educational program preferences. In the process they first ask of the reader, "Where do you stand on human development?" They identify three views on human development: a behavior-environmental view, a maturational-nativist view, and a comprehensive-interactionist view. By selecting from a set of three parallel statements about human development, the reader can identify his beliefs in regard to developmental theory. In the behavior-environmental view, development is seen as an accumulation of learning or sets of responses related to cues that elicit them and reinforcers that sustain them. In the maturational-nativist view, the emphasis is on the role of the individual's genetic make-up that allows development to unfold. The comprehensive-interactionist view sees development resulting from a combination of maturation, experiences, developmental tasks, consultation with other people, and interactions among all of these. Once the reader has determined his point of view on development, he can then use the rest of the report to identify parallel program preferences for early childhood education.[21]

Lawrence Kohlberg and Rochelle Mayer suggest that programs of education differ on the basis of ideologies—prescriptions of practice based upon value assumptions about what is ethically good or worthwhile and theoretical assumptions about how children learn or develop. They identify three ideological thrusts of education, which are not dissimilar from the EPIE views of development: a romantic thrust, a cultural transmission thrust, and a progressive thrust. Underlying the romantic thrust is a conception of development as a process of unfolding. Education is seen as essentially a support for development, as in EPIE's maturational-nativist view of development. The cultural transmission thrust is concerned with transmitting elements of the culture from the older generation to the younger generation. Little concern for maturation is voiced within this thrust, which would be consistent with the behavioral-environmental view of the EPIE report. Within the progressive thrust, development is seen as occurring through an interaction of the individual with his environment, with the individual essentially creating his own development. This thrust is consistent with EPIE's comprehensive-interactional point of view.[22]

---

[21] Educational Products Information Exchange, *Early Childhood Education: How to Select and Evaluate Materials* (New York: EPIE Institute, 1972).

[22] Lawrence Kohlberg and Rochelle Mayer, "Development as the Aim of Education," *Harvard Educational Review,* 42, no. 2 (November 1972), pp. 449–96.

Conceiving of educational programs as based in ideologies rather than in psychological theories alone suggests that programs can be generated with many different goals, yet rooted in the same developmental or learning theory. In early childhood education, we can find the Behavior Analysis Program of Project Follow Through, sponsored by the University of Kansas, geared toward a set of rather narrow goals. This program focuses essentially on social and classroom skills and the core subjects of reading, mathematics, and handwriting.[23] Sidney Bijou, operating from the same theoretical framework in psychology—behavior analysis—has identified a broader set of goals for early childhood programs in the areas of abilities and knowledge, extension of motivation, and the enhancement of self-management skills.

Bijou suggests goals for the development of abilities and knowledge such as body management and control, physical health and safety, self-care, recreation and play, social behavior, aesthetic knowledge and abilities, everyday mechanical know-how, knowledge of how things work in the community, academic and preacademic subjects, and the methods and content of science. The extension of motivation involves the preservation and extension of ecological reinforcers, the development of attitudes and interests in people, and a positive attitude toward school. In the area of self-management skills, Bijou has included personal self-management techniques, and problem-solving and decision-making skills.[24] Bijou's list is quite different from that of the Behavior Analysis Follow Through model, although neither is derived from behavior analysis psychology.

Thus, in assessing early childhood education program models, one needs to know more than just the developmental theory associated with the model. The basic assumptions underlying the model are necessary, including assumptions about the client, the educative process, the school, and the teacher. One needs to identify the long-range and short-range goals of the program, the curriculum and teaching methodology, the style of teaching prescribed, and how the model handles the organization of time, space, physical resources, and human resources. If one is concerned with implementing a model, one should know whether this has been done and how effective the implementations have been. Practical issues regarding costs of implementation, requirements of staff and ma-

23 Don Bushell, Jr., "The Behavior Analysis Classroom," in *Early Childhood Education,* ed. Bernard Spodek (Englewood Cliffs, N.J.: Prentice-Hall, Inc., 1973), pp. 163–75.
24 Sidney W. Bijou, *Child Development: The Basic Stage of Early Childhood* (Englewood Cliffs, N.J.: Prentice-Hall, Inc., 1976), pp. 169–70.

terials, and the availability of supportive services can also affect a decision regarding the worth of a program.[25]

It is not surprising that different programs of early childhood education lead to different learning outcomes when their goals are as diverse as those described above. When assessments are made of these programs in terms of academic achievement alone, some programs seem more effective than others. However, broader assessment techniques show that differences among programs are not just a matter of one program teaching *more* than another, but of programs geared toward different goals.

Project Follow Through has been continually assessed and each year evaluation reports chart the different goals, including noncognitive goals, achieved by children in different models. Site effects have also been studied, suggesting that not only do different models influence children's learning, but different contexts in which they are implemented also influence learning.[26] Programs do not influence all children in the same way. Louise Miller and Jean Dyer, for example, in a study of different Head Start programs, found boys more consistently benefitting from prekindergarten programs.[27] A study of fourth graders in Montgomery County, Maryland, revealed that different types of children thrived in different types of classrooms.[28] All this suggests we might need to learn more about differences in children's learning as well as a program's teaching.

Different programs have different impact on children. One must select a program not only because it works, but because what it achieves is considered worthy, or better than what other programs can achieve. Early childhood programs are manifestations of ethical principles. Our selection of goals and means to achieve them should come from an awareness of the options available and a judgment of the goals we consider appropriate for young children. The match between goals and curriculum method can then be made.

Selections of educational activities are among the choices teachers can often make. The chapters that follow look at the various subject matter areas, presenting a summary of the knowledge available

[25] Spodek, *Early Childhood Education,* pp. 27–34.

[26] Marvin G. Cline and others, *Education as Experimentation: Evaluation of the Follow Through Planned Variations Model, Vol. IIA* (Cambridge, Mass.: ABT Associates, 1975).

[27] Louise B. Miller and Jean L. Dyer, *Four Preschool Programs: Their Dimensions and Effects,* Monograph of the Society for Research in Child Development, Serial No. 162, Vol. 40, Nos. 5–6 (October 1975), pp. 136–37.

[28] Daniel Solomon and Arthur J. Kendall, *Individual Characteristics and Children's Performance in Varied Educational Settings,* Final Report (Rockville, Md.: Montgomery County Public Schools, May 1976).

about each area and a sample of strategies for teaching children that grows out of the basic summary. Organization by subject matter areas is used because it is a convenient way of talking about program content that has been used traditionally in education. While the framework is handy, the reader should continually be on the lookout for ways of crossing these subject lines, of integrating content through activities, and of seeking relationships in terms of children's interests and experiences.

SUGGESTED READING

BALDWIN, ALFRED L., *Theories of Development*. New York: John Wiley & Sons, Inc., 1967.

DEARDEN, R. F., *The Philosophy of Primary Education*. London: Routledge and Kegan Paul, 1968.

EVANS, ELLIS, *Contemporary Influences in Early Childhood Education* (2nd ed.). New York: Holt, Rinehart and Winston, 1975.

PHENIX, PHILIP, *Realms of Meaning*. New York: McGraw-Hill Book Co., 1964.

SPODEK, BERNARD, *Early Childhood Education*. Englewood Cliffs, N.J.: Prentice-Hall, Inc., 1973.

SPODEK, BERNARD, and HERBERT J. WALBERG, *Early Childhood Education, Issues and Insights*. Berkeley, Ca.: McCutchan Publishing Co., 1977.

WEBER, EVELYN, *Early Childhood Education: Perspectives on Change*. Worthington, Ohio: Charles A. Jones, 1970.

Bernard Spodek

CHAPTER FOUR

LANGUAGE LEARNING IN EARLY CHILDHOOD EDUCATION

Perhaps the most important area of learning in the education of young children is that of language. Although reading is obviously crucial to all later school learning, other aspects of language learning—such as speaking and listening—are equally important. As a matter of fact, learning to read is predicated upon a great deal of prior language learning.

From the moment the child enters the classroom he is bombarded with verbal messages from many sources, giving him specific directions for actions, providing information about the world, and offering him opportunities for enjoyment, aesthetic appreciation, and comfort. The child has to act on the messages he receives, understanding and responding to them if appropriate. The child is also sending messages to others. He responds to the teacher and attempts to influence the behavior of his peers; he makes his needs and wishes known to those around him; he expresses the ideas and feelings he has developed. The continual verbal give-and-take of the active school day presents endless opportunities for speaking, listening, reading, and writing. These then become the basis for social interactions as well as for the development of cognitive processes.

THE CHILD COMES TO SCHOOL

School does not provide the child's first language learning situation. The most important part of his learning has taken place before he even arrives at school. The role of the school is to extend and enrich the language learning of the child and to provide remediation if necessary.

This extension and enrichment role is important. In entering the school, the child finds himself in an environment that often requires him to make himself understood in a way not required at home. The communication demands made on the child by both the teacher and other children require him to adjust to an environment less responsive to him than the previous environment he has experienced.

Most young children have learned to use the basic sentence forms of their culture appropriately by the time they enter school. The basic acquisition of grammatical speech is complete by age three and one-half, often before the child enters nursery school. By the time he reaches first grade, he is a competent performer in language. He has probably mastered a listening and speaking vocabulary of several hundred to a thousand words and the basic rules for combining these words in a variety of ways to express different meanings. Although it would not be possible for a young child to parse a sentence or recite the rules of grammar, he has by this time developed an intuitive sense of the structure of the language he continually uses correctly.

Through interaction with others, children have somehow learned, for example, that adding "-ed" to a verb places it in the past tense. The conversational mistakes that teachers so often report grow out of the children's applying rules logically to words that happen to be exceptions to those rules. Rules are seldom misapplied by young children, however. You may hear a child say, "He dided it," but you will seldom hear him add the "ed" to the end of a noun.[1]

Individual children vary greatly in their language development. There are early talkers and late talkers, loquacious children and quiet children. Some differences are a function of the way children react to a specific environment, others are developmental. Psychologists report that sex, class, position in family, and ethnic group membership are all related to the child's rate of language development. Differences reported by psychologists are usually differences in *group trends;* individuals may differ markedly from the norm of their group.

---

[1] Extensive reviews of research in language development are available in many sources. For example, see Francis J. DiVesta and David S. Palermo, "Language Development," in *Review of Research in Education,* Vol. 2, eds. Fred N. Kerlinger and John B. Carrol (Washington, D.C.: American Educational Research Association, 1974); David McNeil, "The Development of Language," in *Carmichael's Manual of Child Psychology,* 3rd ed., Vol. 1, ed. P. M. Mussen (New York: John Wiley & Sons, 1970); Lois Bloom, "Language Development," in *Review of Child Development Research,* Vol. 4, ed. Francis D. Horowitz (Chicago: University of Chicago Press, 1975), pp. 245–304.

HOW DOES LANGUAGE DEVELOP?

The study of language development in children has a long tradition that spans a full century. The earliest of these studies consisted of parents' diaries, often focused upon the first manifestation of a new form of vocalization in their child. Events of the past two decades have been extremely generative of studies of child language development. The field has been spurred by the theories of Noam Chomsky and others, and by the social issues related to dialect differences and bilingualism. Much of the research on language acquisition is not directly relevant to classroom situations at the early childhood or later levels, since it deals with even younger children; also, few studies relate to the effects of environmental manipulations on language acquisition. An understanding of the evolving theories, however, can help in understanding the conflicting prescriptions for educational practice that are available.

Chomsky has proposed a transformational grammar as a way of understanding language. According to his view, two levels of structure exist in language—a surface structure and a deep structure. The surface structure represents the pattern of words that are used; the deep structure represents the pattern of meanings underlying the words. Chomsky also differentiates between language competence and language performance. Competence is a person's knowledge of language; performance represents the use of that knowledge. A child's performance at any language task is only a partial indicator of his language competence.

Chomsky uses transformational grammar to develop his model of language acquisition, which cannot be explained by modeling or repetition alone. Each utterance of an individual, including that of a very young child, is a unique sentence that may never have been articulated before in that particular way. Thus, a child is not repeating phrases and sentences that he hears. Rather, he uses a set of rules to transform components of language that he has heard to create his own peculiar message. The child continually tests the rules he creates about language. The responses he receives allow him to refine and elaborate his language competence and performance. Given a finite set of rules for grammar, any individual can construct an infinite number of sentences.[2]

This view of language acquisition gives an active role to the child as the constructor of his own language within a cultural framework. The ideas and arguments that developed from the articulation of this theory have provided a basis for a range of current language research,

---

[2] Noam Chomsky, *Syntactic Structure* (The Hague: Mouton and Co., 1957).

much of it focusing on how children develop syntactical structures. Ursula Bellugi and Roger Brown's work, for example, focused on the process by which children develop syntax in language as a process of interaction between parent and child.[3]

The parents studied did not develop a series of prescribed lessons for their children. Rather they seemed to use a process called *expansion*. When the child uttered a communicative though incomplete sentence, the parent responded by repeating the statement in syntactically expanded form. The child's utterance, "Mommy, lunch," might be expanded by the parent to "Mommy is having her lunch." Vocabulary might be more directly taught than syntax by parents.

Just how educators can best use the research in language development is not completely clear. Early researchers were concerned with normative studies, attempting to find the regularities in the development of language in children or attempting to discover the language acquisitions of children at different age levels. Later researchers focused more on the theoretical aspects of language development, studying the process of language acquisition or the factors that affect the development of language in children.

Eric Lenneberg has developed a theory of the biological foundations of language that is compatible with the work of Chomsky. He analyzes knowledge of language development in human beings alongside biological knowledge about human and nonhuman animals, synthesizing them into a theory. He suggests that latent language structures are biologically determined and that they need to be actualized within a sound setting through exposure to adult language behavior. The period of language readiness for such actualization, it is suggested, is from two years to the early teens. In this period, the child recreates the language mechanisms of the culture.[4]

While Lenneberg's theories are fascinating and provide great opportunities for speculation, they give little guidance in how best to "actualize" language structures—the key role of language education. Education and child development specialists have developed research related to engineering the social setting to enhance language development.

B. F. Skinner has also developed a theory of language acquisition based upon behavioral principles. He believes the infant's original vocalizations and babblings reinforce themselves. After a while, adults around the infant selectively reinforce sounds that are a part of the na-

[3] Ursula Bellugi and Roger Brown, *The Acquisition of Language,* monograph of the Society for Research in Child Development, 29, No. 2, 1964.

[4] Eric H. Lenneberg, *Biological Foundation of Language* (New York: John Wiley and Sons, 1967).

tive language, thus strengthening them while allowing the others to fade. Language forms are taught through imitation. The child learns grammar and proper word orders as he distinguishes sentences from nonsentences during listening. Thus speech is learned first, followed by grammar. Although Skinner's theory could explain repetition of language, it does not explain grammar-generating rules that have been observed by linguistic scientists.[5] However, this behaviorist approach has been the basis for language learning programs in schools.

Another view that is being tested to explain language acquisition in children sees language as an adjunct to cognitive processes. A number of developmental psychologists, including Jean Piaget and Lev Semenovich Vygotsky, have discussed the relationship between language and cognitive development. Marilyn Edmonds's research seems to indicate a direct relationship between stages of intellectual development and stages of language development in children.[6] There is general agreement that a relationship exists between language and cognition, but just what that relationship is remains open to further study.

Whether specific studies related to language education are directly related to any single theory of language development is questionable. Developmental theories can, however, provide the basis for theorizing about what will work in social engineering that can be transformed into educational hypotheses to be tested in classrooms.

DIALECT

No matter how simple or complex it is, the child will learn the language he most often hears spoken by the significant adults around him. Most American children learn English, and children in Japan learn Japanese just as easily. But the various forms of the English language spoken in American subcultures may differ markedly from one another. These differences are called *dialects*. Naturally the young child learns the dialect spoken most prevalently around him.

The speech patterns of children may differ in many ways. There can be differences in the pronunciation of words or in speech inflections. Differences may exist in the labels ascribed to familiar things, so that what is called a "sack" in one area may be called a "bag" elsewhere. There may also be syntactical differences among dialects, making understanding difficult because the structure of statements carries much of their meaning.

[5] B. F. Skinner, *Verbal Behavior* (New York: Appleton-Century Crofts, 1957).

[6] Marilyn H. Edmonds, "New Directions in Theories of Language Acquisition," *Harvard Education Review,* 46, no. 2 (May 1976), 175–98.

The dialect prevalent in the schools and generally heard over radio and television has been called *Standard American English*. However, many children have been raised in an environment in which different dialects prevail.

The fact that many children enter school with a language background not shared by their teacher and significantly different from the language upon which most school learning is based has many implications for programs and for teaching.

DEALING WITH LANGUAGE DIFFERENCES IN THE CLASSROOM

Some educators suggest that differences in the language backgrounds of children are irrelevant in determining instructional goals; therefore, since the school uses Standard English, one might as well get on with it and teach Standard English, even if it means suppressing the child's language. Others suggest that the child's language is important and should be reflected in the school; one ought not to teach a single system of language, but instead teach the use of language appropriate to the situation in which it is used. Using the Spanish language in school would be justifiable if there were a number of Spanish-speaking children in the class. The black dialect of the urban ghetto could also be recognized as a valid and useful form of verbal communication appropriate to the classroom. More will be said about such situations in chapter 14.

Language serves many purposes in the lives of human beings. These purposes become the basis for establishing the goals of a language arts program in school. One purpose that may unfortunately be of little concern to teachers is language's role in establishing personal and group identity. Speaking a dialect or using a particular style of language establishes an individual as a member of a specific group, and to attempt to change his language system might have significant implications beyond learning the use of proper syntax. Arguments against teaching Standard English may stem as much from pride in minority-group membership as from any other reason.

Both approaches focus on teaching a standard dialect in the classroom, but in one case this would be to the exclusion of all other language systems in school. Within either approach, Standard English might be taught in a number of ways.

USE OF NATURALISTIC METHODS. One way to approach the teaching of Standard English is to model a program on the natural processes of language acquisition. This could be done by surrounding the child with people, both adults and children, who speak the majority dialect. Their natural interactions would help the child acquire this dialect. Still the language of the school might be different from that of the home and children would have the problems of learning to be fluent in two language systems, and continually having to determine which system fit each situation. In addition, the language the child learns in school would not be reinforced in the home or the neighborhood, thus compounding the problem of learning the new language system.

Courtney Cazden reports using a process known as *expatiation* in improving language of children.[7] This process requires the adult to react to the child's utterances by expanding them ideationally rather than linguistically. The child's remark, "Dog bark," may be responded to by, "Yes, he's mad at the kitty." Marion Blank and Francis Solomon also report a naturalistic strategy that is successful in elaborating children's language.[8] Their proposal suggests a one-to-one relationship with the child, basing instruction on his utterance but reflecting open-ended questions that have him move beyond his original statements. This strategy allows the tutor working with the child to make judgments about his level of language development by listening to specific utterances. This information is used in framing the next question, which is designed to move the child along a developmental continuum. The program was not designed to teach a child language per se but to develop within him the linguistic base for thinking.

Naturalistic methods can be used with a range of children in the primary grades as well. The Tucson Early Education Model, developed by Marie Hughes for Mexican-American children, reflects this point of view. The child is given continuous opportunities to speak, and the language he brings to school is valued. The teacher develops a self-conscious style of responding in Standard English that acts as a model for the child. Through the interactions of adult and child, the child's language is expected to be transformed in a naturalistic school setting.

Arline Hobson, working within this model, developed what she characterized as a natural method of language learning—*systematized*. The key to Hobson's approach is that the adult (the teacher) systematically utilizes those elements found within the natural adult–child interaction patterns that support language acquisition. These elements, according to Hobson, are

1. *Corrective feedback*—providing omissions, proper labels, proper word order, and appropriate vocabulary
2. *Summary feedback*—gathering together ideas that have

---

[7] Courtney Cazden, "Some Implications of Research on Language Development," in *Early Education,* eds. Robert Hess and Roberta Bower (Chicago: Aldine Publishing Co., 1968), pp. 131–42.

[8] Marion Blank and Francis Solomon, "How Shall Disadvantaged Children Be Taught?" *Child Development,* 40, no. 1 (March 1969), 47–63.

been expressed by the children, thus expanding the relationships among ideas

3. *Elaboration and extension*—extending language and ideas
beyond the immediate

4. *Extending knowledge*—providing information beyond what
is immediately available

5. *Reinforcing*—providing generous and specific reinforcement
for appropriate language generation

The teacher also uses her knowledge of development and the educational
possibilities in the classroom to provide effective instruction for all the
children.[9]

USE OF SYNTHETIC TECHNIQUES. The Bereiter-Engelmann approach to teaching young children rejects naturalistic strategies.[10] The
teacher uses a series of basic statement forms in Standard English. The
instructional model is closer to that used in teaching foreign languages
to children. It makes no use of the language the children bring to school.

Shari Nedler[11] and Robert Reeback[12] use synthetic approaches
to teach English to non–English-speaking children. The teacher, using
their patterned drill approaches, states a sentence or asks a question and
the children must give the desired response.

Recently Nedler has written a description of the process of
developing and testing approaches to teaching English to non–English-
speaking children. After the experience with two synthetic approaches
to teaching language, which did not have transferable outcomes that the
child could assimilate into his day-to-day verbal interactions, Nedler's
group moved to a more naturalistic approach. This approach was aimed
at teaching English vocabulary and elements of syntactical structure.[13]

The naturalistic and synthetic approaches to language instruction closely parallel the two theories of language acquisition supported
by the transformationalists and the behaviorists. The transformationalists—who view the child as an active participant, generating rules to be

[9] Arline B. Hobson, *The Natural Method of Language Learning: Systematized*
(Tucson: Arizona Center for Educational Research and Development,
University of Arizona, 1973).

[10] Carl Bereiter and Siegfried Engelmann, *Teaching Disadvantaged Children in the
Preschool* (Englewood Cliffs, N.J.: Prentice-Hall, Inc., 1966).

[11] Shari Nedler, *Early Education for Spanish-Speaking Mexican-American Children.*
Paper presented at AERA, March 2–7, 1970.

[12] Robert T. Reeback, *A Teacher's Manual to Accompany the Oral Language Program,* 3rd ed. (Albuquerque, N.M.: Southwestern Cooperative Educational Laboratories, 1970).

[13] Shari E. Nedler, "Explorations in Teaching English as a Second Language,"
Young Children, 30, no. 6 (September 1975), 480–85.

tested and modified to create internal language structures—believe the school should provide opportunities for these language acts to occur, and feedback to allow children to test the rules they create. The behaviorists, on the other hand, see the school as providing an opportunity for a more efficient, more systematic scheme of language instruction than can be provided in the home. By using explicit instructional strategies and manipulating rewards in the environment, the teacher can help the child move quickly through successive approximations toward mature language behavior. To do this, educators must clearly define goals of language instruction as behaviors and determine the conditions for achieving these behaviors.

GOALS OF LANGUAGE LEARNING

Language arts programs in the early years have multiple goals. In general, the goals are as follows:

1. THE DEVELOPMENT OF VERBAL COMMUNICATION SKILLS. The young child is constantly interacting with those around him, transmitting and receiving messages. His ability to function in the world is determined to a great extent by his ability to communicate his wants, needs, ideas, and feelings, and to receive and interpret similar communications from other persons. These two skills are in large part the goals of language arts programs. As the child matures, the communications sent and received are put into written as well as spoken forms—reading and writing become important skills. This requires extended knowledge of vocabulary and structural forms.

2. DEVELOPMENT OF RICH LANGUAGE REPERTOIRE. Language is an extension of the person. To function effectively in the community, the young child must have a sense of the shared meanings of words and of the structure of the language that allows him to be linguistically effective. He needs to learn about the variety of styles and uses of language that are available. Chomsky's "deep structure" becomes important here.

A language repertoire is important not just for communication but as an aid to thinking as well. Since mature thought processes are so closely related to language both in structure and in content, the child's growth in language will also support his growth in thought.

3. DEVELOPMENT OF AN ABILITY TO USE LANGUAGE TO INFLUENCE AND BE INFLUENCED. Until the time a child reaches nursery school age, he is manipulated and manipulates others physically. As he enters school, the manipulation is more by the use of words. The teacher gives instructions in words; language, in this sense, is a tool. The child

satisfies social needs more by talking to other children. The give-and-take of human relationships becomes a function of language. Even in the dramatic play of children, verbal statements soon take the place of actual physical movements. All this suggests that the appropriate use of language is one of the most important social skills the young child can learn.

4. DEVELOPING PERSONAL SATISFACTIONS AND AESTHETIC APPRECIATIONS OF LANGUAGE. Although much of the language arts program in the early school years is primarily utilitarian in nature, aesthetics should not be excluded. The use of literature, poetry, creative dramatics, and other forms of expression can provide great personal satisfactions, aesthetic and emotional, for children.

EXPRESSIVE ORAL LANGUAGE LEARNING

There are many opportunities for oral language learning in the early years of school. Specific times are set aside for group discussion, story reading, and sharing, or "show and tell." Although such large group activities may be suitable for teaching some receptive language skills, they are not efficient for teaching expressive skills, since each child spends too much time awaiting his turn in a large group. Alternate approaches need to be developed. Some of these approaches require a teacher's sensitivity to the time when language learning can occur naturally in a small group setting or in individual interaction. These small settings are usually more appropriate for language learning than are total class instructional settings.

THE ACTIVITY PERIOD

Most nursery-kindergarten programs set aside a good portion of the day for an activity or work period. When primary grades are organized as suggested in Chapter 13, these opportunities are also available. Some of the activities of the work period provide greater opportunities than others to support language learning.

DRAMATIC PLAY

Dramatic play is an important area for language learning. This involves the children in role playing with no predetermined script or plot. It might include family play in a housekeeping area or playing other societal roles reflecting a range of social institutions such as supermarket play, or garage play. In dramatic play a child can put into action his personal constructions of the adult world. The cognitive and effective meanings developed become intertwined in this play.

Although dramatic play is supported most often in nursery-kindergarten activities, similar play interactions can be developed by primary-grade children. These may be more narrowly focused and closely guided and related to specific learning situations. Often social studies activities include dramatic play incidents to explore social roles. Dramatic play is symbolic play. It requires the interaction of children in interlocking roles: they must communicate with one another to carry on the play. Language often substitutes for the actions of the playing. Sarah Smilansky found that a teacher may use specific techniques that work to enrich children's dramatic play.[14]

Educational play requires active guidance by the teacher, although she should allow the children to structure their own play activities within the established theme and the setting. Through observation, the teacher becomes aware of possibilities in the play that are not evident to the children. She may move into the play, momentarily assuming a role, and direct it through verbal interactions. She may ask key questions of the play participants that will suggest new alternatives, or provide additional props if she feels they will move the play forward.

The key to supporting language learning in dramatic play is not in simply setting up the children's play activities and leaving them alone in their corner. Helen Robison and Bernard Spodek used the term *directive teaching* in describing how a teacher might guide the play of children.[15] The teacher functions not only as an observer but also as a guide and a source of information and play materials. In functioning in this manner, the teacher must be careful not to impose too much of herself on the play of children.

OTHER AREAS

Although few activity areas are as productive for language learning as dramatic play, there are other opportunities in the activity period for language learning. More mature block-building often involves verbal and social interaction.

As the children move beyond the manipulative stage of block-building there will be a strong dramatic element to the play. When play takes on this dramatic quality and involves more than one child, it may be used in much the same way as dramatic play to support language learning. Arts and crafts and work in manipulative materials offer fewer opportunities to practice language skills. Teachers can add to available opportunities, however, by holding intimate conversations with the children.

Children who are shy and reticent in a large group situation

---

[14] Sarah Smilansky, *The Effects of Sociodramatic Play on Disadvantaged Preschool Children* (New York: John Wiley and Sons, 1968).

[15] Helen Robison and Bernard Spodek, *New Directions in the Kindergarten* (New York: Teachers College Press, 1965).

will often speak more freely when alone with the teacher. Conversations can be started related to the children's activities or to the materials they are using. Such conversations have the advantage of allowing the child to focus on something outside himself, and to refer to things immediately in front of him as a source of speech content. Teachers can use open-ended questions like, "Tell me what you have there," or "Are there other ways you could make something like it?" to elicit language expressions. These questions can be followed up in a probing fashion to continue the conversation.

Marion Blank designed a tutorial approach that emphasized both language and cognitive goals. The tutorial was essentially a dialogue between the preschool child and the teacher, using the Socratic method. By asking questions about common occurrences and materials, the teacher could extend the child's language and thinking skills. Children's difficulties were attended to and children were helped to deal with ideas on a more abstract level. Tutorial sessions are short but frequent in the Blank approach.[16]

Few teachers could take the classroom time for all children that Blank's method would require, but a teacher can set aside some time within the daily schedule to meet briefly with those children who are having language difficulties. Brief dialogues could be planned relating to occurrences in the classroom and children could be helped to think through and articulate their thoughts about those events. This form of interaction, focusing upon what the child is doing or has around him, could help extend language and thinking skills.

Having the teacher immediately available as a respondent to the child makes these small verbal interactions very useful. If a teacher aide or volunteer is in the classroom, a great amount of teacher–child interaction can take place in an activity period, since two persons can be deployed to support verbal behavior.

DISCUSSION SESSIONS

Most classes set aside periods during the day for discussion sessions, often involving the entire class, as in sharing and "show and tell" periods. Although such discussion sessions have many advantages, there are also disadvantages inherent in their organization.

The sharing period generally requires that each child, in turn, speak to the entire class. He may bring an object from home or discuss something that has happened to him. Such periods, if properly used, can

---

[16] Marion Blank, *Teaching Learning in the Preschool* (Columbus, Ohio: Charles E. Merrill, 1973).

effect a bridge between home and school. If the child is reticent, the teacher can ask questions about the object. During the sharing period the children should be encouraged to ask questions, comment, and make observations on their own.

Teachers using this sharing period should avoid its inherent pitfalls. In some communities the gap between home and school is too great to bridge. The teacher's rejection of objects or incidents from home that might be considered inappropriate at school may actually widen the gap. It may also teach the child that it is safer not to expose oneself in school, and thereby it may limit language learning possibilities.

There is also the danger that limiting the length of each contribution, or having the children take turns or wait for their turn longer than they can bear, may have negative influences on language learning. The children should be learning to be listeners and speakers—this is not easily learned in a situation that supports the negative responses of "turning off" and "tuning out."

Several alternatives to the traditional sharing period exist that can increase the benefits of this type of activity for language learning. One method is to limit the number of children who will speak at each session. Going through the class alphabetically and assigning five children per session, for example, can keep the sharing period to a reasonable limit. Asking that children bring items to class associated with a specific

Bernard Spodek

theme might also limit the range of items discussed and relate the discussion time to other learning situations in the classroom. Children can be asked to bring in something made of wood, something that is attracted by a magnet, something very old, or pictures of objects. The need to focus on some special area or class of object turns the home search for an object into a problem-solving activity for the child as well as the family.

Another alternative is to change the sharing from a whole-class activity to a small-group activity. This would allow a degree of voluntarism to the child's involvement, a greater degree of participation among all the children, and far more interaction among children in the discussion situation. The children themselves might take turns asking about objects and events.

Finally, the discussion session might be changed from a situation in which children talk about things outside the school to one in which they talk about what happened in school. If a sharing time were held at the end of the activity period, for example, the children could then talk about what they made or did during that time.

The children can be called together in a suitable place that is regularly designated for assemblies. Each child can then be asked to talk about what he did or what he made that day. If a product is involved, the child can show it. The teachers or any of the other children may ask questions about it. If there is no product, the child can be asked to describe activities in which he participated. Such discussions have the advantage of avoiding stereotyping, unless the entire program is stereotyped.

As the activities vary, the content of the discussions must also vary. The child and teacher share the same reference so that if there is distortion, misrepresentation, or confusion, the teacher is able to deal with it, since she was witness to the events. *Sharing* in this situation takes on new meaning, for not only does the child have an opportunity to relate things that are important to him, but the interaction and reporting of activity in the school setting can help establish a feeling of community in the classroom, without separating the "haves" from the "have nots."

Many other opportunities for discussions also can be found. Informal discussions between the teacher and a child or group can take place on any occasion and should be regularly encouraged by the teacher. The greater the amount of the child's verbal expression, and the greater the number of adult-child interactions that take place, the greater the opportunities for language learning in the classroom.

CREATIVE DRAMATICS

The school should provide many opportunities for children to interpret the stories, poems, and songs they hear in a variety of ways. Creative drama allows for such interpretations. Unlike dramatic play, which builds upon the general knowledge of children and can move in any direction, this focuses on a particular plot, such as a familiar story with a relatively simple, straightforward plot line. The children can be assigned characters and then can make up their own dialogue, keeping the story line intact. The creative aspect of the dramatic presentation lies in the interpretations of the children, the dialogue they develop, and the actions they assign to particular characters. Children can also base dramatic presentation on their own original stories, which provide them with a greater latitude of plot and character.

Creative dramatic presentations need no audience. They can be organized as a part of the activity period, either started spontaneously by the children or encouraged by the teacher. The teacher and children can assemble the few props needed. The furniture and equipment of the classroom can be made to represent anything: a pair of chairs can be an automobile, a table becomes a bridge, a piece of carpeting turns into an ocean. Odd pieces of drapery material, skirts, and floppy hats can be made to represent all kinds of costumes.

As the teacher directs such a dramatic presentation, she should be careful not to have the children memorize pieces of dialogue or action, but instead to allow the content of the play to be their product. Her job includes providing a story that can become familiar to the children through repeated telling, suggesting actions and sequences, and referring to the original story as a source of dialogue and action. Often a suggestion such as "What happens next?" or "What did he say in response?" is the only guidance a teacher needs to give.

Simple dramatic presentations can be repeated. Children can be encouraged to try new roles and, once assigned, to play them in their own way. Although such productions ought not to be organized primarily as shows for others, if a particular dramatic presentation seems good, there is no reason not to invite another class, the principal, or the children's parents to view it. This can provide the children with a great sense of accomplishment.

As children mature, dramatic presentations can become more elaborate, using more extensive stories and characterizations, and more elaborate props and settings. The same story can often be dramatized in a variety of ways in a class. After interpreting a story in creative dramatics, the children can try it with puppets or flannelgraph illustrations. They could also try acting out the story in pantomime—attempting to communicate with actions alone.

PUPPETRY

Young children enjoy playing with puppets. This is a good way to get a shy child to vocalize, for the puppet becomes the center of

attention rather than the child. A variety of excellent commercial hand-puppets is available in supply houses, and simple puppets can be constructed by the teacher or the children.

Stick puppets can be made by pasting faces the children have drawn on paper to a flat stick. The children then hold and manipulate them in a play situation. Puppets can also be made out of paper bags on which a face has been drawn. If the mouth is drawn on both sides of the point at which the square bottom of the bag is folded, it will open and close when held between fingers and thumb. Such sophisticated puppet manipulations are not really necessary for young children, however.

Teachers and parents can also make interesting puppets out of socks: buttons can be eyes and a piece of felt the mouth. Puppets can be improvised in many other ways. All that is needed is an object to be manipulated that is suggestive of a character. For very young children, a puppet stage is unnecessary, for even if the puppeteer is visible, as in Japanese puppet shows, the audience will focus on the puppets themselves.

Making puppets ought not to be a whole-class craft activity. Puppets should be constructed because some children feel a need for them. Nor should puppet shows themselves involve the whole class. Children can be easily bored if they must sit for periods of time watching the unrehearsed and often uncommunicative manipulations of puppets by each member of the class. Puppet shows are best developed in small groups. In fact, an audience is not always necessary.

With older children, puppet making can become a more extensive craft activity with children using papier-mâché or wood for shaping the puppets' heads. Marionettes—puppets that move by the manipulation of strings—can also be used by children in the upper primary grades. As with creative dramatics, there is no age ceiling on the use of puppets, if their use is varied with maturity.

CHILDREN'S STORYTELLING

Although the teacher generally is considered to be the storyteller in a class, young children should also be encouraged to tell stories. These can be their original stories or stories they have heard. The teacher can ask leading questions, or read part of a story and ask the children to complete it or to fill in portions.

Children can also be encouraged to report on important events. A child may return from a vacation or a trip and be bursting to share his experiences with others. Time should be provided for this, for the sharing of experience is one of the important reasons for developing good language facility. These reports may be given to a small group rather than to the entire class. On occasion they should be written down by the teacher to be read back at a later time.

Teachers should be willing to take dictation from children. The children's observations of the process of dictating, recording, and reading back stories gives them an understanding of what reading and writing are, and the reasons for our concern for learning these skills. The phrase "writing is talk written down" comes vividly to life in this process. Meaningful associations between their verbal utterances and the books around them are created in this process.

RECEPTIVE ORAL LANGUAGE LEARNING

The skills of a receptive language become increasingly important. Most children spend less time speaking and acting and more time listening and watching as they move through school. Opportunities must be provided for children to listen.

Children listen at different times for different purposes and with varying degrees of depth. Levels of listening have been classified as marginal, appreciative, attentive, and analytic.[17] Listening to sounds in

[17] National Council of Teachers of English, *Language Arts for Today's Children* (New York: Appleton-Century-Crofts, Inc., 1954).

the background can be characterized as marginal; listening to music or to a story is appreciative listening; attentive listening is listening for directions; analytic listening requires a more active role of the individual, who dissects and evaluates what is heard. Unfortunately the activities in too many classrooms support marginal listening alone.

When children are constantly bombarded with messages and instructions, not all of which may seem relevant to them, they tend to tune out. In many crowded, noisy homes children learn this skill as a survival mechanism that may be brought to school and applied indiscriminately.

Teaching children to listen is a worthwhile goal for early childhood education, but it is sometimes difficult to determine whether it has been achieved. Children who are watching will usually provide visual cues of their attention: their eyes are focused and their faces turned toward the object being viewed. The child's ears do not give the same clues of attention. A child may be listening while looking away from the speaker, even engaged in other activities. Too often what is accepted as listening behavior in young children is simply an outward manifestation of conformity. The only way we can actually tell whether a child is listening attentively is to ask him a question that requires him to reflect some element of what he heard, or to do something with what he heard. Young children can be involved in the processes of appreciative, attentive, and analytic listening in schools. Storytelling and discussions about stories will help.

TELLING STORIES TO CHILDREN

Storytelling, both with and without books, has a firm, well-deserved place in school programs. A large body of children's literature providing a wealth of resources for storytelling has developed in the last few decades in our country. Unfortunately, the availability of books for children often creates a situation in which the teacher only reads stories, rather than telling them. This is probably easier than having to worry about content or plot, but reading books should never completely eliminate telling stories. Teachers can familiarize themselves with stories from children's books, which they can retell in their own words.

The story might be a fanciful, contemporary tale or a traditional story culled from the folk literature. Stories may also be the outgrowth of the children's experiences. Retelling the happenings on a trip or another experience the children have had, or even an occurrence from the childhood experience of the teacher, provide excellent resources for stories.

Teachers often find that props or pictures help them dramatize a story. Simple figures for use on a flannel board, simple objects, or pictures are commercially available.

READING TO CHILDREN

Any nursery or kindergarten class should have a good stock of well-written and well-illustrated books for children. Collections of stories, or anthologies, even when not illustrated, are also useful. Teachers can get help in selecting books from other teachers and supervisors, librarians, and local colleges and universities. In addition, several printed resources are available to help teachers select books. These include

> *Best Books for Children.* New York: R. R. Bowker.
> *Bibliography of Books for Children.* Washington, D.C.: Association for Childhood Education International.
> *Books for Children.* Chicago: American Library Association, n.d.
> Eaken, Mary K., *Good Books for Children* (3rd ed.). Chicago: University of Chicago Press, 1967.
> Guilfoile, Elizabeth, *Books for Beginning Readers.* Champaign, Ill.: National Council of Teachers of English, 1962.
> Larrick, Nancy, *A Parent's Guide to Children's Reading* (rev.). Garden City, N.Y.: Doubleday, 1964.
> Reid, Virginia M., *Reading Ladders for Human Relations* (5th ed.). Washington, D.C.: American Council on Education, 1972.
> Rollins, Charlemae H., *We Build Together* (3rd ed.). Champaign, Ill.: National Council of Teachers of English, 1967.

In addition, each spring *Young Children* publishes a series of annotated bibliographies of outstanding new books for young children.

Books should be selected carefully; it is important that they be of interest to the children. When information books are chosen, they should be accurate and authoritative—accuracy of information may take precedence over literary style. The teacher might select stories to prepare children for a future study, or a book because the theme concerns her. Books are also read simply for good fun.

Good children's literature has themes that are the central focus of young children's concerns. Books provide a way of learning about things outside the immediate in time and space, thus expanding the child's horizons. Persons different in manner and dress can be introduced to children through books. And certainly the world of whimsy and fantasy should be a part of the child's literary experience.

Books can often help the young child deal with the resolution of his own problems and conflicts; they may have a mentally healthful

Bernard Spodek

effect by showing the child that the problems he encounters are not his alone. Some educators have suggested that teachers systematically use books and discussions to help children cope with the problems they encounter. Such an approach, called *bibliotherapy,* is seen as having preventative powers as well as therapeutic values in maintaining a child's mental health.

In addition, books that depict children from minority groups in realistic ways are becoming increasingly available. Although such books are no substitute for an integrated classroom, they help the majority culture member realize that people who may seem different are really not that different. Providing such books in school also shows the minority-group child that members of his group are worthy of being depicted in the national literature.[18]

It is important that the teacher be familiar with the book she is reading to the children. New teachers often find it helpful to take books home and practice reading them aloud. The stage should then be set for

[18] For information about books dealing with minority children, see the list of books suggested earlier in this chapter, as well as Bernard Spodek and others, *A Black Studies Curriculum for Early Childhood Education* (rev.) (Urbana, Ill.: ERIC Clearinghouse for Early Childhood Education, 1976); and *Interracial Books for Children Bulletin* (Council on Interracial Books for Children, 1841 Broadway, New York, N.Y. 10023).

a pleasurable reading experience with the children. An informal arrangement helps; seating the group informally on a rug so that each child has an undisturbed line of vision to the teacher is helpful. Chairs can also be informally arranged for reading—especially if a picture-story book is being read.

It is disturbing to have to interrupt a story constantly to admonish a child who is misbehaving or inattentive. Teachers sometimes use the tactic of placing obstreperous children near them to forestall the need to interrupt. Making story listening a voluntary activity, with choices of other non–noise-producing activities available, is also useful. It is interesting to note how often a child will begin to pay attention simply because he is not required to do so.

Teachers generally read stories to children themselves, but it is beneficial to have an aide or a volunteer parent come to school and read. If more than one person is available, a story-reading time need not involve the entire class. Actually, making the story-reading period more intimate is helpful in developing language learning. Children in the upper grades may be invited to read to the class, as may the better primary readers.

The reading of a story will often engender a discussion. Teachers sometimes also like to ask questions of the children to see if they have understood the story. Although this is a good technique for ferreting out the misconceptions of children, it can be overdone. Care must be taken to see that the story-reading activity remains a pleasant one and does not become burdensome to children.

BROWSING THROUGH BOOKS

Children need opportunities to look at books themselves, to get the feel of books even before they are required to learn to read them. A good library area has books attractively displayed and available for children. Books may be laid on a shelf or placed in a rack so that the child can easily see covers in order to select books that seem interesting. There ought to be a place where the child can comfortably look through the books, examining the pictures, reading, and discussing them with other children. A rocking chair, a table and chairs, a group of pillows on the floor, or even a small rug all make inviting settings for browsing through books. Of course, lighting must be adequate and there should be a degree of isolation to the area. The books available in the classroom can be organized so children can care for them. When books are changed at frequent intervals, some new and exciting reading material is always available.

It is useful to allow children to take books home if possible.

Particularly when there is a suspicion that the child has few books at home, the teacher should try to arrange to lend books. Inexpensive reprints of good children's books are available that make the cost of this activity reasonable. If books are to be taken home, it is a good idea to encourage the parents to read to nonreading children. Sometimes a simple instruction sheet sent home to the parent is enough; at other times, the teacher might wish to devote a parent meeting to working on the specific skills needed by the parents in reading to their children.

POETRY FOR YOUNG CHILDREN

Children enjoy listening to poetry, for it combines the rhythmic flow of words with a concern for their sounds. A range of poems for young children from Mother Goose rhymes and A. A. Milne to the works of many contemporary poets can be introduced. The repetitive quality of much of children's poetry will sometimes help the children learn the poems themselves.

Often, reading poetry in a class will lead children to an interest in the sounds of words. Rhyming and alliteration may fascinate some children who simply enjoy the sounds of the words and the way they feel on their tongues. Play with words should be encouraged, but teachers should be forewarned that young children can be terrible punsters. Poems should be read aloud so that the rhyme and rhythm become apparent.

Teachers of young children often use poems along with finger plays. These activities often lack literary value, but they are useful as time-fillers and are enjoyed by children. Finger play has a venerable tradition in early childhood education, originating in Froebel's kindergarten.

USING AUDIO-VISUAL AIDS

In most classrooms the teacher, being alone, is limited in her ability to provide a great variety of listening activities for the children. If she reads a story to the children, her entire attention is consumed and she can do nothing else, thus, story times too often become total class activity times. This is not necessary in a well-organized classroom. Many teachers have found that using audio-visual aids can extend their ability to provide receptive language activities under a variety of conditions and with smaller groups of children.

Commercial recordings of many children's stories are available. In addition, teachers have found it helpful to make their own sound recordings of stories. Most children at the nursery level can learn to handle a cassette tape recorder on their own. Providing children with a tape recording of a book along with the book itself allows them to listen to the story and look at the pictures at the same time. Recording an auditory signal for turning the page is helpful.

Many classes are equipped with *listening centers.* Such a center consists of headphone attachments to a phonograph or tape recorder. Multiple jacks are available so that more than one child can listen at a time. Although some listening centers are designed with carrels to separate the children, such separations are unnecessary and possibly even a hindrance unless there is a severe attention problem. Listening to a story can and ought to be an experience a child can share with others. The headsets are used primarily so that the sounds of the record do not interfere with other activities that may be occurring in the classroom.

Motion pictures and sound filmstrips can also be used to extend children's receptive language experiences. A number of excellent children's stories are now available in these media and rooms can be arranged and equipped to allow viewing by a single child or a large group.

TELEVISION AND CHILDREN

Most children spend a large proportion of their waking hours viewing television, but we are still not sure what they learn from it; certainly they seem to learn a lot. Any parent can report stories of young children identifying packages of advertised products, or of having the children badger them for toys they have seen advertised on that medium. While educators may not be sure of the impact of television on children's learning, advertisers seem to have a lot of faith in it.

We know that children's vocabulary is affected by television, because many of the words young children use daily are accessible only through this medium. It is doubtful that television similarly influences syntax, however. Although Standard American speech is broadcast continually on television, children of minority groups who are constantly exposed to it still do not master the syntax. This exposure apparently does not affect their speech patterns. Perhaps this is due to the lack of interaction in televiewing, which is a relatively passive act, as well as to the fact that much of the listening is on a marginal level.

Educational programs have, on occasion, been developed for young children, but often these are local shows operated on meager budgets. Few national programs of educational value exist for children. *Sesame Street* and *Misterogers' Neighborhood* are distributed nationally on public television, and *Captain Kangaroo* is distributed commercially; these have all demonstrated that television programs can be entertaining, educational, and mentally healthy while appealing to large groups of children. It is difficult to determine the full educational impact of such programs, however.

Existing programs for children are designed primarily for home viewing. Whether it would be profitable to provide television instruction in school is open to question. The amount of time available to most early childhood classes is little enough as it is. It would be unfortunate to limit interactional possibilities by substituting passive listening and viewing. Television scheduling also limits the teacher's flexibility in class, although this may change as videotape recorders become more readily available.

USING THE NORMAL OCCURRENCES OF THE DAY

Teachers can find many opportunities in all situations to support language learning throughout the school day. Continual language instruction, however, requires a sensitivity to the potentials of learning in each situation.

A cooking activity might start with a planning discussion: "What needs to be done?" "How will we go about it?" "Who will do each task?" "What materials and equipment are necessary?" These questions can be used to elicit responses in a planning discussion from all the children. Recipes need to be read several times, during both the planning and the cooking. The teacher can review the entire cooking sequence at its termination and perhaps write a chart describing the experience.

In dramatic play situations, signs can often be made by the teacher and used by the children. In music, the teacher might have the children listen carefully to the words of a song, then talk about the sounds of the words as well as their meaning. She might even use the singing of a repetitive verse to teach new words, or ask the children to create their own verses. The need for finding rhymes will help the children learn to listen to the word endings and to compare the sounds of words. Each activity needs to be plumbed to determine the depth of language learning that can be found therein.

OTHER LANGUAGE-RELATED ACTIVITIES

In addition to the areas already discussed, many other opportunities exist for language learning in the classroom. In most classrooms, a number of manipulative materials are provided in support of language learning. The use of these materials can extend an understanding of specific language attributes.

Lotto games are a good example. In playing Lotto, children have to identify a picture, label it, and match it with another picture on a card; thus Lotto games can be used to teach names of categories of objects, names of objects, or names of actions, in addition to teaching visual matching skills. *See-Quees* puzzles, in which the scenes from familiar stories must be placed in proper order, help children learn the sequence of events in a story. Then they may be asked to relate the story after the pictures are ordered. There are also many reading-readiness materials that can be used. Three-dimensional letters allow children to make up words and learn the names of the letters without coping with the problem of forming the letters themselves. They also provide a tactile experience in perceiving the shape and form of letters. A number of reading-readiness games and materials can also be included here.

Many of the games in the manipulative material area can be used by children individually or in small groups. Once children have mastered the skills needed in using the materials and the rules for their use, they can often work independently, with the teacher periodically checking on the accuracy of the activity. This independence of operation allows the manipulative materials to be used during many different times of the day.

The child's continued involvement in oral language activities, discussions, creative dramatic productions, and listening to stories and poems has a direct connection with his involvement in written language activities. There is less separation of the language arts in life than in school programs, which are too often segmented and compartmentalized. Reading and writing must go hand in hand with listening and speaking in the classroom.

WRITTEN LANGUAGE LEARNING

Primary teachers in particular are concerned with the mechanics as well as the expressive content of reading and writing. Much activity in the area of written language learning can be approached informally. However, teaching the skills of reading and writing requires some systematic approach to learning.

WRITING

Most schools today teach young children to write in manuscript, a simple form of calligraphy using unconnected letters. The switch to cursive writing, in which all the letters in a word are connected, usually comes at the end of the primary grades or the beginning of the intermediate grades—typically about the middle of second grade. Children often begin writing in kindergarten by learning to write their names.

Sometimes they have learned this skill at home. It is helpful if kindergarten children can learn to use manuscript rather than block printing to avoid an additional transition.

The beginnings of letter writing actually start even earlier. Children in nursery school and kindergarten have already had experiences using crayons and paint brushes. If the teacher has helped the children learn to hold and use these implements properly, the transition from drawing to writing is simplified. Children can be provided with pencils in the kindergarten for both drawing and beginning writing. They can be helped in informal situations to make the strokes necessary for manuscript writing—these strokes include the circle and the horizontal, vertical, and slant strokes. They can often be identified in the child's existing paintings and drawings. The child's ability to control his painting, drawing, or writing implement will aid him later in forming letters.

A variety of techniques can be used to teach the formation of letters, including the use of template, wooden, or sandpaper letters. This lets the child experience a feel for the shape and form of letters. Children can then copy letters the teacher writes or those printed in work sheets or exercise books, or go over letters formed by the teacher. Letters can be formed in the sand or on a blackboard before using paper and pencil. Teachers may also give a child models printed on paper placed under acetate sheets so that his first writing is directly on the model. When such activities are provided, they should be provided only to those children who are interested and who can benefit from them. It is unwise to make such printing activities a whole class assignment.

One intriguing sequence in teaching children to write was observed in an English infant school. Children from the day of admission (about age five) were given a book of their own, several sheets of paper stapled together along the left edge. Each day every child was to "write" in his book. The "writings" at first were pictures drawn by the children. The teacher would write a short narrative about the picture as dictated by the child. Later, the children were asked to write with a pencil over the teacher's writing. Still later the children copied the teacher's narrative directly below her words on the paper. Finally, the children were expected to write their own short narratives with the help of the teacher or another child.

In many cases, children will be able to *use* writing long before they have perfected the ability to write each letter clearly, legibly, and without error. They should be encouraged to do so, since unnecessary attention to the mechanics of writing without any concern for its use may lead them to lose interest. It is useful to have the children write words, sentences, and stories as early as possible.

Many kindergarten and primary classrooms have primer typewriters available. Their large type and simplified form of the letters make them an extremely useful addition to the classroom. Children can begin early to type their own stories on these machines, and they can be read by other children with ease. The typewriter frees the young child from his concern with coordinating the muscles of his hand to form the letters. Words come out with ease. In its introduction, the typewriter often stimulates children to play with the forms of letters and punctuation marks. Soon children will move from this exploratory stage to a more goal-oriented stage, using the typewriter as a writing implement. More than one child might wish to be at the machine at the same time—for dialogue as well as discourse can be typed by children.

If the teacher has been taking the dictation of children, it is an easy matter to move slowly to the children's writing. She might begin by having them dictate a short story, using only a few words that they can copy. The children might also be given the opportunity to illustrate the story on large sheets of paper. The copying of short stories can be extended as stories are elaborated and lengthened. Groups of children can write stories together. They should be encouraged to begin to write their own stories as soon as possible.

The stories children write should be used. They should be read, either to the teacher or to other children. They may also be sent home. It is helpful to collect the writings of children to show progress in school and to read for pleasure. These writings can be stapled together into a book with covers and illustrations done by the children. The total volume can be displayed or put into the reading area so that others can read these stories as well. The need for clarity and precision in writing becomes evident—it is for the other children's convenience.

Providing the children with thin writing tablets at the beginning of the year gives them a sense of writing a book. Care should be taken that there are not too many pages in these tablets; otherwise, completing them will seem an overwhelming task. A home-made book, used in the infant school as described above, is often sufficient.

The school day is filled with opportunities for writing and children should be encouraged to write as much as possible. They can write about experiences out of school as well: starting with reporting incidents may help the children become writers. As time goes on, they can become more creative in the writing and add the composition of fanciful tales and poetry to their accumulated skills.

In the beginning, spelling is not too important and should not be stressed. Children need to feel comfortable in writing and this is not easily accomplished. Premature criticism can stifle the child's early attempts. The work can be corrected later by the teacher or by other children. Eventually children will develop the habit of proofreading their written work before submitting it to the teacher. It is helpful to provide them with primary dictionaries so that they can begin to look up the spelling of words. A file box and a set of cards or a notebook with each page devoted to a single letter of the alphabet can help them develop their own dictionaries or word lists. Children can put into their dictionary new words that they have learned to spell and define. They will soon begin to use one another as well as the teacher as resources for proper spelling. In the primary grades, more formal work in spelling can be included in the program.

There is not complete agreement in the field as to when a systematic program of spelling construction ought to begin for children, nor is there agreement as to the nature of such a program. In the past, many spelling programs consisted of providing children with lists or books of words used in their particular age-groups. Since it was felt that English spelling was highly irregular, most programs had the children memorize the spelling of lists of words in some fashion. Sometimes pretests were given weekly and children wrote the words they could not spell periodically until they were retested at the end of the week. Often the length of the word was the criterion for determining its suitability for children, with young children asked to learn shorter words. They were often helped to focus on the visual aspects of the word to enhance retention.

Studies by Paul and Jean Hanna and others have shown a high degree of regularity in the spelling of English words.[19] This would suggest that spelling patterns can be abstracted and words taught to children in a more rational manner than has been the convention. It also suggests that the errors of children who spell words as they sound could also be used to greater advantage by teachers, for even when mistakes are made, some errors may be more logical than others.

GRAMMAR

Recent changes in linguistic theory have had a profound effect on the teaching of grammar at the secondary school and college level. It is only possible to speculate about the extent to which these changes call for modification of early childhood programs. Current theory conceives of grammar as a process by which an infinite variety of sentences can be derived by transformation from a limited number of basic sentence forms.[20] The theory of transformational grammar as postulated by Noam

---

[19] Paul R. Hanna, Jean S. Hanna, Richard E. Hodges, and E. Hugh Rudorf, "A Summary: Linguistic Cues for Spelling Improvement," *Elementary English*, 44 (December 1967), 862–65.
[20] Noam Chomsky, *Syntactic Structure* (The Hague: Mouton and Co., 1957).

Chomsky and others would suggest that grammar ought to be taught not as a series of rules that lead to "proper" language usage, but as a series of rules from which new structure can be generated.

In the early years we are concerned with having children become good users of language rather than scholars of the structure of the language. From this point of view, the teacher's concern needs to be about how the newer grammar could provide insights that would help to extend children's language.

One possible approach is to provide children with opportunities to "play" with the structures of language just as they often play with the sounds of words. Children can be given simple sentences and asked to transform them in a variety of ways. Given a declarative sentence, children could be asked to state it as a question or as a command. They could add modifiers to noun or verb phrases, thus becoming more specific in their language use. They could also be asked to place words in different sequences to try to change the meaning of sentences or to become sensitive to grammatical and ungrammatical structures.

Teachers need to be aware of the beauties of the language that can be found in the personal ways children express themselves. Often the idiosyncratic phrases of children in the nursery years are subdued because they do not fit into the formal structure of the language program. Subcultural groups have expressions that have enriched our language, yet we often exclude these from our schools. Teachers should support and cherish these rather than try to eliminate them. The beauty of the language is enhanced when communication is a personal statement rather than a stereotyped series of phrases.

English primary schools can be characterized by the amount of writing in which the child engages. American schools can be characterized by their emphasis on reading. Carol Chomsky suggests that the natural order of progression is from writing to reading. Starting written language instruction through writing makes the child aware that the written work is an extension of his consciousness. Beginning reading can grow out of the child's writing. Beginning spelling can be invented by the children following the sounds of words, thus making them aware of letter–sound associations. More formal spelling instruction can take place later.[21]

One can debate whether writing should precede reading; however, instruction in the two language areas needs to go hand in hand. Having the children write early is consistent with a number of methods of teaching reading reviewed in the next chapter. It can also help the class-

[21] Carol Chomsky, "Write Now, Read Later," *Childhood Education,* 47, no. 6 (January 1971), pp. 296–99.

room teacher develop an integrated approach to the language arts in her classroom.

READING

Reading and writing are two sides of the same coin. As we wish to develop writers through our primary programs, we also wish to develop readers. Therefore, reading has to become a meaningful and personally satisfying experience. This can happen only when the child reads because he wants to rather than because he has to. If a child is to become "hooked on books," the book has to be introduced early in his reading experience.

As we mentioned earlier, children need to be provided with opportunities for free browsing and reading. They should be able to determine what they will read, when they will read, and for how long. Even nursery-school children need opportunities to look at books and get their feel before being required to learn and to read them. Once children develop reading skills, they should have many opportunities for independent study.

The books available in a class should range broadly in topics and reading levels. If a book is interesting, a child will be able to read beyond his level as well as beneath it. A child needs a place to sit or stretch out and read undisturbed. Conversation should not be limited in a reading area, for if a child is truly interested in a book, he will want to share its contents with others. If the school has a library, it is important to schedule times for children to read or select books in it. However, a school library is a supplement, not a substitute, for a classroom library. Children need continual access to books. If they are reading independently, a record-keeping system will enable teacher and children to keep track of books read.

Children learn as much by observing the behavior of teachers as by listening to their admonitions. If a teacher wishes to teach them to enjoy reading, she must be a reader herself and able to communicate her enjoyment of reading. Reading stories to the class is one way of showing this enjoyment. There are other ways as well. A teacher can bring special books into class on occasion and tell the children about them, or feature them in a display. She can have conferences with the children, asking them to describe the books, telling if they enjoyed them and why. She can allow the children to write about the books they read, and can schedule time for them to read books of their choice during the school day.

More than anything else, the climate of the classroom and the values the teacher's behavior reflects will determine the nature of the language program. The same room with the same materials can be a dull setting or it can be an exciting place with children eagerly learning, listening, reading, talking, and writing. It is what the teacher does with the materials at hand that makes the difference.

SUGGESTED READING

ANDERSON, PAUL S., *Language Skills in Elementary Education.* New York: Macmillan, 1964.

BURNS, PAUL C., and ALBERTA L. LOWE, *The Language Arts in Childhood Education.* Chicago: Rand McNally, 1966.

CAZDEN, COURTNEY B., ed., *Child Language and Education.* New York: Holt, Rinehart and Winston, 1972.

_____, *Language in Early Childhood Education.* Washington, D.C.: National Association for the Education of Young Children, 1972.

CHUKOVSKY, KORNEI, *From Two to Five.* Berkeley: University of California Press, 1963.

DAWSON, MILDRED A., and GEORGIANA G. NEWMAN, *Language Teaching in Kindergarten and Early Primary Grades.* New York: Harcourt, Brace and World, 1966.

HOBSON, ARLINE B., *The Natural Method of Language Learning: Systematized.* Tucson: Arizona Center for Educational Research and Development, University of Arizona, 1973.

HUCK, CHARLOTTE S., and DORIS A. YOUNG, *Children's Literature in the Elementary School* (3rd ed.). New York: Holt, Rinehart and Winston, 1976.

SHANE, HAROLD G., JAMES WALDEN, and RONALD GREEN, *Interpreting Language Arts Research for the Teacher.* Washington, D.C.: Association for Supervision and Curriculum Development, 1971.

STRICKLAND, RUTH G., *The Language Arts in the Elementary School* (3rd ed.). Lexington, Mass.: D. C. Heath, 1969.

TOUGH, JOAN, *Talking, Thinking, Growing: Language with Young Children.* New York: Schocken Books, 1974.

Bernard Spodek

CHAPTER FIVE

TEACHING BEGINNING READING

In recent years, the number of alternative approaches to beginning reading instruction seem to have increased. New textbooks and programs have appeared and older programs have been revised and updated. To the legion of reading specialists producing instructional materials have been added linguists, psychologists, special educators, media specialists, and many others. Concern about the schools' failure to educate poor and minority children has heightened developmental activities for teaching reading, especially in the area of early instruction and prereading education.

For all the interest and activity, the fact is that *there is relatively little dependable knowledge about how children learn to read and what instructional programs seem to be most effective.* A decade ago, the U.S. Office of Education conducted an extensive study of reading in the first grade designed to collect data about the effectiveness of many programs. In general, the findings suggested that no single approach to reading instruction was outstanding compared to others in all aspects of reading. Although there were differences in results, children learned certain phases of reading better by one method, and other phases better by other methods. Furthermore, it was suggested that more variability existed among teachers than among programs in terms of successful reading achievement.[1] Therefore, it is quite possible that variables other than the particular methodological approach used in reading instruction are crucial in getting children to read. This presents an interesting point

---

[1] Guy Bond, "First Grade Reading Studies: An Overview," *Elementary English,* 43, no. 5 (May 1966), 464–70.

for speculation and research. What are the crucial elements of an effective reading program? Are there classroom characteristics, teacher characteristics, pupil characteristics, or community characteristics that must be taken into account in developing an optimal program? More careful analysis needs to be made of classroom variables other than the instructional method before we can make use of these findings.

First, we must distinguish between reading as a mature process and learning to read. Just as a good bicycle rider does not attend to or do all the things a beginner feels are important, so the mature reader attends to different things and reads differently from the novice reader. An analysis of reading will help in understanding the goals of the reading program. The ways in which these goals are achieved cannot be directly derived from this description.

DEFINING READING

Some of the controversy about reading instruction arises from the way in which the reading process is defined. Some educators contend that it is basically a decoding process—learning the relationship between written symbols and spoken sounds. Once these associations are learned, the child is a reader. Since the young child already has a body of knowledge available to him in relation to meanings and processes in oral language, beginning reading teachers need not worry about these. What the child does with the information gleaned from the written page is not considered the domain of reading. Further, the goal of reading instruction, according to this point of view, is to provide children with the key letter-sound associations that will unlock the written code.

Although few will disagree with the need for the successful beginning reader to learn letter-sound associations, many suggest that the reading process is more than "code cracking." Different experts extend their interpretations of the reading process and include much more. Some claim that reading is "gaining meaning from the printed page." They take reading one step beyond the first approach, suggesting that *interpreting* the sounds associated with the letters is also a part of the reading process and needs to be included in any program of instruction. Educators supporting this theory even suggest that the derivation of meaning for the printed word, rather than "code cracking," be emphasized in any reading instructional program.

Still others suggest that the reading process is really an extension of intellectual processes, for the interpretation of meaning is a significant part of reading also. Critical reading, problem solving, and other complex processes need also to be included in any reading program.

Frank Smith sees reading as gaining meaning from the printed word. He identifies two ways of achieving comprehension in reading. The first, *immediate comprehension,* is accomplished by going directly from the visual features of writing to their meaning. The second, *mediated comprehension,* requires a prior identification of words. The fluent reader reads primarily by way of immediate comprehension, using alternative sources of redundant information to speed the process along. This information comes from word forms, syntactical structures, and the context of words. Only when difficulties arise does the fluent reader use mediated comprehension.

Smith believes the problems of the beginning reader are compounded by a lack of experience with the reading process and suggests that traditional programs allow him to achieve the experience he needs to create rules of reading for himself. The fact that the redundancy of information is used by mature readers may explain why different programs stressing different reading skills may be equally successful in teaching beginning reading.[2]

These points of view are not contradictory, for they deal with the relationship of reading to the language and thinking process of the individual. It is quite possible that, as Smith suggests, the reading process is different at different age or grade levels. For the teacher of young children, some of the discussion about reading may seem irrelevant, for much of it relates to its nature in more mature individuals. The teacher of young children, though concerned mainly with the beginning processes of reading, needs an understanding of the relationship between early and more mature processes to put beginning reading instruction in the proper perspective.

RELATIONSHIP OF READING
TO LANGUAGE

When discussing language, one needs to include the four modes of communication: speaking, listening, reading, and writing. The linguists study written language as a way of expressing oral language in visual symbols. The writer takes oral language and encodes it into a series of characters that can be decoded in order to ascertain their meaning.

There are many ways of encoding language. Early people used pictures to illustrate the things they wished to communicate. Some people eventually developed abstractions of these pictures, replacing them with

[2] Frank Smith, *Understanding Reading* (New York: Holt, Rinehart and Winston, 1971), pp. 3–9.

a set of symbols, each symbol reflecting a single idea. The advantage of this ideographic approach was that the symbols could be combined to create representations of abstract ideas and actions. The Chinese written language is composed of such ideographs. While the written symbols relate to the spoken language ideationally, they have no relationship to the sounds of the language. The advantage of such a written system is that it allows one to communicate across languages and dialects without sharing a common spoken language. The disadvantage lies in the large number of symbols that need to be learned to establish basic literacy, let alone the vast number needed for a person of scholarship.

In our system one can read any material, no matter how complex, by mastering a set of twenty-six symbols and their multiple sound relationships. The symbols reflect sounds in the spoken language rather than ideas or objects. The need to crack the code of letter-sound association, therefore, becomes obvious, for the written symbols carry no meaning outside their oral counterpart. Some reading specialists suggest that one of the major problems in reading stems from the fact that a sound can be represented by more than one letter, and letters or combinations of letters can represent a multitude of sounds. Still, there is a high degree of regularity between the sound symbols and the visual symbols of our language.

Reading is a part of the language process that deals with decoding written symbols. The written word in our language is derived from the spoken word, but this does not mean that the reader must translate each word read into a word heard. Rather, once reading skill is achieved, the individual has two parallel forms of receptive language available. In the early years of schooling, the child may have to move from the novel (for him) written symbol to the more familiar spoken symbol before meaning is achieved. At this point, the meanings gained from the written word are usually those the young child has already learned in relation to his knowledge of the spoken word. Only as he approaches maturity does his reading vocabulary outstrip his listening vocabulary. Few books developed for reading instruction under any system contain a vocabulary that is beyond the listening vocabulary of the children for whom the book is designed. In some cases, advocates of the code-cracking approach to reading have described very young children reading Shakespearian plays or other similarly sophisticated written matter. This is a distortion of the reading process, for few reading experts at any level would support a child's learning to read to the exclusion of understanding.

Defining the process of reading does not solve the issues inherent in reading instruction, though it is a necessary first step. The crucial issues relate to *how* the child can best learn the reading process. Is meaningful or meaningless material best for teaching the code-cracking system? This is one question that even the proponents of "phonics only" or linguistic approaches to reading raise. Another relates to the appropriateness of using cues other than letter-sound associations in gaining meaning from the printed page. Yet other issues relate to the form, organization, and materials of instruction in reading. Some of these issues might be clarified if we fully describe the process of reading.[3]

THE READING PROCESS

Even in its simplest form, the reading process seems to involve a broad range of perceptual, associative, and cognitive elements. While these processes may be analyzed and described separately, they are intertwined so that the individual does not practice each one separately as he reads. Nor is reading simply a matter of making a series of letter-sound associations. The scene of the preschool child roaming the aisles of a supermarket and identifying and reciting labels of packages made familiar through television commercials is not unusual. Although this might not be labeled *reading,* much early reading seems to mirror this process, for in attempting to gain meaning from the written page, the young child uses a variety of approaches and clues.

Young children can learn a reasonable number of words without using any analytic techniques. The associative learning technique used in the "look-say" method has proved successful and is probably responsible for the very young child being able to read product labels. The continually repeated association between the picture of the product and its name on television helps the child learn the words and recall them when he sees the symbol. Other techniques can be used for associating visual cues with the sounds of words.

The shapes of beginning and ending letters provide clues to the word. Using these visual cues, the child can be helped to make the association between the written symbol and the spoken word. Children also learn to use a word's context as a clue to reading it. The structure of the language and the meaning of phrases have a degree of regularity that creates a fairly high chance of success in the use of context clues.

As the child begins reading instruction he learns other tech-

---

[3] For an interesting discussion about the relationship of reading to language from a number of viewpoints, see Irene J. Athey, "Language Models and Reading"; Doris R. Entwhistle, "Implications of Language Socialization for Reading Models and Learning to Read"; and Ronald Wardhaugh, "Theories of Language Acquisition in Relation to Beginning Reading Instruction," *Reading Research Quarterly,* vol. 7, no. 1 (fall 1971).

niques of word recognition. Structural analysis—the breaking of large words into their parts—is an important one. Phonetic analysis, one way the child can identify letter-sound associations, is another important technique. Phonetic analysis is not the *only* method, however, that the young child can use in learning to read, nor is it necessarily the first. It would be unfortunate if we did not provide the child with as many different ways of unlocking the mystery of the written word as he can use, for it is the synthesis of many skills that helps make a competent reader.

It is important to note that word identification, although important, is just one part of beginning reading. Meanings must become evident to the child. He must associate the written words with the spoken words and move quickly from reading *symbols* to reading *ideas.*

John Carroll has identified the necessary elements of a reading instructional program. He suggests that the disagreements about how reading should be taught are actually disagreements about the order in which these skills should be taught. The skills identified are

1. The child must know the language that he is going to learn to read.
2. The child must learn to dissect spoken words into component sounds.
3. The child must learn to recognize and discriminate the letters of the alphabet in their various forms.
4. The child must learn the left-to-right principle by which words are spelled and put in order in continuous text.
5. The child must learn that there are patterns of highly probable correspondence between letters and sounds.
6. The child must learn to recognize printed words from whatever cues he can use.
7. The child must learn that printed words are signals for spoken words and that they have meanings analogous to those spoken words.
8. The child must learn to reason and think about what he reads.[4]

APPROACHES TO READING INSTRUCTION

While a multitude of different reading instructional programs is available today from which teachers may choose, many are actually quite similar

---

[4] John B. Carroll, "The Nature of the Reading Process" in *Language and Reading,* ed. Doris V. Gunderson (Washington, D.C.: Center for Applied Linguistics, 1970), pp. 31–33.

in approach, if not in the skills developed. In analyzing reading programs, we should look at the dimensions upon which these programs might differ. Essentially, the differences can be categorized into the following scheme:

1. Differences in the stress on letter-sound association
2. Differences in the conception of reading in relation to other language arts
3. Differences in the organizational pattern of instruction

The various approaches to reading instruction can be analyzed within these three dimensions.

PROGRAMS THAT FOCUS ON LETTER-SOUND ASSOCIATIONS

Several kinds of programs can be grouped in this category, including the various phonics programs, the newer linguistics programs, and the programs that use a transitional alphabet or orthography to provide a greater degree of regularity in the relationship between letters and sounds.

Teaching reading through phonics may require the children to sound out the letters in a word and then blend the sounds to create the word, or to analyze speech sounds in words and then relate them to letter representations. Although some programs depend upon phonics entirely, it is usually taught in combination with other reading skills. One often finds a phonics workbook added to a basal reading program. Phonics lessons are also outlined in teachers' manuals and in most basal series reading textbooks.

In recent years a number of programs labeled "linguistic" or "modified linguistic" approaches to reading instruction have reached the market. These programs attempt to teach the child the rules of letter-sound associations in the language. They often start with those letters that have a regular relationship to specific sounds in the English language, progressing slowly to letters with less regular relationships, and from there to those with the most irregular relationships. Instruction in this approach may place little reliance on understanding meaning as a way of learning to read, so reading might be taught through the use of nonsense words as well as meaningful words.

Approaches that use artificial orthographies cannot truly be classified as programs that teach letter-sound associations, since an orthography can be used in many ways. Because these orthographies tend to produce a greater degree of regularity between written symbols and the sounds they represent, and because this aspect has been highlighted by most developers, they are discussed here. The most widely known of all the artificial orthographies is the Initial Teaching Alphabet (*ita*). First introduced into British schools, this approach to reading has had a good deal of exposure in American schools. It consists of a forty-four–symbol alphabet that, while not completely regular, is more regular in its letter-sound associations than our traditional twenty-six–letter alphabet. The child is introduced to both reading and writing instruction with materials using this alphabet. After he has achieved a degree of competency with it, he is helped to make the transition to the traditional form of reading and writing. At present, one can find both simple trade books and reading textbooks available in *ita*.

While *ita* is the most popular of the artificial orthographies being suggested as aids to beginning reading instruction, it is only one of several similar approaches. Although different in its operation, the *Words in Color* approach to reading also fits into this category. In this approach, a sound is associated with a color in which it is presented no matter what its spelling, thus providing a regularity of relationship between spoken sounds and their presented counterparts.

RELATING READING
TO OTHER LANGUAGE ARTS

The one program of instruction that seems more than any other to relate reading closely to the other language arts is the Language Experience Approach. Basically, this conceives of reading as integral with writing, speaking, and listening as a unified whole of language experience in the life of the child. Of all the possible approaches to reading, this one places the least emphasis upon learning the code-cracking skills in some systematic fashion. Some proponents of the Language Experience Approach would caution teachers that premature focus on reading skills will thwart rather than help the child's acquisition of them. Since focusing on a single word or part of a word would slow down the child's rate of reading and is counter to the natural way mature readers function, teachers are cautioned not to start the child with improper reading habits. Word attack skills are often taught to individuals and small groups as the need arises.

The Language Experience Approach works most effectively in a classroom that is filled with stimulating learning opportunities. As the child involves himself in classroom activities, he feels the need to communicate what he is doing. Early communication takes the form of speaking and listening, then a natural transition to reading and writing takes place. The child first dictates stories about his experience to the teacher, who will write them on experience charts; the child learns to read from these charts.

The child is also encouraged to write early. Soon he is writing his own stories rather than having the teacher do the writing for him. These stories become the content of the child's reading. Since he has written the material himself, he seldom has difficulty with vocabulary, for even difficult words are remembered.

The next transition is from reading his own writing to reading someone else's writing, and the child is encouraged to read other children's work as well as many books available in the classroom. Stories and experience charts can also be written as a group endeavor.

The Language Experience Approach to reading does not deny the need to crack the code of letter-sound associations. Rather than being learned from lessons designed specifically to this end, however, they are learned through the organic activities provided. The process of learning to read more closely parallels learning a native language than a second language.

DIFFERENCES IN ORGANIZATIONAL PATTERNS OF TEACHING READING

The most popular of the two basic organizational patterns in teaching reading is the *group* method, most often exemplified in the use of the basal reading approach. The other, less popular, is the *individualized* reading program.

The *basal approach* consists of instruction in reading through a series of ordered reading textbooks. Along with the textbooks and often available from the same publisher come workbooks and other instructional aids, such as flash cards, pictures, films, filmstrips, and records. In most classrooms, the children are divided into groups for instructional purposes based upon reading ability: one group of high ability, another of low ability, and a third, usually the largest group, in the middle. Group instruction is organized to limit the range of ability within each instructional unit, a range that would be great in most classrooms.

Most basal reading programs are carefully designed, eclectic ones. Teachers are provided with a highly detailed manual of instructions about the content of the program and the method of instruction to be used. The use of textbooks and related activities may be carefully prescribed for the teacher. In addition, the books are carefully graded so that a teacher needs only to take her class through the books and related exercises provided her to successfully carry on the program. Generally, all groups are offered the same reading program, but the pace of instruction differs.

Some basal reading programs are changed from edition to edition over the years to mirror the changes that take place in current reading instruction theory. Recent changes include a greater focus on phonics and a concern with the linguistic analysis of initial vocabulary. Changes in the content of some basal readers also reflect the changing social scene. Many have begun to change their illustrations to reflect more honestly the multiracial nature of our society. Newer reading series (such as the *Bank Street Readers, Skyline Readers,* and the *Chandler Reading Series*) have been developed in which the story lines relate to an urban context not found in the more popular readers. Additional changes include newer format designs for basal reader series, especially the use of smaller books and integrated audiovisual aids.

Most basal reading series begin by providing pupils with a limited sight vocabulary of words and names of characters in the stories. The vocabulary is carefully limited and constantly repeated. As the child's sight vocabulary reaches a minimal level, he is introduced to a variety of word recognition skills, including phonics and structural analysis.

Although basal reading programs have been discussed as a group here, there is considerable variation in methodological emphasis and textbook content among basal reader series.

Individualized reading programs have been conceived of to deal with the inherent problem of the inappropriate fit of instructional programs to the diverse needs of children in any group. Within a single group of children there are differences in learning skills, styles, interests, and reading abilities. While grouping might limit the range of differences in one dimension, differences in children continue to exist in other dimensions.

Individualizing reading instruction provides neither a single medium nor a single organizational framework for instruction. Instead, a great variety of books are provided for the children—both trade books and basal readers. Trade books vary in topics and level of difficulty, and so are selected by the child as he sets his own learning pace.

Central to the organization of the individualized reading program is the pupil-teacher conference. Several times each week the teacher meets with each child in conference. The conference is used to review the child's progress in reading and to plan new work for the future. The teacher often asks children to read aloud, and asks questions about what the child has read to check on his degree of comprehension.

An individualized program requires an extensive amount of record-keeping and planning. The teacher keeps records on the books the child has read as well as on the content of her conference. These records might include notes about the child's progress in reading and the problems encountered that need to be dealt with. Planning consists of selecting and providing an adequate array of books, then suggesting specific books for particular children. This requires that the teacher have some degree of familiarity with a wide range of books and be knowledgeable about the reading level and content of each book.

If more than one child manifests the need for instruction in a particular set of reading skills, the teacher may organize a group for instructional purposes. The group is convened for a particular task and may include children of different levels of reading ability but with the same instructional needs. When the instructional task is completed, the group may be disbanded. Practice in reading skills may also be provided through worksheets and other materials. Some teachers may begin a program of instruction with individual lessons, but more often such a program is designed to extend from some form of group instruction. As the children show competence in reading skills, they are allowed greater degrees of freedom in reading.

Although significantly different from the individualized reading program described above, another method that has been developed for individualizing instruction is called *Individually Prescribed Instruction* (IPI). This system is organized to provide for individually paced instruction in a classroom setting. The focus is on reading skills rather than on other aspects of the reading program. At the beginning of each instructional unit the child is given a diagnostic test, and on the basis of the results of the test, is provided with his own instructional prescription—a worksheet he completes that is then checked by a classroom clerk supervised by the teacher. He may then be allowed to move at his own pace to the next set of instructional tasks or be provided with remedial work. In the IPI model, no child is asked to work on a lesson if he has already mastered the skills that are the goals of that lesson.

Computer-assisted instruction and *programmed instruction* have also been used to individualize reading programs. Each of these approaches allows the child to move through set instructional programs at his own speed. Computer-assisted instruction also has greater flexibility in the presentation of material based upon the analysis of the child's learning weaknesses.

These two types of instruction are vehicles for teaching, and represent no single instructional approach. Phonics, linguistics, contextual analysis, and other skills can be taught through this kind of teaching program. Programmed instruction may use a teaching machine or may be incorporated into a workbook. Computer-assisted instruction may make use of both visual and auditory channels and require many different forms of children's responses.

While these approaches to individualization have proven to be effective teaching tools, they are probably best used in conjunction with other program elements. The high cost of computer-assisted instruction and the continual need for adult intervention raise the question of its practicality. Program writing and rental of computers and coaxial cables often makes computer-assisted instruction prohibitive for use in early educational programs. At present, the computer does have a role to play in researching early education, although its role in producing continual instruction to young children still needs to be demonstrated.

The three dimensions of reading instruction have been discussed separately, but we should note that all programs combine elements of the three. The *Distar* program, for example, focuses on teaching letter-sound associations and uses elements of artificial orthography. Teaching is done in a small group setting. Thus the range of programs that can be developed to teach reading is infinite, based upon the possible combinations of these elements, plus others that authors add.

EVALUATING APPROACHES
TO READING INSTRUCTION

Considering the number of possible approaches to beginning reading instruction and programs available within each approach, it becomes exceedingly difficult for the classroom teacher to decide which program to institute in her classroom. In many school systems the teacher has little choice, for the decision has already been made by the administration or by a curriculum committee, usually selecting one reading program to be instituted in all classrooms.

Teachers are usually involved in program selection procedures. They can also supplement any adopted program in their own classroom. Selection should be made among program alternatives, considering evidence of program effectiveness, practicality, content, and the willingness of teachers to use the program. A framework for comparing and evaluating reading programs is presented in chapter 16.

A READING PROGRAM FOR THE EARLY YEARS

The First Grade Reading Studies described above suggest that the best results could probably accrue from a program that uses a combination of approaches for teaching beginning reading. This might lead a teacher to organize her class instruction around a basal reading series. In addition, a supplementary program of phonic materials could be used. To round out the program, elements of a Language Experience Approach could be included, such as having the children write stories and using experience charts for instructional purposes. Finally, ways of individualizing the program could also be devised. Such a program could be implemented by the majority of teachers who are best able to use published instructional materials.

A teacher with a knowledge of the reading processes and methods of reading instruction, a desire to provide creative experiences in her classroom, and a willingness to develop her own methods and materials could probably do just as well by eliminating the basal readers and providing a wide range of language experience, using many trade books. If the class is average or above-average in intelligence, such an alternative might significantly increase the children's reading abilities. It would also allow increased creative expression and independence in reading. Because this alternative program is difficult to implement, especially for teachers who are unsure of their ability to teach reading, it is not recommended for all.

The combined approach suggested should not be merely a basal reading program with a few chart stories used at the beginning and a few trade books available for children to read as time fillers. In the program proposed, the range of classroom activity available at any time would be great. The combination program would not be a basal program, but would use basal reading materials. George and Evelyn Spache, in their book *Reading in the Elementary School,* describe what could be considered a realistic combination program and provide an excellent description of its content in the primary grades.[5]

BEGINNING A READING PROGRAM

A reading program begins long before the child attempts to make sense out of the first preprimer. Reading is an extension of the language process. As such, reading instruction begins in the infant's babbling stage. The child's first reading teacher is usually his mother, who has a profound effect on his reading achievement in many ways—she helps him develop language skills and provides the motivation for learning to read. Few schools concern themselves with attempting to influence the child's reading patterns so early in life, but the idea is not as far-fetched as it might seem. Several projects have developed ways to reach the child as an infant and toddler and provide him with home instruction through teaching the parent specific ways of playing and interacting with him to increase his intellectual and language skills.

---

[5] George D. Spache and Evelyn B. Spache, *Reading in the Elementary School,* 3rd ed. (Boston: Allyn and Bacon, 1973), pp. 293–399.

Most schools, however, wait until the child is old enough to be enrolled in an institutional group program before beginning any kind of formal instruction. The age at which a formal reading program might be provided for the child is open to controversy, and it is doubtful if any single age limit would be appropriate for all children.

BEGINNING READING INSTRUCTION

When should reading instruction begin for the child? It is impossible to provide legitimate answers, although there are those who provide glib answers for the public. As has been mentioned, articles in lay magazines in the past decade have suggested that even infants can learn to read. Research reports have been circulated describing reading instruction for two-year-olds. Montessori programs have been held in esteem by some because, as described, reading instruction begins when the child enters the program. (Actually, much of what is labeled "reading instruction" by some Montessorians is what other educators have called a reading-readiness program.) In many school systems where dissatisfaction has been felt with the current reading program beginning in first grade, a program of reading instruction has been instituted in the kindergarten with reported positive results. All this suggests that it might be possible to begin reading instruction at some point earlier than has been traditional.

On the other hand, a large number of educators suggest that reading instruction should begin no sooner than the first grade. In some kindergarten classrooms of the recent past, teachers were not even allowed to display any written material, for written language was the province of the first grade. Few basal reading programs are designed to begin formal reading instruction prior to first grade, although they might include readiness materials for use in the kindergarten.

In the United States, the traditional age for beginning reading instruction is at some time during the child's sixth year. Some countries postpone reading instruction until age seven, while still others begin at age five. Generally, the age at which children begin to learn reading is related to the age at which most children in the community enter the primary school.

In the area of beginning reading instruction, one also can see the operation of an "educational mythology." In many books on early childhood education and beginning reading instruction, it has been traditional to state that children cannot benefit from beginning reading instruction until they have achieved a mental age of six years and six months. An attempt to find the source of this statement leads to a single study done in a Chicago suburb many years ago which found that children in the Winnetka schools with a mean age of six years and six months benefited from reading instruction.[6] A study conducted a short time later by Arthur Gates, however, suggests that the necessary mental age for beginning reading instruction is not rigid, but is related to the size of the group and the flexibility of the program.[7]

The answer to the question of when to begin reading instruction is complex. It depends, to begin with, on the child's maturity, his level of intelligence, and his language background and capability, which is also related to intelligence. The decision to begin instruction must also depend on the particular program of reading instruction and the way in which it is organized. Not all classroom situations or teachers can provide the individual attention or flexibility needed to support an early reading program.

A question might also be raised about the effort needed to teach young children to read and the ensuing benefits. There is research to support the contention that children who are taught to read early do seem to benefit from such instruction. These studies seldom, however, compare formal reading instruction with other attempts at enriching the program. Whether the results of an early reading program fade in the

[6] M. V. Morpell and C. Washburne, "When Should Children Begin to Read?" *Elementary School Journal,* 31 (March 1931), 496–503.
[7] Arthur Gates, "The Necessary Mental Age for Beginning Reading," *Elementary School Journal,* 37 (March 1937), 497–508.

James L. Hoot

years beyond the primary grades is still open to further research. Certainly, a program of early reading that provides an educational advantage that is not exploited by later programs is a worthless one. Too often the cry for early reading instruction is a substitute for the more difficult task of reforming the programs of primary and intermediate education in our schools.

Nevertheless, the question of when a child might begin formal reading instruction is best answered on an individual basis. If children can receive individually or in small groups beginning reading instruction at the time they seem most receptive to it, this is probably the best method of matching a program to the children's capability.

Teachers can assess the readiness of the child to benefit from such instruction in a variety of ways. One way is to use reading-readiness tests. Although they correlate well with successful results on reading achievement tests in first grade for *groups* of children, these are not accurate enough to predict the success of any single child. Teachers may also make their own personal assessment of a child's readiness to read. Spache and Spache present the following checklist as a guide to observation:

READINESS CHECKLIST

VISION

Good binocular acuity, near
Good binocular acuity, far
Able to shift focus easily and accurately
Good binocular coordination
Good visual discrimination
Good hand-eye coordination, near

SPEECH

Free from substitutions and baby talk
Able to communicate in conversation and with group
Reasonable fluency and sentence structure

LISTENING

Able to attend to and recall story
Able to answer simple questions
Able to follow simple directions
Able to follow sequence of story
Able to discriminate sounds of varying pitch and loudness
Able to detect similarities and differences in words
Sufficient auditory vocabulary for common concepts

SOCIAL AND EMOTIONAL BEHAVIOR

Able to work independently or in group
Able to share materials
Able to await turn for teacher's attention
Able to lead or to follow

INTEREST IN LEARNING TO READ

Shows interest in signs and symbols
Interested in listening to stories
Can tell some stories and recite some poems or rhymes
Likes to look at pictures in books
Can attend to the continuity in a sequential picture book
Makes up stories about pictures
Asks to take books home; brings some to school
Tries to identify words in familiar books[8]

The results of the First Grade Reading Studies suggest that the attributes of children that correlate most with reading success include auditory discrimination, visual discrimination, familiarity with print, intelligence, knowledge of letter names, and the ability to discriminate between letter sounds. These attributes should be kept in mind and observed by the teacher when she is making judgments about beginning reading instruction for a particular child.

READING READINESS

The term "reading readiness" might most simply be defined as the predisposition to benefit from reading instruction. The term has been used in so many ways that its meaning is often unclear. To some, it has been seen as a maturational state in a child. If readiness is a function of maturation alone, the teacher who identifies a child as not yet ready to read has no recourse but simply to wait until the child ripens. Little in the school curriculum has any effect on the rate of maturation of the human organism.

Educators have, however, become aware of the inadequacy of the maturation approach to readiness. Success in reading achievement is correlated not just with intelligence, physical maturity, or wrist-bone indices of maturation, but with specific learned skills such as auditory and

---

[8] George D. Spache and Evelyn B. Spache, *Reading in the Elementary School,* 3rd ed. (Boston: Allyn & Bacon, 1973), p. 76. Reprinted by permission of the publisher.

visual discrimination, familiarity with print, and knowledge of letter names. These are not functions of maturation alone, but are a result of the child's specific learning before he is introduced to formal reading instruction. Our knowledge to date suggests that even intelligence as we measure it is not a function of maturation alone, but is also related to the learning opportunities available in the child's environment. A purely maturational approach to reading readiness is wholly inadequate today.

Actually, formal reading instruction should be considered not the beginning of a reading program but an extension of a program of language learning, in the school or at home, that provides children with a large number of requisite skills and information that are put to use through reading instruction. Some children arrive at school already knowing what is necessary, having been taught by siblings, peers, or parents or having picked up this knowledge on their own. If they have not yet mastered the prerequisites for formal reading instruction, it is the responsibility of the school to create a program of instruction to foster this readiness.

DESIGNING A READING-READINESS PROGRAM

Much of the composition of a readiness program for reading has already been described in the previous chapter on language learning. Reading should be seen as an extension of the language process rather than as a set of exercises in a workbook. The child's ability to be involved in the production and reception of oral language is important in his ability to learn to read. He needs to develop fluency in speaking and listening abilities. The focus on oral language helps the child develop an extensive speaking and listening vocabulary that can be a resource in developing a reading vocabulary. He will also have developed a familiarity with print and printed material. Stories will be read to him and he will have an opportunity to handle books and to see how one can get information from the printed page, if only from pictures at first. The child can develop simple skills such as how to hold a book, open it, turn its pages, and care for it.

The suggestions provided here are consistent with Dolores Durkin's proposal for a language arts approach to beginning reading.[9] The nursery school and kindergarten day are full of opportunities to ex-

---

[9] Dolores Durkin, *Teaching Young Children to Read,* 2nd ed. (Boston: Allyn and Bacon, 1976), pp. 159–77.

pand language activities. Many of the activities suggested in the previous chapter can be used to provide a beginning to reading and help children see the relationship between the written language that is new to them and the oral language competencies they already have.

Most important, the child will develop a concept of what reading is and that the written word has the same power to express meaning as does the spoken word. He will have many opportunities to dictate his own stories to a teacher who will read them back at a later time. These informal and formal language activities will help the child as he moves into actual reading.

In addition to these, teachers can provide learning activities that help develop the specific skills upon which the reading process is built. Many of these will be in the area of visual and auditory discrimination.

VISUAL DISCRIMINATION. Many nursery and kindergarten classrooms include a wealth of materials that help a child develop visual discrimination skills. In using parquetry puzzles, he must relate the shape of each piece to the shape of the space in which it is to be inserted, and to the rest of the picture. Pegsets, beads, strings, and similar materials can also be used in teaching visual discrimination. Teachers can develop design cards for children to model. A simple pattern of one red and one blue peg alternating along the length of a line of holes in the pegboard is one that children can model, with more complex patterns following. Similar patterns can be made with beads on a string. A series of cards beginning with simple patterns and including complex designs, and design cards used with parquetry blocks of different shapes and colors, are other models. These can be used at the children's own pace, with more complex tasks being offered as they succeed in the simpler tasks.

Children can also be asked to copy specific patterns from models using crayons or pencils. Etch-a-Sketch boards help children copy models provided by the teacher. Using an Etch-a-Sketch is a complicated task, since it requires coordination of both hands. Form discrimination tasks can be given to children, starting with simple geometric forms on form boards and continuing to writing letters with letter templates. A number of visual discrimination and perceptual motor programs are available on the market that may be used for this purpose.

As children learn to discriminate letters, they should also learn the names of letters. Not only is this a good reading readiness task but it also improves communication between teacher and child by providing the class with a common verbal referent. Although copying patterns and filling in outlines are suggested here, none of these activities are to be considered as a substitute for an art program concerned with creative expression.

AUDITORY DISCRIMINATION. Music affords many opportunities for this, since the child must distinguish and reproduce pitch in music as well as learn to listen to the words of songs. Instruments can be provided to allow the children to recreate patterns of sound that differ in pitch and rhythm according to models provided by the teacher. Again, this is not to be considered a substitute for a creative music program.

A number of other techniques for auditory discrimination exist. Books such as the *Muffin* series can be read to make children more aware of sounds. There are many records and sound filmstrips that can similarly be used—for example *Sounds Around Us* (Guidance Associates). Teachers can also create games for teaching listening skills such as sound recognition and discrimination. They may make their own auditory discrimination materials using tape recorders or a *Language Master*.

Most importantly, teachers need to make children aware of the sounds they hear in the language around them. Word sounds can be the basis for much fun, because children enjoy alliteration and rhyming. While many opportunities for learning may be found in the classroom, teachers should be aware of the need to exploit situations as they arise as well as to create situations for particular purposes.

As in formal reading activities, children differ in their ability to profit from reading-readiness activities. Requiring a child to participate in an activity for which he has no need or is not yet ready is wasteful. Such formal requirements for total class participation are doubly wasteful, for the child neither profits nor is able to be involved in a more useful activity.

FORMAL READING INSTRUCTION

The move from a reading-readiness program to a formal reading program should be gradual, almost imperceptible. If the children have been writing stories and charts, it is an easy move for the teacher to begin to use simple short charts for reading. This can be done with individual children or with small groups as the teacher identifies their ability to profit from reading instruction. Such a beginning will build upon the language knowledge that a child already possesses and will keep reading from seeming like an exotic skill. The charts can become longer and more elaborate as each child progresses. The teacher should have pupils write their own stories on smaller sheets of paper, rather than have all experiences transcribed onto large charts. She can also start children reading books at this time.

DEVELOPING WORD-RECOGNITION SKILLS

Chart reading should involve more than the children sounding out words previously memorized. With the presentation of charts, teachers must help them develop a range of word-recognition skills. Many of these skills can be introduced in conjunction with reading experience charts. Because the content of the chart is so close to the child's experience, teaching him to use context clues seems natural. The child's intuitive knowledge of sentence structure and the fact that he has shared in the experience recorded on the chart make this an effective technique.

Informal phonics instruction can also be provided in the program. The child should be made aware of the sounds of words. Initial consonants can be identified and related to sounds. Experience charts have the disadvantage or advantage, depending on one's point of view, of extending beyond limited word vocabulary. Children's experiences and interests are so broad that they cannot be limited to those that can be described with only a small number of words. A formalized linguistics or phonics program becomes difficult to introduce to children if only experience charts are used. Children's writings and reading will contain a sprinkling of fairly sophisticated, complicated words. The teacher using these methods should accept this fact, and realize that some words will not be fully learned by the children. Independent of experience charts, teachers can provide more systematic instruction in phonics and structural analysis.

USING A BASAL READING SERIES

Most teachers in the primary grades establish a reading program based upon the basal readers. Yet Russell Stauffer reports that in every instance in which the basal reader approach was compared with other approaches in the First Grade Reading Studies, the basal reader came out second best.[10] Although these books may not be bad in themselves, they are often used in such a stereotyped fashion that the reading programs that result are boring to children. Basal readers must be seen as a resource to be used in the teacher's program rather than as a program by themselves. Slavish adherence to teachers' manuals and to the traditional grouping practices should be avoided.

Teachers need to take into consideration their pupils' abilities

---

[10] Russell G. Stauffer, ed. *The First Grade Reading Studies: Findings of Individual Investigations* (Newark, Del.: International Reading Association, 1967), p. vi.

in planning the reading program. The First Grade Reading Studies suggested that bright children did better in more individualized programs, while slow readers seemed to profit from a basal reading approach. This might suggest that a teacher's use of basal readers needs to be differentiated. Brighter children will develop the basic techniques of reading rapidly and should be allowed the freedom to select books to read under the guidance of the teacher. Those children who need the help provided by the basal readers, with their controlled vocabularies, should be given the opportunities to use them. But even then, a great degree of flexibility and alternative resources must be employed.

When teachers use the basal readers, they do not need to operate in the traditional "three-reading-groups-everybody-reads-aloud-today" fashion. Opportunities can be provided for silent reading, and conferences can often supplant the group experience. Teachers can use the pupil-teacher conference even when the reading program is not fully individualized and task grouping can supersede ability grouping.

Nor does the teacher need to follow a workbook step by step. In the discussion of reading readiness, no mention was made of using readiness workbooks. Readiness skills can best be taught in an experience context where children learn to use their language skills through interacting with the human environment. Children differ in their educational needs and patterns of learning. Skill learning and practice ought

Bernard Spodek

to be a part of a beginning reading program, but this does not necessarily mean that these skills are best taught by having all the children systematically go through a set of prescribed exercises. Although some teachers prefer this so that children "won't miss anything," the practice is too often wasteful.

Spache and Spache suggest that instead of using a single workbook, the teacher should order a few copies of a number of different workbooks and skillsheets.[11] These can be organized into sets of related exercises for each skill area, and placed in heavy acetate folders on which the children can mark their answers.

USING A CLASSROOM LIBRARY

The availability of a classroom library has been continually emphasized in this book. If children are to learn to read, they must learn not only the basic skills, but also the uses of reading. The more children practice reading, the more they will master the rules for gaining meaning from the written page. Most reading is an intimate personal experience based upon a person's interest and need for knowledge. Classroom reading, from its moment of introduction, should reflect this. As soon as children have mastered a rudimentary vocabulary, they should be introduced to a range of books. Fortunately, books are available that even the first-grade child can read independently. If he does not know how to read all the words in a book, he can practice his developing word recognition skills. Books should be carefully selected, with a relatively small number in the room at any one time, and with the selection constantly changing during the year.

USE OF READING
IN OTHER SUBJECT AREAS

While the appreciation of literature is an important aspect of a reading program, there are other uses of reading. Reading in specific subject areas for particular purposes will help increase the children's comprehension and help them learn to use reading skills flexibly, reading differently for different purposes. Many information books are available in the various subject areas, written at a primary grade level.

In addition, children can begin to use reference books. Encyclopedias, dictionaries, atlases, and other reference books are available in simplified children's forms. This will require that children learn cer-

---

[11] Spache and Spache, *Reading in the Elementary School,* p. 330.

tain techniques for seeking information. Alphabetization becomes important, since topics are often listed in alphabetical order. Children also need to learn to use the table of contents and index to seek out specific information. These skills, often part of a reading program, take on greater significance when the child can see the need for learning the skill and it has a fairly immediate payoff.

Teachers can help children to use information books by phrasing questions to guide their reading. At first these questions may be related to the specific content of the book. As the children develop skills in informational reading, more critical elements need to be included in the questions so that they learn to read carefully and make judgments about what they have read. Often, asking children to read and compare material from two different sources on the same topic is helpful.

The previous discussion might appear to make teaching reading seem a simple, seldom problematic activity. In reality, a number of children do learn to read very easily and some even learn to read without a teacher's aid. But a large number of children have difficulty learning to read, sometimes for reasons that seem beyond the comprehension of educators. There are also those for whom we compound the problem of learning to read.

Teaching a child to read requires more than presenting learning activities in some sequential order. The teacher needs to make use of the child's current language competence and be aware of any disabilities that might inhibit his learning. Most important, she has to sense the forces that would create a desire to read in a child. Children for whom the reading material is irrelevant, dull, or even insulting may not progress readily through the stages of reading instruction. Yet we often present suburban, middle-class–oriented materials to urban, working-class children and female-oriented material to boys. We sometimes make demands on children, for the sake of the reading method rather than the reading process, that are unnecessary and create discomfort or confusion. We sometimes ask children to read in a dialect or language that is foreign to them. This can compound the problems of learning to read, for a new language as well as a new coding system must be assimilated; the cues to unlock language that have worked for children before may no longer have any power at all.

The reading teacher must know not only methods of instruction but also her children—their competencies and their backgrounds. Special procedures must be used with children who have special needs. These techniques, often newly developed, have met with a range of success. Some of these will be discussed in chapters 11 and 12.

SUGGESTED READING

DURKIN, DOLORES, *Teaching Young Children to Read* (2nd ed.). Boston: Allyn and Bacon, 1976.

GUNDERSON, DORIS V., ed., *Language and Reading: An Interdisciplinary Approach.* Washington, D.C.: Center for Applied Linguistics, 1970.

LEE, DORRIS M., and R. V. ALLEN, *Learning to Read Through Experience* (2nd ed.). New York: Appleton-Century-Crofts, 1963.

MONROE, MARION, and BERNICE ROGERS, *Foundations for Reading.* Glenview, Ill.: Scott, Foresman, 1964.

PFLAUM, SUSANNA WHITNEY, *The Development of Language and Reading in the Young Child.* Columbus, Ohio: Charles E. Merrill, 1974.

SMITH, FRANK, *Understanding Reading.* New York: Holt, Rinehart and Winston, 1971.

SPACHE, GEORGE D., and EVELYN B. SPACHE, *Reading in the Elementary School* (3rd ed.). Boston: Allyn and Bacon, 1973.

STAUFFER, RUSSELL G., *Directing Reading Maturity as a Cognitive Process.* New York: Harper & Row, 1969.

Lois Duncan

CHAPTER SIX

SCIENCE
IN THE EARLY YEARS

Almost from the moment of birth the young child reaches out to his surroundings through his senses in an attempt to gain information about the world in which he lives. At first the child's understanding of the physical world is limited by his perceptual field. Things not perceived do not exist; things perceived often seem to have no explanation.

As the child begins to mature and his experiences with the world increase, he becomes aware of the existence of order in the world. A degree of regularity exists to events and objects with which he has contact. Some cause-and-effect relationships soon become evident. Items heretofore dealt with as discrete phenomena are now classed with other, similar items and treated accordingly. The child will even try to create order where order does not exist. He develops concepts, both physical and social, about the world that allow him to accumulate knowledge from experience and develop new powers of understanding.

It is easy to see how early observers in the field of child development conceived of the child's intellectual development as following the pattern of the development of cultural knowledge; the parallels are striking. Early humans also viewed occurrences as discrete, attributing changes to magical powers beyond human understanding. From that point human society moved through a series of progressions whereby a person could explain, understand, and to some extent deal with the world of people and things through the development of concepts. The concepts allowed whole classes of objects to be treated as equivalent. Generalizations could then be developed about regularities of relationships among concepts. Systems of knowledge could be created by relating concepts and generalizations to one another.

As knowledge was created it could be accumulated and transmitted from generation to generation. In time, knowledge systems became quite complex, and divisions were established leading to an increase in specialization of inquiry and to a more efficient system of knowledge storage and retrieval. This specialization has evolved into the *scholarly disciplines* as we know them today, with separations based upon the subject studied, the basic sets of assumptions, and agreed-upon ways of accumulating and verifying knowledge in each area.

One of the basic purposes of school is the transmission of significant portions of this knowledge to the young. This allows each generation to grasp what we know at present about the world, so that they can deal effectively with it, building upon what is already known and, in time, accumulating greater knowledge about it.

School subjects—sciences, social studies, mathematics, and others—closely parallel the scholarly disciplines. Recent activities in the area of curriculum development have illustrated the parallels between the ways children develop knowledge of the world and how the scholarly disciplines have developed. Science, mathematics, and the social sciences have been viewed as the results of intellectual processes by which the physical and social world can be explored. Science is not the only method we have for exploring the world, but it is an important one. Science deals with the physical properties of the world. It orders these properties, identifies relationships among them, and establishes theories that can be empirically tested to explain the relationships identified. These theories allow us to predict events and the consequences of acts, and thus to develop a technology to harness natural phenomena. Philosophy, literature, and religion are a few of the other tools we have for knowing about the world. Unlike science, knowledge in these areas is personal, often not generalizable, and cannot be validated by recourse to public, empirical testing. Paul Hurd and James Gallagher have identified the ability to comprehend science as:

> (1) the ability to grasp the central theme of a set of observations;
> (2) the ability to look at data from a variety of vantage points;
> (3) the ability to recognize the effect of changing one variable
> at a time; (4) the ability to discount irrelevancies and focus on
> the useful aspects of information; (5) the ability to formulate
> useful hypotheses and test them; (6) the ability to search for new
> evidence; and (7) the ability to reason logically from a model.
> A good imagination is also helpful.[1]

[1] Paul DeHart Hurd and James Joseph Gallagher, *New Directions in Elementary Science Teaching* (Belmont, Ca.: Wadsworth Publishing Co., Inc., 1968), pp. 5–6.

These skills represent a high order of intellectual development. As newer conceptions of intellectual development were promulgated, these higher mental processes were seen as deriving from a long train of maturational stages and prior experiences. Thus, the ability to think scientifically does not suddenly appear in a youngster at maturation, but requires nurturing from the early years on. As a result of this realization, the new curriculum development movement began to turn its attention to programs in the primary grades. The theories of Jean Piaget provided one framework within which science concepts could be generated in children; learning theory provided another. Models of curriculum development paralleled the beliefs about what and how children could learn, models now evident in the newer science programs. Basic to this development in science education is the belief that schools should teach science as an intellectual activity.

THE NATURE OF SCIENCE EDUCATION IN THE PAST

Science was one of the later subjects to be included in the curriculum of early childhood education. In many of the pioneering approaches we do find nature study—the observation of natural phenomena primarily for the sake of appreciation rather than comprehension. Teachers were admonished to keep a section of their outdoor play space reserved for a garden to be cultivated by the children. Small animals were kept as classroom pets, and the children cared for them. Interesting natural objects such as rocks and leaves were brought into the classroom and arranged on a table for the children to observe. Nature stories were read and pictures exhibited to further children's learning.

All this activity had as its prime purpose the development of children's reverence for the outdoors and appreciation of the wonders of nature to be found around them. In urban schools nature study was often considered a form of compensatory education, needed because city children had less opportunity for encounters with nature than did rural children. Since young children were seen as being so natural themselves, nature study seemed a logical inclusion in the program. Although direct observation in a natural setting is one strategy of modern science, observations of the "wonders of nature" were seldom used in the past as the basis for thinking scientifically about the surrounding world.

After the first quarter of the twentieth century, the study of science began to replace nature study in the curricula of elementary schools and in early childhood education. Science education became concerned less with appreciation and more with understanding scientific concepts and the scientific method, even at a rudimentary level. Vestiges of nature study continue in early childhood classes today, with teachers still displaying materials for observation and appreciation on science tables, reading anthropomorphic nature stories, and using an incidental approach to science education.

Although teaching an appreciation of nature, providing opportunities to observe natural phenomena, or using incidental occurrences to further children's learning are all worthwhile activities in a science program, they are not adequate as a total science program. Teachers need to develop activities that improve children's observational skills, for example. They should also teach children that an appreciation of nature might require social action based on an understanding of how to preserve nature and the consequences of technological activities on nature.

Knowing what science is allows us to use everyday occurrences in a classroom to build a science program. Using flasks, test tubes, or technical measuring devices in a class does not make a science program; nor does bringing animals and plants into a classroom, or using the scientific names for phenomena. The careful inquiry that takes place in a classroom, and the use of scientific approaches to generate and test ideas, make a science program. Careful observation, description and measurement, development and testing of hypotheses, acceptance of multiple explanations of happenings, adequately explained—this is the stuff of which science programs are made.

SOME MODERN CONCEPTIONS
OF SCIENCE EDUCATION FOR THE EARLY YEARS

What and how one decides to teach in science programs depends to a great extent upon how science is conceived by the curriculum developer—what he sees as the purposes of science education and how he conceives the nature of early learning. At the early childhood level teachers are not concerned with preparing children to be scientists. Rather, science education is considered part of general education. All persons in our society ought to have some knowledge of science to use in their daily activities. Equally important is an understanding of the nature of scientific inquiry and the role of science in modern society. Scientific literacy is an educational goal for all children in schools today.

SCIENCE AS SYSTEM OF KNOWLEDGE

Science has been conceived of by some educators as a body of knowledge about the physical world. The curriculum, from that point of view, could contain selective scientific facts most useful to children and adults. Determination of the scope and sequence of such a curriculum would be made by deciding which facts could be learned at what age and dividing the information so that it is all covered by the time a child completes school.

The problem with developing a program based upon this point of view is that so many scientific facts have been and continue to be accumulated that it is difficult to select the most significant ones. The number of facts an individual would have to be taught and later have to remember would make science education a formidable task. In addition, new scientific facts are continually discovered and information thought to be true is continually discarded. Teaching a body of scientific fact to children becomes a cumbersome, never-ending task of questionable ultimate value.

Because of the difficulties within this approach to science teaching, it has generally been discarded in favor of a view of science as a set of organized concepts and generalizations. Most scientific information can be organized into a systematic set of concepts that help to order the facts of science. The concepts give meaning to the facts, putting them into a more generalized perspective that allows a person to relate pieces of information to a conception of knowledge about the world.

In addition, science is conceived as a method of generating and verifying knowledge. The methods used by the scientist in observing phenomena, in testing hypotheses, in controlling variables, and in careful reporting and replicating of experiments are all part of what may be considered the *structure* of science. Teaching this structure is the goal of the newer science programs.

The organizing of the content of science into a conceptual structure is not a completely new idea. Gerald Craig's research in science education in the 1920s was aimed at developing a unified science program for children based upon generalizations that cut across the boundaries of separate disciplines.[2] This work led to the development of a conceptual scheme for education that is still in use today:

1. The universe is very large—*Space*
2. The earth is very old—*Time*
3. The universe is constantly changing—*Change*
4. Life is adapted to its environment—*Adaptation*
5. There are great variations in the universe—*Variety*
6. The interdependence of living things—*Interrelationships*
7. The interaction of forces—*Equilibrium and Balance*[3]

[2] Gerald S. Craig, *Certain Techniques Used in Developing a Course of Study in Science for the Horace Mann Elementary School* (New York: Teachers College Press, Columbia University, 1927).

[3] Gerald S. Craig, *Science for the Elementary School Teacher* (Boston: Ginn and Company, 1958), pp. 93–101.

This scheme became the source of a textbook series based on an elementary school science program authored by Craig and his associates that was adopted by many schools. Other textbook-based programs have also been built around conceptual schemes. For example, Paul Brandwein and his associates recently developed a similar conceptual scheme for science teaching:

1. When energy changes from one form to another, the total amount of energy remains unchanged.
2. When matter changes from one form to another, the total amount of matter remains unchanged.
3. Living things are interdependent with one another and with their environment.
4. A living thing is the product of its heredity and its environment.
5. Living things are in constant change.
6. The universe is in constant change.[4]

Within this framework, Brandwein and his colleagues have designed an integrated science program for the kindergarten through the sixth grade. While the conceptual organization may be similar to older ones, the science content and the approaches to teaching have been modernized.

Such conceptual schemes are beneficial for education. They are useful in integrating information into meaningful concepts and generalizations. In addition, almost all scientific knowledge and information fits into a category, programs at different levels can be articulated with one another, and the entire content of science education for the school can be integrated by fitting each science experience into a concept and then determining the level at which it could best be taught. In this way what is taught in the kindergarten can be related to what is taught in the third grade, with little danger of too much overlap in the content of instruction from grade to grade.

This approach is, however, still based upon a conception of science primarily as a body of knowledge and information. Scientific concepts are not taught directly but through the teaching of elements of knowledge that reflect these concepts. The concepts, however, order this knowledge and allow for its greatest transferability. This does not allow us to test the concepts' truth or their usefulness.

---

[4] Paul F. Brandwein, Elizabeth K. Cooper, Paul E. Blackwood, and Elizabeth B. Hone, *Concepts in Science* (Grade I, Teacher's Edition) (New York: Harcourt, Brace and World, Inc., 1966), pp. 8–9.

Other programs of science education have focused on the phenomena of science, the concepts of science, or the strategies of scientific inquiry rather than on scientific knowledge. Robert Karplus and Herbert Thier have characterized the differences in three science curriculum projects as follows:

> The interested reader is urged to examine in detail the course material produced by these three groups and by others. He will find a variety of approaches to the curriculum. For example, the units produced by the SCIS and the parts written by the AAAS form a complete and integrated curriculum, while the ESS is creating self-contained units that may be fashioned into a curriculum by local teaching groups. He will also find that there are significant differences in emphasis on the three elements—concepts, phenomena, processes—which make up the science course. Thus, the ESS stresses the child's involvement in the phenomena and is confident that he will thereby gain practice with processes and achieve understanding of valuable concepts even though these are not made explicit. The SCIS stresses the concepts and phenomena, with process learning an implicit by-product of the children's experimentation, discussion and analysis. The AAAS stresses the child's practice with the processes and uses the phenomena only as vehicles and the concepts as tools. An added difference is that the AAAS program attempts to appraise the children's progress more systematically and in greater detail than do the others.[5]

Differences in programs, however, reflect not only differences in content emphasis but in ideas about how children learn and develop, and in how people conceive of the nature and purpose of school.

Although it is easy to emphasize differences in programs, there are also a number of common attributes found in newer programs. Generally they are all based upon modern conceptions of science: they conceive of the child as an active learner and require his participation in science experiences, and provide materials for learning and instructions to teachers for developing activities with these materials.

A brief sketch of the three science programs discussed by Karplus and Thier should help to illustrate the likenesses and differences among newer programs. The American Association for the Advancement of Science has developed the program *Science—A Process Approach* (S—APA). The *Science Curriculum Improvement Study* (SCIS) was

---

[5] Robert Karplus and Herbert D. Thier, *A New Look at Elementary School Science* (Chicago: Rand McNally, 1967), p. 8.

developed at the University of California under the direction of Dr. Robert Karplus. The *Elementary Science Study* (ESS) is a product of the Educational Development Center.[6]

These are but three of many science programs available today. Barbara Waters presents six different early childhood science programs in greater detail for teachers to analyze in choosing a program.[7] In addition to those programs generated as part of the curriculum reform movement, a number of science programs are available for kindergarten and primary grades that have been developed by textbook publishers. Often teachers' manuals and kits of materials go along with the textbooks. The three that have been selected here for presentation and analysis have been chosen because each is well conceived, well developed, and represents a distinct point of view about what science is and how children best learn it.

SCIENCE—A PROCESS APPROACH

The American Association for the Advancement of Science, in the primary science curriculum it has developed, conceived of the processes of scientific inquiry as the essential elements of science that one wishes to communicate to children:

> The basic processes of science appropriate for children in the primary grades are identified by the following terms:
> 1. observing
> 2. using space-time relationships
> 3. using numbers
> 4. measuring
> 5. classifying
> 6. communicating
> 7. predicting
> 8. inferring
>
> A principal aim of the program is to develop skill in the careful

---

[6] More complete descriptions of the content of the various science programs and the materials developed are available from their educational publishers. For information, contact the Webster Division, McGraw-Hill, Manchester, Mo., for *Elementary Science Study;* Rand McNally, Chicago, Ill., for *Science Curriculum Improvement Study;* and Ginn & Co., Waltham, Mass., for *Science—A Process Approach.*

[7] Barbara S. Waters, *Science Can Be Elementary: Discovery—Action Programs for K–3* (New York: Citation Press, 1973).

and systematic use of these processes in the primary grades as a necessary preliminary to undertaking more complex science learning in the later grades.[8]

The more complex science learning of the intermediate grades includes the skills of formulating hypotheses, defining operationally, controlling variables, experimenting, formulating models, and interpreting data.

Activities in the S—APA primary program are carefully designed to teach children the above processes. Young children observe objects and identify color, shape, and texture within them. They observe weather phenomena, and the various parts of a plant, then describe their observations. In the area of space/time relationships, children learn to identify two- and three-dimensional shapes and angles and deal with concepts of speed. Number work includes identifying and comparing sets, finding the sum of two numbers, and dealing with number relationships. Measures of length, weight, area, and volume are explored by the children, in making comparisons and using standard units of measurement.

Specific experiences are provided to help children classify objects by visible attributes, moving from single stage to multistage classifications. Communication requires identifying and naming objects, using graphs, and describing experiments to others. Children are required to draw inferences from information and demonstrate how they may be tested. They also learn to make and test predictions.

The program is hierarchically structured, with simpler activities followed by more complicated ones. Prerequisites for later activities are encased in earlier activities. In the area of observation, for example, early activities include identifying and naming attributes of an object— is it rough or smooth, large or small, or of primary or secondary colors? Later activities require the identification and naming of two or more characteristics of an object, such as roughness and smallness. Similarly, early identification of two- and three-dimensional shapes leads to the identification of two-dimensional shapes that are the components of three-dimensional ones.

This approach conceives of science education as helping children learn the process of scientific inquiry that can be identified through a task analysis of the scientist's role. The facts of science continually

[8] American Association for the Advancement of Science, *Description of the Program: Science—A Process Approach* (New York: Xerox Educational Division, 1967), p. 3.

change. However, the basic processes of scientific inquiry remain relatively constant even though changes in technology affect the way these processes are used.

The method of teaching scientific processes in the program leans heavily on behaviorist learning theory rather than developmental theory. Readiness is identified as the achievement of prerequisite learnings rather than the attainment of a maturational state. Upon successful attainment of one level of skill development, the child moves up to the next level. What a child can learn is a function of what he already knows. If he is unable to master a scientific process then he needs to go back and master the prerequisite skills.

BEHAVIORAL OBJECTIVES

The S—APA program has been organized toward the achievement of specific observable behavioral goals. Identified within each lesson or element of instruction are the goals the child is expected to achieve, specified in behavioral terms. Since these behaviors are directly observable by the teacher, immediate evaluation becomes possible and she can then judge the effectiveness of the program.

"The process skills of the program are readily described in terms of component skills which correspond to observable performances or behaviors of the child."[9] The evaluation of learning for the whole class as well as for the individual child is related directly to these behavioral goals.

> Appraisal helps determine whether a majority of the children in the class have satisfactorily attained the behavioral objectives of an exercise. . . . Tests designed to evaluate individual achievement are called competency measures. Each task included in a competency measure tests the attainment of one or more objectives of the exercise.[10]

An illustration of the goals and evaluation technique is provided from the lesson *Observing I—Perception of Color*. The objectives of the lesson are as follows:

> At the end of this exercise the child should be able to
> 1.   IDENTIFY the following colors by sight: yellow, orange, red, purple, blue, and green.

[9] AAAS, *Description of the Program*, p. 3.
[10] Ibid., p. 6.

2. NAME the three principal colors—yellow, red, and blue.
3. IDENTIFY other colors as being like one of the colors yellow, red, and blue.

The appraisal of the group is based upon the following tasks:

Ask each of about six children to bring a box of crayons and sit together in some place convenient for you. (The boxes of crayons must include red, green, yellow, blue, orange, and purple.)

Ask each child to match one crayon with some article of clothing that someone else is wearing. For example: Find a crayon whose color is most like Jane's skirt. If Jane's skirt is pale blue, the child should point to the blue crayon.

Before each group of children leaves the activity, ask each child individually to name and point to the red, blue, and yellow crayons.

Competency measures for each child include:

TASKS 1–3 (OBJECTIVE 1): Show the child in turn each of three blocks: a yellow (1), a red (2), and a blue (3). Each time ask, "What is the color of this block?" Give one check in the acceptable column for each correct name.

TASKS 4–6 (OBJECTIVE 2): Name the colors of three blocks which are in front of the child: an orange (4), a green (5), and a purple (6) one. As you name each one, say, "Put your finger on the block as I name the color." Give one check in the acceptable column for each correct identification.

TASK 7 (OBJECTIVES 2, 3): Give the child three paper plates: one yellow, one red, and one blue. Show him a piece of pink paper and say, "Put this on one of the three plates— yellow, red, or blue. Which color is it most like?" Give one check in the acceptable column for placing the paper on the red plate.

TASK 8 (OBJECTIVES 2, 3): Repeat this procedure with a light blue piece of paper. Give one check in the acceptable column for placing the paper on the blue plate.[11]

Critics of this approach are concerned that while it does teach some of the basic processes in science, it omits other important ones, which include thinking creatively about phenomena, inventing concepts, and developing divergent notions about aspects of the world. The lack of concern for children's stages of intellectual development has also been

[11] American Association for the Advancement of Science, *Science—A Process Approach*, Part A, Observing 1 (New York: 1967).

criticized. Further, one may criticize the teaching of science, an open-ended field, within a closed system of instruction.

SCIENCE CURRICULUM IMPROVEMENT STUDY

Another approach to teaching science conceives of it as a way of thinking about the world through developing and testing theories. The Science Curriculum Improvement Study of the University of California sees science education as a way to help children form "a conceptual framework that permits them to perceive phenomena in a more meaningful way. This framework will also help them to integrate their inferences into generalizations of greater values than they would form if left to their own devices."[12]

The topics of the SCIS program have resulted from an identification of basic concepts in science. The organization of units reflects an acceptance of a Piagetian framework of intellectual development. Level I corresponds to the transition from preoperational to concrete operational thought in the child; level II reflects concrete operational thought; level III reflects the transition from concrete operations to formal operations; and level IV requires facility with formal operations.[13]

Materials, activities, and concepts are compatible with the child's reasoning ability at each level, and science learning is seen as providing a bridge between personal explorations and interpretations of the world and an understanding of scientific concepts.

> The child's elementary school years are a period of transition as he continues the exploration of the world he began during infancy and builds abstractions with which he interprets that world. With a careful introduction to scientific abstractions at this time, he will later be able to relate them to the real world in a meaningful way. As he matures, the continual interplay of interpretations and observations will frequently compel him to revise his ideas about his environment.[14]

Units in the SCIS program are designed to be taught in a specific sequence. Each unit includes a teacher's guide, student manuals, and a kit of equipment and materials to serve one teacher and thirty-two children. Each unit covers a number of topics and contains *invention*

[12] Karplus and Thier, *A New Look at Elementary School Science,* pp. 20–21.
[13] Ibid., p. 35.
[14] Science Curriculum Improvement Study, *Teachers Guide: Systems and Subsystems* (Preliminary Edition) (Lexington, Mass.: Raytheon Educational Co., 1968), p. 1.

lessons and *discovery* lessons. Invention lessons allow the teacher to define new terms or concepts; discovery lessons permit the children to apply these new ideas. Optional activities are also provided.

In each lesson children are given specific sets of materials and asked to experiment with them. All the children in the class are usually working on the same experiments, either individually or in small groups. The children may record the results of their experiments in their individual manuals. Some lessons in the program are left completely open-ended; others may terminate in classroom discussions. Teachers are often advised to guide discussions with questions and comments requiring reflection as well as response, such as, "Tell us what happened in your experiment," or "How did the objects change?" Since specific behavioral objectives are not stated, a range of outcomes could be expected from any of the experiences provided and often no specific immediate outcome is expected from a single experience. Goals are to be achieved cumulatively over long periods of time.

In the *Interactions* unit, for example, each pair of children is given, to begin with, a box containing:

Cupped vial with water
Colored candy spheres
Scissors
Paper clips
Rubber band
3" x 5" card
Plastic clay
Small magnet
Battery
Flashlight bulb
Aluminum wire
Two "mystery pictures"
Sharpened pencil with steel eraser band

The children are allowed to experiment with the objects from the box, and the teacher guides individual experiments by asking questions and making suggestions. Later the children are asked to record their experiments and a discussion is held in which they can demonstrate their experiments to the class. This work is preliminary to the lessons, in which the interaction concept is *invented* through reference to these experiments and demonstrated with magnets and roller skates, and water, vinegar, and bromothymol blue solution in tumblers.[15]

[15] Science Curriculum Improvement Study, *Interaction and Teaching Guide* (Preliminary Edition) (Boston: D. C. Heath, 1967), pp. 28–34.

ELEMENTARY SCIENCE STUDY

The products of the Elementary Science Study are a series of units, each of which can be used at several grade levels, rather than a specified program of science instruction. A particular model of science education underlies the project. David Hawkins, former director of ESS, defines three phases of science instruction in a program. The first is one in which children primarily "mess about," freely exploring the materials and making their own discoveries in an unstructured environment.

In the second phase the work is externally guided but still highly individualized. This can be done, according to Hawkins, through the use of "multiply programmed" materials—materials that contain written or pictorial guidance for the student but are designed for the greatest variety and ordering of topics. Consequently, for almost any way a child may evolve, material is available to help him move along in his way.

The third phase of science instruction moves children from concrete perception to abstract conceptualization. This phase of theorizing must be built upon experience and experimentation, but abstraction does not develop without special attention. Although each of these phases is described discretely, actually they all represent central tendencies of the phases and each includes activities reflecting the other.[16]

The "messing about" phase can be illustrated in the directions for getting started provided in the *Teachers Guide for Geo Blocks.* In the Geo Blocks unit, children are provided with a set of blocks smaller than the traditional kindergarten unit blocks. They are designed as units so that a number of small blocks equal the size of a larger one. Many small blocks and fewer larger ones are provided so that children are forced to develop equivalences. The blocks are used to build towers, ramps, three-dimensional maps, and other constructions. Specific problems are provided for the children to work through with the blocks. In the introductory instructions, however, the teacher is advised not to structure prematurely:

> Before beginning any formal work with Geo Blocks, the children should have ample opportunity to familiarize themselves with the composition of the Basic Set. We recommend, therefore, that you begin by making the blocks available to your class during periods of free time, without giving directions and without commenting on their use. Put the blocks in an easily accessible

[16] David Hawkins, "Messing About in Science," *Science and Children,* 2, no. 5 (February 1965), 5–9.

place with an open space (floor or table) nearby where your students will have room to spread out the blocks and explore their nature and possibilities. At times, these early investigations may be noisy, and they may last for months rather than weeks, but they are as much a part of the learning process as are the later activities in which you may participate more actively.[17]

Teachers are asked to observe but not intervene in these early explorations, although they may make informal suggestions for elaborating the use of the blocks. Later, more directed use can be developed by the children as a result of the teacher's questioning. Questions may deal with building, counting, shapes, slopes, grouping, surface area, and volume. In addition to Geo Blocks, a number of other units have been prepared by ESS. Some of these are appropriate for young children, others are designed for the intermediate grades. Units include *Small Things, Growing Seeds, Batteries and Bulbs, Mirror Cards,* and *Light and Shadows,* among others.

While the S—APA and SCIS programs tend by their structure to support whole class activity, the ESS units can be used by a small group. The ESS program also uses "discovery" techniques as an instructional strategy to a greater extent than do the others. Children are placed in direct contact with scientific phenomena with a minimum of prestructuring by the teacher. Although the teacher does play an active role in helping children build scientific concepts, it is not in the first phase of the learning situation. Her role relates more to the organization of the environment to facilitate children's "discovery."

SELECTING A SCIENCE PROGRAM

The three programs discussed here represent only a sample of the programs in science available today. In addition to those of the national curriculum development projects, textbook publishers offer programs that reflect many of these new developments. The *Concepts in Science,* published by Harcourt Brace Jovanovich, mentioned earlier, is one example. The newer programs generally contain up-to-date science content. In addition, they make provisions for active participation of the child in the learning process so that science instruction goes well beyond rote memorization.

The first decision that needs to be made is to include science

---

[17] Elementary Science Study, *Geo Blocks—Teachers Guide* (Trial Edition) (Newton, Mass.: Educational Development Center, 1967), p. 3.

in the classroom program. Too often at the kindergarten and primary levels, teachers are so concerned with teaching children to read and write that they use all their classroom time for academic skill instruction. The art program may then be relegated to Friday afternoons; physical education becomes a way of helping to rid children of their excess energy; and science and social studies may be offered only erratically and superficially.

Evidence has accumulated that the current science programs can have an important impact on children's thinking and academic achievement. Increases in scores on IQ and achievement tests have been noted as a result of children's immersion in a science program. Mary Rowe, who summarized a number of studies detailing these positive gains, suggests that too often those children who can benefit most from science programs, including the poor and the handicapped, are the ones who are denied them.[18] If teachers could provide enriched educational opportunities for all children in these early years, perhaps there would be fewer learning difficulties in the upper grades.

Once a teacher opts to include a science program, she needs to decide which to include. Selection could be based on an analysis of

[18] Mary Budd Rowe, "Help Is Denied to Those in Need," *Science and Children,* 12, no. 6 (March 1976), 323–25.

James L. Hoot

available programs, then judgments could be concerned with the content emphasis (for example on content, concepts, or skills) as well as assumptions made about child learning and development. This would require a study of the program itself.

Most important, the science program should be compatible with the rest of the classroom curriculum. The S—APA program as a whole, for example, would be more difficult than the ESS program to fit into an open education approach. It would, however, fit into a more formal, behavioral-oriented classroom since it is based on behavioral principles. The SCIS and ESS programs derive from a Piagetian view of cognitive development and could be implemented by teachers who support this view. None of these programs would fit into a textbook-oriented classroom where children are expected to read books, listen to lectures, and watch demonstrations for their science activities. These programs all require children to "do" science, to engage in inquiry-oriented activities.

The Hawkins paradigm of science teaching closely parallels that of the *integrated day*. "Messing about" is followed by other elements of instruction as the child shows an interest and the ability to move ahead. The teacher can then provide him with formal or informal assignments that will move his inquiry into greater depth. The "multiply programmed" effect that Hawkins suggests is closely akin to that gained from the use of the *assignment cards* in English primary schools. Each card raises a question for children to pursue or suggests some activity to further their learning. For the very young, these suggestions could just as easily be provided orally by the teacher.

Teachers can also sit down with children in group discussion sessions, asking what they have been doing and leading them to develop generalizations and theories about their experiences. Such sessions can be brief, organized informally during the activity period or integrated into a time when children are describing and evaluating their work. Such a discussion could take place with a single individual or a group. The key in fruitful discussions rests in the teacher's serving a guidance function, leading the discussion and asking clarifying questions without offering conclusions to the child or structuring his thinking too much. Although not all teachers would select this program, the other programs available can also be modified to be more *open*.

SELECTING A SCIENCE PROGRAM
FOR YOUNG CHILDREN

At the kindergarten and primary levels, a number of completely developed science programs are available that have the potential of providing significant science learning for young children in the classroom.

Often the decision of what to teach under such circumstances is not the teacher's, for a school system may adopt a single textbook series or program to insure continuity of learning through the grades with a minimum of unnecessary duplication of experiences. The newer science programs often provide a better learning potential than some of the traditional school curriculum guides, although many textbook programs have followed their lead. In most instances, the newer programs were developed by teams of scientists, psychologists, and teachers, and have been tested and refined before final dissemination. Such professional services are often far beyond the resources of the curriculum committees of most school systems.

A PROGRAM
FOR THE NURSERY SCHOOL

The nursery-school teacher has fewer guidelines to follow in selecting a science program. Some nursery-school teachers skim off a number of experiences from a science program intended for older children and offer these to their classes. This approach can lead to a lack of significant learning, since the activities are unrelated to each other and the intended meanings of the experience may actually be beyond the young child's capability for understanding. Other teachers use a nature study approach, creating displays of leaves, rocks, small animals, or other "science material" in the classroom, and also talk to the children about weather and seasonal changes. Still others provide children with scientific labels for everyday phenomena.

Science education, however, is more than memorizing multi-syllabic names for simple phenomena. Nature study can provide a good beginning if the teacher capitalizes on the possibilities of various activities. Displays can be designed in cooperation with the children who organize materials as a result of their observations. Rocks placed together will highlight likenesses and differences. Leaves can be arranged so that the individual differences among a set of similar leaves can become apparent. The care of animals provides a legitimate source of science study. Teachers can begin to ask questions that alert children to significant occurrences rather than *tell* them what they ought to know.

The key to science is helping children *do* something with what they observe of the natural world. The new science curriculum projects can provide guidelines for structuring a science program at the nursery-school level, since they all seem to have common prerequisites.

Each program requires that the children be able to make and describe observations of physical objects, know how to categorize objects by certain attributes, and discriminate between groups of objects that fit into a category and those that do not. A significant program could be built around experiences that help children to observe, describe, and categorize physical phenomena. These activities could be balanced with others in which children freely explore scientific materials and their use in a range of classroom experiences.

FOCUSING ON THE EXPLORATION
AND DESCRIPTION
OF SENSE PERCEPTIONS

Each person receives information about the external world through his five senses: sight, sound, touch, taste, and smell. This information can be identified and categorized. Visual properties of things can be differentiated in terms of size, shape, color, and other qualities. Sounds can be identified by pitch, intensity, quality, and regularity. Sounds can also be related to their producers. Touch sensations can be described as hard or soft, rough or smooth, warm or cold, sharp or dull. The qualities of taste and smell, although not as precisely identifiable, can also be differentiated. These properties are listed as examples and are not to be considered exhaustive.

For each sense there are manipulative activities and related language experiences that would help children identify, categorize, and differentiate experiences and begin to describe objects by their sensory properties. This is the beginning of scientific thought. Language activities can be related to manipulative activities so that children learn descriptive language that allows them to symbolize and to communicate their sense experiences.

EXAMPLES OF ACTIVITIES. At snack time, the teacher might want to vary the traditional serving of milk or juice and crackers and bring in a variety of foods for the children to taste. Children can eat these foods and talk about how they smell, taste, and feel. Fruits make excellent samples, as do many vegetables, including those seldom seen by children in their natural form and not often tasted raw, for example, carrots, potatoes, celery, turnips, and spinach. A variety of breads and crackers, as well as many other foods, can be included.

As the children taste these foods they should be asked to talk about their sense experiences, focusing on taste, texture, smell, and so on. Foods can be described as sweet or salty, or soft or crisp. Children often associate their current sense experiences with something in their past. A description of cookies as "like my grandmother used to make" should be accepted as a legitimate, vivid, description.

The teacher might wish to cook some of these foods, especially the raw vegetables, to show children the process of change that takes place when heat is applied. Cooked spinach looks different from raw spinach. Cooked carrots feel different from raw carrots. Even mixing foods together often makes significant differences in the way they look, taste, and feel. Sugar dissolved in water still tastes sweet, but no longer has a granular feel. Flour also changes consistency when mixed with a liquid. Foods can be used in an endless variety of ways.

Children should be asked to describe the changes they see taking place in foods as they are processed, and make charts of the descriptions. These could be mounted on the wall or the bulletin board to be referred to later.

The children may arrive at generalizations as the result of their observations and descriptions. A generalization that seems wrong to the teacher but fits the children's observations should be accepted. The teacher can then provide experiences that complicate the observations and increase dissonance in the hope that a new and more accurate generalization will be forthcoming.

Experiences with many other materials can help children become aware of the attributes of things. Providing similarly shaped objects of lead and aluminum helps them differentiate between heavy and light objects. A touch board made with sandpaper, velvet, absorbent cotton, a piece of aluminum foil, and other such everyday items displays different textures. Setting up a "feeling box" containing an object hidden from view that can be touched by the children helps focus on tactile perception. Teachers can talk about the colors and shapes of a number of things, bringing in samples of primary colors and specific shapes and using everyday objects around the school. Block structures can be identified as larger or smaller, wider or narrower than other block structures.

Children can focus on the different elements of their perception in the free, less structured activities of play situations, or in more structured activities specifically designed to help them learn a particular category or name for an attribute. Once attributes are learned, children can be helped to make finer and finer discriminations and to begin to categorize things by their attributes. The same objects can be used to teach different kinds of categorization. A box of buttons, for example, might be given to a group of children to be separated by color, size, or on the basis of the material from which they are made.

INCLUDING SCIENCE MATERIALS
IN CLASSROOM ACTIVITIES

While conducting an "attribute" program, the teacher should also be concerned with feeding science materials into children's play activities so they can discover properties and relationships and use them. Setting up a pulley system in the block area for the children to use in building will help them learn about force and how it can be increased or changed in direction. The child should be allowed to verbalize the experience in his own way. It is less significant that he learn such terms as *friction, inertia,* or *mechanical advantage.* More important is that the child has intuitively learned through experience that a pulley will make it easier to lift things and that this is always the case with pulleys.

A doorbell and buzzer operated on batteries could be included in the housekeeping area, stimulating dramatic play as people come and go, and helping children see the effects of electricity and the need for a circuit in operating electrical devices. Battery-powered electric lights complete with switches could also be placed in a playhouse. A bulb, battery, and a couple of lengths of wire can be placed in a box for the children's free manipulations and discovery. Magnets, magnifying glasses, and other items can be made available to children for "messing about" or for inclusion in their play activities.

It would be helpful if the teacher asked the child to explain what happened when he used these materials. The key to the child's response is not its formal accuracy, but the fact that he has been able to provide *his* explanation that reasonably explains *his* experience from *his* point of view. The teacher then knows what the child understands, and what confusions still exist in his mind. She must then determine whether to leave the adequate though erroneous explanation alone for a while, or to engage the child in other experiences that will lead him to discover his errors.

Children might also be given opportunities to grow things from seeds, tubers, and cuttings. They should be able to describe things growing as well as what they and the teacher did to help them grow. Fish and small animals, in appropriate containers, can also be placed in a classroom for the children's observation.

It is important in all science inquiry that children be given opportunities to ask questions about what they see and to be able to find the answers. Sometimes the questions are unanswerable. "What is electricity?" might best be answered by the teacher who says, "I don't know, but we can see some of the things that electricity can do." It is better to answer questions honestly than to be caught providing inaccurate or semimagical answers. Children need to become comfortable with the unknown.

In using everyday classroom activities to further the science program, we break down artificial barriers between subjects. Most problems that we deal with cannot be labeled "science problems" or "social science problems," but rather spill over into many areas. Ecological issues, for example, may have a biological base, but the tools needed to resolve them grow out of a knowledge of economics and politics also.

Science activities can enhance the language arts program. The observations and descriptions needed in science enable children to use words better. Their descriptions will be more accurate and vivid. Their vocabularies will increase and they will use more adverbs and adjectives. Measurement used in science can benefit the mathematics program as well. Even drawing and modeling as a way of recording observations tie science to the arts. Both science and social studies units can provide themes to help integrate the early childhood program.

SCIENCE ACTIVITIES IN THE CLASSROOM

Whether or not a teacher selects a particular science program, she still must organize her classroom so that science learning can take place in an area that is identifiable by the children and has a degree of isolation. The center should have within it or near by some closed storage space, such as a cabinet, in which the teacher can keep science materials not currently in use. If these materials are readily available, the teacher is able to use the children's cues to move into a science topic that happens to interest them, thus exploiting their personal motivation for learning. If a range of materials is not available, the teacher may have to postpone an experience or even allow a critical moment for learning to pass right by.

Bernard Spodek

In addition to storage, there ought to be some open shelf space where children have access to a range of science materials. A display area, including a bulletin board and a display table, might be available in this center. Space should be available for children to work at problems. If the center is relatively isolated, a teacher can set up a problem and allow the children to work on it individually or in small groups. Since scientific inquiry is the important goal of science instruction, most of the science work ought to be done by individuals or small groups.

USING DISPLAYS

Teachers of young children often place displays on a "science table." Simply *having* a display is inadequate for science education in the early years, for the key to its effectiveness is how the display is used. Teachers should organize their displays for the children's use.

Bulletin-board displays can be organized to demonstrate a scientific concept. Leaves of the same kind of tree can be pinned up to show diversity of foliage. Pictures of a plant at different periods in its growth demonstrate the process of growth. Objects of varying size show the concept of "bigger than" or "smaller than."

Materials on a science table can be organized so that they can actually be used by the children. The children might organize a group of rocks by texture, color, or form. Different types of lenses allow children to look at objects and discover the effect on their apparent sizes. Children can discover the properties of magnets on both magnetic and nonmagnetic material.

Displays can be organized in many other ways. The crucial element is that the child use the display in learning to develop modes of scientific thinking. Simply exhibiting materials for children to examine is a waste of materials and classroom space.

Displays that are effective are changed regularly. If the content of a display reflects the children's concern with particular areas of scientific inquiries, it can be changed to keep up with shifts in the focus of science learning in the classroom.

PROVIDING DEMONSTRATIONS

Actual experiments, in the traditional sense—including the use of laboratory controls—are seldom carried out in the classroom. Often little is to be gained from such experiments that cannot be gained from freer experiences with the same materials. Experiments using a certain degree of control over conditions to highlight comparison can answer a child's question about the consequence of certain variables in a situation, but teachers often use demonstrations instead.

Demonstrations can be a way of *telling* children about science, a variation on direct verbal instruction, or they can be a part of legitimate scientific inquiry, depending upon how they are set up. If the demonstration is performed and followed only by an explanation, this accomplishes no more than an illustration. Even when followed by a form of superficial inquiry in which the children guess what the teacher wants them to know—a form of academic "twenty questions" often played in school—it remains a form of telling.

Demonstrations lead to inquiry when followed by a legitimate questioning and discussion session. Teachers can stimulate such sessions by asking questions such as, "What happened?" "Why did it happen?" "How do you know?" "Did you see anything else happening?" "Can you think of other ways we can explain what happened?" "How can we tell that our explanation is correct?" These questions need to be a part of honest inquiry, because without them there may be blocks that are insurmountable, and improper answers might be accepted that are unsupported by some form of evidence. For honest inquiry to occur, the children must have access to the information that can be used to test their conclusions. If such information is not directly observable by the children, their responses may border on the magical rather than the scientific.

For example, a child who is told that the flame of a candle in a jar went out because it had used up all the oxygen has not been told anything useful, from a scientific point of view. There is no way the absence or presence of oxygen can be demonstrated to that child. The explanation must be accepted on faith, which is in itself unscientific. It is important that the explanations teachers provide be in keeping with the information available to the young child.

Demonstrations should be considered ways of helping children focus their observations so that they can better see a phenomenon, without its being masked by other phenomena. If children can perceive a thing or action more clearly they can more easily abstract the ideas embedded from the physical world and thus understand them. Rather than explanations, questions such as those suggested above would be more appropriate. If children are not able to answer these questions, then it is possible that the demonstration did not serve its purpose. It might have been beyond the level of the children's understanding or the ideas might have been presented in a confusing or obscuring way.

RECORDING THE RESULTS
OF INQUIRY

One of the important elements of science is that the products of inquiry be recorded and communicated so that ideas can be retested and the results of earlier inquiries can be compared to those of later inquiries. Thus, children learn to record the results of their investigations in such a manner. With children in the upper primary classes, this generally presents no problem, since they can write with a sufficient amount of competence to begin to develop science notebooks, which reflect their science activities. For the younger child, this requirement presents a bit of a problem, but teachers can devise many ways of helping children record their scientific activities.

Children can dictate materials into tape recorders or to the teacher to record on experience charts or in individual books; they can use paintings and drawings to record their experiences in some symbolic fashion. The teacher should set aside time for discussion and recording, because the language and symbolic aspects are important for the child's continued learning.

The records developed for science activities provide one way of interrelating subject areas. Helping children draw objects accurately or use words that accurately represent an observation can help a child become a more creative artist or writer. As the child gains mastery over ways of recording and representing his observations and experiences, he is able to control his medium and do more with it. He also learns the uses of records so that the acts of reading and writing become more meaningful to him.

PROVIDING OPPORTUNITIES
FOR INQUIRIES

This chapter has emphasized science instruction as a part of the curriculum that requires children to be actively involved in forms of inquiry. Science has been viewed not as a set of labels or concepts, but as a way of conceiving of the world—a way of thinking about things. This point of view makes it imperative that at every point in the curriculum children actively think about the experiences provided for them and that their thought processes about physical and natural phenomena parallel their acquisition of scientific information. The ramifications for classroom organization are that activities must be organized so that children can *act upon* materials and experiences and arrive at their own conclusions. This requires that most activities be organized for individuals and small groups. The teacher should not spend a great deal of time telling children about science, but instead continuously provide them with opportunities to find out on their own.

In this approach, the teacher must be both sensitive to the child's thought processes and an observer of what he does in class. The important element of science learning is not necessarily the product of scientific inquiry—the conclusions that the child arrives at or the kinds of categories he develops—but rather the process by which he arrives at these conclusions and the reasons and methods of developing a set of categories. This approach should support a great deal of diversity in the classroom—diversity in achievement, goals, and activities.

A good early childhood science program requires more than a set of apparatus and some instructions for its use. It demands a climate of inquiry pervading the class. Lazar Goldberg defined the characteristics of such a climate as

> antiauthoritarianism and democracy; high tolerance for dissent, argument, error and failure; regard for aesthetic reward; absence of fear and humiliating measures; emphasis on cooperation rather than competition; respect for manual as well as intellectual effort; and above all interesting and significant activity. It is not a climate where "anything goes." Rather it is one which is humane and reasonable. It is a climate in which children cultivate valid criteria for choosing among alternative beliefs.[19]

Such a climate can support the achievement of "autonomy based upon reason" in young children.

SUGGESTED READING

ALTHOUSE, ROSEMARY, and CECIL MAIN, JR., *Science Experiences for Young Children* (10 booklets). New York: Teachers College Press, 1975.

BLOUGH, GLENN O., and JULIUS SCHWARTZ, *Elementary School Science and How to Teach It*. 5th ed. New York: Holt, Rinehart and Winston, 1974.

DUNFEE, MAXINE, *Elementary School Science: A Guide to Current Research*. Washington, D.C.: Association for Supervision and Curriculum Development, 1967.

GOLDBERG, LAZAR, *Children and Science*. New York: Scribner's, 1970.

HAWKINS, DAVID, "Messing About with Science," *Science and Children*, 2, no. 5 (February 1965), 5–9.

HURD, PAUL D., and JAMES J. GALLAGHER, *New Directions in Elementary Science Teaching*. Belmont, Ca.: Wadsworth Publishing Company, 1968.

---

[19] Lazar Goldberg, *Children and Science* (New York: Scribner's, 1970), pp. 14–15.

KARPLUS, ROBERT, and HERBERT D. THIER, *A New Look at Elementary School Science*. Chicago: Rand McNally, 1967.

ROWE, MARY BUDD, *Teaching Science as Continuous Inquiry*. New York: McGraw-Hill, 1973.

WATERS, BARBARA S., *Science Can Be Elementary: Discovery-Action Programs for K–3*. New York: Citation Press, 1973.

Bernard Spodek

CHAPTER SEVEN

MATHEMATICS
FOR YOUNG CHILDREN

Just as the child enters school having learned much about the language he speaks and his physical world, so he comes to school with a broad background of experiences in mathematical learning. The child has been living in a world of quantity and been made conscious of its quantitative characteristics. He has experienced "too small," "too large," and "all gone." His parents may have taught him to count before he entered nursery school, although saying number names in order might have been taken for counting. The child probably has little experience with mathematical operations and much of his understanding is at an intuitive rather than an analytic level.

Robert Rea and Robert Reys studied the competencies of entering kindergartners in geometry, numbers, money, and measurement. A wide range of abilities was identified, exhibiting some overall patterns that can provide reasonable expectations for teachers to follow. Nearly three-fourths of the children correctly identified the numerals 1, 3, 4, and 5, and between 50 percent and 80 percent were able to point correctly to the appropriate numeral when the number names one through eight were presented. When a sequence such as 1, 2, 3 or 5, 6, 7 was presented, about 90 percent of the children could provide the next number in the sequence. Over half the children were able to form groups of three and seven discs, count up to five items on a card, identify the number of items in a group up to eight, and point to the first and last item in a sequence when asked. About three-fourths of the children could also compare the number of items in two groups containing up to four items each.

Rea and Reys also found that the majority of the children could identify penny, nickel, and dime coins and distinguish between one, five, and ten dollar bills. More than half knew that a penny bought the least and a half-dollar the most of all coins, and that ten dollars bought the most of all the bills. The children also possessed a wide range of geometric knowledge.[1]

An inventory such as this can only sample a limited range of the knowledge of groups of children. Some children know more than others about the items tested. Many things known by children may not have been sampled. But such a study does point out that many children have much mathematics knowledge before they even enter kindergarten. That they already know much does not by itself suggest they should be taught more, but it does suggest that they are capable of mathematics learning.

The work of Jean Piaget has been used to illuminate the capabilities of young children in mathematics more than in any other curriculum area. This is partly because of the close proximity of mathematics operations to the formal mental operations that have been studied by Piaget and his colleagues.

The operations that can serve as the basis of an early childhood program have been characterized by Constance Kamii as logico-mathematical and spatio-temporal knowledge. They are structured from the child's own actions and the logical sense of these actions. Thus, they are constructed by the child himself. The three areas of logico-mathematical knowledge include classification (finding similarities and differences among objects, and grouping and separating objects according to them), seriation (ordering things according to relative differences), and number (judging "same," "more," or "less," and conserving quantity). In relation to time and space, the child needs to structure time in sequence and develop topological structures at the representational level.[2] These are essentially the mental operations needed by children as they approach mathematics instruction in school. A number of books have been written for teachers by mathematics educators who have attempted to translate the implications of Piagetian theory to mathematics education for children.[3]

---

[1] Robert E. Rea and Robert E. Reys, "Competencies of Entering Kindergartners in Geometry, Number, Money and Measurement," *School Science and Mathematics,* 71, no. 5 (May 1971), 389–402.

[2] Constance Kamii, "A Sketch of a Piaget-Derived Preschool Curriculum Developed by the Ypsilanti Early Education Program," in *Early Childhood Education,* Bernard Spodek, ed. (Englewood Cliffs, N.J.: Prentice Hall, Inc., 1973), pp. 216–18.

[3] For example, see Richard W. Copeland, *How Children Learn Mathematics: Teaching Implications of Piaget's Research,* 2nd ed. (New York: The Macmillan Company, 1974); and Kenneth W. Lovell, *The Growth of Understanding in Mathematics: Kindergarten Through Grade Three* (New York: Holt, Rinehart and Winston, 1971).

In addition to the impact of Piagetian research on mathematics education, the new curriculum development movement of the 1950s and 1960s had its greatest gains in the areas of science and mathematics. These two subjects, possibly more than any others, were said to be out of phase with recent developments in their parent fields of scholarly inquiry. The mathematics developed in the last hundred years could not be found anywhere in the teachings of elementary and secondary school. In addition, much of the mathematics that was taught in schools relied heavily on rote learning with the goal of developing computational skills. Little emphasis was placed on mathematics as a logical system, a symbol system, or a system of inquiry, and little was done to teach problem solving in mathematics.

Although the new vocabulary of the modern mathematics movement was quickly embraced by teachers, the spirit of modern mathematics was often lacking in classrooms adopting new programs. Instead of learning mathematical concepts as a result of inquiring into the nature of numbers and number relationships and abstracting generalizations and concepts from their own experiences, children were asked to memorize new sets of words and new operations. They often memorized the new vocabulary without having the opportunity to gain an understanding of it. The "new" mathematics differed from the traditional only in its use of less familiar language. In addition, topics for mathematics study were often added to the curriculum because they were exotic rather than because they were useful to children or could help build better mathematical understandings.

In recent years there has been a backlash to the new mathematics in the school. Part of the negative reaction is probably the result of excesses in some instructional programs, in which too little attention was given to the computational skills in traditional arithmetic and to its uses in everyday life. Negative reaction is also due to the implementation of poor programs and poor teaching in mathematics. Where teachers learned the new math vocabulary but not the meanings of the words, and where teachers did not understand mathematical reasoning themselves, instruction in the new mathematics became an empty, meaningless ritual.

THE CONTENT
OF MATHEMATICS PROGRAMS

What should be the nature of the mathematics program for young children? Howard Fehr suggests that elementary school mathematics should be a "study of number and of space, and the relating of these two ideas through the use of measurement . . . presented in a well-balanced program of mathematical concepts, computational procedures and problem solving."[4]

W. W. Liedtke and L. D. Nelson suggest that at the preschool level, beginning mathematics experience should relate to the skills of classification, one-to-one correspondence and ordering, or seriation.[5] In England, the Mathematics section of the Association of Teachers in Colleges and in Departments of Education suggests that mathematics at the primary level (ages 5–11) include the following topics:

> Addition, subtraction, and one-digit multiplication for numbers up to two digits
> The use of money in daily life
> All common aspects of time and date
> Familiarity with the use of metric units
> Meanings of percentages and averages
> Understanding statistical graphs
> Rough estimates of size, distance, and costs
> Rounding off measurements.
> Reading graduated scales[6]

Although the proposals of the English Association and of Fehr go beyond the early childhood level and the Liedtke and Nelson proposal is probably too limited considering the mental operations young children manifest, taken together they can help provide the basis for the scope of an early childhood mathematics program. Such a program would include the study of "sets," or collections of objects; learning cardinal and ordinal numbers; one-to-one correspondence; the operations of addition, subtraction, multiplication, and division; as well as the concepts of fractions; informal geometry; developing concepts of measurement of two-dimensional space, volume, and weight; and learning about time.

INCIDENTAL VERSUS PLANNED TEACHING

With the development of new mathematics programs, there was a revolt against teaching mathematics through "incidental activities" in the classroom. Earlier programs for young children had often admon-

---

[4] Howard Fehr, "Sense and Nonsense in a Modern School Mathematics Program," *The Arithmetic Teacher,* 13, no. 2 (February 1966), 87.
[5] W. W. Liedtke and L. D. Nelson, "Activities in Mathematics for Preschool Children," *The Arithmetic Teacher,* 20, no. 7 (November 1973), 536–41.
[6] K. L. Gardner, J. A. Glenn, and A. I. G. Renton, eds., *Children Using Mathematics* (London: Oxford University Press, 1973), p. 30.

ished teachers not to be tied to a textbook but rather to use the environment of the child and his daily activities as a source for mathematics learning. Often the teacher was expected to wait for a significant natural occurrence that could be exploited for its inherent learning opportunities, too often a function of chance.

Newer programs did not rely upon chance classroom occurrences. Specific lessons or experiences were planned for the children with particular learning goals in mind. Courses of study were carefully detailed and the sequence of learning was specifically ordered. Specifically designed textbooks, workbooks, and manipulative materials were developed and incorporated into planned programs.

Unfortunately, in their desire to remove themselves from the anarchy of incidental learning, many of these planned program developers ignored the many rich opportunities the child's daily life provides for mathematics learning. There are systematic ways of using the real world surrounding the child as a source of mathematics learning. These require the teacher to assess carefully the learning possibilities available in each situation, as well as understand the goals of mathematics education for young children.

A planned program need not necessarily be a formal program. Teachers can plan many fruitful mathematics experiences without recourse to textbook or to lecture and recitation sessions.

Kenneth Lovell, operating from a Piagetian point of view, suggests that all elementary mathematics programs move from a formal approach where the teacher talks to the entire class, to an approach in which children work with materials and games individually or in small groups. He also recommends that teacher-child and child-child interaction be nurtured, combining dialogue with physical actions. Lovell recommends that the determination of direction and initiative for instruction come from the teacher, that there be an appropriate degree of structure to the activities, that appropriate symbolization be introduced, and that there be opportunities for practice.[7] Although Lovell argues for a somewhat formal program at the elementary school level, these attributes ought to characterize the informal activities provided to young children in an equally systematic fashion.

Almost all areas of the early childhood program provide opportunities for children to group things and to count limited numbers of objects. In the block-building area children can make comparisons and show one-to-one correspondence by matching two walls of a block construction. Similarly, the woodwork area can provide experiences in com-

---

[7] Kenneth R. Lovell, "Intellectual Growth and Understanding Mathematics: Implications for Teaching," *The Arithmetic Teacher*, 19, no. 4 (April 1972), 277–82.

paring lengths of wood or counting nails. Arts and crafts areas also allow for grouping and comparisons: of the volume of clay being used, or of the various shapes of paper for collage and their attributes. Sand tables and water play areas can be planned to include a variety of containers so that children experience and compare different measures.

In addition, a great range of manipulative materials may be given children in a game setting so they can gain experiences with numbers, size, shapes, and the like. Various structured mathematics materials such as the Stern blocks, Cuisenaire rods, or Montessori beads may be used. Puzzles using geometric inserts, peg-sets, and sets of beads and strings can be used for counting, showing numbers, and patterning. The endless opportunities available in any classroom for counting, comparing, and measuring provide children with a wealth of opportunity to do mathematics.

Organizing these mathematics materials as an activity center in one section of the classroom supports their regular use. Directions for using manipulative materials should be available in such a math center. In this way individuals or small groups can engage in mathematics learning activities independent of the teacher. Richard Copeland provides a fine set of suggestions for organizing and equipping a mathematics laboratory, which can be used in creating a classroom math center.[8]

Experiences with real things in their environment, if used appropriately, can keep children from feeling that mathematics is totally theoretical and alien to their lives, a feeling that can be communicated when it is taught in a rigid, abstract way. It is disheartening to see some young children labeled incapable of understanding mathematics when they go to the store each day, order groceries for their families, pay the grocer, and count the change, being sure to check the transaction along the way so that they are not cheated. Often it is the way mathematics is taught rather than the nature of mathematics that creates learning difficulties.

TEACHING BASIC MATHEMATICS CONCEPTS
IN THE EARLY YEARS

Although it is simple to order the range of mathematics learning for the early years and to assign grade placements for each topic, such an exercise is not productive. One might approximate the age at which concepts can be taught, but there ought to be an acceptable degree of variability.

---

[8] Richard W. Copeland, "The Mathematics Laboratory—An Individual Approach to Learning," in *Mathematics and the Elementary Teacher*, 3rd ed. (Philadelphia: W. B. Saunders Company, 1976), pp. 356–82.

The child beginning school earlier need not be held back from pursuing a topic because others do not have the necessary background. It is important to note also that concepts are not learned in an all-or-none fashion. Starting with intuitive responses to the environment, children go through a series of successive approximations of mature concepts. Continued experiences with an idea and its various manifestations and examples help children understand the concept in greater depth. Therefore, no age or grade placements are suggested for topics discussed in this chapter. Teachers need to be sensitive to the children's level of understanding and to the prerequisites for understanding a particular concept.

Assessing a child's level of understanding is more difficult than assessing his ability to produce specific responses. The teacher may find that a child can complete a page in a workbook but will not be able to perform similar operations in another situation. One way of assessing his level of understanding is to see if he can use what he has learned in other situations. Important clues can be gained by listening carefully to his responses to questions. If the response is incorrect, the teacher can attempt to infer the child's level of understanding. Incorrect responses may be a result of inattention, but more often they reflect an inability to grasp concepts. Teachers can diagnose a child's difficulties and either present activities that will clarify misconceptions or gear their teaching more closely to his ability to understand.

GROUPING

In developing young children's concepts of quantity, the teacher can begin by having them group things. Children could group all the pencils in a box, all the red beads in a bead set, the pieces of a puzzle, containers of milk, or the children in a class. Such a group may be called a *set*. Sets can be made up of dissimilar things, but it is less confusing for the children in the beginning to use objects with common elements.

Young children can also begin to compare the number property of sets by matching the members of a set. As the children set the table for snack time, for example, they can compare the set of napkins with the set of straws laid out. In matching, they might discover that the two sets have the same number of elements, or that one set has more elements. Learning the concepts of *more, fewer,* and *same* precedes knowing *how* many more or *how* many fewer there are. Such a use of sets and the comparison of sets has practical application for the children, making the uses of mathematics obvious to those who may now have to modify their environment on the basis of increased mathematical knowledge (provide more napkins or more straws).

The matching of sets to teach one-to-one correspondence may also be done with pictures and charts. However, it is helpful for children to have real objects to manipulate in the beginning. With manipulative objects, they can line up two sets of objects, matching a member of one set with a member of the other, even before they can count.

COUNTING

Children often come into nursery school or kindergarten "knowing how to count." What too often passes for counting is the ability to recite the names of numbers in sequence without any understanding of the idea of the number that corresponds to a given name or numeral.

Young children need experiences that help them associate names or symbols with the numbers they represent. They see little difference between a physical representation of number and the idea of number. They can be helped to make these associations through the experiences described above. At first, children can be given manipulative materials and asked to build sets of two and three. It is easiest for them to begin to match their constructed sets with those provided as models. The spoken symbol for the number can be learned immediately; the written symbol may be learned later. Although much has been made about the differentiation of number and numeral, emphasizing such a differentiation may be confusing to the young child.

Many experiences allow children to build sets of two, three, four, and so on. They can match these sets to other sets, matching either groups to other groups, or groups to pictures of groups. They can also match sets of objects to symbols of these sets. As children begin to write—numerals as well as letters—they can begin to match the numerals they write with the correct number of objects in a set.

From this point, children begin to construct new sets by adding one more object to a set already constructed. They can also be given opportunities to order sets in relation to the number of objects in each group. Through a series of such experiences, children will learn that the numbers one to ten fit into a special order from smallest to largest quantity. This is the beginning of counting and understanding ordinality. A range of materials may be used to move children along, and a number line with numerals written from 0 to 10 may help them in their final ordering.

THE NUMBER SYSTEM

Once children begin to count beyond nine and record these numbers, they must become aware of our numeration system. This system has its own peculiarities, but it is simple enough to allow notation of extremely large numbers with only ten digits. The children are already aware of the number named by each symbol or digit, 0, 1, 2, . . . 9. They must now learn that the numeration system has a base of ten and that the place of each digit in a numeral represents its value. A whole range of activities in which children learn to substitute ten unit elements for an element valued at ten using rods, beads, chips, or markers can help them develop this concept of equivalence. Then, working with columned paper or pocket charts, they can study the role of position in relation to value. The notation of two-place numerals can be presented at this time.

Three-place numerals and other ways of representing numbers would be taught next. One-place numerals are easily represented by squares and sets of squares lined up to ten, or by a variety of three-dimensional rods or sets of beads. Two-place numerals can be represented in like fashion. A set of ten rods of ten values each equals one hundred.

Larger numbers become rather cumbersome in concrete representation. The Montessori golden beads represent one thousand as a cube—ten beads long, ten beads wide, and ten beads deep. Children soon become aware of the need for more efficient representation of numbers, especially large numbers, and are ready to represent and read large numbers in the arabic notation system.

NUMBER OPERATIONS

It is a relatively simple matter to go from counting, comparing, and noting numbers to the basic operations on numbers. At the primary level, we are concerned mainly with the basic rudiments of addition, subtraction, multiplication, and division. By counting up or down, the child can develop the basics of the addition and subtraction operations. For centuries people have used counting up and down as the basis for addition and subtraction, as evidenced in the use of the abacus. With this rather sophisticated yet simple device, counting beads allowed a person to go through complicated mathematical procedures.

Similarly, beginning addition- and subtraction-type problems can utilize the process of counting objects. Only later, when the child has developed an understanding of the process, does he move to the use of shortcuts, or *algorithms*. After understanding is developed, he can be offered practice activities to improve computational skills. The failures in early mathematics programs too often occur when teachers forget that the acquisition of mathematical knowledge must be based upon understanding. Then, drill will lead to mastery. When drill alone is the basis for the program, simple facts are easily forgotten, since they were meaningless from the beginning.

Children should be provided many situations in which they can put together sets of objects to establish the facts of addition, and gain an intuitive understanding of it. At this point, the process can be formalized and the appropriate language of mathematics introduced. Too early an emphasis on the formal aspects of arithmetic may thwart the children's intuitive acquisition of sophisticated concepts and operations. If children are too often told they are wrong, or that they are not saying it correctly, they may stop saying it altogether. Continued practice with the operations will lead to their mastery.

Similar approaches can be used in teaching subtraction, beginning with the opportunities to actually "take away" members of a large group and see how many are left. The children can then count down on an abacus or similar device, moving objects over, then comparing larger sets with smaller ones. The proof of the correctness of response is immediately available.

If children have already learned the concept of place and understood the equivalence of one ten to ten ones, for example, it becomes relatively simple to move from addition and subtraction of one-place numbers to two-place numbers, since the readiness for this learning has already been developed.

Multiplication and division are usually introduced in the primary grades. These processes, too, can be approached by the use of concrete manipulative materials and by recourse to prior mathematics learning. Children have probably already learned to count by twos, fives, and tens before multiplication is introduced. They have also learned to add. If they are asked to put together five groups of two blocks each, for example, they can visualize the process of multiplication. Many experiences such as these are helpful to begin with. Later the multiplication facts can be organized into tables.

Asking such questions as, "If I want to make groups of three out of this pile of twelve beans, how many groups will I have?" or "I want to give the same amount of pretzels to each of the five children here. I have ten pretzels. How many will each child receive?" is an appropriate beginning of division. Using real situations, involving the children in the manipulation of concrete objects, and having them act upon their environment provide the basis for later mathematics learning.

GEOMETRY

Almost from birth, children have been developing an understanding of spatial relationships. They are beginning to grasp the basic concepts of topological geometry in their intuitive constructions. Copeland suggests that this form of geometry might best be presented to children informally prior to their introduction to aspects of Euclidian geometry. Among the basic topological concepts that can be taught are *proximity,* the distance of objects from one another; *separation,* the lack of nearness; *order,* the arrangement of objects in space; *enclosure* or *surrounding;* and *continuity.*[9] Any number of experiences with blocks, beads, or other manipulative materials could be used to illustrate these concepts. Children separate blocks or beads as they move them away from one another. They often talk about objects or persons being far and near. The ongoing activities of the class help provide the basis for teaching these concepts if the teacher is aware of them and makes them explicit.

Copying the pattern of beads, blocks, or other manipulative materials or placing objects in a pattern can help the children understand the concept of order. Dealing with the idea of in and out ("Put the crayons *in* the box; put the box *between* the other two on the shelf.") can help the child use the concept of surrounding or enclosing. It is important that children operate on these materials and that teachers ask them questions about the objects' relationships to one another, to help them formalize their understanding of these concepts.

[9] Copeland, *Mathematics and the Elementary Teacher,* pp. 220–31.

James L. Hoot

In the geometry program young children can also learn to identify and compare basic shapes: square, circle, and triangle. Rectangles and other shapes, more difficult to identify, can be introduced at whatever point children are able to compare the measurements of sides and angles of objects. In identifying these shapes, the children learn to count sides and angles, or "corners." They can later compare sides, as well, so that they can differentiate between a square and a rectangle.

Later, as the children learn to measure, they will begin to compare perimeters and areas of different objects and shapes. Problems such as which shape of several has the greatest perimeter or how many things it takes to cover the top of a table (a problem in area) can be worked out by children who have been provided with the proper manipulative material and learned how to set out to solve problems of this nature. Children can also learn to classify objects by shape and to find geometric shapes in familiar objects around them. The concrete presentation of geometry makes it a natural part of the program since they can handle things, ask questions, and test their ideas on elements of physical reality. Although proper vocabulary is important in teaching geometry to children, the language should be an outgrowth of experience. Otherwise, the content becomes abstract and, unfortunately, meaningless.

DEVELOPING MEASUREMENT SKILLS

One way to integrate the mathematics learning of the early years and to concretize quantitative and spatial concepts is to use measurement. This allows the young child to use his developing mathematical knowledge as a vehicle for understanding his immediate world. Measurement can be approached simply and intuitively by young children. Teaching measurement begins with teaching the comparison of things to one another, and moves to comparisons of things to a common arbitrarily established standard, to comparison and quantification in relation to commonly established standards. Each area of measurement has its unique set of problems.

LINEAR MEASUREMENT

When they are very young, children come up against problems of linear size. The problems of matching the heights of two sides of a block structure or of finding a piece of wood that fits in a woodwork construction are examples of children's experiences with problems of linearity. It is a simple matter to give children sets of wooden rods and ask them to find the longer one or the shorter one, or even to have them stand beside one another and judge who is taller. The words "tall," "taller," "short," "shorter," "long," and "longer" can be taught in this connection.

A somewhat higher order of linear comparison is reached in asking children to compare things that cannot be placed next to one another: block structures on two sides of the block area, or the heights of the sink and the woodwork bench. In this case, they have to somehow record the measurements and compare the recording of one object with another. A length of wood might be marked to record the height of one block building and later moved to the other block building so visual comparison can be made. After many such experiences, regular measuring devices can be introduced, such as primary rulers and yardsticks. As children learn to count they can be taught the numbers on the ruler and the unit "inch." Before fractions are introduced, length can be reported as "between _____ and _____ inches long."

After time with inches, children may be taught the concepts of "foot" and "yard." Unfortunately, our measurement system is still not metric and the relationships between various units of measure are nonregular (for example, there are twelve inches in a foot, three feet in a yard, and thirty-six inches in a yard). These relationships may take some time for children to master.

Once children have learned to measure objects there is no end to the amount of measuring they can do and, with these measurements, no end to the amount of practice in addition and subtraction that can result. Floors, walls, furniture, materials, and people are all objects to be measured. Children can compare the measurements and make spoken and written statements about them.

MEASUREMENT OF WEIGHT

Weight is somewhat less directly perceivable than length. Placing an object in each hand and comparing weight is exceedingly tricky, for the volume of the object distorts our perceptions. A pound of feathers, for example, does not *feel* as heavy as a pound of lead. External aids to judgment are most necessary in teaching children about weight comparisons.

A simple balance is a useful tool in helping young children begin to make weight comparisons. This can be either purchased from an educational equipment company or made by using a length of wood, some string, and a couple of pie tins. If the teacher makes such a device she should be certain that the two ends of the balance do indeed balance when empty.

Again, the measurement of weight begins by comparing objects. When the child places two objects in the balance pans he makes a visual judgment about which is heavier and which lighter by noting which pan is lower. The child's next step can be to make comparisons with arbitrary standards with which the weights of objects can be measured. These standards might be anything—large metal washers, fishing line sinkers, or rocks. Later metal weights representing units of measure can be introduced—one-ounce weights, half-pound weights, and one-pound weights.

When children are introduced to measurement of weight they again find that the relationships between units are complicated; they simply have to be learned arbitrarily. At this point, it is useful to bring in a scale for determining the weight of objects. This introduces children to indirect measurements, for in reading the pointer on the scale, they are observing weight translated into the distance or movement of the pointer from zero.

It is helpful if the children first have the experience of direct measurement before moving on to indirect measurement. A limitless number of objects in the environment of the school can be weighed. These weights can be added up, subtracted from one another, or compared. Statements about these activities are communicated orally and in writing. The language of measurement, including concepts such as "lighter than," "heavier than," and "the same weight as," become important.

MEASUREMENT OF VOLUME

In learning to measure volume, children can be provided with containers of all sizes and shapes to fill and to transfer the contents from one to another. It is a good idea to include containers of the same volume, but different shapes. Using these the children can learn that volume is not simply a function of the height or width of a container. In time, containers of standard volumes should be introduced: one cup, half-cup, pint, quart, and gallon. The sand table and water play area are excellent places to introduce measurement of volume.

One of the complicating factors in teaching measurement at this particular time is the movement toward the metric system. We will be using more and more metric measurements in our lives while we continue to use the more familiar traditional units. States are presently mandating the teaching of the metric system in schools while children are being overwhelmingly confronted with pounds, feet, and Fahrenheit degrees of temperature in their everyday lives. They may not care that their milk was poured from a container that holds .95 liters, or that the cottage cheese was scooped from a package weighing 227 grams, or that their fathers must drive no faster than 88.7 kilometers per hour (one quart, one-half pound, and 55 miles per hour respectively). Although the interactions of the two systems during this interim period will require that people learn to convert from one system to the other, it is probably best to teach metric measurement directly, parallel to teaching measurement with traditional units.

This will require the teacher to engage the children in measuring activities using metric units, perhaps duplicating measurement equipment. There will need to be meter sticks as well as yard sticks, weights for the pan balance in grams as well as ounces, thermometers showing the Celsius scale and the Fahrenheit scale, and containers based on liters as well as quarts and pints. Since units in the metric system are based on the decimal system, conversion from smaller to larger (as from millimeters to centimeters to meters) or the opposite should be easier than in our present system with its irregular set of relationships. The fact that time units will not be going metric means that children will still have to learn complicated time units, but at least there will be no need for conversions here.

MEASUREMENT OF TIME

Much attention in the early years is given to the measurement of time. Time is measured indirectly, making it a difficult dimension for young children to measure. Teachers do a lot of classwork with calendars and clocks. Unfortunately, the work is ineffectual in too many cases. All too often the children are inattentive or make only arbitrary responses.

There are two processes involved in learning to measure time that need to be addressed separately. One is reading clock faces and calendars; the other is measuring something that cannot be seen or felt. The passage of time is perceived subjectively. All of us have experienced periods of time that have dragged on interminably and others that have moved too quickly. Time is a difficult concept for a child to grasp. Until his entrance to school, he has seldom had much awareness of time, except for the passage of day and night and the regularity of daily occurrences, including viewing television programs. There have been few expectations for him to be "on time," or to do things at a particular time. He has also experienced few cycles of seasonal change. With the beginning of school, the child's life suddenly becomes ordered in time, and time takes on increased psychological importance.

Many of the problems that children face in clock and calendar work stem from the fact that they are being asked to read fairly sophisticated material on the clock or the calendar without being taught the symbols and systems by which they are ordered. Other problems stem from the complicated relations of time segments to one another, as well as from the child's lack of knowledge of the benchmarks needed for the measurement of time. Often the only alternative left to the child is to memorize the material offered without ever really understanding it. It is amazing how few curriculum guides ever take the time to analyze and identify the elements needed to insure successful learning in this area of measurements. Lassar Gotkin's article demonstrates the systematic development of a curriculum to teach time to children.[10]

One of the ironies of modern technology is the availability of digital clocks and watches. Direct reading of hour and minutes may soon make learning the face of the clock obsolete.

OTHER TOPICS IN MATHEMATICS

A number of additional topics will be touched upon in our discussion of a mathematics program for the early years. Although generally not treated as extensively as the ones described above, they are still important elements. Included are the study of fractions, the use of graphs and charts, and money.

FRACTIONS

Once they understand whole numbers, young children can also be helped to understand simple fractions as equal parts of a unit. They can learn the meaning of one-half, one-fourth, and one-third. Their first understanding is of the number of parts of a unit, without concern for their equality. The teacher will find many opportunities to use fractions in the classroom: sharing snacks, giving out materials for craft work, and children's work in the block area or at the woodworking bench.

Understandings in this area, as in other areas, grow slowly in young children. A nursery school child's concept of "half" comes from seeing objects divided into two parts. The fact that the parts must be equal to be considered halves is a part of the definition that comes later. Children's understandings, however, grow as a result of many encounters with their environment, beginning long before they are able to grasp complex sophisticated meanings.

---

[10] Lassar G. Gotkin, "A Calendar Curriculum for Disadvantaged Kindergarten Children," *Teachers College Record,* 68, no. 5 (February 1967), 406–17.

Bernard Spodek

GRAPHS AND CHARTS

As children learn to communicate in writing they may become aware that some things are communicated more efficiently in ways other than through the use of words. Geography requires written communication of topographical information through maps. Quantitative information, similarly, might best be communicated using graphs and charts. Helen Robison, in her study of economics in the kindergarten, used graphs to communicate quantitative information.[11] Ida Heard also described her use of bar graphs and picture graphs in the kindergarten.[12] A variety of graphic representations can be used in the early years. They might start simply as ways of comparing children in the class in just two columns, such as the number of boys versus girls, those who go home for lunch versus those who stay at school, or those who live in houses versus apartments. Beginning graphs can be three-dimensional representations. A line of building blocks or wooden cubes representing each group, with

[11] Helen F. Robison, "Learning Economic Concepts in the Kindergarten" (unpublished Ed. D. project, Teachers College, Columbia University, 1963).
[12] Ida Mae Heard, "Making and Using Graphs in the Kindergarten Mathematics Program," *The Arithmetic Teacher,* 15, no. 6 (October 1968), 504–6.

each block or cube standing for one person, can be used at first; later, two-dimensional representations can be added.

The children can then move on to more complicated graphs: of children's birthdays (by months), heights, weights, color of hair, interests. Line graphs can be made of the morning temperature of the room or the outdoors over a period of time, of the number of children absent each day, or of the number of cars passing the school in a five-minute interval. This will require the collection of information from which the graphs will develop and will often be a part of a more extensive study. Using graphs in this fashion demonstrates that their study is not an abstract, theoretical exercise, but a practical way of recording and communicating information.

MONEY

Another topic often included in the primary mathematics program is the study of money and money equivalence. Since our monetary system is based on the unit of ten, just as our system of numeration, once the relative value of coins and paper money is learned, little new knowledge or skills are required for children to develop skills of monetary computation. As a matter of fact, the use of real or fake money is a helpful resource in teaching the numeration system itself to the very young.

In the early years, the main concern is teaching children to recognize coins of different values and to exchange coins properly. Manipulations with real coins are necessary to some extent, although play money can be used. Opportunities for using coins in play, as in a mock supermarket, or in real situations, such as shopping trips, and experiences in purchasing, making, and selling objects are helpful.

USING A MATHEMATICS VOCABULARY
WITH YOUNG CHILDREN

Psychologists and educators have become very much aware of the importance of language development in children and the relationship of language to thinking. In the area of mathematics, there has been an increased concern with language because the vocabulary used in many new mathematics programs is so different from that in older programs. This strangeness has often created a "mathematics generation gap" as parents, taught in an older arithmetic tradition, are unable to communicate with their children about school work.

It is important that children learn to use the language of

mathematics with some degree of precision. It is also important that they find mathematics meaningful. Children will use new words appropriately if they understand them and when to use them. When new vocabulary that is more appropriate for graduate school than kindergarten is given the children, the teacher has overstepped the bounds of reasonable innovation and may find them rejecting the new words.

The understanding that mathematics is a language system is as important as are computational skills. The children are confronted with a whole new notation system. The symbols of mathematics allow people to write rather complex statements in a simple form with a degree of clarity and specificity that would be difficult to match if they were limited to words alone. As children become appreciative of written communication, they can be helped to become appreciative of the language of mathematics and learn to use it appropriately.

USING REALISTIC EXPERIENCES

The nursery school and kindergarten are replete with opportunities for infusing mathematics learnings into the day's activities. The entrance of children into school provides the chance to tally those in attendance. Marks can be made for each boy and girl and these can later be grouped and added. Other routine activities also hold similar promise. Setting up for snack time gives opportunities for seeing one-to-one relationships and for counting. Work in the block area requires a mathematical sense, as do woodworking and crafts activities. Music, dance, and games all allow counting and matching. Dramatic play activities can offer a storehouse of mathematics activities: playing store requires using money, counting, and measuring, and playing at bus driving or housekeeping offers similar opportunities.

As the children move up into the primary grades, less fanciful activities are available to them in the classroom and the teacher needs to employ realism in mathematics. Most classrooms are full of things that can be compared, counted, added, weighed, and measured. It is important to give children both the chance to involve themselves in these operations and direction in doing it. One of the instruments used in English infant schools for this purpose is the assignment card.

Assignment cards have written simple problems or activities in which children can engage. The provision of assignment cards allows individualized instruction and provides many learning activities without constant teacher supervision. A small file box will contain a large number of assignment cards, numbered in order of difficulty and coded by topic. Such things as weight, linear measure, clock work, counting, writing equations, measuring volume, and geometry can all be taught through assignment cards. Teachers can set up a simple chart for each area of assignment cards on which children can check off those they are using. This simplifies record keeping. The teacher also needs to devise a way to check the accuracy of the completed assignment.

While some assignment cards may list closed-ended tasks, others may be open-ended, allowing opportunities for creativity and discovery in mathematics. The key to developing good assignments is to analyze the environment in which the children live and work and the activities in which they and others around them engage. Then the teacher should look for areas in which children can practice and extend the mathematical skills and concepts they have gained in the more formal parts of the school program. Such assignments can also allow for opportunities to relate mathematics tasks to other subjects. Thus a child could use a graph for quantitative representation, then represent the idea in another way, writing a story or drawing a picture. Examples of assignment cards follow.

WEIGHT

Place a cup of rice in one pan of a balance and a cup of beans in the other. Which is heavier? Write a story about these.

Choose two things that look the same size and weigh them. Do they weigh the same? Now choose two things that seem to feel the same weight, but are different in size. Weigh them. Are they the same in weight? Which is easier to guess, equal weights or equal sizes?

Take your shoe and place it in the scale. Weigh it to the nearest ounce. Record the weight. "My shoe weighs _____ ounces."

LINEAR MEASURE

Measure the length of your desk. Measure the length of the teacher's desk. Which desk is longer?

Measure the heights of all the boys in the class. List the boys in order of height, starting with the tallest.

VOLUME

Using a one-cup measure, fill up a quart container. How many cups does it take?

COUNTING

Count the number of windows in the room. How many can be

opened? How many must remain closed? Do more windows open or close?

Count the number of books with blue bindings in the library.

GRAPHS

Make a graph using unit blocks for each person. Show the number of persons in the class that have a birthday during each month of the year. Write a story about it.

AREA

Cover the top of your table with index cards. How many are needed?

SHAPES

How many things can you find in the room that have circles in them? List them.

Draw a design using ten squares. How many different designs can you make?

Such assignments allow the children to grasp mathematical relationships in the world around them. They will gain new mathematical insights and be able to practice the knowledge they have already acquired. In the area of measurement, dual assignment cards can be constructed reflecting metric units and conventional units used in the same problem. Assignment cards, like other such devices, must be used wisely. When used in a stereotyped way, they are no better than workbooks. Used with imagination, they can point out the learning opportunities in the surrounding world. The use of the environment as a resource of learning mathematics opens up new vistas for children's mathematical understandings.

USING MATERIALS

Although many opportunities exist for learning mathematics in the environment, teachers cannot depend on natural occurrences as the only source of mathematics learning. Additional sources should be infused into the program.

In the primary grades, one usually finds a great deal of dependence upon mathematics textbooks and workbooks. If used flexibly, these provide an excellent source of learning activities. Textbooks may offer the teacher as well as the children a guide to learning. The selection of a single textbook series should assure a certain degree of continuity of learning from grade to grade. Textbooks also present a large number of instructional and practice activities.

Mathematics instruction must go beyond the textbook, however. Manipulative materials can help the children understand concepts and processes through practical application with concrete examples of the ideas taught. A large number of these materials are commercially made. Many teacher-made materials should be included. Although the quantity and type of materials provided depends on the needs of the class at any time, it is helpful to have a mathematics center available in the classroom where mathematical material can be kept and used. The materials should be easily accessible and well organized so that cleanup is not cumbersome.

In spite of the material and supplies provided, it is still the teacher who remains the key to the success of the program. Although she needs to be knowledgeable in mathematics and methods of teaching mathematics, her sensitivity to children is more important. For within the framework of her knowledge she is constantly in the decision-making role—planning activities, assessing progress, diagnosing difficulties, and providing additional sources of learning for some while looking for enrichment activities for others. It is the teacher who can make the subject of mathematics a vital and meaningful area of inquiry in the early years of schooling.

SUGGESTED READING

BIGGS, EDITH E., and JAMES D. MACLEAN, *Freedom to Learn*. Don Mills, Ontario: Addison-Wesley, 1969.

CALLAHAN, LEROY G., and VINCENT J. GLENNON, *Elementary School Mathematics: A Guide to Current Research* (4th ed.). Washington, D.C.: Association for Supervision and Curriculum Development, 1975.

COPELAND, RICHARD W., *Mathematics and the Elementary Teacher* (3rd ed.). Philadelphia: W. B. Saunders Company, 1976.

DEVAULT, M. VERE, and THOMAS E. KREIWALL, *Perspectives in Elementary School Mathematics*. Columbus, Ohio: Charles E. Merrill, 1969.

DIENES, ZOLTAN P., *Mathematics in the Primary School*. London: Macmillan, 1966.

FEHR, HOWARD F., and JO MCKEEBY PHILLIPS, *Teaching Modern Mathematics in the Elementary School*. 2nd ed. Reading, Mass.: Addison-Wesley, 1972.

GARDNER, K. L., J. A. GLENN, and A. I. G. RENTON (eds.), *Children Using Mathematics*. London: Oxford University Press, 1975.

GROSSNICKLE, FOSTER E., and LEO L. BRUECKNER, *Discovering Meanings in Elementary School Mathematics*. 6th ed. New York: Holt, Rinehart and Winston, 1973.

KAMII, CONSTANCE, and RHETA DE VRIES, *Piaget, Children and Number*. Washington, D.C.: National Association for the Education of Young Children, 1976.

LOVELL, KENNETH, *The Growth of Understanding in Mathematics: Kindergarten Through Grade Three*. New York: Holt, Rinehart and Winston, 1971.

PAYNE, JOSEPH N., ed., *Mathematics Learning in Early Childhood, 37th Yearbook*. Reston, Va.: National Council of Teachers of Mathematics, 1976.

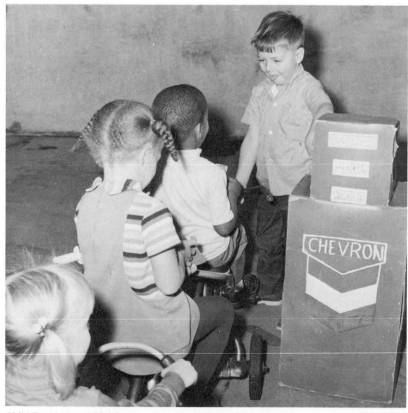

Child Development Division, Los Angeles Unified School District

CHAPTER EIGHT

SOCIAL STUDIES
FOR YOUNG CHILDREN

Schools for young children attempt to help them understand themselves, the world around them, and their relationship to it. The child learns about himself through feedback from the outside world; thus, his self-knowledge depends upon that relationship. He tests his powers on the physical and social worlds. He influences and is influenced by others. He becomes aware of the context in which he lives and strives to understand it, becoming more a part of that context as he defines the boundaries between himself and the world around him.

As the child makes sense of his surroundings, he develops knowledge and skills that are useful both for his everyday life and as a prerequisite for future learnings. His approach to the physical world is direct. He can test what he knows about physical things by touching them, listening to them, or viewing them directly. Because of the transitory nature of human behavior, the social world is more elusive. Although he has direct contact with people and can observe their behavior directly, it is the *meaning* of behavior that is important rather than the observable behavior alone—and the meaning is not directly accessible. The products of social behavior and the context in which behavior takes place, however, are more accessible to him.

ELEMENTS OF A SOCIAL STUDIES PROGRAM

A strong social studies program must actually contain all these elements: social science concepts and knowledge, applications of these concepts to social problems, and the socialization of children. The socialization and problem solving, however, are not the sole domain of social studies, but can be found in many portions of the school program.

INTELLECTUAL PROCESSES

Using the Piagetian construct of knowledge presented in chapter 3—including physical knowledge, social knowledge, logico-mathematical knowledge, and representation—one can identify the intellectual elements in a social studies program. Physical knowledge includes knowledge of the real world. This can probably best be gained by direct contact with that world, such as field trips, observations, and interviews. Texts, audiovisual material, and simulations can approximate this direct source of physical knowledge. Social knowledge includes the knowledge of social conventions, symbols, values, rituals, and myths; it is knowledge of what is considered right and what is taboo. This can be told to children either directly or indirectly.

Creation of logico-mathematical knowledge requires that a child use his thought processes to act upon information. Categorizing and ordering objects and events, observing and stating relationships, and putting things into the proper time/space context are included in this. Representing ideas and feelings belongs in the fourth area of cognitive knowledge. Pictures, maps, play activities, and stories are forms of representational knowledge.[1]

An inquiry-oriented social studies program must include all areas of cognitive knowledge. Most important, it should require that children collect data, order data, interpret data, and finally represent the products of inquiry.

SOCIALIZATION

Socialization is one of the prime goals of early childhood education. But though they can certainly contribute to the socialization process, the social studies should not be identified as the prime vehicle for the socialization of the child. There are too many other learning opportunities in the school day. The classroom teacher is concerned with helping the child find his role in the school community and in the larger community. While there is some transfer in learning socialization strategies from one area to the other, there are enough significant differences in these two forms of socialization to warrant their separate treatment.

Within the classroom, the teacher not only creates a range of

---

[1] Bernard Spodek, "Social Studies for Young Children: Identifying Intellectual Goals," *Social Education*, 38, no. 1 (January 1974), 40–45.

conditions that helps the child learn his role of pupil but also teaches him the rules, expectations, mores, and values of the school. The child's awareness of the way the teacher organizes the class, the rules she makes, the way these rules are enforced, the amount of freedom provided, the kinds of activities rewarded, and the rituals of daily life all lead to his socialization. But there is more to socialization. At times group efforts are allowed in the classroom; at other times children are expected to work alone. They soon learn the need for sharing, and that physical conflict is frowned upon. Children also learn that there are appropriate ways of interacting with and addressing a teacher. The lessons of the socialization process are sprinkled throughout the entire program.

The social studies program can play an important part in helping the child find his role in the larger community. He needs to understand how society is organized, to learn the shared values, rituals, symbols, and myths. The school's attention to holidays, to stories of historic figures and heroes, to the reading of traditional stories and the singing of traditional songs all contribute to the process. Activities that allow children to inquire into social phenomena can help the child better understand the organization of society and thus be better able to act out his role in appropriate ways.

VALUES

All education is concerned with values. The very fact that we provide an environment for children's learning and invest resources in materials and personnel is proof that we feel what happens in school is important. In addition, a specific set of goals is identified for the children to achieve in school. These goals—the understandings, attitudes, and skills achieved by the children—are valued by our society. Requiring children to become involved in the activities of the school indicates to them that these activities are important.

The basic social values that we wish to communicate to children include concern for the worth of the individual, concepts of freedom and responsibility, the importance of democratic decision making, and concern for the safety of persons and property. All these can be taught in the school. They cannot, however, be taught as a separate subject, for they are communicated as much by the way the teacher organizes her classroom and deals with individual children as through separate lessons. If children from minority groups are not respected and valued for the contribution they make in the classroom, then typical patriotic exercises take on little meaning. If rules of behavior are arbitrarily set by the teacher, children learn not to value rational decision making as a basis for developing behavior controls.

Children learn what to value from inferences drawn from the

behavior of significant adults in their lives, by imitating their behavior and assimilating perceived values. Values are learned constantly, not just in single segmented subject-oriented periods. The teacher, therefore, is transmitting her values to the children all day long. The social system within the classroom and the school operates as an educative force that may be more powerful than any curriculum in developing values.

Bernice Wolfson suggests that values can be learned by young children through role playing, creative dramatics, literature, and art experiences. She concludes that value development is promoted by providing a wide variety of opportunities for individual selection of goals and activities, by allowing children to consider alternatives and possible consequences of acts and of their own feelings.[2] This may be seen as a beginning step in the analysis of value systems. The level of analysis that can be expected of young children, however, is a function of their level of intellectual as well as moral development.

In addition to teaching values in the traditional sense—that is, helping children become aware of acts considered proper or for which the culture has a high regard—schools have often been concerned with their moral education—helping them distinguish right from wrong. The issue of whether schools ought to deal with moral education or to what degree is unresolved. While there is a common moral code, the sources of morality are varied in our country. The home and church are separate institutions concerned with the moral education of children. Nor are we at all sure how effective schools can be in teaching morality. Since moral issues cannot be resolved by recourse to a single source, some educators suggest that their teaching is not the domain of the public schools.

In the education of young children one must also be concerned with their readiness to deal with learning. How much can they gain from moral education in the traditional sense at this point? Lawrence Kohlberg has identified three levels, with two stages at each level, of moral development in children.

I.   PRECONVENTIONAL LEVEL. The child is responsive to cultural rules and labels of good and bad, right and wrong, but interprets them in terms of either the physical consequences of action (punishment and reward for example) or the physical power of those who enunciate the rules. This level is divided into the punishment and obedience orientation stage and the instrumental orientation stage.

II.   CONVENTIONAL LEVEL. Maintaining the expectations of the individual's family, group, or nation is perceived as valuable regardless of immediate and obvious consequences. The attitude is one of con-

---

[2] Bernice J. Wolfson, "Values and the Primary School Teacher," *Social Education,* 31, no. 1 (January 1967), 37–38.

formity, of loyalty, of actively maintaining the order. This level is divided into the interpersonal concordance or "good boy—nice girl" orientation stage and the authority and social order maintaining orientation stage.

III. POSTCONVENTIONAL, AUTONOMOUS, OR PRINCIPLED LEVEL. There is an effort to define moral values and principles apart from authority and apart from the individual's own identification with a group. This level is divided into the social-contract legalistic orientation stage and the universal ethical principle orientation stage.[3]

While Kohlberg's framework provides a way of identifying the levels at which children judge moral dilemmas, it does not identify levels of moral behavior. Since most children in their early years would be operating no higher than stage two or three, that is, not beyond the early stage of the conventional level, it is doubtful that value clarification techniques could be used profitably in early childhood education. Children can be helped to see what is proper behavior but their discourse about why it is proper will not be related to higher-order ethical principles. Discussions about the reasons for moral judgments might help the teacher identify the children's present stage. Questioning children about their reasons might help move them up to the next stage.

The role of the teacher should be less teaching moral behavior directly and more setting a moral atmosphere in the classroom that allows children to move beyond their present stages of moral development. This role, too, goes beyond the confines of the social studies or of any portion of the curriculum but must pervade the entire environment of the classroom.

SELF-AWARENESS

A number of educators have voiced concern that all programs, but especially those at the early childhood level, concern themselves with the affective aspects of development. Children can be helped to explore their self-concepts, deal with feelings about themselves and others, and develop appropriate means of expressing themselves and interacting with others. Such goals can be achieved through discussions, role playing, storytelling, and other techniques by which children are stimulated to express their feelings or concerns with the teacher, alone, or in a group. Programs are available in affective education, based on behavioral principles of learning, on psychodynamic principles, or on principles of humanistic psychology.

[3] Elliot Turiel, "Stage Transition in Moral Development," in *Second Handbook of Research on Teaching,* R. Travers, ed. (Chicago: Rand McNally, 1972), pp. 733–34.

It is important that children learn ways of dealing with their emotions and develop a heightened awareness of themselves, but teachers should be cautioned not to go beyond their own capabilities in exposing feelings with which they themselves might have difficulty in coping. The key to success in these programs is to focus on educational outcomes rather than on cathartic effects.

APPROACHES TO SOCIAL STUDIES

Over the years, many approaches to teaching social studies to young children have been used in schools. Early in the century, history and geography were taught separately, often to older children.

As educators became aware of the concrete nature of young children's learning, it was proposed that the young child deal with elements of his immediate world as a basis for social studies education, leaving the more remote in time and space to older children. The same areas of human activity could be studied within a more expanded concept of humanity as children matured. Out of this approach grew the "here and now" school of early childhood education, this being the most immediate arena of human activity.

Unfortunately, the "here and now" approach was distorted in time so that although the *topics* for study (home, school, and neighborhood) remained in the tradition of early childhood education, the *method* of study (acting as laboratory scientist) disappeared. Gathering, recording, organizing, and analyzing data from the outside world were complex and time-consuming operations.

Textbooks often so watered down the content of social studies that there was little relationship between the social studies programs in young children's classrooms and the actual social sciences. The "here and now" approach was divorced from the reality of the child's life and treated in the most remote way possible in these books.

A number of curriculum development projects in the social studies have been mounted in the past decade, including some at the kindergarten-primary level. The results of these programs are presently being disseminated.

Many of the projects attempted to look at the social studies as a total field, integrating ideas from the various social sciences within them. The University of Minnesota *Project Social Studies* and the Taba *Elementary Social Studies* program are examples. Other projects like the *Anthropology Curriculum Project* of the University of Georgia and the *Developmental Economic Education Program* of the Joint Council for Economic Education concerned themselves with only a single discipline. Some projects concentrated primarily on developing resource units—

outlines that could be disseminated to teachers and schools—while others, such as *Materials and Activities for Teachers and Children (MATCH)*, developed boxes of multimedial materials, including books, films, and manipulative materials to be used in carrying out teaching units.

Some programs were primarily cognitive in orientation, such as Lawrence Senesh's *Economic Education Program,* while others, like the *Intergroup Relations Program* of the Lincoln Filene Center for Citizenship and Public Affairs, concerned themselves with the affective domain.[4]

Each of these projects has its own rationale from which a unified, often sequential program has been developed, covering either a few grade levels or the entire spectrum of public education. In all the projects there is greater recourse to social science materials than has been the case in earlier social studies programs. Many of the materials are directly available from the projects themselves, and a number of commercial publishers are producing them.[5] Some program evaluations are also available.[6] In addition to the many specific projects, the movement has also brought about changes in textbook publishing.

A number of programs also exist in the area of affective early childhood education. The materials come in sets that range from those including a teacher's manual and curriculum guides to those also providing worksheets or sound filmstrips. One set even includes puppets and role-playing cards. The teacher's selection of a set of materials should be determined not only by their worthiness but by her own ability to use them to achieve the program's goals. Some of the activities may seem quite ritualized. Teachers who are new to an approach might need the specificity of prescribed encounters until they feel comfortable going beyond the prescriptions. In that way, using the program becomes a form of teacher self-education.

[4] See Bob L. Taylor and Thomas L. Groom, *Social Studies Education Projects: An ASCD Index* (Washington, D.C.: Association for Supervision and Curriculum Development, 1971).
[5] For example, see The Educational Research Council of Greater Cleveland, *Concepts and Inquiry* (Boston: Allyn and Bacon, 1970); Hilda Taba, *Elementary Social Studies* (Menlo Park, Ca.: Addison-Wesley, 1967); Lawrence Senesh, *Our Working World* (Chicago: Science Research Associates, 1964); Vincent and Carol Presno, *Man In Action Series* (Englewood Cliffs, N.J.: Prentice-Hall, Inc., 1967); and Frederick H. Kresse and Ruth Green, *MATCH* (Boston: American Science and Engineering).
[6] Morris Serdus and Marlin L. Tank, "A Critical Appraisal of Twenty-Six National Social Studies Projects," *Social Education,* 34, no. 4 (April 1970), 383–449. Descriptions and evaluations of many social studies programs are also available from Social Science Research Consortium, 1424 15th Street, Boulder, Colo. 80302 (see chapter 16).

Peter Martorella has done a comparative analysis of four programs of affective education designed for early childhood education. These include the *Developing Understanding of Self and Others* (*DUSO-1*); *First Things: Values*; *Human Development Program*; and *Dimensions of Personality*.[7] He studied structural characteristics, the specified learning outcomes, the theoretical bases, and the degree of consistency between the theoretical base and the instructional strategies provided in each program. Field test data as well as internal analyses of programs were collected.

The DUSO-1 program contains a teacher's manual, two story books, a set of posters, puppets, recordings and related activities cards and props, role-playing cards, and group discussion cards. The cycles of activities are organized into units to support understanding of self, feelings, others, and attributes of motivation. The *First Things: Values* program is a collection of filmstrips, records, and teacher's manual that focus on moral dilemmas; children discuss, arrive at a position, and justify it. The *Human Development Program* contains a theory manual, a curriculum book, and a set of daily instructional strategies focused on "magic circle" discussions related to awareness, mastery, and social interaction. The *Dimensions of Personality* program includes students' and teacher's manuals, group activity sheets, and a set of ditto masters. Work activities and group discussion are used to build positive self-concepts, competency in work in noncompetitive supportive groups, and basic social competence skills.

Martorella's comparative analysis of the four programs is presented in figure 8-1, in which the teaching models, affective themes, and key roles expected of students and teachers are summarized for each program. Martorella warns teachers about using the various programs, suggesting that basic issues related to each program are confused by the absence of any explicit and thorough examination of their theoretical bases and their failure to consistently operationalize program objectives. The lack of teacher-training techniques to use the experiences provided and to assess outcomes also presents a problem.[8] Martorella's analysis would suggest that teachers wishing to implement a program of affective

[7] Bessell and Palomares, *Human Development Program* (San Diego: Human Development Training Institute, 1970); *Dimensions of Personality* (Dayton, Ohio: Pflaum/Standard, 1972); *First Things: Values* (Pleasantville, New York: Guidance Associates, 1972); and Don Dinkmeyer, *Developing Understanding of Self and Others* (Circle Pines, Minn.: American Guidance Service, 1970).

[8] Peter H. Martorella, "Selected Early Childhood Affective Learning Programs: An Analysis of Theories, Structure and Consistency," *Young Children*, 30, no. 4 (May 1975), 289–301.

Figure 8-1 Summary Comparisons of Early Childhood Affective Programs

	Developing Understanding of Self and Others (DUSO-I)	First Things: Values	Human Development Program	Dimensions of Personality
Basic Teaching Model(s)	Awareness training; Laboratory method; Operant conditioning	Developmental	Awareness training; Operant conditioning	Laboratory method
Basic Affective Theme(s)	Emotion arousal; Focus on self	Emotion arousal	Focus on self	Focus on self
Key Student Role(s)	Spectators, actors, role players	Taking, justifying, and defending moral stands; considering and challenging competing arguments	Group participant	Group participant
Key Teacher Roles	Group discussion leader; clarifier and summarizer; puppeteer and dramatizer; behavior reinforcer	Organizing discussion groups; encouraging role taking; "devil's advocate"; diagnosing stages of moral reasoning	Organizing discussion groups; group discussion leader; behavior reinforcer	Organizing discussion groups; group process observer

Reprinted by permission from Peter H. Martorella, "Selected Early Childhood Affective Learning Programs: An Analysis of Theories, Structure, and Consistency," *Young Children,* Vol. 30, No. 4 (May 1975), p. 300. Copyright © 1975, National Association for the Education of Young Children, 1834 Connecticut Avenue, N.W., Washington, D.C. 20009.

education should evaluate their own capabilities in this area as well as the purpose, materials, and structure of formal programs available to them.

DECIDING WHAT TO TEACH

In developing a social studies program for young children, educators must decide what to teach and how to teach it. Often these decisions are made in relation to research reporting children's present level of knowledge.[9] Such research assesses what children know without benefit of an educational program; it cannot offer guidelines as to what they can or should be taught.

Maxine Dunfee, however, in reviewing research on social studies education, identified a number of studies showing that children in the primary grades had a greater knowledge of social studies information and concepts than was supposed. Often children already knew what they were to be taught prior to instruction. Even the one researcher who interpreted her evidence somewhat differently concluded that first grade children are ready to learn concepts that require only a single criterion of classification.[10]

Goals for the social studies must be related to overall goals of early childhood education. Instructional programs should be based upon concepts of readiness. Children should be given material that is appropriate, in a way that is consistent with their specific level of development. Knowledge of a child's readiness tells us to what degree we can expect him to master concepts and skills rather than what concepts and skills ought to be considered in the program's goals.

Children at the nursery school level, for example, can begin to deal with sociological concepts such as *self* or *group* as they explore themselves in relation to others in school and at home. Their level of understanding of these concepts will be quite different from that which can be expected from a primary-grade child. Similarly, young children can deal with historical events, putting them into a framework of "now" and "long ago" before they can deal with chronological time and the periodicity of history. If teachers conceive of the goal of social studies instruction as achieving a series of successive approximations to more sophisticated cognitive structures, then a concept of readiness becomes a helpful tool of instruction rather than a limiting one.

IDENTIFYING GOALS OF INSTRUCTION

The process of defining what and how to teach in an early childhood class is rather complex. It involves setting goals for instruc-

---

[9] For example, see Louise B. Ames, "The Development of the Sense of Time in the Young Child," *Journal of Genetic Psychology,* 68, no. 1 (1946), 97–125; and Joy M. Lacey, *Social Studies Concepts of Children in the First Three Grades* (New York: Teachers College Press, Columbia University, 1932).

[10] Maxine Dunfee, *Elementary School Social Studies: A Guide to Current Research* (Washington, D.C.: Association for Supervision and Curriculum Development, 1970), pp. 25–26.

tion, identifying topics to be used as vehicles for achieving these goals, and developing instructional units or programs based upon these goals and related to the topics. Materials and resources need to be gathered; activities need to be planned and implemented. Some way of judging the program's effects on the degree of achievement of the goals should also be a part of the process.

One way for kindergarten-primary teachers to deal with this decision is to adopt a total program—either one from a textbook publisher or one from a curriculum development project. Goals and activities are provided in a sequential framework, which simplifies the decision. However, selecting an appropriate program can be difficult. No one program serves all the purposes of social studies. A program should be selected based upon the match of its goals with the teacher's or school's priorities.

In many of the new social science curricula, the relationship of social studies to the social sciences has been emphasized. The goals of instruction may be concerned less with gaining factual knowledge about the topic under study and more with understanding basic concepts, generalizations, or conceptual schemes.

A conceptual scheme might be identified for the social studies as an integrated field. Paul Brandwein has identified the following "cognitive scheme" in the social sciences:

1. Man is a product of heredity and environment.
2. Human behavior is shaped by the social environment.
3. The geographic features of the earth affect man's behavior.
4. Economic behavior depends upon the utilization of resources.
5. Political organizations (governments) resolve conflict and make interaction easier among people.[11]

Other conceptual schemes have been developed that underlie a number of curriculum guides or programs in the social studies.

The advantage of a conceptual scheme such as Brandwein's is that it provides unity to a set of diverse activities. It also helps the teacher fit unplanned learning opportunities into the program. The scheme itself is never learned by children, but becomes a tool for the teacher's use.

Social studies goals cannot be conceived in terms of concept attainment alone. Hilda Taba, in her elementary social studies program,

[11] Paul F. Brandwein and others, *Principles and Practices in the Teaching of Social Sciences: Concepts and Values* (New York: Harcourt, Brace & World, 1970), pp. T–16–17.

identifies four categories of objectives: (1) basic knowledge, (2) thinking, (3) attitudes, feelings, and sensitivities, (4) skills. Basic knowledge includes basic concepts, main ideas, and specific facts. Thinking includes concept formation, the inductive development of generalizations, and application of principles and knowledge. Attitudes, feelings, and sensitivities include the ability to identify with people in different cultures, self-security, open-mindedness, acceptance of change, tolerance of uncertainty and ambiguity, and responsiveness to democratic and human values. Skills include both academic skills, such as map-reading, and research and social skills, such as the ability to work, plan, discuss, and develop ideas in groups.[12]

Although goals need to be identified for a program, a set of worthy goals does not necessarily lead to a worthy program. Often a program's stated goals seem to have little relationship to the activities. Sometimes older, traditional activities appear in programs espousing currently fashionable goals. For example, the topic of "community helpers," a venerable topic in primary social studies, is now being used to teach "career exploration."

IDENTIFYING TOPICS FOR STUDY

In the early childhood years there have traditionally been a limited number of topics for social studies programs. No topical themes are identified in the literature for the nursery school social studies, so teachers at this level have probably been freest to choose topics for study independently. At the kindergarten-primary level, these have usually revolved about the immediate environment of the child in school. Generally accepted topics consist of home and family, the school (including the classroom), the neighborhood (stores, supermarkets, filling stations), and the community (community services, agencies, and workers), as well as transportation and communication. Sometimes comparative studies of communities are suggested, such as the urban community versus the rural or suburban community.

In recent years curriculum guides, textbooks, and curriculum development projects have suggested the widening of topics for study by young children. These include family life in far-off countries such as Israel or Japan, broader comparative community study, and the study of specific concepts or conceptual schemes from the social sciences, such as "consumers" and "producers" and how they are related—derived from

---

[12] Hilda Taba, *Teachers' Handbook for Elementary Social Studies* (Menlo Park, Ca.: Addison-Wesley, 1967), pp. 7–10.

economics—or an understanding of actions and interactions among people—derived from sociology. Many social science concepts can be adequately studied through observation of social phenomena within the children's immediate environment.

The expansion of topics for early childhood social studies to include themes not associated with the "here and now" approach is laudatory. However, there is a danger that concepts related to these themes will be learned shallowly by rote because of a lack of direct data sources available for the children's personal inquiry. When topics dealing with the remote in time and space are offered to young children, care must be taken that they have the requisite learning necessary to establish their own meanings from the experiences and that they have access to appropriate data sources. The topic's appropriateness is as much a function of our concerns as of children's interests. A program focused on inquiry skills requires that opportunities be provided for collecting and acting upon information. Concepts and generalizations abstracted from such inquiry can later be applied to more remote topics, having few or no opportunities for direct collection of information.

A unit on families in a foreign country can provide meaningful study if the children have some understanding of family structures, roles, and relationships. This might best be achieved through a study of families in their own immediate environment. Teachers can alternate topics dealing with the immediate environment with related topics dealing with the remote in time and space, giving the children an opportunity to apply concepts and generalizations to new situations and to broaden their concepts as new data are fitted into already developed conceptual schemes. When dealing with topics unrelated to the immediate environment of the child, a broad range of resources should be available for his study, including books, audiovisual materials, and collections of artifacts and simulated materials.

Given these considerations, a teacher can decide that a prepared program will fit her class needs. A number of program evaluations are available to help in the choice. Martorella's analysis of affective learning programs, described earlier, could help a teacher decide among the four studied, if such a program is judged appropriate.[13]

The National Council for the Social Studies has also produced an analysis of the many newer social studies programs. These include a number designed in whole or part for the kindergarten-primary grades, all so different from one another that direct comparisons are

---

[13] Martorella, "Selected Early Childhood Affective Learning Programs," pp. 289–301.

difficult to make. Rather, each needs to be judged first as to the match between its goals and the teacher's priorities. Then information regarding quality becomes useful.[14]

USING RESOURCES
IN PRIMARY SOCIAL STUDIES

Once decisions about program goals and topics for study are made, teachers must organize for instruction. Planning at this point includes deciding about classroom activities, and identifying and organizing resources to be used by both teacher and children in the instructional program.

It is important for the teacher to realize that she is probably the single most important resource in the classroom. She serves as a model for teaching values and behaviors to the children through direct observation and imitation. The types of questions asked by the teacher can either further inquiry or lead to stereotyped responses. In addition, she sets up the classroom organization, deciding on the activities to be included and the range of behavior permitted. She uses her knowledge of the children, the resources available, and the topic under study to further the learning of the children.

Inquiry is important in early learning, but exposition still plays an important role. The teacher's role as teller—as source of information—is never to be underestimated.

Books also can provide a wealth of information not directly accessible to children. More children's information books are becoming available that are well written at a level children can understand and that accurately reflect reality. Fictional books are useful in that they, too, reflect the social world, often with greater insight than do many informational books. Children need to learn to use these important sources of information.

The oral tradition is important in social studies. Verbal descriptions offered by children and adults are useful sources of information. Group discussions help children clarify ideas, and can provide the teacher with feedback about the concept and the misconceptions the children might have from their activities. A group discussion cannot determine the truth of a child's statement. The vote of a kindergarten

[14] NCSS Curriculum Committee and Social Science Educational Consortium, "Evaluation of Curriculum Projects, Programs and Materials," *Social Education,* 36, no. 7 (November 1972), 712–71.

class cannot determine the sex of a rabbit. Having a child check his assertions against those of others, however, can help him become less self-centered and more aware of the external criteria of truth.

Although language is the most often-used symbol system in the social studies area, nonverbal symbol systems are also used, providing a useful resource for the children as both a source of data and a way of recording and communicating data. The most used nonverbal symbol systems are the map and the globe. Primary globes that show the world represented in simple form should be introduced early in school. The globe is a more accurate representation of the world than a flat map. Charts and graphs are other nonverbal symbol systems children must learn to use.

Maps are an important symbol system in the social studies. Children can learn to understand maps by developing their own, mapping field trips and other experiences. Children might begin mapping with three-dimensional representation—blocks—and later use pictures, and finally pure symbolizations. They could even invent their own symbol systems as they move to higher levels of abstraction.[15]

USING CONCRETE MATERIALS

The concrete materials of the social studies are representations of social science phenomena. Those we make available to children are either artifacts out of which we must infer behavior or symbolic representations of social science phenomena.

For the study of geography, a teacher may bring a map into the classroom, or, for a more realistic view of the terrain, a three-dimensional model. She may show slides or a movie of a particular area. These materials help make the children familiar with geographical areas which, more often than not, they cannot visit and explore.

In studying the family life of an Asian country or the culture of an African people, the teacher is again limited in what she presents for study. She can describe different family patterns, roles, and relationships. She can display pictures of the families in action, but seldom can she bring the family members into the classroom for interaction with the children, or even have the children visit families in the field. Even if they could visit, the children would not necessarily witness the behavior being studied or understand its meaning.

The earliest development of concrete materials for use by

---

15 Betty Richards, "Mapping: An Introduction to Symbols," *Young Children*, 31, no. 2 (January 1976), 145–56.

young children in social studies education was in the Montessori Method. In addition to tactile globes, Montessori devised map puzzles representing the world's political units. By playing with the map pieces, children became familiar with the names of countries and their boundaries. Each puzzle piece had a small knob attached to it to facilitate the children's handling. Similar geographic puzzles are available today (without the knob) from educational equipment suppliers.

With the development of the reform kindergarten movement in the United States during the first third of the twentieth century came the development of new educational materials. One of the most useful and flexible of these is *building blocks*.[16] Two basic variations were developed. In the "Conduct Curriculum Classes" of Patty Smith Hill, a set of large floor blocks was devised. Long blocks could be fastened to corner posts with pegs to create structures for children's dramatic play. The structures were large enough to allow children to play within them, and sturdy enough to take the occasional knock from a group of robust five-year-olds. The stability of any structure built with these blocks allowed the children to use them over a period of time so that their dramatic play could be extended and elaborated. Several variations of this type of block are available today, including hollow blocks, variplay sets, and Sta-Put blocks.

Unit blocks were developed by Caroline Pratt about the same time. The unit block, looking much like a length of 2″ × 4″ lumber, is based upon a unit of measure. Each block is either the size of the unit, a multiple, or a fraction of that unit. Thus there are half-units, quarter-units, double units, and quadruple-unit blocks. Various shapes are added, such as columns, wedges, curves, and semicircles, to make a set. A good set of unit blocks is constructed of hardwood that will not splinter or wear excessively, and is finished carefully so that each block is in exact proportion to the unit. This allows the children to construct complicated buildings that will stand securely for a time.

Because unit blocks are much smaller than the floor blocks, they cannot be used for dramatic play. With unit blocks, the child miniaturizes the world and plays with, not *in*, this miniature world. In the early stages of block play, found in the nursery school, the young child is content to build abstract structural designs. This type of block-building gives way to the building of individual structures, then large, elaborate, interrelated structures. These may represent either the child's fantasy world or the real world, depending upon the guidance that has been offered, as well as his present mood or needs.

---

[16] For an extensive analysis of blocks and their uses in early childhood classes, see Elizabeth S. Hirsch, ed., *The Block Book* (Washington, D.C.: National Association for the Education of Young Children, 1974).

Block constructions in social studies learning help children represent a home or a school. More elaborate structures can be used to represent a complex such as a shopping center, a neighborhood, a harbor area, or an airport. There is virtually no limit to the elaborateness possible in block representations, providing enough blocks and freedom of ideas are available to the children, and that the construction activity can continue over a long period of time. Block-building of this kind has a legitimate place in the primary grades as well as in the nursery school and kindergarten.

Children can incorporate other materials to elaborate on block construction; these can be purchased or improvised by the teacher. Miniature wooden or rubber people representing different family or community roles can be utilized, as can toy cars, trucks, boats, and airplanes. Traffic signs and street lights add to the reality orientation of a construction. Signs written by teacher or children can identify places; strips of paper or plastic represent streets or rivers. A ball of twine can help the children build a suspension bridge. Imaginative use of many everyday materials enhances the building and provides an outlet for the children's creativity.

Blocks are simple things. They become arbitrary symbols to be used as the children and teacher see fit in representing portions of the world. A block construction as a concrete representation provides a good

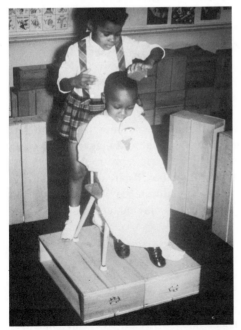

Preprimary Demonstration Unit, University of Illinois

transition to the children's use of maps and other forms of symbol learning in the classroom.

Blocks are only one kind of concrete material used in early school to support social studies learning. Teachers can help children make models of places using cardboard cartons, papier-mâché constructions, or other kinds of materials. Also available are commercial sets such as *Kinder City* or *Playschool Village,* and tabletop construction sets such as *Lincoln Logs* and *Lego.*

Other concrete materials used in support of children's dramatic play also provide a useful resource for social studies education. The traditional housekeeping area of the nursery school and kindergarten can encourage the exploration of family roles and relationships. Dress-up clothes and play props that suggest many situations support dramatic play; hats representing different occupations, in particular, are helpful. A ladder and a length of hose inspire children to work as firemen. A table, cash register, some paper sacks, and empty food containers suggest a supermarket. Sometimes the article in play does not even have to look like what it is representing. A bicycle pump, for example, can be used as a gasoline pump in a service station, or a fireman's hose. If the teacher is imaginative in her uses of concrete materials, the children will soon match, if not surpass, this imaginativeness in play.

AUDIO AND VISUAL REPRESENTATIONS

A range of simple to complex audiovisual representations can also provide resources for social studies teaching. Still photographs stimulate discussions and provide information. A number of sets of pictures for use in developing discussions are available from commercial sources.[17] Pictures should be large enough to be viewed by a group of children and contain enough detail without clutter so they can easily focus on what is important. The availability of commercial picture sets means the teacher does not have to hunt through old magazines for useful pictures. Pictures can be shown to children in a group discussion setting or placed on bulletin boards. If bulletin boards are used, care should be taken that the arrangement helps the children see what is important. Pictures may also be combined with other display materials on the bulletin board.

---

[17] For example, see Allonia Gadsden, *Concept Picture Charts: Exploration in Beginning Social Studies* (New York: Harcourt, Brace & World); Fanny and George Shaftel, *Words and Actions: Role-Playing Photo-Problems for Young Children* (New York: Holt, Rinehart and Winston); and Betty Atwell Wright, *Urban Education Studies* (New York: John Day Co.).

Magnetic and flannel boards are also useful, because they allow the children or teacher to manipulate the materials and change the organization, thus allowing a more active use than simple picture displays provide. Commercial flannel board and magnetic board materials are presently available.

While commercially produced pictures provide easily accessible resources, they may not contain the specific elements needed to study a particular environment. These materials can be supplemented by locally developed and often teacher-developed materials. Fortunately, audiovisual technology is at the point where much good material can be produced by persons having little technical skill.

Polaroid cameras allow teachers to take still pictures that are immediately available. Relatively simple cameras such as the Kodak Instamatic produce color slides that can be projected on a screen and viewed by an entire class, or placed in a viewer for individual study. Eight-millimeter movies can be made just as easily. The cost of motion pictures unfortunately often limits their classroom use.

Sound recordings also provide a good resource for learning. Commercial recordings of songs and stories can be an authentic mirror of a culture. Children can supplement these records by making tape recordings of their own songs and stories. A trip is recaptured in a classroom through the sounds and pictures recorded. Upon return from an airport visit, for example, children could listen to the announcements of flight arrivals and departures and the roar of the jet engines as a plane taxis to the runway and takes off. Tape recordings can also be made of interviews with resource persons or of class discussions. Audio and visual resources combine very effectively.

Planned arrangements of materials are often useful in communicating information. Exhibits should vary with the topic under study. Studying a service station, for example, might suggest an exhibit of things used and sold there, or an exhibit about petroleum and petroleum products. The first exhibit might include containers for products sold for automobiles, collections of small spare automobile parts, road maps, and simple hand tools used by mechanics. The petroleum exhibit could include a chart of petroleum products and refining processes. Containers of crude oil, lubricating oil, diesel fuel, home heating oil, kerosene, petroleum jelly, and paint thinners could be brought into the room for exhibition. Care should be taken with these materials since they are flammable and dangerous if swallowed. Pictures of these products or their uses can be substituted if deemed wise.

A study of families in Israel might include materials reflecting the culture of that country, with pictures of the area as it looked long ago. Displays should be used by the children rather than simply becoming a decorative part of the classroom.

Teachers generally collect materials and arrange displays by themselves, but children and their parents can profitably be involved in this enterprise. Sometimes commercial sources are willing to provide display materials for school use. A survey of resources available in a community is wise. Care must be taken that commercially available materials are not distorted by advertising messages, however.

In some areas, local museums lend displays of social studies materials to schools. Dioramas or artifacts may come in kits, some of which are commercially available.

USING COMMUNITY RESOURCES

Teachers need to look beyond the classroom for learning resources. Resource persons are often quite willing to come to school to meet with a group of children. Such people could be representative of community workers (such as a garbage collector or a fireman), have a particular skill or area of knowledge (a weaver or an anthropologist), or possess something of interest to the children. A hobbyist, a visitor from a foreign country, a member of a particular ethnic group under study, or an older person who has first-hand historical knowledge might be of great interest.

In using resource persons, the teacher should be sure that both the children and the visitor know the purpose of the visit and that basic ground rules for participation are laid down. Children enjoy acting as hosts in their classrooms.

Field trips into the community need to be properly planned. In addition to the technical planning, the children should be aware of the purpose and particular focus of the trip. Although chance occurrences can enhance a trip, it is not wise to leave its organization to chance. Field trips need not be elaborate excursions. Often the simplest trip is the most meaningful to young children. A walk to the corner to watch the traffic control operations or a visit to a local supermarket can provide a fruitful experience. Even though children may have had the same experience outside of school, the focus provided by the teacher and the preparation can open new learning opportunities as new aspects of a familiar situation are unfolded.

USING TEXTBOOKS
AND CURRICULUM GUIDES

An increasing number of social studies textbooks are becoming available at the kindergarten-primary level. Often a textbook series at this level takes the form of workbooks with pictures for the earliest units, and becomes a social studies reader at later levels. While many texts follow a story line, newer ones present social science materials directly to young children.

However, a textbook can provide only a limited amount of information and should not be the only resource for learning. Textbooks can be used as resources for a program, as a way of providing common knowledge, or for pulling together knowledge from a variety of sources. A good teachers' manual may also provide helpful suggestions for resources and instructional procedures. Rather than simply reading about concepts from a book, the children should actively inquire about and develop concepts on their own. Teachers may not want to order a single set of textbooks for an entire class, but it is often useful to have available several copies of many textbooks for the children's use.

Curriculum guides are seldom considered instructional resources because they are not used directly by the children. A good curriculum guide can help a teacher develop significant instructional activities, however. Curriculum guides vary in scope and organization. Some provide a generalized scheme of the subject matter area and are more suggestive; others can be highly prescriptive, describing in detail the work that is supposed to take place in a classroom. Still another kind of guide takes the form of resource units, containing outlines for classroom study and information for planning activities. Often resource units contain much more information than a teacher can use at any one time, thereby allowing her greater freedom and flexibility without imposing too great a need to seek out materials and instructional ideas.

In most states and large local school systems, curriculum guides and resources are generally developed and made available to teachers. Where such materials are not available, teachers must use their own resources. Teaching units are available commercially and can also be found in such magazines as the *Teacher, Early Years,* and *Instructor.* Teachers need to assess the worth of available units in terms of the significance of the goals, the practicability of the suggested activities, the availability of resources, and the applicability of the program to the particular class of children. At the preschool level, few resource units are available and teachers must generally rely on their own ingenuity for developing classroom activities.

INSURING SIGNIFICANCE IN THE USE OF RESOURCES

A lot of activity can take place in schools that does not produce learning or that causes children to learn the wrong things. Merely amassing resources and materials and providing children with activities does not insure learning. Although children's involvement is important, the achievement of instructional goals is the prime criterion by which we judge the success of schooling. Teachers need to select carefully from the range of resources available, using only those that help children achieve significant and worthwhile goals.

Teachers frequently use free and inexpensive materials because they are readily available, but they should judge the worth of materials as much by the benefits that accrue from using them as by their cost. Criteria for selecting resources include the material's usefulness for achieving instructional objectives, its possible effectiveness compared to other resources, and its appropriateness to the maturity level and background of the particular children. In addition, teachers need to consider the ease of operation of the resources and the cost of the materials in relationship to gains, in terms of both initial expense and time and effort expended by children and teacher.

INTEGRATING SOCIAL STUDIES
WITH OTHER ASPECTS OF THE CURRICULUM

Although the social studies program has been described independently, it often loses its distinctiveness as it becomes merged with other portions of the program. In the nursery school and kindergarten, portions of the social studies program should be integrated into a general activity period. Children can build with blocks, act out social roles, and look at pictures as a part of the social studies program at the same time other children are busy in other curriculum areas. Even in the primary grades, social studies can integrate a wide range of learning so that the school day is not made up of a string of distinct disparate activities. Other parts of the early childhood programs have much to offer the social studies.

Social studies activities often include the construction of models or dioramas by children. Many arts and crafts activities can be related to social studies, providing the children with opportunities to develop expressive skills. At the same time, the products become useful tools for social studies education. Drawing a picture of a supermarket, devising a decorative chart, or making Indian handicrafts are examples of how this can be done. The children can also use paintings, drawings, and constructions as a way of telling what they have learned.

Music and literature of a culture can provide a key to understanding its symbol system and values. Ethnic music, songs, stories, and poetry have an important place in the social studies program. Good literature for children (and adults) provides insight into people, institutions, and social relationships that are hard to describe in straight exposition.

Children can empathize with persons by sharing their feelings long before they can intellectually understand them.

The basic concepts of topological geometry, discussed in chapter 7, are just those concepts necessary for an understanding of geography and maps. Being able to locate places, and to determine proximity and separation are needed in map reading.

Language arts in general provide an excellent resource for the social studies. Children can create dramatic presentations or puppet shows in relation to a social studies unit. They can use dramatic play to act out roles and relationships, and tell or write stories that express the insights gained in a program. They also need to develop command of language skills to be effective in gathering information and communicating the fruits of their learning to others.

EXAMPLE OF A SOCIAL STUDIES UNIT
FOR YOUNG CHILDREN

The following is offered as a generalized approach to a social studies unit that could be taught at various age levels. It is an example of what it is possible for teachers to do; however, it is not meant to suggest that this is the only way or the best way to organize a social studies unit.

TOPIC: The Community
CONCEPTS: From Geography—Perpetual Transformation
GOALS OF THE PROGRAM:

A. Concepts and generalizations
   1. Change takes place in the geography of an area through people's social processes.
   2. These changes can be understood in a framework of time, and become evident through observations spaced in time.
B. Competencies
   1. Developing a sense of the passage of time
   2. Learning to use observation as a source of information
   3. Learning to compare observations made at different times
   4. Learning to use pictures, films, and models as sources of information

ACTIVITIES

1. The teacher may begin this study by reading to the children from Virginia Lee Burton's The Little House. After the reading, a discussion can be held about the changes that occurred to the house and the area around it. The teacher should attempt to elicit from the children the concept that

things change over time. Children's own recollections of moving into their neighborhood or of changes they have seen can personalize the experience and make the concept of change more meaningful. The children can then draw or describe in stories a list of changes that have taken place in their community. These descriptions can be grouped under *manmade changes* and natural changes, or changes in houses, the street, and in people who live in these houses. The groupings provide a basis for a display.

2. Plan a field trip to some place in the community that is undergoing change: an area of urban renewal, a new subdivision, construction of a street or highway, or some similar kind of construction that can dramatize change for the children. Have them observe the site and the work in progress. If possible, try to get a worker from the project to talk to them about what is happening and why. Take pictures of the site. Plan to visit it at some time in the future. If a visit with the children is impractical, the teacher can go alone, taking more pictures of the work as it then looks, and report to the children, showing the pictures and comparing them with the ones taken earlier. If it is possible to procure a picture of the site before the work began, this is also helpful. Have the children look at the different sets of pictures and discuss what is the same and what is different in each set. See if they can visualize what the completed project will look like. Pictures the children draw may be discussed. Since none of the children will really know how the project will come out, there is no one right picture. A display of different pictures might be interesting.

3. Set up a similar work project in the classroom using toy machines and blocks or a sand table. If possible, help the children fashion machines of their own. Simple trucks, cranes, and bulldozers might be improvised at the woodwork bench. Allow the children to play freely with the materials. You might wish to talk with them as they play, asking questions about the uses of the machines and the purposes of their play. You could also suggest uses of the machines similar to those seen on the field trips. Books and filmstrips about machines can be brought into the classroom for display at this time (e.g., Zaffo, *The Big Book of Real Building and Wrecking Machines*). Children may then draw or describe in words different kinds of machines, different in both purpose and operation.

4. Identify a resource person from the community who has lived in the area a long time. Invite him into the class to talk with the children about the neighborhood as it looked a long time ago, comparing it to the neighborhood as it looks today. If he has photographs or old newspapers, ask him to bring them along. Develop a display of pictures and relics from the neighborhood as it once looked. In many areas one does not have to go too far back to find observable change.

5. Ask the children to ask their parents what they remember about the neighborhood as it was long ago. If the community is a stable one, it will be easy to get information and memorabilia from families. Have the children dictate or write stories about the things they were told, illustrating their stories with their own pictures or those from other sources, so that each child has a personal history book. The stories and pictures could be placed along a time-line so that children begin to visualize the chronology of change.

6. A local museum or historical society may have displays of things from long ago that are related to the locality. A visit to such a display or its inclusion in the classroom could be coupled with the showing of the personal history books.

This unit deals with the neighborhood in a geographic framework. Many other topics could have been used and other social sciences could have provided equally adequate frameworks for study. Many of those traditionally studied in early childhood classes can provide opportunities for significant social studies learning.

If a study of community workers is well organized, then children can analyze what people do at work, separate the production of goods from the production of services, and relate production to the idea of consumption—who consumes the goods or services, where they are consumed, and why they are needed. The idea can also be developed that goods and services must be paid for, either directly or indirectly, and that we sometimes do without goods or services because we can't pay for everything we want. Children can be helped to see that choices are involved even when they are not evident. A study of families of children in the class (done carefully and with permission) can help children see that there is great diversity in social structures within a community as well as similarities and differences in the functions of family units. For each topic the teacher must view social studies as a method of inquiry rather than as a body of information to pass on to children. Additional topics can also be used, such as a unit on Black Americans, taught within a framework of anthropology, that presents significant learnings from both a social science and human relations point of view. A Black Studies curriculum has been developed with units in social studies—as well as language arts, art, and music—that could be easily integrated into a social studies program.[18] Studies of other ethnic groups are also worth including in the early childhood program. Ours is a multicultural nation. Too often teachers and schools include only elements of the majority culture, helping children become socialized by behaving as if they were all a part of that majority culture. While a certain amount of such "as if" programming is legitimate and even necessary, the exclusion of elements of other cultures from the program impacts on children of both the minority and the majority groups. It limits the opportunities for children to cope with a multicultural existence and to enjoy the benefits of this diversity, and it hides the problems with which they may later be faced.

A social studies program in the early years might not help children learn the names of presidents in order or the capitals of countries throughout the world. It should, however, help them gain a better understanding of themselves in relation to the social world in which they live. In addition, it should provide children with reasonable and verifiable ways of finding out about their social world. Linked with an understanding of the physical world, such knowledge helps them begin to make reasonable decisions about some of the things that happen to them.

SUGGESTED READING

CHASE, LINWOOD W., and MARTHA TYLER JOHN, *A Guide for the Elementary Social Studies Teacher* (2nd ed.). Boston: Allyn and Bacon, 1972.

FENTON, EDWIN, "Moral Education: The Research Findings," *Social Education,* 40, no. 4 (April 1976), 188–93.

HANNA, LAVONE A., GLADYS L. POTTER, and ROBERT W. REYNOLDS, *Dynamic Elementary Social Studies.* New York: Holt, Rinehart and Winston, 1973.

HOFFMAN, ALLAN J., and THOMAS F. RYAN, *Social Studies and the Child's Expanding Self.* New York: Intext Educational Publishers, 1973.

JAROLIMEK, JOHN, *Social Studies in Elementary Education* (4th ed.). New York: The Macmillan Company, 1971.

MICHAELIS, JOHN U., *Social Studies for Children in a Democracy* (5th ed.). Englewood Cliffs, N.J.: Prentice-Hall, Inc., 1972.

MITCHELL, LUCY SPRAGUE, *Young Geographers.* Orig. pub. 1934. New York:

---

[18] Bernard Spodek and others, *A Black Studies Curriculum for Early Childhood Education,* rev. ed. (Urbana, Ill.: ERIC/ECE, 1976).

Bank Street College of Education, 1971. Distributed by Agathon Press, New York.

MORRISETT, IRVING (ed.), *Concepts and Structure in the New Social Science Curricula*. West Lafayette, Ind.: Social Science Education Consortium, 1966.

ROBISON, HELEN F., and BERNARD SPODEK, *New Directions in the Kindergarten*. New York: Teachers College Press, 1965.

SEIFELT, CAROL, *Social Studies in Early Childhood Education*. Columbus, Ohio: Charles E. Merrill, 1977.

SPODEK, BERNARD, et al., *A Black Studies Curriculum for Early Childhood Education* (rev. ed.). Urbana, Ill.: ERIC Clearinghouse in Early Childhood Education, 1976.

Courtesy of The Brooklyn Museum

CHAPTER NINE

EXPRESSIVE ARTS IN THE EARLY YEARS

The expressive arts have traditionally held honored positions in early childhood education. The early Froebelian kindergartens included music and art activities in the form of the *Occupations* and the *Mother's Songs and Games*. Both of these were carefully patterned according to explicit directions and gave children opportunities to be actively involved in making and doing, even though the results were not creative products.

Such is the case in the art activities found in many contemporary programs for young children. The kindergarten that gives every child exactly the same paper construction or asks students to fill in the spaces outlined on a sheet of paper by the teacher leaves no room for the child's interpretation of reality or his outpouring of ideas and feelings. Nor is creativity nurtured by stereotyped rhythm band activity, in which a teacher plays the piano and each child is supposed to carefully follow the established beat, adding stress at preassigned points in the composition. Music, movement, and art serve as vehicles for creative expression, but used improperly, they can support conformity and the suppression of individual style. Properly used, they enhance individuality and creativity, as do other subjects and activities in the early years.

A distinction needs to be made between formal and stereotyped teaching. When we speak of *formal teaching*, we mean teaching in a situation in which subject or activity areas are kept separated, where activities and goals are determined by the teacher, often prior to the activity, and where the relationship between the teacher and the children is hierarchical and formally defined. *Stereotyped teaching* occurs when activities or lessons are provided to children without concern for their purposes, interests, or abilities. The same activities may be presented class after class, year after year. Stereotyped teaching can take place in formal or informal settings. Formal teaching can be responsive to the needs, abilities, and interests of children.

There are those who believe that creativity flourishes only when children are given free rein with material, and that any requirement for their activity is an unnecessary and stifling imposition. Others feel that children left unbridled cannot develop the inner discipline and self-reflection necessary for creative activity. In reality, children can benefit from a variety of structures and degrees of adult intervention. Formal relationships between teacher and children do not necessarily lead to stereotyped activity. It is interesting to note that involvement in a Froebelian kindergarten and training in the prescribed use of blocks—one of the Froebelian *gifts*—is seen as having a major formative influence on Frank Lloyd Wright, one of the most creative of American architects.[1]

The arts are to be valued in school as a way of knowing rather than for their cathartic effects. It is not a child's unbridled outpouring of feelings through the use of media that makes the arts important in his education, but rather his use of feelings, sensitivities, and understandings that require expression in a nonrational, often nonlinear form. Shaping the child's expression into two- or three-dimensional constructions, into sound patterns, or into the deliberate development of movement patterns extends his way of understanding the world in a manner not possible through the sciences or conventional verbal description. This is a personal way of knowing, but one that can be shared with others.

CREATIVITY

Mary Marksberry identifies three types of creative products: unique communications, plans or proposed sets of operations, and sets of abstract relations.[2] Music, movement, and art activities generally produce creative products in the first category. A painting, a piece of sculpture, a musical selection, or a series of movements are of this nature. Other areas of the curriculum, such as language arts—including the child's own stories, poems, or special descriptive phrases—are unique communications. Personal interpretations of other people's works might also be so considered.

The other two types of creative products can be found throughout the program. The techniques for learning science and social

[1] Robert B. Clements, "A Case for Art Education," *Art Education,* 28, no. 3 (March 1975), 2–7.
[2] Mary Lee Marksberry, *Foundation of Creativity* (New York: Harper & Row, 1963), pp. 10–13.

studies, discussed in chapters 6 and 8, lead children to create plans and proposed sets of operations that often result in the creation of sets of abstract relations.

To speak of creativity in the classroom is really to refer to the total program. But teaching music, movement, and art cannot be understood only in terms of creativity, for in dealing with them, one must deal with concepts of aesthetics as well. The young child needs to be surrounded by beautiful things to begin to appreciate and understand beauty. He also must learn to criticize his own work and that of others constructively to develop criteria of aesthetic appreciation. Such criticism need not be negative, nor does it require that the children have sophisticated tastes and mature sensitive appreciations, for these too develop as a result of experience and guidance. As children experience the creative process themselves and share their expressions with others, and as they mature to the point that they can separate themselves from their products, they can learn to become critics and accept criticism themselves.

Elwyn Richardson describes how children develop sensitivity to aesthetic components as a result of the criticism of their art work. Such criticism heightened their appreciation of the individuality of others and helped them develop more artistic approaches to materials.[3]

THE CREATIVE PROCESS

Gladys Andrews suggests that the creative process involves three phases: "(1) The child and his creative power, feelings and imagination, (2) the action or interaction of his experience, (3) and his outward form of expression."[4] Too often teachers focus almost exclusively on the third phase, to the exclusion of the others. The experience of putting one's expressions into concrete form through words, paints, musical rhythms, or movement through space is the culmination of a chain of events and cannot be considered in isolation. The teacher who wishes to foster creative expression must do much more than provide paint and paper. It is in the attitude pervading the class and in the uses she makes of the child's perceptions and experiences that creativity begins.

Each aspect of the creative process needs to be supported in the classroom in its own way. The child's feelings and imagination are outside the teacher's direct reach. She can support their development in direct ways. The child must be given opportunities to freely use his imagination, with the products of this imaginative thought accepted and cher-

---

[3] Elwyn S. Richardson, *In the Early World* (Wellington, New Zealand: Council of Educational Research, 1964), pp. 15–48.
[4] Gladys Andrews, *Creative Rhythmic Movement for Children* (Englewood Cliffs, N.J.: Prentice-Hall, Inc., 1954), p. 21.

ished. To use his power, he must feel a degree of acceptance in a climate in which he is viewed as a competent individual, important and worthy. This acceptance of the uniqueness of the individual and the importance of each person's contribution to the classroom can boost creative power.

The teacher should provide the children with the stimulation of a broad range of experiences. The child who can see, hear, taste, smell, and touch a great variety of things has access to the raw material of creative expression. These sensory perceptions are meaningless, however, when provided in isolation. Giving the child a set of color chips, a range of tone blocks, or a board covered with various textured materials may help him become aware of differences in sensory experiences or learn to name and categorize them, but the creative process may be thwarted if these isolated sensory explorations become the sum and substance of his education. Creativeness grows out of experiencing the rich fabric of sensory images woven into the complexities of real life. The child who is taken to the docks of a seaport and can not only perceive the visual images of ships, cargo, and machines but also have his experience heightened by the smell of salt water, the feel of damp air on his skin, and the sounds of seagulls and shouting stevedores has a rich experience. He may select those portions that are personally meaningful to represent through the art media.

Similarly, the child who is allowed to sit for long periods of time watching the movement of a lonely insect in a field—seeing how it travels from place to place, how it eats and collects its food—has a perception of the natural world far richer than that provided through a book. Experiencing the world in its realistic state is an important part of the creative process.

The opportunity to interact with his environment is just as important for the child. This interaction may be physical, as he moves out and talks to people or touches things. It can also be intellectual, an internal process that allows him to reflect on his experience and abstract significant aspects for further study. He can compare a recent experience with one he remembers from an earlier time, or compare his perceptions and interactions with those of other people. The abstraction of personal meaning from the world surrounding him provides the raw material from which creative expressions are derived, while the expressive act serves as a way to integrate these meanings into mental structures.

As the child develops an outward form of expression, he learns to master media so that the expression is deliberate rather than accidental. This means that he learns to use himself—his body for movement, his hands for painting and modeling. He learns to control the media with which he works. Paints and brushes become an extension of him, as do musical instruments, words, and all the raw material out of which he creates artistic products. This is not to say that he becomes insensitive to the attributes of the materials or that he rejects ideas stimulated from experiences with the medium alone. The child who is given modeling clay needs to explore the dimensions of the material and test ways of using it in order to achieve mastery.

Thus the quality of the materials and tools we provide in early childhood classes takes on added importance. They must be able to become an extension of the child's body, extending rather than limiting his possibilities. A sturdy brush for painting is better than a string or a piece of sponge if it allows greater control of the expression. Modeling clay that is malleable and responsive is more useful than oil-based Plasticine because the child has greater control over it. The attractiveness of the final product is not the criterion for an art project's success. The degree to which the product—painting, pot, movement pattern, or song-theme— was a deliberate outgrowth of the child's intent and to which it extended his ability to express himself in that particular medium determines both the success and the worthiness of the activity.

The young child is to some extent stimulus-bound. His use of a medium of expression becomes a significant experience that, in effect, transforms itself. Colors dripping into each other on a painting may elicit new forms and new colors that will stimulate him to explore opportunities not even present when he first stood at the easel. These explorations should be supported, for it is through the individual exploration of the medium that the child develops control.

DEVELOPMENTAL STAGES
IN ART AND MUSIC

Improving artistic expression is not merely a matter of teaching children control. The stages of human development influence the child's creations as much as anything else. A concept of stages in development suggests that a substantive difference exists between the child and the adult that cannot be explained on the basis of experiences alone. Every person goes through a series of metamorphoses in development so that each level is different in kind from the one preceding it and those following it.

Levels of artistic development have been identified as being similar to those of intellectual development. Victor Lowenfeld, over three decades ago, devised a scheme of stages in the artistic development of children. The levels of development that are roughly approximate to the early childhood period would include the *scribbling* stage (ages two to four), the *preschematic* stage (ages four to seven), and the *schematic* stage (ages seven to nine).[5]

Between the ages of two and four, the child, usually in the scribbling stage, has a kinesthetic experience through drawing. He moves through longitudinal, then circular motions, becoming more coordinated as he matures. The child first experiments with the materials, then finds likenesses within his drawing to objects in the real world, thus coming up with a "name" to give the drawing.

Between the ages of four and seven, the child in the preschematic stage discovers the relationships between drawing, thinking, and reality. Although a continuous change occurs in the symbols he creates in his drawings, the child starts out with an idea of the object he wants to represent. He begins to develop representational forms, although they may not be related in the picture as they are in reality. He also is developing form concepts.

When the child moves to the schematic stage, between seven and nine, he begins to create realistic representations of people and things. He learns to use color and space realistically, and to depict movement in his pictures. He then moves on to more mature stages of artistic development.

Lowenfeld's conception of stages in art closely parallels Jean Piaget's stages of intellectual development. It is quite possible that art as an expression of the child, built upon his perceptions and conceptions and his level of muscular control and coordination, is to some extent a function of general intellectual development.

The implications of the stage theory of development apply to other areas of creative expression as well. Children may go through various stages in the use of movement and music. Frances Aronoff uses Jerome Bruner's conception of three modes of learning—*enactive, iconic,* and *symbolic*—in her framework of music education: "(1) the enactive through action and manipulation; (2) the iconic through perceptual organization and inquiry—aural, kinesthetic and visual; and (3) the symbolic through words and symbols."[6] She suggests that the enactive and iconic modes are the ways in which young children know music. They respond readily to the elements of music through movement and play. Without the use of symbols they are able to organize their perceptions of and responses to music, forming mental structures that become the basis for understanding, remembering, and creating music. This use of a

---

[5] Victor Lowenfeld, *Creative and Mental Growth* (New York: The Macmillan Company, 1947).

[6] Frances Webber Aronoff, *Music and Young Children* (New York: Holt, Rinehart and Winston, 1969), p. 7.

Brunerian framework, built upon a Piagetian conception of development, also suggests the development of concepts in music as a function of general intellectual development.

Geraldine Dimondstein identifies some of the negative results of applying a developmental stage concept to art education. The use of stages to explain changes in children's art products, she contends, has tended to inhibit the teachers' fresh perceptions of the specific qualities of an art product. It has also perpetuated the myth that the teacher should leave children to grow through these stages, limiting her role to providing materials for them.[7] These dangers grow from a conception of development as maturation rather than as a result of an interaction of internal and external forces. Given an interactionist view of development, a conception of stages can help a teacher establish tentative expectations for children. It can also help her interpret children's products and determine what are the best next steps for them and how they can be helped to take those steps. Thus assessment and future planning for increased learning can be enhanced by a realistic use of a stage theory.

What a child does or how he develops does not predetermine how he should be taught or what the content of instruction ought to be. It does, however, establish a framework within which goals can be determined and expectations set. It also *suggests* directions for education, for the teacher should be concerned with helping him move through present stages to more mature stages. A child in nursery school, for example, should not be expected to create representational paintings and drawings. Nor should a kindergarten child be expected to be able to draw his room with all the objects shown in proper size and place relationship to one another.

The concept of stages taken by itself does not suggest that the teacher ought to simply sit back and wait for the child to mature. The teacher's role is to guide the child and help him arrive at more mature ways of handling media and creating expressions. The guidance function of the teacher is as important with young children as with mature adults. A knowledge of stages of development provides a series of benchmarks that the teacher can use in directing the child's learning.

ARTS AND CRAFTS

Arts and crafts activities are often considered less important in the primary grades than in the nursery school and kindergarten. Too often the

---

[7] Geraldine Dimondstein, *Exploring the Arts with Children* (New York: The Macmillan Company, 1974), p. 57.

arts and crafts work is designed solely to insure that a finished product will be presentable and each child will have something to take home. This makes for good public relations, for parents can see that the children are doing *something* in class.

There is no denying the importance of sound public relations for a school. There are also times when it is appropriate to have the children make a product for the home such as the Christmas or Mother's Day gift. It is unfortunate, however, when concern for the image of the school takes precedence over the child's learning, for it is not the product that is the important goal of the school, but the child's growing mastery over materials. Using them to express feelings, perceptions, and ideas is important, though intangible. The completed work of the child has significance only in that it provides the teacher with insights into what he has learned and what difficulties he still must master.

The media of art most productive for children in the early years are those that can be used at any age level. Naomi Pile identifies the basic art materials as paint, clay, and drawing and collage material. These are basically formless in themselves and offer endless possibilities for change, mastery, surprise, and self-reflection.[8] Paints, clay, drawing, and collage, for example, can be used by the three-year-old as well as by the mature artist. One does not limit a medium to a particular age level. Nor does the child's prior experience with the material need to concern the teacher, because in his developing competency, the young child will continue to see fresh possibilities in these media that represent an outgrowth of his increased mastery and the more mature stage of artistic development he is entering. The materials, however, do need to be introduced in fresh ways through the years.

TWO-DIMENSIONAL ART WORK

Much of the art work we provide for children in the early years relates to the use of materials on a flat surface. Paints, crayon, and collage material are concerned with only a single plane, although collage work can have depth as a result of overlaying various materials and textures. The child's concern is primarily with form and color.

Painting is one of the mainstays of the early childhood program. In many classrooms, an easel is accessible to the children for a good part of the day. While an easel is handy for painting, the top of a table or a bit of floor space is just as good. The level surface, as a matter of fact, will limit the amount of dripping that occurs during the painting.

[8] Naomi F. Pile, *Art Experiences for Young Children* (New York: The Macmillan Company, 1973), p. 13.

Teachers should organize the area used so that cleanup is as simple as possible, having children spread papers under the painting and making sponges and paper towels readily available. Keeping paints in containers that can be covered enables art work to continue with a relative degree of administrative simplicity.

Tempera paints may be either powdered or liquid in form. If powdered, they should be mixed thickly enough so that the colors will be rich and the paint opaque. With young children, a few colors at a time are adequate; more and different paints can be added later. Colors other than primary can be purchased or mixed in class. The mixing can lead the children to make new discoveries about color.

The children at this stage prefer to experiment with form and color, allowing the movement of their own arms to stimulate the shapes that form on the paper. These experiments often have rhythm, balance, and interest. Many children appear to have an instinctive aesthetic sense and their abstract paintings sometimes resemble works of art. The teacher can use her judgment in recognizing these artistic productions, thus encouraging children to evaluate their own efforts along these dimensions.

Although the young child should be encouraged to explore and experiment, simple techniques can be demonstrated for him. Wiping the brush so that it is not overloaded with paint, cleaning brushes before using them for other colors, mixing colors in specific proportions to achieve desired results, and placing the right brush into the right container of paint are simple skills that young children can learn. Teachers need to be willing and able to use the accidents of painting, however. A color mixture that results from an improperly placed brush or an accidental drip can lead to exciting learnings.

Brushes should be large and rather stiff so they respond easily to the movements of the child. Several sizes should be available. Most of the painting in classrooms is done on unprinted newsprint. The standard size used is 18″ × 24″. Teachers ought not to limit themselves to this kind of paper, for a different size, shape, or even texture will stimulate new ways of painting. The classified section of a newspaper or a piece of wrapping paper with a small design might also be used for painting.

Tempera painting is usually considered a quiet, individual activity. Each child has his own paper and paints and interacts little with others. Even when two children are painting together at the easel, they are seldom interacting, for their work is separated.

Children do, however, enjoy painting side by side or in groups. A double easel or the floor supports painting as a group activity. Involving the children in mural painting is another way of creating a group experience.

Murals can be painted on large sheets of brown wrapping paper, which many schools keep available. At first, the murals of young children will actually be a collection of individual paintings, with any consistency growing out of the teacher's organization rather than their work. There is usually little group planning, and teachers often find it useful to simply allocate space on different parts of the paper to different children. As the children mature and gain experience in this work, they can begin to plan toward a unified product.

The teacher's role in painting is not to have the children copy models she provides but to encourage them to explore the media, to observe their progress and guide it, providing new techniques consistent with their development and needs.

Many teachers of young children shy away from the use of transparent water colors in the classroom. Although this medium is more difficult to control, young children can use and benefit from it. The flow of color over color can also add interesting dimension. Oil paints are much more difficult to use and are best avoided.

Wax crayons are almost universally found in early childhood classrooms. Their use requires little teacher preparation; they seldom create much of a mess, and they are easily available. Large hexagonal or half-round crayons are available that allow the very young child to make bold, controllable strokes and that will not roll off the table. Children may be given their own sets of crayons, or crayons may be kept in a class pool. Large sheets of manila paper are useful for coloring with crayons, but other kinds of paper can be used as well.

As the children learn to use crayons, they can also be encouraged to mix crayoning with other media. The waxy crayon drawing provides a surface to which tempera paint will not adhere, so covering the surface with a single coat of paint allows the crayon drawing to stand out in interesting relief.

Using colored or white chalk at a blackboard, the child has a freedom to cover a large surface without concern for creating a product, for he knows his work will soon be erased. Chalk can also be used on paper; wetting the paper with water or buttermilk makes the colors show up more brilliantly, and spraying a fixative on the chalk drawings keeps them from rubbing off the paper.

Cutting, tearing, and pasting paper to create interesting designs has long been a school activity. Papers of adequate stiffness can be folded to create three-dimensional shapes; the Japanese art of origami creates three-dimensional forms out of a single piece of paper without any cutting. Although this form of art work may be too complex for the young child, it does give one an idea of what can be done. Interesting designs can also be created at the two-dimensional level. For very young children, the teacher could prepare various-shaped pieces of colored paper to be pasted on a background, and as children develop competency in using scissors, they can create their own shapes. White school paste is all that is needed for children's collage work.

Other kinds of materials can be added to the pool of colored paper to increase the variety of textures, colors, and shapes in collage. A teacher might pick up many scavenged materials in her daily travels rather than order them from a supply house. A variety of these, organized so that teachers and children can select them without too much difficulty, enhances an art program.

Various kinds of special paper and cardboard, pieces of fabric of various sizes, shapes, colors, and textures, bits of rope and yarn, feathers, buttons, colored sawdust, metal foil, and almost any other kind of material can be shaped, cut, pasted, and otherwise included in a creation. Children should be offered a limited variety of these materials at any one time, but can also be encouraged to think of new materials. As new materials are used, the teacher must provide other ways of attaching them, since school paste may be inadequate. Rubber cement, white glue, staples, and cellophane tape may need to be added to the resources of the class.

Finger paints are often difficult for children to control, but they offer the child a release that cannot be matched by other media. The child has direct contact with the medium since he has no brush, scissors, or other implement between him and the paper. Often a child's finger painting is important because of the process of exploration it provides rather than increasing his control over the media.

For finger painting, a glossy nonabsorbent paper is available from school supply houses; glazed shelf paper may also be used. Sometimes the painting can be done on the plastic surface of a table—this allows it to go through many design changes. When the child is through painting, he may wash the surface of the table to complete the cleanup, or if the teacher wishes to preserve the finger painting, she can print the product by carefully placing a paper over the painting, pressing it down firmly all over, and carefully lifting it off.

There are many ways of printing designs. Dipping an interesting textured or shaped object into a shallow dish of tempera paint and pressing it firmly on a sheet of paper works well. Sponges, grainy ends of wooden boards, and vegetables such as carrots or potatoes are among the many materials that can be used. A design can be carved into these materials to enhance the printing. The process is similar to that of a linoleum block printing or a woodcut, but not as complicated. With the youngest children, the teacher can create the designs and let the children print. Varying designs through the use of different colors and patterns makes this an interesting medium.

THREE-DIMENSIONAL
CONSTRUCTIONS

Although depth can often be added to the two-dimensional media, for example, by adding whipped soap suds to tempera paint so that it dries with a degree of depth, the three-dimensional constructions created by children are quite different. In the early years, the three-dimensional media include woodworking, cardboard box constructions, clay modeling, and the creation of mobiles and stabiles.

Children get a great deal of pleasure out of working with wood—the simple activity of hammering and sawing is often enough to satisfy the very young child. It is not uncommon, for example, to find children in a nursery class sawing piece after piece of wood from a board until there is nothing left of the original; they may even bring home wood constructions that seem to contain more iron in the form of nails than wood.

Unfortunately, teachers in many classes hesitate to include woodworking, usually because they lack experience with carpentry and tools. Hammers, saws, and other tools, if improperly used, can injure children. The greater the ignorance of the teacher, the greater her fear of possible bodily harm to children. But young children can develop a respect for tools and skills and learn to use them safely.

Regina Weilbacher

A woodworking area needs to be organized to promote positive activities and avoid danger; it requires a certain amount of isolation from other activities. Tools and supplies should be stored so they are readily accessible, and be in good order and in proper repair, with saws sharp and hammer handles firmly embedded in the heads. A good supply of soft wood such as common pine is necessary. Wood can often be collected from the scraps of local lumber yards. A number of accessories can be included as the children mature in their ability to use wood and tools.

Lightweight but good quality hammers and short crosscut saws should be provided. Sandpaper, block planes, rasps, and wood files help children smooth their woodwork. A brace and drill bits and hand drill are useful. Screwdrivers can be added as children learn to use screws as well as nails for fastening boards together. A woodworking vise, workbench or saw horses, and "C" clamps are useful, too.

Children usually begin by building simple constructions. These can often be put together with nails, and later, screws with large heads and white glue. As the projects are elaborated, teachers can add dowels, empty paper rolls, spools, and just about anything she and the children find useful. Woodworking projects can be painted with tempera and then covered with shellac or lacquer so the color will not run. More responsible children might be given enamels for painting. These, however, are harder to work with and to clean up.

Clay modeling has been a mainstay in early education for many years. Potter's clay is soft and malleable, and can be used over and over. If it has dried out, water can be added to it; if it is too wet, it can be left to dry.

Very young children enjoy the sheer fun of manipulating clay. They knead it, pound it, roll it into balls or snakes, flatten it, break it up, and push it all together again. Just playing with the clay often takes precedence over actually creating something. Later, children learn to make pinch pots, pulling the clay into shapes and tearing off pieces. They create figures, adding pieces of clay—heads, arms, and legs—to a rolled body to create people and animals. After a while, they can even learn to build pots, using the coil or slab method.

After the children are through working with clay, they are often content to put it back into the crock. When they wish to save what they have made, however, the clay can be dried slowly and then painted. If a kiln is available in the school, it is exciting to watch the clay transformed by the heat. Care should be taken, however, that work to be fired in a kiln is sturdy and will not explode or come apart. If the children have worked over the clay for a while, it may not need to be wedged. The pieces should not be too thick and the appendages should be securely attached. The teacher might even wish to glaze some of the children's work.

In some classrooms, other modeling material such as Plasticine, an oil-based clay, is sometimes substituted for clay. Although Plasticine is not as responsive to modeling, and the children's work cannot be preserved, it can be used again and again and will not dry out. Some teachers also use modeling dough. It can be purchased commercially or made out of simple household ingredients—salt, flour, and water.

Simple constructions—houses, cash registers, rocket ships, or model automobiles—can be made out of cardboard boxes and cartons that are cut up, pasted together, elaborated with paper, and painted and colored. The skills the children have developed in two-dimensional work can be elaborated and used in endless constructions. Thick corrugated cardboard is now available that can be worked like wood to create sturdy constructions. This "cardboard carpentry" is a welcome addition to the resources of schools.

Mobiles and stabiles are three-dimensional designs. Mobiles are designed to move; stabiles remain stationary. They are created by combining a variety of material in interesting fashions—dowels, tongue depressors, wire coat hangers, pipe cleaners, metal foil, yarn, balls, sponges, rubber bands, and so on. Bases for stabiles can be easily fashioned out of clay or styrofoam; mobiles are designed to hang, and do not need a base.

Young children can weave on simple looms early in their school careers. "Loopers," using cotton loops and simple metal looms, are a beginning. Teachers can also make simple looms out of squares of corrugated cardboard. Half-inch-deep slots in two opposite ends allow the child to thread the loom; the yarn can then be woven back and forth until a square is completed. Simple looms can also be made by driving nails into the edges of wooden boxes or frames.

Children can begin to sew designs onto pieces of burlap with tapestry needles. In time, these can be combined with sewn pieces of felt or a similar fabric to create interesting pictures.

THE CLASSROOM AS A STUDIO

In using arts and crafts activities in the classroom, the teacher is concerned with teaching techniques; but techniques need not be taught in isolation. A child needs opportunities to explore each medium and set of materials. Skill in use of materials and respect for their potential and limitations grows out of personal exploration. Technique can be provided as the child feels the need to push his use of the material beyond what he has already accomplished. This is true for the mature artist as well.

The teacher should not be concerned that every project the child works on lead to a finished product worthy of display. If a child experiments, he should be allowed to experience failure, and if he is busy practicing one technique in a complex project, he may not even be concerned with product completion.

The classroom should be a place where a child can explore his abilities and the uses he can make of material. Accomplishment can be acknowledged and criticism provided, but only in the spirit of guidance and to move children to further accomplishments. The work of the child is his way of expressing himself. As an extension of himself, his art work becomes personally important.

MUSIC

Aronoff defines the discipline of music as including "concepts of music, skills and knowledge for applying them, and concepts about music dealing with the uses of music in the past and ongoing culture. Their interrelationship is in fact the structure of music."[9] Music study, then, involves the development of factual knowledge and concepts, analysis, and skills and repertoire. Skills include listening, singing, playing, moving, and reading and writing music. A music program in early childhood education, therefore, should provide children with opportunities to listen to music, learn to understand its elements, reproduce these through singing and playing instruments, and relate bodily movement to musical expression. Creation of musical compositions or movements should also be included. The music program must relate to other parts of the curriculum, especially the language arts and social studies, to help children learn about the uses of music in any culture. Such a program provides opportunities for them to deal critically with music, to learn to reproduce it, and to learn to express themselves through it.

Creative music and movement are difficult to teach because they are noisy activities—a teacher cannot allow a child to experiment with the sounds of a drum while a reading lesson is in progress. Specific times should be set aside, and musical noise and movement controlled so that real learning can occur.

Too often music and movement sessions are organized as large group activities. While such organization may be valid, children also need times to work alone or in small groups. In an activity-based program at the primary and preprimary levels, these opportunities can be provided during the activity period. A portion of the room can be set aside for movement. Musical instruments can be furnished for use by a few chil-

---

[9] Aronoff, *Music and Young Children*, p. 19.

dren; others can listen to a phonograph, using earphones if they are available. The music that children create in their ongoing activities should be recorded or transcribed by the teacher. A multipurpose room, the play yard, an auditorium, or a gymnasium are often available for a portion of the day for such activities.

Music in school during the early years generally consists of singing, playing simple instruments, listening, and creative movement. Often creative movement involves children in mime and creative dramatics. Although musical activities may be primarily the responsibility of a music teacher, the classroom teacher always has some obligation to the music program. There are too many opportunities in a school day that support music education and too many ways to integrate music into children's learning to allow teachers to avoid this area of instruction.

SINGING

Almost all children enjoy singing. They sing loudly, often with more exuberance than skill. Young children pick up songs they hear and repeat them to the best of their ability, sometimes repeating a phrase over and over, and mispronouncing or not completely learning the words. At times the pitch is off, but this seldom deters a young child in his continued singing. A teacher should capitalize on this enthusiasm and exuberance. Greater adherence to melody and verse comes with experience and repetition. Teaching songs to children can be fun as well as educational.

Robert Smith has designed a singing program to develop and improve children's vocal accuracy, range, and quality. Songs chosen to help this development, according to Smith, should continue to appeal to children after many repetitions; there should be melodic phrase repetition, repeated word phrases, and the appropriate range for the child's particular stage of vocal development.[10]

The piano and other instruments such as the autoharp, guitar, or ukelele can be played to accompany the children's singing. However, some music educators feel that instrumental accompaniment is unnecessary for singing, even with young children. The Kodaly method suggests that human voices be used to accompany other human voices, leading to a program of unaccompanied singing and simple two-part singing for primary children.[11] The Kodaly method offers a sequential system of sight singing leading to an understanding of musical notation.

[10] Robert B. Smith, *Music in the Child's Education* (New York: Ronald Press, 1970), pp. 10–24.
[11] Geoffrey Russell-Smith, "Introducing Kodaly Principles into Elementary Teaching," *Music Educators Journal,* 54, no. 3 (November 1967), 43.

Carl Orff has developed an approach to music education beginning with young children. The program's basic premise is that feeling precedes intellectual understanding. The early focus is on rhythm—through the rhythm of speech and movement, children are encouraged to explore music. Some educators have suggested the integration and adaptation of Orff and Kodaly methods as an approach to music education for children.[12]

A focus on rhythm and movement is certainly a possible approach to teaching music in the early years and is one that has been suggested by early childhood educators in the past. Teachers who want to adopt and adapt Orff and Kodaly approaches, however, might need specific training in formal music theory, performance, and music education. All teachers can help children develop rhythmic awareness. Listening to natural speech, poetry, rhymes, and jingles, children can learn to identify rhythmic patterns. They can clap out the rhythms they hear and improvise movement patterns to follow them. Musical instruments might also prove helpful.

Teachers who need help beyond these simple techniques can find resources. A number of elementary music textbooks and books of children's songs are available on the market. Some of these are listed at the end of this section. Teachers who cannot read music may be able to learn children's songs from records; some music textbooks have accompanying records.

Sources of children's songs are varied. Many, of course, are written especially for children. Popular songs should also be welcome in class. The folk tradition is rich in children's songs, which include the nursery rhymes as well as the vast array of folk songs from all over the world. Many of these are quite simple, contain much repetition of musical phrases and words, and are easy for children to learn.

Too often, unfortunately, the music of the school is far removed from the music the child hears at home. Children should have opportunities to explore many kinds of music. Much contemporary music is rich in line, harmony, and meanings. Jazz, folk, and rock should not be avoided by the teacher, but included in both singing and listening activities.

Many of the ethnic traditions composing American culture ought to be used as resources for songs as well; for example, the music of black Americans, Spanish-speaking people, Native Americans and people of various European heritages should be included in the repertoire of the class. The teacher should select songs that she likes, that also

---

[12] Lawrence Wheeler and Lois Raebeck, *Orff and Kodaly Adapted for the Elementary School* (Dubuque, Iowa: William C. Brown, 1972), pp. xix–xxviii.

meet Smith's criteria, stated earlier. Songs can be selected to fit a particular area of study in the program, such as African songs as related to a black studies program, or holiday songs at appropriate periods of the year.

Although most portions of the singing program are concerned with the recreation of musical experiences, singing has creative aspects as well. Children can compose their own verses to familiar songs and can write new songs. Teachers can write these songs in musical notation, reading them back to the children, or use tape recorders to capture their creations.

PLAYING MUSICAL INSTRUMENTS

Early childhood classes should provide opportunities for children to play many musical instruments. Group playing may be desirable at some times, but the children should not be restricted to this, for they need to explore the use of musical instruments independently. It is a good idea to make a few instruments available at different times for the children to use. On these occasions, they should not be required to beat out a particular rhythm, but should be given the freedom to experiment. Drums, tambourines, rhythm sticks, maracas, and tone blocks are all instruments simple enough for young children to use.

Some commercially made instruments should be provided, because many homemade instruments do not achieve a high quality of tone. Children can create their own instruments as well. These can be as simple as shakers made out of milk containers or plastic boxes holding beans or sand; different objects in the box give different tones to the shaker. Sandpaper attached to wooden blocks and rubbed together makes a suitable instrument. Many objects found around the house or salvaged from the trash heap can also be fashioned into instruments—pot covers and automobile brake drums make percussion instruments, for example. An imaginative teacher will come up with a long list of such items. All instruments, whether purchased or homemade, should be treated with respect.

In many classes for young children a heavy emphasis is placed upon the use of rhythm instruments. Simple tonal instruments should also be included. Although teachers should avoid those that must be placed in the mouth to be played, since this could spread infection, many tonal instruments can be used. Tone blocks in small sets, xylophones, marimbas, and tuned bells can be provided for the children. The use of these instruments encourages exploration of tonal as well as rhythmic relationships, and the children often begin to play simple tunes by themselves.

James L. Hoot

If the classroom has a piano, the children can be taught to use it with care and then be allowed occasional access to it. Often they experiment with the keyboard, sometimes playing only black or only white keys, or scales up and down the keyboard. They may even attempt to pick out simple melodies.

Musical instruments can be used to accompany the children's singing or movement, to reproduce rhythmic or melodic patterns, or to create original compositions. They also provide an avenue for free musical exploration. Sometimes merely leaving an instrument on a table is enough to stimulate a child to begin to "mess about" with sound. A teacher can direct this type of activity by helping him extend from simple explorations. Sometimes the child can abstract patterns from the world around him: the sound of running, the noise of the mimeograph machine, and activities in the streets. The pattern of children's names, objects, or words in a story can also be reproduced on a percussion instrument.

Children can also listen to songs, abstracting the meter or the accented beat and reproducing it. Changes in tempo should be felt and produced by the child. Individual explorations lead to group playing, with children playing in unison or even against one another as in a dialogue.

As children play instruments, they should attend to the range of sounds that can be made with each instrument. A drum struck with the hand sounds different from the same drum struck with a stick. When it is struck in the center it emits a different tone from when it is struck at the edge. Children can learn to create different effects using the same instrument.

As children move into the primary grades, the teacher who knows how can begin to teach them aspects of musical notation. They can clap out different note values, or run, walk, and skip to different rhythms. They can even learn to follow the melody line of a song as the music rises and falls in tone. The teacher, moving her hand up and down, illustrates changes in tone; or, she may mark a blackboard accordingly. The extension of the child's musical ability at this level is as much a function of the teacher's capability and creativity as of his.

Children should not be forced into a rigid pattern of music production. Activities with instruments need to be a function of the children's interest and willingness to try out new ideas in sound. In the early years, the teacher should help the children explore and discover the rich area of music through the use of instruments.

LISTENING TO MUSIC

Listening is a basic skill in the music program. Children, listening to the world around them, abstract the sounds as a way of knowing about the world. They can also learn to listen for elements of music such as pitch, intensity, and rhythm, as well as for patterns and themes. Attentive listening helps characterize music and determine its mood. In addition, listening is a skill needed for other musical activities such as singing or developing creative movement.

As children listen to music, live or on records, they soon become aware of various qualities. Some music is loud, some is soft; some is fast in tempo, some is slow; musical pitch rises and falls. Teachers can help children become aware of these differences and learn to characterize the elements, design, and texture of music.

Children can also learn to distinguish the various musical instruments and identify their sounds. Differences between families of instruments—brass, woodwinds, strings, and percussion—can be noted first, and later, differences among the instruments in each family. Records of musical pieces highlighting the various instruments are useful, as are pictures and charts of them. The teacher might also be able to bring live musicians to class to play for the children.

Children often listen to music actively in the early years, responding to rhythm and melody with bodily movement. Sometimes they respond through the use of musical instruments or voice. These forms of active listening extend naturally into creative expression. At other times children are expected to listen to music more passively, attending to it the way they would attend to a story.

Teachers can develop discussions that enhance attentive listening and lead to critical listening. Children should begin to talk about the feelings generated by pieces of music and the kinds of activities that might be evoked. They can also talk about the *uses* of music: for relaxation, to accompany dancing, to facilitate work, to set a mood, or accompany a story. Music often exists solely for sheer pleasure. The teacher should help children explore their music preferences and help them discover which elements appeal to them most.

Almost every aspect of the music program is built on the development of listening skills. If children are to learn to sing properly, they must accurately reproduce the pitch and rhythmic pattern of a song; this requires that they attend to it and are able to recall it. Creative movement activities in which children respond to music require that they listen.

Although music recorded for children is plentiful, they should have opportunities to hear live musicians as well. Sometimes a teacher is talented enough to play for her class. Parents or older children might be found who are willing and able to perform. In some communities, local symphony orchestras or ensembles are contracted to perform in schools. Sometimes young children are considered too immature to be included in the audience, but this is an unfortunate attitude, for they can profit from this experience. The one problem that may be encountered is that young children sometimes do not manifest "proper" audience behavior. They may make noise or move during a performance. Some parts of audience behavior can be taught: although children naturally move in response to music, they can learn that there are times when it is appropriate to sit quietly.

SONG BOOKS FOR YOUNG CHILDREN

Dietz, B. W., and T. C. Parks, *Folk Songs of China, Japan, and Korea*. New York: John Day, 1964.

Fowke, Edith, *Sally Go Round the Sun*. Garden City, N.Y.: Doubleday, 1969.

Glazer, Tom, *Eye Winker Tom Tinker Chin Chopper: Fifty Musical Fingerplays*. Garden City, N.J.: Doubleday, 1973.

Jenkins, Ella, *The Ella Jenkins Song Book for Children*. New York: Oak Publications, 1969.

Landeck, Beatrice, *Songs to Grow On*. New York: William Morrow & Co., Inc., 1950.

————, *More Songs to Grow On*. New York: William Morrow & Co., Inc., 1954.

Langstaff, Nancy, and John Langstaff, *Jim Along, Josie*. New York: Harcourt Brace Jovanovich, 1970.

Seeger, Ruth Crawford, *American Folk Songs for Children*. Garden City, N.Y.: Doubleday, 1948.

————, *Animal Folk Songs for Children.* Garden City, N.Y.: Doubleday, 1950.

Sendak, Maurice, *Maurice Sendak's Really Rosie: Starring the Nutshell Kids.* New York: Harper & Row, 1975.

Winn, Marie, *The Fireside Book of Children's Songs.* New York: Simon & Schuster, 1966.

————, *What Shall We Do and Allee Galloo!* New York: Harper & Row, 1970.

MOVEMENT

As children learn to respond to music and to their feelings about it, they can become quite creative in using their bodies as vehicles for expression. This requires that they become aware of themselves in different ways and learn to control their movements. As in other areas of creative expression, movement develops out of children's intuitive responses and explorations. These should be nurtured as they expand their physical capabilities.

A distinction needs to be made among the uses of movement as a way of helping children gain greater control over their own body patterns, as a means of creative expression, and as a way of developing understandings about the surrounding world.

Lydia Gerhardt reports on a study that analyzed how the young child orients himself in space and uses movement to understand concepts of space, time, length, shape, and direction. She also offers suggestions for enhancing the early childhood curriculum through the use of movement. Concepts of topological geometry, geography, and the measurement of time, space, and weight can all be encountered through movement exploration.[13] Such an educative use of movement in the early years is consistent with a Piagetian view of cognitive development. It suggests systematic ways in which motor patterns generated early by children can be integrated into cognitive schema. This allows movement education to serve an integrating purpose in the curriculum. Betty Rowen's book on movement education contains examples of strategies for using movement as an aid to learning about language, science, social learnings, and number concepts.[14]

Movement education is concerned with helping children gain an understanding of the structure of movement and improve their bodily

---

[13] Lydia A. Gerhardt, *Moving and Knowing: The Young Child Orients Himself in Space* (Englewood Cliffs, N.J.: Prentice-Hall, Inc., 1973).

[14] Betty Rowen, *Learning Through Movement* (New York: Teachers College Press, 1963).

skills and coordination. They learn to adapt movements to factors of space, different tempos and speeds, different levels, various numbers of people, variations of force and intensity, and different shapes of small and large objects. The activities of dance, gymnastics, and games are introduced in the early years to achieve these goals.[15] Conceptions of basic movement are used to integrate learnings within these three areas.

Basic movement is best seen in a developmental framework. The body's maturation interacts with the child's learning of specific skills and techniques to increase his ability as he continues to grow. We do know that the body undergoes major developmental changes during the early years. We also know that a number of movement techniques are learned by each child. Several physical educators are attempting to develop norms for the children as regards weight, strength, agility, and particular skills. Caroline Sinclair, for example, has identified norms for a group of fifty-seven children in Virginia in relation to certain movement tasks and patterns.[16] This approach is in its initial phases of development, and basic patterns and skills worth studying need to be agreed upon. Such norms, no matter how well validated, should not be taken as goals to be achieved by all children at any age.

The area of gymnastics includes developmental exercises, stunts, tumbling, and performing on small and large apparatus. At the nursery-kindergarten level, these activities are generally provided informally. Adequate space is needed both indoors and outdoors for running, jumping, walking, and crawling and for other large-muscle activities. Equipment should be available for jumping, grasping, and climbing with stairs, ladders, and ropes. Balancing beams, hoops, rings, ropes, bicycles, scooters, and wagons all contribute to these skills at this level. As children move into primary grades more formal activities might be introduced. An exploratory approach to gymnastics is wise in the primary grades, in contrast to the more formalized physical education programs still found in some elementary schools.

Formal games have no place in the nursery schools since children are generally not able to stay with game rules or goals for any length of time. As children move into the primary grades, rudimentary games, having a low level of organization, can be introduced. The use of games in early childhood education is discussed in relation to all play activities in the next chapter.

Teachers can help children use movement to express ideas

---

[15] Evelyn L. Schurr, *Movement Experiences for Children,* 2nd ed. (Englewood Cliffs, N.J.: Prentice-Hall, Inc., 1975), pp. 40–44.

[16] Caroline B. Sinclair, *Movement of the Young Child Ages Two to Six* (Columbus, Ohio: Charles E. Merrill, 1973).

and feelings. Joan Russell has grouped the dimensions of movement thus used under four main headings: the body, the instrument of expression; effort, how the body moves; space and shape, where the body moves; and relationship, relationship of body parts to each other, of dancers to each other, and of groups to each other. Russell has built upon the work of Rudolf von Laban to develop a program of creative dance aimed at helping children develop competency in movement through a series of basic themes.[17]

Movement also helps children explore the structure of music. The Eurythmics of Émile Jaques Dalcroze provided the basis for the music program developed by Aronoff, mentioned earlier. Although most teachers lack the specialized training of a Dalcroze teacher or a dance instructor, they have many ways to encourage children to explore movement. Simply playing music on a phonograph or piano often stimulates them to move, and varying the pitch, intensity, and rhythm leads them to move in different ways. Sometimes just a drum beat stimulates them. It is even possible to encourage movement without any musical accompaniment by using descriptive phrases, or asking them to show a soft movement, a hard movement, high steps, or a close-to-the-ground movement—all allowing them freedom of expression within a framework established by the teacher.

Such experiences are often enhanced with simple props. Hoops or fine silk scarves affect children's motion, often enabling them to make more flowing movements. Asking them to move in ways that represent specific things can also extend their movements. A child can be a jet, a slithery snake, a boat, or a flower growing. Each object calls forth certain associations for the child, which he should be able to interpret in his own way. Having the children all move in the same stereotyped way stifles rather than supports creative expression. Indeed, individual interpretation is essential in these rhythmic activities. The teacher's role in the early years is to elicit movement and to encourage new ways of using one's body rather than to teach specific forms and techniques.

However, there should be opportunities for other kinds of dance activities as well. Rhythmic games coupled with songs or chants are enjoyable and can be learned by young children. Such games as "Looby-Loo" or "Bluebird, Fly Through My Window" are simple to direct and so full of repetition that they can master them with ease. Many of these activities grow out of folk tradition, and the teacher sometimes finds that children know versions somewhat different from the one she is teaching. This may also occur when she introduces a folk song. These

---

[17] Joan Russell, *Creative Dance in the Primary School* (London: Macdonald and Evans, 1965), pp. 19–30.

differences are interesting to study, for they represent a portion of the folk tradition in American society. It may be easier, however, for the teacher to learn the local version than to teach a foreign version.

Play party activities can soon give way to folk dancing, of both American and European derivation. Children can learn the simple basic steps of folk or square dances and then do the patterns as called by the teacher. Records and books are available that provide music and directions for the simple dances. More formal dances should probably be postponed until later in the child's school career.

The child's exploration of his body's uses, and the extension of his ability to express feelings and ideas through his body and through instruments and media, are the goals of this portion of the program. Children in the early years are not being prepared to become musicians or artists any more than they are being prepared to become scientists and mathematicians. Learning to express themselves and to appreciate the expressions of others, and to find beauty in themselves and in their surroundings, are discoveries that can last throughout their life.

SUGGESTED READING

ARONOFF, FRANCIS W., *Music and Young Children*. New York: Holt, Rinehart and Winston, 1969.

DIMONDSTEIN, GERALDINE, *Exploring the Arts with Children*. New York: The Macmillan Company, 1974.

GERHARDT, LYDIA A., *Moving and Knowing: The Young Child Orients Himself in Space*. Englewood Cliffs, N.J.: Prentice-Hall, Inc., 1973.

JONES, ELIZABETH, *What Is Music for Young Children?* Washington, D.C.: National Association for the Education of Young Children, 1969.

LOWENFELD, VICTOR, and W. LAMBERT BRITTAIN, *Creative and Mental Growth* (4th ed.). New York: The Macmillan Company, 1964.

PILE, NAOMI F., *Art Experiences for Young Children*. New York: The Macmillan Company, 1973.

RICHARDSON, ELWYN, *In the Early World*. Wellington, New Zealand: Council of Educational Research, 1964.

RICHARDSON, MARION, *Art and the World*. Peoria, Ill.: Chas. A. Bennett Co., Inc., 1952.

RUSSELL, JOAN, *Creative Dance in the Primary School*. London: Macdonald and Evans, 1965.

SHEEHY, EMMA D., *Children Discover Music and Dance*. New York: Teachers College Press, 1968.

SMITH, ROBERT B., *Music in the Child's Education*. New York: Ronald Press, 1970.

Steve Herzog

CHAPTER TEN

CHILD'S PLAY AS EDUCATION

Play activities or their derivatives have been part of early childhood educational programs since these programs were first implemented in any systematic way. The original Froebelian kindergarten included the manipulation of *Gifts,* the use of craft activities or *Occupations,* and the involvement of children in the *Mothers' Plays and Songs,* all described in an earlier chapter. Although the children did not engage in freely expressive forms of play, the activities were manipulative and derived from the free play of children. The source of kindergarten activity was the natural play of German peasant children. The essential elements of the play, as identified by Friedrich Froebel, were abstracted and systematized to insure that they would be given to all children.

Maria Montessori, in the development of her educational method, similarly abstracted the essential elements from the natural play activities of children, reconstructed them, and systematized them as an instructional method. Activities in these two instances were meant to achieve different instructional goals. Froebel wanted children to gain the spiritual meanings symbolized by the materials and the activities. Montessori, however, wanted them to gain a greater understanding of the properties of the objects themselves as well as specific skills through manipulating them. In both instances, the elements of the activity considered educationally productive were abstracted and many of the qualities of play, including actual *playfulness*, were eliminated from the educational method.

Playfulness means the *fun* aspects of play activities—a quality that pervades all types of real play. J. Nina Lieberman has identified five characteristics of playfulness: physical, social, and cognitive spontaneity, manifest joy, and a sense of humor.[1] All these should characterize children's play activities to some extent.

It was only with the advent of the reform kindergarten movement and the modern nursery-school movement in the first quarter of the twentieth century that the organic play of children became accepted as a vehicle for learning. No attempt was made in these educational systems to abstract distinct separate elements from the play. Instead, the children's natural play activities were supported and nurtured as being educationally significant in their own right. However, in neither of these newer educational institutions was play considered the only way for children to learn.

The use of children's play for educational purposes created some changes in the play. Eva Neumann suggests that this places constraint on the play activities. These constraints are a result of creating a specific setting for play and providing adult supervision, as well as selecting specific objectives and specific objects for play.[2] The reform kindergarten movement accepted these constraints while taking care, at least theoretically, that the children's play was not completely distorted in the school.

With the advent of these new forms of early childhood education, equipment and materials were designed for fostering play in classrooms, intended to be used by teachers to stimulate and elaborate the play activities. Even a cursory glance into a nursery school or kindergarten classroom reveals many of these objects. Almost all classrooms at the preprimary level have some sort of doll corner or housekeeping area. In these areas miniature representations of kitchen equipment—play pots, pans, and dishes—household furniture, dolls, cleaning equipment, plastic food, and other similar items are available to the children to help them act out their representations of home life. The block area is another place having equipment designed to foster children's play. In addition to the equipment in these areas, one might also find dress-up clothes, steering wheels, toy cars and trucks, and innumerable other devices for supporting play activities.

In recent years, new programs in early childhood education have been developed that question the place of play in the school curriculum. This is especially true of those programs concerned with the achievement of intellectual goals and the remediation of learning deficits.

---

[1] J. Nina Lieberman, "Playfulness and Divergent Thinking: An Investigation of Their Relationship at the Kindergarten Level," *Journal of Genetic Psychology*, 107, no. 2 (December 1965), 219–24.

[2] Eva A. Neumann, "The Problem of Play" (unpublished Doctoral dissertation, University of Illinois, 1971).

While play may be all right for normal children when we are not concerned with their intellectual development, the argument states, play has no place in an intellectually oriented program, for it does not foster intellectual development or, if it does, not with any great degree of potency. Alternative approaches to play may be supported on the basis of the self-evident nature of learnings possible through more direct methods or, at most, on the basis of relatively short-range evaluations. A review of the theories of play and an analysis of the ways the teacher can use play in support of intellectual and other forms of learning will be useful.

THEORIES OF PLAY

Play is not only hard to understand but also extremely difficult to identify and define in any systematic way. Play appears in the behavior of adults as well as of children—even in animals. Attempts to define it have ended in the diffusion of definitions. However, play can generally be identified easily when observed. Elmer Mitchell and Bernard Mason have gathered many of the definitions of play traditionally used. These include the following:

SCHILLER: The aimless expenditure of exuberant energy.

FROEBEL: The natural unfolding of the germinal leaves of childhood.

SPENSER: Superfluous actions taking place instinctively in the absence of real actions. . . . Activity performed for the immediate gratification derived without regard for ulterior benefits.

LAZARUS: Activity in itself free, aimless, amusing, or diverting.

HALL: The motor habits and spirit of the past persisting in the present.

GROOS: Instinctive practice, without serious intent, of activities that will later be essential to life.

SEASHORE: Free self-expression for the pleasure of expression.

DEWEY: Activities not consciously performed for the sake of any result beyond themselves.

SHAND: A type of play directed at the maintenance of joy.

DULLES: An instinctive form of self-expression and emotional escape valve.[3]

Neumann has attempted to develop a definition of play that synthesizes elements from other definitions and is useful in defining play in a variety of settings. This definition includes the *criteria* of play—

[3] Elmer Mitchell and Bernard S. Mason, *The Theory of Play,* rev. ed. (Cranbury, N.J.: A. S. Barnes, 1948), pp. 103–4.

characteristics that differentiate play from nonplay; the *processes* of play—their form and method; and the *objectives* of play—the elements toward which play is directed.

The *criteria* for play include internal control, internal reality, and intrinsic motivation. To the extent that these characteristics—as opposed to external control, external reality, and extrinsic motivation—are dominant in an activity, that activity may be considered play. The *processes* of play include the operations—repetition, replication, and transformation, and the *modes*—sensorimotor, affective, oral, or cognitive.

The *objectives* of play include subjects, functions, and locations. The *subject* may be the player himself, other children, or adults. The *objects* of play may be real objects, toys, instructional materials, or multipurpose materials. The *functions* may be information seeking, social learning, sensorimotor activity, emotional expression, or sensorimotor expression. The *location* of play may be internal (within the organism) or external (within the environment.)[4]

Mitchell and Mason have identified six classes of theories of play. These include the surplus energy theory, relaxation theory, preexercise theory, recapitulation theory, cathartic theory, and self-expression theory.[5] J. Barnard Gilmore, building upon this taxonomy, has divided the theories into two groups: the classical theories and the dynamic theories. While the classical theories attempt to explain why children play, the dynamic theories concern themselves with the content of the play.[6]

THE CLASSICAL THEORIES

SURPLUS ENERGY THEORY. This postulates that a quantity of energy is available to the organism and that the organism tends to expend that energy either through goal-directed activity (work) or through goalless activity (play). Play occurs at any time the organism has more energy available than it needs to expend for work. In this theory, the content of the play activity is not important and one form of play could easily be substituted for another.

RELAXATION THEORY. This postulates that play is used to replenish expended energy. After a period of fatiguing activity (work), the organism needs an opportunity to be involved in a relaxing activity (play). According to this theory, play occurs when the organism has little

---

[4] Neumann, "The Problem of Play."
[5] Mitchell and Mason, *The Theory of Play*, pp. 48–85.
[6] J. Barnard Gilmore, "Play: A Special Behavior," in *Current Research in Motivation*, ed. R. N. Haber (New York: Holt, Rinehart and Winston, 1965).

energy left rather than when it has too much energy. Again, one kind of play activity could be substituted for another as a replenishing device.

PRE-EXERCISE THEORY. According to the pre-exercise theory, play is instinctive behavior. The child instinctively involves himself in play activities that are, in essence, a form of some more mature behavior he will later have to assume. The content of play is therefore determined by the content of mature future adult activity. Play may be conceived of as preparation for future work.

RECAPITULATION THEORY. From this position, play must be understood, not in terms of the future activities of the individual organism, but in relation to past activities of the race. Play becomes an instinctive way of ridding the organism of the primitive and unnecessary instinctual skills that have been carried over through heredity. The stages of play correspond to the stages of development of the human race, going from the most primitive to the relatively sophisticated. By allowing the person to rid himself of primitive activities, play prepares him for modern work activities.

It is interesting to note in these examples how the same activity—play—can be understood through a series of opposing theories. Play represents either surplus energy or an energy deficit. Play can be either a form of pre-exercise for sophisticated action or the purging of primitive action forms found within the organism. Either alternative offers a legitimate and testable possibility.

THE DYNAMIC THEORIES

The dynamic theories of play do not attempt to understand why children play; they simply accept the fact. They focus on attempting to explain the *content* of play. The two most elaborate dynamic theories of children's play are found in the works of Sigmund Freud and Jean Piaget.

PIAGETIAN THEORY. Piaget believes the development of the human intellect involves two related processes: *assimilation* and *accommodation*. In the process of assimilation, the individual continually abstracts information from the outside world and fits it into the organized schemes representing what he already knows. He also modifies these organizational schemes when they do not fit adequately with his developing knowledge. The latter process is called accommodation. According to Piaget, play is a way of taking the outside world and manipulating it so that it fits a person's present organizational schemes. As such, play serves a vital function in the child's developing intellect and remains, to some extent, always present in human behavior.

Piaget has defined three distinct stages in the development of play. The first is the sensorimotor stage of infancy based upon existing patterns of physical behavior. The second is a level of symbolic play, representing the stage of dramatic play that we find in young children. The third is the stage of playing games that have rules, representing the play behavior of older children.

FREUDIAN THEORY. Freud considered play a cathartic activity, allowing children to master difficult situations. The child can use the fantasy play situation to act out adult roles, gaining a feeling of mastery that allows him to cope with reality situations. The child can use play to act out personally painful occurrences and to master the pain by coming to grips with it in the fantasy of the play situation. This same mastery in fantasy can help children cope with the affective elements of more positive life situations as well. Lois Murphy, in her book *The Widening World of Childhood,* presents some vivid descriptions of young children using play activities to cope with problems of living.[7]

Michael Ellis adds another dimension to the theories of play.[8] He characterizes as modern theories those that view play as a function of competence motivation and those that view play as an arousal-seeking device. Traditionally, psychological theories conceive of man as passive in his natural state. Thus human activity needs to be explained usually in terms of external rewards and punishments or internal drives. Robert White's theory of competence motivation suggests that people receive satisfaction from developing competencies, independent of whether external rewards are gained in the process. From this point of view, human activity can take place without external reinforcement. Play is one way that children act on their environment, becoming more effective in their actions and receiving more personal satisfactions. The activity of playing from this point of view is self-rewarding.

The arousal-seeking theory suggests that human beings normally need to be continually involved in information-processing activities; hence their normal state is active. The absence of stimuli in one's environment will lead to discomfort that will cause him to increase the amount of perceptual information available. This can be done by seeking additional stimulation externally or by creating it internally, possibly by daydreaming. Too much stimulation leads the individual to attend less to his environment. Play is seen as a vehicle by which the child can seek and mediate the amount of external and internal stimulation available to create an optimal balance.

Studying play from a cognitive-affective framework, Jerome Singer considers the imaginative play of children an effort to organize

[7] Lois Murphy, *The Widening World of Childhood* (New York: Basic Books, 1962).
[8] Michael J. Ellis, *Why People Play* (Englewood Cliffs, N.J.: Prentice-Hall, Inc., 1973).

their experiences while utilizing their motor and cognitive capacities. The child shows interest, alertness, and positive emotional reactions as he interacts with novel play materials, and shows the positive emotions of joy and laughter as he becomes familiar with and masters materials. The play of children is seen by Singer as a vehicle for exploration, the achievement of competence, and the development of creativity.[9]

These dynamic and modern theories of play, if properly understood and used, can provide us with an understanding of the power of play that can be useful in designing educational programs that support children's development. Our concern as teachers needs to be with the content of play and how to move it in desired directions. From Freud we learn that the content of play has a strong affective tone; from Piaget we learn that it has a strong cognitive tone. Learning can be supported in both these domains. Play can also have an important socializing role, a third significant domain.

According to George Herbert Mead, children use play as a way of developing their concept of *self*—what they are. They learn this by actually trying on the roles of those about them in dramatic play. The concept of the "generalized other," upon which mature socialization is built, develops in the next stage as children play games. The games are based upon rules and require, for the child to perform them properly, that he internalize the role behavior of others as well as his own in the games.[10]

A final note on the school and play may be derived from Lieberman's research. In her study of kindergarten children, she found a relationship between playfulness in children's behavior and their divergent thinking ability, or creativity. This research suggests that it might be possible to use play activities to improve creativeness in children.[11]

EDUCATIONAL USES OF PLAY

The theories of play discussed here are descriptive theories. They attempt to explain play as it exists, but provide no guide for action. Teachers are not interested as much in how children play in natural settings as in how to modify the play to achieve educational goals. An understanding of these theories can allow us to extrapolate guides for action appropriate to use in teaching situations.

[9] Jerome L. Singer, *The Child's World of Make-Believe* (New York: Academic Press, 1973), pp. 20–26.
[10] George Herbert Mead, *Mind, Self and Society* (Chicago: University of Chicago Press, 1934), pp. 152–73.
[11] Lieberman, "Playfulness and Divergent Thinking," pp. 219–24.

Young children play whenever they are able to be active and have some degree of freedom, whether alone or in a group. Evelyn Omwake has distinguished between *spontaneous* and *structured* play activities for children:

> Spontaneous play by younger children is universal wherever children happen to be. It can develop in an empty basement, city dump, elaborately furnished living room, expensively landscaped lawn, or a nursery school especially arranged and equipped to invite and promote play. A unique feature of such spontaneous play is the subtle, frequently nonverbal communication among the players as to theme, the assignment of roles and the rules. While an adult may be needed as a stage hand, prompter, audience, or to make certain the cues are understood, the inspiration and ideas come from the children's own interests and experiences. Another characteristic of such play is the children's ability to endow whatever is at hand with the features and functions of the things they want it to represent. . . .
>
> Although the organized setting in the nursery school provides opportunities for spontaneous play, its curriculum also features structured play suited to the educational needs of young children. These structured play activities are especially planned and presented with regard to the developmental capacities, interests and experiences of the group of children. At the same time such planning depends upon attention to the differing developmental rates of the individual children.
>
> The two forms of play can be differentiated by the degree and nature of adult participation. In this structured form, teachers decide the time and place and provide the materials to be used, establishing appropriate limits for their use.[12]

Omwake's distinction between structured and spontaneous play is very attractive. In analyzing the kinds of activity that would be labeled as *structured* or *spontaneous* play, however, we find that her distinction seems to be between dramatic play activities (activities in which a child assumes a role in a situation and plays it through) and all other activities that might be included in a nursery school or kindergarten curriculum. Dramatic play has been labeled spontaneous; all other activities are labeled structured play. Many of Omwake's structured play activities

---

[12] Evelyn Omwake, "The Child's Estate," in *Modern Perspectives in Child Development*, eds. Albert J. Solnit and Sally A. Provence (New York: International Universities Press, 1963), pp. 581–82.

may not be play at all, such as science projects or stories, while other play activities, such as block-building, might contain a high degree of spontaneity. In addition, dramatic play loses some of its spontaneity when it occurs in a school situation, for the teacher decides the time and place of such activity, provides the appropriate materials, and sets the limits. The teacher's guidance limits the spontaneity of the play situation even further. It may well be that for the teacher, spontaneous and structured play are not a very useful pair of concepts.

A more productive distinction might be made between *educational* play and *noneducational* play. The difference is not in the activities or the degree of enjoyment that a child may receive, but rather in the purposes ascribed to the play by those persons responsible for the child's activities. Educational play has as its prime purpose the child's learning. Such play must still be fun for the child, for without giving the prime personal satisfaction, the activity stops being play. Educational play activities are supported, however, because they serve an educational purpose rather than because of their personally satisfying qualities. Thus a child in the housekeeping area of a classroom is receiving personal satisfactions from playing out the particular role he has ascribed to himself interacting with persons in other roles, and using various play properties in innovative ways. The value of this play is that it helps the child explore and understand role dimensions and interaction patterns, thereby supporting his further understanding of the social world and helping him to build a realistic sense of *self*.

Educational play may take many forms. The key role of the teacher here is in modifying the natural spontaneous play of children so that it has educational value while maintaining its qualities as play. She must also set up less spontaneous educational play activities. Such play is evaluated not only by the child's degree of involvement but by its effectiveness in achieving educational aims.

In most nursery school and kindergarten classrooms one can usually find four kinds of educational play: manipulative, physical, and dramatic play, and games. In manipulative play the child handles relatively small pieces of equipment such as puzzles, Cuisenaire rods, or peg sets. The actions are relatively self-contained; that is, there is no necessary interaction between the manipulative activity and other kinds of activities, nor is there a dramatic element to the play. The goals of manipulative play activities are achievable directly through the child's handling of the material. The use of Montessori apparatus, although defined as "work" by Montessorians, provides a good example of educational manipulative play. A child may be given a series of wooden cylinders and a case into which they fit. By comparing cylinders and attempting to fit them in the case, he begins to learn to make size comparisons and to seriate. Manipulative play activities generally have fairly narrowly defined educational goals.

Physical play involves children's large actions, such as running, jumping, or riding a tricycle. The goals of these activities are to help children increase their physical skills or learn to use them in new situations. Physical play can have a dramatic component to it and teachers can elaborate the play either by making the physical activities more challenging or by providing social content to the play.

Dramatic play requires that the child assume and act out a role, often in relationship to other children playing their roles in informal dramatic situations that may represent true life experiences. The housekeeping area (or doll corner) is the most readily observable setting for play. In this area children act out the roles of family members in actions representing home situations. The teacher may set up other dramatic play situations to enable the children to play many roles.

At times, rather than becoming the performer in the dramatic play situation, the child manipulates things that represent the characters. Informal puppet play allows him to act out a role through a puppet. Children, building with unit blocks, are involved in miniature dramatizations. In this, the teacher must provide adequate properties, enough time for children to go beyond the manipulative building, and ideas as sources for dramatic themes.

Games are a form of play activity, but of a different kind from those discussed above. They are highly structured activities that include specific rules to be followed. Games have often been excluded from early childhood activities because they were considered inappropriate for this age level. Actually children at the four- and five-year-old levels are beginning to move into a stage where game playing is possible. Simple games or musical activity containing elements of games are quite appropriate for children. Games that young children play must include certain elements if they are to be played successfully and to be educational. Children need to be taught the strategies of game playing (gamesmanship). The teacher needs to be continually involved in guiding the game, for she is the only one mature enough to maintain its rules and to help the children understand rule-appropriate behavior.

Although many educators accept play as a part of nursery school or kindergarten classroom activities, they are hesitant to recommend it as a part of the primary school program, with the exception of the physical education program. Play, however, has equally valid uses with primary children as with children at lower educational levels. The "messing about" of the science program is a form of play, as are many of the newer materials-oriented programs in mathematics. Dramatic play is often a useful avenue of social studies education and a support for language learning. Appropriate play activities can be integrated in almost all areas of learning in the primary school.

MANIPULATIVE PLAY

A manipulative play center is desirable in the nursery or kindergarten class. In the primary grades, manipulative materials are generally organized along subject-matter lines. A manipulative play center may have materials placed on open shelves, so they are readily accessible. A set of tables and chairs can also be included, but many of the materials can be just as easily used on the floor, preferably with a rug. The shelves can hold the following materials:

PUZZLES. A wide range of children's jigsaw puzzles is presently available, including puzzles that have just three or four pieces, each representing a single item, and rather complex puzzles made of two or three dozen pieces. The "See-quee" puzzle, which contains a set of pictures that children put in sequence to represent a story, is another useful type of puzzle. Sturdy puzzles can be purchased that are made out of wood or masonite and will stand much use. It is a good idea to have a number of puzzles ranging in difficulty. If a puzzle rack is used for storage, the children can easily learn to carefully take out and replace puzzles, limiting the number of puzzle pieces that get lost. Marking the backs of each puzzle's pieces with a common symbol also helps children locate missing pieces. When losses do occur, teachers can shape substitutes out of wood putty, painting them to match the rest of the puzzle.

The teacher should organize the puzzles according to their order of difficulty and check the children periodically to see how they have progressed in their ability to complete puzzles. Although most children have had some experience in working with puzzles prior to school, some have not learned the appropriate skills. Teachers should not take skills for granted, and a session or two at the beginning of the year explicitly teaching children the procedures of puzzle completion may be useful.

PARQUETRY BLOCKS AND PEGBOARDS. Parquetry blocks with wooden pieces of varying shapes and colors, and pegboard sets with pegs of different colors, are useful materials for teaching form and color discrimination and retention. Many of the skills gained can later be used for formal reading and mathematics instruction. Although children need opportunities to manipulate these materials freely, teachers can make model cards for the children to replicate with their manipulative materials. These cards should also be ordered from the simplest to the most complex and presented to children in order of difficulty to support mastery. Pegboard sets can also be equipped with elastic bands with which the children can create various shapes.

CONSTRUCTIVE MATERIALS. Small sets of constructive materials such as *Lego* or *Lincoln Logs* are useful additions to the manipulative play area. Children can either make fanciful creations or construct small buildings with these. A large variety of construction materials is available from manufacturers for this purpose.

SCIENCE MATERIALS. Plastic boxes containing sets of science materials can be profitably included in the manipulative materials center. A battery, bulb, and a couple of lengths of wire could constitute one set. A magnet with some small bits of material, some magnetic and some not, could constitute another set. A plastic jar covered with a rubber membrane, half-filled with water, and containing a medicine dropper; a small basin of water and materials that float and some that sink; and a box of variously textured materials, are all examples of the wide range of manipulative materials that can be included for science exploration.

MATHEMATICS MATERIALS. Cuisenaire rods, Stern Structured Mathematics Materials, counting frames, simple measuring devices such as a balance, primary ruler, a set of measuring cups and spoons, and materials to be measured or counted can all be fruitfully incorporated into the manipulative materials center.

MONTESSORI MATERIALS. Many of the Montessori didactic materials are ideally suited for the manipulative play center. They can generally be used independently by the children and are self-correcting in nature. Montessori materials need not necessarily be used according to orthodox Montessori prescription.

OTHER MANIPULATIVE MATERIALS. A quick glance through an educational equipment supplier's catalogue can provide some further ideas for this center. Teachers might have ideas as they rummage through their own homes or through hardware stores and see materials that can be included in the classroom. Often some of the most stimulating and exciting materials for educational purposes result from the teacher's ingenuity.

MANIPULATIVE PLAY WITH NATURAL MATERIALS. While generally not included in a manipulative materials center, natural materials such as sand and water are important adjuncts to play. Although specially designed sand and water tables are available commercially, a galvanized tub or a plastic wash basin can also be used. Children need freedom in using these materials, but must also learn how to care for them and know the necessary limitations on their use. A number of accessory materials including containers, spoons, and shovels should go with the water and sand. Wet sand can be molded in many shapes; dry sand can be sieved and run through funnels. Equipment for cleanup such as sponges, a floor brush, and dustpan should be readily available for children to use.

Regina Weilbacher

PHYSICAL PLAY

Physical play generally requires much more space than manipulative play. Much of children's outdoor play in early childhood classes falls in this category.

OUTDOOR PLAY. The content of outdoor play depends as much upon the climate and weather conditions as upon space and other considerations. In some schools in the United States, outdoor play consists mainly of sledding and building with snow during the bulk of the school year. In other areas, there are possibilities for free exploration and a wide use of materials, because the weather remains temperate during the school year. Teachers should vary outdoor play with the possibilities created by local conditions.

Outdoor space—both soft- and hard-surfaced areas—should be available and easily accessible to the classroom. Teachers should provide outdoor storage space for equipment; but they can also bring classroom materials outdoors.

Outdoor play activities and equipment should allow opportunities for climbing, running, jumping, riding on large pieces of equipment, and digging. Many school yards contain either no equipment at all or just the stereotyped slides, swings, and jungle gyms. These severely limit the range of children's play activities and should be supplemented or replaced by other kinds of materials. Recent concern about playgrounds for young children has brought about the design of many more exciting pieces of equipment to support creative physical activities and social interaction in outdoor play. Some of these may be permanently installed and require little maintenance. In addition to permanent structures, other equipment should also be available, including

> Sand pit for children's digging
> Play houses and platforms
> Wheel toys, including tricycles, wagons, wheel barrows, and boxes on casters
> Movable equipment for climbing, such as saw horses, walking boards, barrels, packing crates, and ladders
> Balls and jump ropes to be used for games

INDOOR PLAY. Many of the same physical play activities that are offered to children outdoors can be provided indoors as well. Sometimes they need to be scaled down to the space available. In some schools a multipurpose room is available for the children to use for more vigorous play, especially on days when inclement weather keeps them inside. In other situations, classes are limited to their own rooms. In any event, some physical play can take place indoors.

Teachers can often include some climbing apparatus in their classrooms. Boards, sawhorses, and ladders can be combined into rather elaborate exciting edifices that require relatively little storage space and are fun for the children. Wheel toys can also be provided indoors for younger children, but these should be smaller than the ones used outdoors—sturdy wooden trucks or variplay boxes rather than tricycles and wagons. In many cases schools have built playhouses with elevated platforms, ladders, staircases, slides, and other artifacts into small spaces in a classroom.

BLOCK PLAY. Falling somewhere between the categories of physical play and dramatic play is block play. Two basic kinds of blocks are used in early childhood education: the smaller unit blocks, which allow the child to miniaturize his world, and the larger hollow blocks, or comparable variations on the Patty Hill blocks, which allow him to build large structures suitable as stages for dramatic play.

Caroline Pratt and Jessie Stanton describe children going out into the neighborhood of the school and returning to symbolize their perceptions of it in block structures.[13] Lucy Sprague Mitchell,[14] and Helen

---

[13] Caroline Pratt and Jessie Stanton, *Before Books* (New York: Adelphi Co., 1926).
[14] Lucy Sprague Mitchell, *Young Geographers,* 1934 (reprint, New York: Bank Street College of Education, 1971; distributed by Agathon Press, New York).

Regina Weilbacher

Robison and Bernard Spodek,[15] provide examples of blocks being used to further the young children's geographic understanding. Blocks can also be used in relation to science and mathematics learning. As children mature in their use of blocks they move through various stages of block building. An awareness of the stages, as originally identified by Harriet Johnson or as modified by others—beginning with just carrying blocks around and advancing to simple constructions and to building elaborate structures that suggest dramatic content—is useful for teachers as an aid in guiding children's block building.[16]

If blocks are to be used effectively, teachers must provide a large number of them as well as adequate space for block-building. In addition, it is helpful if children can work on a block structure for longer than a single period or a single day, to further elaborate it.

DRAMATIC PLAY

Dramatic play is seen most often in the housekeeping areas of nursery schools and kindergartens. The children assume various adult roles in their play, which unfolds with a great deal of spontaneity. In these situations the children are generally acting out roles as they perceive and understand them, although elements of fantasy often move the play far from reality.

---

[15] Helen F. Robison and Bernard Spodek, *New Directions in the Kindergarten* (New York: Teachers College Press, 1965).
[16] Elizabeth S. Hirsch, ed., *The Block Book* (Washington, D.C.: National Association for the Education of Young Children, 1974).

Richard E. Farkas

In setting up an attractive housekeeping area, the classroom teacher stimulates the role playing of the children. The materials reflect the home life of a family and little else, so the ensuing play generally remains in the realm of family play. However, the total adult world is the legitimate scope of school play situations, including work as well as family living.

For a play situation to be educationally useful it should be guided by the teacher. This guidance does not require the teacher's interference in children's play. It does, however, require the teacher's awareness of and sensitivity to their play activities, a sense of the goals of play, and an ability to move into the play on occasion, make suggestions, even become a player if that can be done without distorting it.

Most important, the teacher's responsibility is to provide the information that will move the play ahead; reading books or showing films and filmstrips often provides this information. Discussions, resource persons, and trips are all legitimate sources of new information for children in their play, allowing the activity to shuttle between fantasy and reality in a wholesome way.

GAMES

A wide range of games can be used in early childhood classes. Some games are oriented only toward physical movement; others require little movement but a great deal of attention to problem solving. Different games can be used for different purposes.

In the nursery school and kindergarten years, games should be rather simple, with uncomplicated rules. Games at this level can include activities accompanied by singing and simple physical games in which children must follow a few directions. Lotto and other table games also have a place at this level. As the children move into the primary grades, more complicated physical activities requiring strict adherence to rules, and many of the traditional games of childhood, can be incorporated into the school day. In the classroom, teachers can use games to provide practice opportunities in the academic areas. Games such as these are often suggested in the teacher's manuals of textbook series and in teacher-oriented magazines such as *Instructor, Early Years,* or *Teacher.* Board games can also be used. Those requiring evolving strategies and planning before making moves, such as checkers, can help children develop thinking skills.

Although some games require specific equipment or sets of materials, many require little besides direct instructions from the teacher and her supervision. Often a piece of chalk or a ball is all that is needed to keep children involved in playing a game for a long period of time.

GUIDING EDUCATIONAL PLAY

Most discussions of play necessarily focus primarily on the activities of the children themselves. If play is to be educational, the teacher has a prime role in setting the stage for play, in guiding its direction, and in modifying it. She must be aware of this important role and of the way she can facilitate the extension of educational play. Preparation for educational play, careful planning, and guidance are necessary.

PLANNING FOR EDUCATIONAL PLAY

Although extremely satisfying play can erupt spontaneously in almost any class, adequate preparation greatly increases the chances of productive play activities occurring. The teacher must be aware of topics for play—topics that are of interest to the children and have the possibility for rich educational experience. Play activities revolving around various social roles can help children explore the functions of these roles and their limitations. Store play can help children understand economic principles. Block play can help them become aware of geographic relationships in their community. Play at being a builder gives them practice in measurement skills.

In planning for play, the teacher should assess the learning potential of the play activity, then search for resources to help children gain information about it. The teacher may look for informational books, films, filmstrips, and recordings on the topic. Picture files can provide graphic information. A search of the community might produce field trip possibilities or resource persons who can be brought into the classroom. A phone call to a museum or educational resource center may bring the loan of dioramas or other resource materials.

The teacher will not use all the resources identified in the classroom, or introduce everything to the children at one time. But a careful search will allow her to choose deliberately those materials that can provide enough information to stimulate the play and to carry it forward over time. In planning, the teacher should also identify the play materials that will be used: articles of clothing for dramatic play, manipulative materials, and raw materials to allow the children to create their own props. Many of these things can be used from year to year by different classes, so teachers often develop extensive collections of play materials over time.

The kinds of materials the teacher brings into the classroom affect children's play activities. Mary Ann Pulaski's study demonstrates that children engage in a greater variety of make-believe games when the playthings presented to them are minimally structured (novel toys will also elicit children's attention).[17] Singer suggests that there is probably a curvilinear relationship between the degree of realism of a toy and its usefulness in stimulating a child's imaginative behavior. Toys without definite structure, such as building blocks, because they are relatively nonspecific and flexible, may lend themselves best to long-term use and can be mixed with more specific playthings to stimulate make-believe play.[18]

The teacher should also think through the strategies that can be used for stimulating play, and the goals that ought to be achieved. An understanding of these goals can provide her with guidelines for the constant evaluation and guidance of the play activities.

INITIATING PLAY ACTIVITIES

Simply setting out new materials in the classroom is often enough to start the children's play. If new materials are introduced into

[17] Mary Ann Pulaski, "Toys and Imaginative Play," in *The Child's World of Make-Believe*, ed. Singer, pp. 74–101.
[18] Singer, *The Child's World of Make-Believe*, pp. 236–42.

a situation in which children are offered choices, the teacher might initiate new play activities in two areas at the same time. This will keep the whole class from focusing on just one exciting area and allow small group play to develop without undue coercion.

The introduction of new materials and equipment frequently requires a certain amount of direction. Teachers may want to talk with their students about how the materials are used and what limitations are to be placed upon their use. A short meeting prior to the introduction of the materials can prevent problems from occurring later.

In generating play activities, the teacher can look for ways to stimulate the children's imagination. Dramatic play activities are often initiated through a field trip, the showing of a film, or the reading of a book related to the topic of play. This initial infusion of information gives the children ideas for the use of materials provided and will also suggest themes for play.

GUIDING THE PLAY OF CHILDREN

Insuring the educational significance of any play activity requires that the teacher be actively concerned with the play. Although this does not require her to hover constantly over the children's activities, it does suggest that she not consider the play periods the time for the completion of records or leaving the classroom. Teachers should be aware of the processes of play that unfold and use the cues they get from their observations as the basis for supporting or modifying the play.

Techniques that are useful in guiding children's play can be identified by observing effective teachers. Since parents serve as children's first teachers, observations of parents should be a productive source of such information.

Burton White describes the role of the more effective mothers in his study of the influences of the environment on the development of competency in very young children:

> What they seem to do, often without knowing exactly why, is to perform excellently the functions of designer and consultant.
> By that I mean they design a physical world, mainly in the home, that is beautifully suited to nurturing the burgeoning curiosity of the one-to-three year old. It is full of small, manipulable, visually detailed objects, some of which were originally designed for young children (toys), others normally used for other purposes (plastic refrigerator containers, bottle caps, baby-food jars and covers, shoes, magazines, television and radio knobs, etc.).

It contains things to climb, such as chairs, benches, sofas and stairs. It has available materials to nurture more mature motor interests, such as tricycles, scooters, and structures with which to practice elementary gymnastics. It includes a rich variety of interesting things to look at, such as television, people, and the aforementioned types of physical objects.[19]

The role of the teacher in a classroom is also one of designer and consultant. She creates a world in which children can learn through play, modifying play opportunities to increase their educational value. The teacher, however, will play a somewhat more active role in guiding educational play than did the mothers described in White's study.

The teacher should guide play by modifying the situation. In dramatic play this might mean either adding new materials or withdrawing some when their use no longer seems productive; in manipulative play, terminating one form of play and suggesting another. The teacher may also modify the situation through social engineering: easing left-out children into the play situation by suggesting important roles for them, or simply modifying the play situation to include them. Children who are disruptive might be eased out of the situation. At times teachers might want to determine the membership in play groups to support specific social learnings. They might also use a play situation for what Omwake has called "play tutoring." In such a situation the teacher works with a single child to help him learn *to* play or learn *through* play.

The infusion of more knowledge helps guide children's play activities. Observing the play of the children sometimes shows the teacher that they lack some necessary information or are operating under certain misconceptions. Providing information by telling, or by having children read information books or look things up in resource books, can effectively clear up their confusions. Sometimes a field trip or the visit of a resource person also provides significant information that will modify the play.

There are occasions when the teacher becomes an active player in the children's activities for varying periods of time. She may have to remain an active participant in the games introduced in early childhood classes. This can allow her to modify the direction of the play by introducing new elements. It can also limit disruptive behavior. The teacher provides a role model for the play of the children. She can ask

[19] Burton L. White, Jean Carew Watts, and others, *Experience and Environment: Major Influences on the Development of the Young Child*, vol. 1 (Englewood Cliffs, N.J.: Prentice-Hall, Inc., 1973), p. 243.

clarifying questions in this way that will allow them to better understand the content of the play and the meanings of certain behaviors. In becoming an active player, she must take care not to distort the children's play, and to leave them ultimately in command, otherwise her involvement becomes a disruption and the play activities may terminate.

Sylvia Krown presents a report of a program for Israeli children that includes delightful descriptions of how their play changed over time. In the beginning the activities were highly stereotyped. Two years later, the children had modified and enriched their play. Four basic strategies were used to stimulate children's play:

1. The teachers spent time "startling children out of vagueness into purposeful activity," sometimes inviting themselves into the play activities for a period of time, then withdrawing (as in play tutoring).

2. The teachers added new materials to the play situation as needed to move the activities on.

3. The teachers asked questions to stimulate more detailed observations to be used in play and to help children recall and associate past experiences.

4. Some teachers developed discussions to stimulate more detailed observations and play. They provided additional information to children through books, trips, and the like.[20]

Thus the teachers influenced the play of children while still allowing them to maintain control over the play situation.

These strategies can be used by all teachers in their guidance of play. The "startling of children" into purposeful activities can be accomplished in a variety of ways. The teacher's short-term involvement in a play situation, interacting with the children in the context of the play while asking questions about the play plot, can cause enough cognitive dissonance to extend both the play activities and the children's thinking about those activities. New materials, like new ideas, stimulate new play activities. Questioning techniques used by the teacher can help the children become more aware of what they already know and of how they can use that knowledge, comparing play situations to real situations and applying previously acquired knowledge to new situations. Finally, teachers

---

[20] Sylvia Krown, *Three and Fours Go to School* (Englewood Cliffs, N.J.: Prentice-Hall, Inc., 1974), pp. 94–101.

can find many ways to provide children with additional information that will feed into current play structures and extend them.

The decision of when to intervene or how far to go in extending children's play can be made only situationally. The judgment must be based upon knowledge of children in general and of the particular children involved. The potential of a play situation for learning must also be assessed. Too much intervention can stop play or distort it; the absence of intervention can keep a play situation from realizing its potential. The teacher must continually strive to achieve an appropriate balance. This sensitive, provocative balance, and design, consultation, and intervention, can help generate educational children's play. Learning can thus occur in the context of playfulness. The essence of good teaching lies in the ability to plan learning goals for children, to respond, to intervene without unnecessary interference and distortion, and to change direction when appropriate. Perhaps this requires an adult who brings a quality of playfulness as well as a respect for children to the classroom.

SUGGESTED READING

BIBER, BARBARA, *Play as a Growth Process*. New York: Bank Street College of Education, 1959.

CAPLAN, FRANK, and THERESA CAPLAN, *The Power of Play*. Garden City, N.Y.: Anchor Press/Doubleday, 1973.

CASS, JOAN E., *Helping Children Grow Through Play*. New York: Schocken Books, Inc., 1973.

CHERRY, CLARE, *Creative Play for the Developing Child*. Belmont, Ca.: Fearon Publishers, Inc., 1976.

ELLIS, MICHAEL J., *Why People Play*. Englewood Cliffs, N.J.: Prentice-Hall, Inc., 1973.

HILL, DOROTHY M., *Mud, Sand, and Water*. Washington, D.C.: National Association for the Education of Young Children, 1977.

HIRSCH, ELIZABETH S., ed., *The Block Book*. Washington, D.C.: National Association for the Education of Young Children, 1974.

KROWN, SYLVIA, *Threes and Fours Go to School*. Englewood Cliffs, N.J.: Prentice-Hall, Inc., 1974.

MATTERSON, E. M., *Play and Playthings for the Preschool Child*. Baltimore: Penguin, 1965.

MURPHY, LOIS, *The Widening World of Childhood*. New York: Basic Books, 1962.

PIAGET, JEAN, *Play, Dreams, and Imitation in Childhood*. 1945 reprint. London: William Heinemann Ltd., 1951.

SINGER, JEROME L., *The Child's World of Make-Believe*. New York: Academic Press, 1973.

SPONSELLER, DORIS, ed., *Play as a Learning Medium*. Washington, D.C.: National Association for the Education of Young Children, 1974.

Rose C. Engel

CHAPTER ELEVEN

YOUNG CHILDREN WITH SPECIAL EDUCATIONAL NEEDS: I

Including two chapters on children with special educational needs is in a way inconsistent with one of the major assumptions of this book: that *all* children have special educational needs. Although each classroom contains a range of individual children, each of whom needs to be dealt with in a specific personal manner, there are identifiable groups of children for whom education in conventional classrooms poses distinct problems for teachers. Many of these children have been identified as "exceptional" through individual diagnosis. Others belong to groups for whom conventional educational programs have been judged inadequate or inappropriate. These include children from low income families and from minority populations of our nation.

Although the differences among these groups are great, there is a history of confusion and confounding of educational problems that suggests that programs for these groups of children might best be discussed in a related fashion. This chapter addresses itself to the bases for identifying children with special educational needs based upon individual characteristics and to programs for them. The characteristics of teachers to work with these children will also be considered. Concerns for children with special educational needs based upon social or cultural characteristics will be discussed in the next chapter.

DETERMINING SPECIAL EDUCATIONAL NEEDS

Generally children have been identified as having special educational needs (often judged not capable of being met in conventional school programs) based upon one or more of the following criteria:

1. The child has some defect or illness that makes it difficult for him to function in a normal classroom.
2. The child somehow falls beyond the range of normalcy on some personal attribute that is considered educationally important.
3. There is a conflict between the demands of the conventional educational setting and the values or capabilities of an individual or his cultural group.

Each of these criteria can affect the educational expectations set for an individual, his educational placement, and the instructional techniques that are considered appropriate for him.

THE CHILD WITH A DEFECT OR ILLNESS

Children with clearly observable problems make up a large part of the population of "exceptional children" in early childhood classes. These include perceptually impaired children (those whose sight or hearing is seriously or totally impaired), speech impaired children, and physically handicapped children. Children with diseases that seriously limit their activities might also be included here. The problems of these children may be genetically determined, may result from difficulties during birth or pregnancy, or may be the result of childhood accident or illness. Whether children having severe learning disabilities or emotional problems should be considered in this category is open to question. Such children are often identified by physicians or community agencies and recommended for special education classes.

The function of educational programs for exceptional children is not necessarily remedial, since many of the difficulties cannot be remedied, at least not through education. Rather, the concern is to teach these children to make the greatest use of the capabilities they do have, and to use prosthetic devices that can extend their capabilities, if appropriate. Since these educational goals are not the concern of children developing normally, special activities and methods may need to be provided.

While these children might often be considered handicapped, the handicap might be created or increased by their physical environment, thus causing a conflict between the expectations of the institution and the capabilities of the children. When doorways to classrooms are widened, ramps installed to supplement stairways, and grab bars provided in bathrooms, children with orthopedic problems become less handicapped. Modification of furniture, facilities, and educational equipment, or of educational activities, can dispell or create handicaps. Thus these children's ability to function competently is related as much to their environment as to their capabilities.

CHILDREN BEYOND THE RANGE OF "NORMALCY"

Often children are identified as exceptional because they have a set of normal attributes to an exceptional degree. Children labeled intellectually gifted or mentally retarded are thus identified because they are considered to have much more or much less of an attribute all humans have: intelligence. Thus their exceptional abilities have a statistical as well as physiological basis.

Mathematical studies of probability have demonstrated that events occurring by chance are distributed "normally" so that most of the occurrences fall close to the average, with consistently fewer events falling farther from the average.

If you were to measure the height of adult males in a community, most men would fall in the average range, say between 5' 7" and 5' 11"; fewer men would measure between 5' 11" and 6' 3"; and even fewer between 6' 3" and 6' 7". The man who measured over 7' would be relatively rare in any community. Again, while this relationship might hold true for a normal community, it might not reflect the measurements in a particular community—for example, a basketball camp.

This distribution of random characteristics has been illustrated by the *normal distribution curve,* a hypothetical curve of the frequency of occurrences, which is bell-shaped and symmetrical. This curve shows the relationship of a single individual to a total population with reference to some attribute. You are considered short, for example, only in relation to the height of all the other members of a group, or a slow learner only if most other people learn faster. Not all human characteristics are thus distributed. The annual income of adults in the United States, for example, are not normally distributed.

Scores on intelligence tests are related to the normal distribution curve. Mental age was originally determined by the average of scores achieved on an intelligence test by a representative sample of children at that age. The intelligence quotient or IQ was the relationship of that mental age to a child's physical age ($IQ = \dfrac{\text{mental age}}{\text{chronological age}}$). More recent measures of intelligence transpose test scores into IQ by comparing the individual test score to the scores of all children of that age arranged according to the normal distribution curve. Children scoring at or around the mean are considered to have normal intelligence (IQ = 100). The further from the mean a test score falls, the less normally intelligent the child is considered.

There are several ways of classifying retarded children. Frank Hewett, for example, divides retarded children into four groups: borderline (IQ 75–85), educable (IQ 50–75), trainable (IQ 25–50), and profound (IQ below 25). Hewett reports, however, that his classifications are different from those used by the American Association for Mental Retardation, which identifies five classes of retardation: borderline (IQ 70–84), mild (IQ 55–69), moderate (IQ 40–54), severe (IQ 25–39), and profound (IQ below 25).[1] This discrepancy in classification schemes suggests a degree of arbitrariness in the delineation of mental retardation.

Another set of discrepancies arises out of information about the incidence of mental retardation in the general population. One would assume that since mental retardation is a concept based upon a measure of native ability, it would be distributed equally throughout the total population (one of the assumptions of the normal distribution curve). Yet this is not the case. Studies of the incidence of mental retardation suggest that it varies with age. Relatively few retarded people are identified either below or above the age of school attendance.[2] One could explain the paucity of cases prior to school enrollment as resulting from poor screening in the early years. The low incidence of retardation after school age suggests that other variables are operating. Persons considered mildly retarded become less visible in society than in school, suggesting that they are capable of making an acceptable adjustment to society's demands, and further that the concept of retardation might result as much from a conflict between child ability and school expectation as from a personal deficiency in the child.

In addition, regarding school-age children, more from poverty areas are identified as mentally retarded than from areas of higher socioeconomic status. About 60-80 percent of pupils classed as retarded are from low-status backgrounds and many are members of minority groups for whom standard English, the language of the intelligence test, is not always the prime language. This awareness of the class, ethnic, and racial overtones of the process by which mentally retarded children are identified was one of the considerations that led to a call for "mainstreaming" children—educating mildly retarded children in classes with normal children.[3]

---

[1] Frank M. Hewett, *Education of Exceptional Learners* (Boston: Allyn & Bacon, 1974), pp. 77–78.

[2] Ibid., pp. 78–79.

[3] Lloyd M. Dunn, "Special Education for the Mildly Retarded—Is Much of It Justified?" *Exceptional Children*, 35, no. 1 (September 1968), 5–22.

Further evidence of problems in identifying and labeling children as retarded can be found in court cases reported in California, where it was argued that intelligence tests used to place children in programs for the retarded were culturally biased and linguistically inappropriate. Other cases in other jurisdictions in the United States have challenged the use of traditional standardized tests as the basis for placement of retarded children.[4]

Not only does the possibility of discrimination exist in the tests used to assess retardation, but the judgments made as a result of testing may also be tinged by discrimination. Arlene Burke, for example, found in a study of placing handicapped children in one school system that more black children than expected were observed in educable mentally handicapped classes and more white children than expected were observed in learning disability classes. This was true at the elementary, junior high, and senior high school levels.[5] The awareness that class, ethnic, and racial bias has operated in identifying retarded children has led Lloyd Dunn to propose that children labeled mildly retarded or as having mild general learning disabilities include no more than 1.5 percent of each racial and ethnic subgroup in a school population.[6] This recommendation does not address itself to the question of the appropriateness of present screening devices, including IQ tests, for identifying retarded children. The biases shown in placements are inherent both in the instruments and in the use of the instruments. Addressing one aspect of the problem and not the other leaves much to be desired.

While this discussion of special needs based on an assumption of exceptionality from the norm has focused on the retarded child, it must be noted that deviation in the opposite direction is also viewed as exceptionality. Children at this extreme are generally labeled *gifted* or *talented*. Segregated programs for these children have also been established in schools. Such programs tend to enroll larger numbers of white and middle-class children; the label gifted seldom has the same stigma as retarded.

CHILDREN WHOSE ATTRIBUTES CONFLICT WITH SCHOOL EXPECTATIONS

While the children described above have to some extent been identified as children whose needs have conflicted with school expecta-

---

[4] Lloyd M. Dunn, "An Overview," in *Exceptional Children in the Schools: Special Education in Transition,* 2nd ed., ed. Lloyd M. Dunn (New York: Holt, Rinehart and Winston, 1973), pp. 45–48.

[5] Arlene A. Burke, "Placement of Black and White Children in Educable Mentally Handicapped Classes and Learning Disabilities Classes," *Exceptional Children,* 41, no. 6 (March 1975), 438–39.

[6] Lloyd M. Dunn, *Exceptional Children in the Schools,* pp. 129–31.

tions, we find even more prevalent conflicts in children from minority group and poverty-stricken families. These children speak a language different than the language of instruction. Their cultural patterns and values may differ from those expected of *all* children in school. Such children have conflicted with the schools for generations. Traditional school responses to them have been to expect them to conform, to identify them as retarded or as behavior problems, or to allow them to drop out. With changes in the laws relating to schools and schooling, many of these responses are no longer viable, and attempts have been made to provide more meaningful programs for these children.

In recent years we have seen an upsurge in the availability of programs for bilingual/bicultural children; some states sanction such programs and others mandate them. Proposals for special programs for "disadvantaged" children and even for teaching reading in Black English, a minority dialect, have been discussed seriously by educators. Thus conflicts between groups of children and school expectations are being mediated so that children's educational needs rather than the schools' institutional needs are receiving priority. Forms of such mediation are discussed in the next chapter.

Even with exceptional children, problems can occur as a result of conflict. Children with behavior disorders are often considered to have behavior inappropriate for the school setting. While the requirement is usually stipulated that the child's behavior should change, the expectations of schools might also need to be modified.

M. Stephen Lilly, in an attempt to put exceptional education into its proper perspective, has suggested that there is a need to move from defining *exceptional children* to defining *exceptional situations within the school*. Exceptional situations occur in the school when there is a breakdown in the student-teacher relationship that results in a disruption in the normal educational routine:

> An exceptional school situation is one in which the interaction between a student and his teacher has been limited to such an extent that external intervention is deemed necessary for the teacher to cope with the problem.[7]

Accepting the implications of exceptional school situations could have a profound effect not only on the definition of problems, but on the way they can be resolved. Exceptionality is viewed as being situationally based and the responsibility for change is not on the child alone, but on the total setting, including child and teacher. This would suggest

[7] M. Stephen Lilly, "Special Education: A Teapot in a Tempest," *Exceptional Children,* 37, no. 1 (September 1970), 43–45.

the need for an ecological approach to understanding and dealing with children with special educational needs. By that, it is meant that the child, the teacher, and other individuals interacting with them in the educational setting must be understood in relation to one another and in the context of the situation in which they operate. Solutions can be suggested that would require modification in the behavior of the child, the teacher, or of other adults as well as in various other aspects of the setting as a way to improve the child's learning capability, whether he be physically handicapped, bilingual, or gifted.

IDENTIFYING EXCEPTIONAL CHILDREN

The same influences that led to an extension of early childhood programs for all children during the 1960s and beyond have led to a broadening of educational services for exceptional children. Some states, such as Illinois, now provide educational opportunities for handicapped children as young as age three within the public schools, even though normal children are not the responsibility of public education until age five or six. Community screening programs—using volunteer and professional personnel, and referrals from pediatricians and social agencies—identify those children who are eligible and who can benefit from such services. Such a thrust makes it difficult to remember that not too many years back handicapped children were generally excluded from public school programs.

In addition, one of the major national early childhood programs, Project Head Start, originally designed for "disadvantaged" children, was mandated in 1972 to enroll handicapped children as not less than 10 percent of its total population.[8] This is one of the major efforts to integrate handicapped children into classes of normal children. Programs are also being developed specifically for the handicapped at the early childhood level. A range of model programs for handicapped children is presently being supported by the U.S. Office of Education for development and national dissemination.

These efforts do not represent a new thrust in early childhood education any more than Project Head Start represents the first time early childhood education has been provided for children in slum areas. There have been programs that have addressed themselves to the needs of handicapped and gifted children for decades. There have also been numerous nursery schools and kindergartens in which handicapped chil-

---

[8] Jenny W. Klein and Linda A. Randolph, "Placing Handicapped Children in Head Start Programs," *Children Today,* 3, no. 6 (November–December 1974), 7–10ff.

dren have been integrated with normal children. The present situation, however, reflects a greater general acceptance of early childhood education for handicapped children and of the integration of exceptional children into regular classrooms. This is a change in the educational scene.

SCREENING THE EXCEPTIONAL CHILD

In earlier days, teachers of young children often had exceptional children in their classroom who were not so identified. Often, with a mildly or moderately disabled child, the parents become so used to his manner of performing that they compensate for any disability without developing an awareness of its existence. In addition, the parents may not have any children available for direct comparisons to judge what is normal and what is exceptional. Sometimes deviation from the norm becomes evident only when the child is included in a group of similarly aged children under the observation of an impartial adult. The demands that school places upon children might also provide the basis for a judgment of exceptionality for a child of whom demands never have been made.

The current change in attitude toward early identification and treatment of handicapped persons might make teachers more aware of the existence of handicaps in their students. Certainly the newer attempts at screening preschool children will identify more handicapped children than have been generally thought to exist.

One of the first tasks traditionally required in working with exceptional children is identification and assignment to an appropriate category of exceptionality. The categories enable educators to assign children to appropriate classes and develop appropriate educational opportunities based upon the nature of the exceptionality. In addition, state aid for handicapped children is often provided based upon a set of traditional categories. Many labels are used to distinguish groups of exceptional children. However, labels considered appropriate seem to change over time, much like fashions in clothing. This is not to say that the labels are totally arbitrary, but rather that the assumptions upon which categories of exceptionality are based have been changing over time, and no greater stability of concepts on special education is apparent in the foreseeable future. For example, Robert Smith and John Neisworth have identified fifty-seven different categories of exceptionality in a five-year survey of the literature of special education.[9] Sometimes the same essential set of

---

[9] Robert M. Smith and John T. Neisworth, *The Exceptional Child: A Functional Approach* (New York: McGraw-Hill, 1975), p. 147.

attributes is given different labels by different educators. It is doubtful if the "hyperactive" is any different from the "hyperkinetic" child, or the "socially defective" any different from the "socially maladjusted" child.

More standard are the nine categories presented by Hewett, although even this list of exceptionalities presents problems. Hewett's list included

> Emotionally disturbed children
> Children with learning disabilities
> Mentally retarded children
> Socially and economically disadvantaged children
> Visually handicapped children
> Hearing disabled children
> Speech handicapped children
> Physically handicapped children
> Gifted children[10]

Some of these categories can be challenged as inappropriate. As has already been suggested, the distinction between retarded children and learning disabled children seems to be a difficult one to make, although the label of retardation carries with it a greater stigma. In addition, the inclusion of socially and economically disadvantaged children is spurious, though it is often found in the literature of special education. The assumption of genetically limited intelligence or limited intelligence due to a deprived background has been challenged in a number of places.[11]

Labeling children has serious consequences in relation to educational expectations for exceptional children. It is questionable whether it has similar consequences for the determination of educational experience. The placement of a child into a category is at best imprecise. Children within the same category often suffer from difficulties with quite different etiologies, for which educational prescriptions may be diverse. In addition, children from different categories might benefit from the same kind of educational experience.

Some special educators have tried to take a more functional approach to dealing with exceptional children, moving away from the traditional categories and attempting instead to identify those attributes that have implications for educational programming. Ira Iscoe and Sherry Payne suggest that children differ in several dimensions of basic impor-

---

[10] Hewett, *Education of Exceptional Learners*, p. ix.
[11] For example, see Herbert Ginsburg, *The Myth of the Deprived Child* (Englewood Cliffs, N.J.: Prentice-Hall, Inc., 1972).

tance: physical, adjustment, and educational dimensions. Each of these dimensions can be further broken down. The broad categories include

PHYSICAL STATUS

Visibility of physical deviation
Locomotion capabilities and limitations
Communication capabilities and problems

ADJUSTMENT STATUS

Peer acceptance
Family interaction
Self-esteem

EDUCATIONAL STATUS

Motivation
Academic achievement
Educational potential[12]

These categories are useful in identifying information about the child that can help in making educational decisions for him. His physical status, for example, can help educators assess to what extent he can be accommodated in a class, what kinds of modifications might need to be made for him, and what kinds of learning difficulties he might encounter. Similar judgments can be made on the basis of information on his adjustment status and educational status.

CURRICULUM CONCEPTS
IN EDUCATING EXCEPTIONAL CHILDREN

Within the field of special education, two concepts have been developed and are receiving major attention at this point that have importance for teachers of young children: *normalization* and *mainstreaming*. Although each is a distinct idea, they enhance one another and need to be considered in relationship to each other.

---

[12] Ira Iscoe and Sherry Payne, "Development of a Revised Scale for the Functional Classification of Exceptional Children," in *Readings on the Exceptional Child,* eds. E. P. Trapp and P. Himelstein (New York: Appleton-Century-Crofts, 1972), pp. 7–29.

Normalization refers to the creation of educational environments for exceptional children that are as close to generally normal environments as possible. One of the purposes of education for exceptional children is to help them cope as well as possible with everyday circumstances, interact as well as possible with a range of people, and live as normal lives as possible. Given these goals, the school is expected to design educational experiences to enable the child to develop coping skills. Contact with a range of children becomes important. But even in circumstances in which the child is educationally segregated, the educator is expected to make that learning situation as close to normal as possible.

Mainstreaming refers to the education of exceptional children in unsegregated facilities, integrated with normal children as much as possible. A hierarchy of possible placements ranging from maximum integration to maximum segregation has been identified by Evelyn Deno. In essence it is as follows:

1. Regular classroom assignment, possibly with classroom modification and supportive services provided
2. Regular classroom assignment plus supplementary instructional services (a resource room or itinerant teacher might provide these)
3. Part-time special classes with the remainder of the day spent in a regular class or resource room
4. Full-time special class with the child segregated into a separate class in a conventional school
5. Special day school
6. Homebound instruction
7. Institutional or residential assignment[13]

Each succeeding level of placement provides a more segregated and less normal educational environment for the child. Because of the nature of some educational exceptionalities and the demands placed upon children by schools, it is not possible for all children to function in regular classrooms, regular schools—or even homes, for that matter. Current practice calls for placing children into a setting that is the least restrictive possible. It is suggested that most exceptional children can be educated in normal settings with the classroom teacher providing help directly, or receiving special outside help. Fewer and fewer children need the more restrictive settings that are lower on the list. A further goal is

[13] Evelyn Deno, "Special Education as Developmental Capital," *Exceptional Children,* 37, no. 3 (November 1970), pp. 229–37.

for children to move from current settings to those that are closer to the normal educational setting.[14]

While there is not total agreement in the field as to the desirability of mainstreaming exceptional children, this idea is being heavily advocated. With the move toward normalization and mainstreaming, more teachers in conventional classes will have responsibility for educating children with a range of exceptionalities. This will certainly increase the demands placed on classroom teachers. An understanding of the types of exceptionalities that exist and the educational possibilities related to each should be helpful to teachers.

EXCEPTIONAL CHILDREN

For this discussion, six categories of exceptional children are used: gifted children, mentally retarded and learning disabled children, emotionally disturbed or behaviorally disabled children, children with sensory problems, children with communications problems, and children with physical or motor problems. Given the nature of the various exceptionalities and the state of knowledge in the field, these categories seem to be reasonable.

GIFTED CHILDREN

Children are considered gifted who have a high degree of talent, intelligence, and imagination. They can be identified through a number of procedures including teacher observations, achievement on school tasks, and the use of intelligence tests. While for educational purposes giftedness has been linked primarily to high intelligence, there can be gifted children who excel in almost any area of human endeavor. Schools seldom reward or accommodate children who are gifted in physical activities or the arts in the same way they do those gifted in the intellectual or academic realm. Children with high IQ do, however, tend to be generally superior developmentally. The Lewis Terman study of gifted children, for example, showed them to be heavier at birth, manifesting greater height and strength, and walking and talking earlier than average.[15] Terman's follow-up study showed these children continuing in their giftedness into adulthood.[16]

---

[14] Dunn, *Exceptional Children in the Schools,* pp. 36–39.
[15] Lewis M. Terman, *Genetic Studies of Genius,* vol. I (Stanford, Ca.: Stanford University Press, 1925).
[16] Lewis M. Terman and Melita H. Oden, *The Gifted Child Grows Up* (Stanford, Ca.: Stanford University Press, 1947).

Gifted children tend to learn rapidly in school and retain what they have learned. They tend to be verbal and enjoy reading, developing reading skills early and acquiring an extensive vocabulary. They gain facility with thinking skills and gather a rich background of information. Although intelligence and giftedness are generally considered closely related, Jacob Getzels and Philip Jackson were able to separate high IQ from high creativeness for purposes of study—two dimensions of giftedness often thought to go hand-in-hand.[17]

The education of gifted children in the early years is usually based upon one of two approaches: enrichment and acceleration. Very often gifted children are placed ahead a grade or admitted into school earlier. In regular classes, teachers tend to give these children additional or advanced work, allowing them to move through the standard curriculum more quickly or enriching and extending their studies.

There have been a number of special programs for young gifted children, beginning at the nursery-school level. However, no evidence exists that these special programs are more enhancing for their students than the strategies of enrichment and acceleration. Advanced placement, though the basis for controversy over the years, seems to leave no ill effects. Gifted children who are advanced a grade are generally able to keep up, both academically and socially.

THE MENTALLY RETARDED
AND/OR LEARNING DISABLED CHILD

The assumption underlying the label of mentally retarded is that the individual lacks the capacity to learn what a normal child can learn. The assumption underlying the label of learning disabled is that there is a discrepancy between the individual's capacity and his actual learning achievement. Although the judgment of capacity might be made accurately for severely and profoundly retarded children, the accuracy of such judgments for mildly and moderately retarded children has been open to question.

Achievement is assessed by some observation of what a person actually has done. But how can we assess what an individual is capable of doing, unless we rely on what he has already done? Thus, no judgment of capacity can presently be made that does not rely heavily on observed achievement. The intelligence test uses achievement to judge capacity. Such a judgment is based upon the assumption that every child

[17] Jacob W. Getzels and Philip W. Jackson, *Creativity and Intelligence* (New York: John Wiley, 1962).

has had an equal opportunity to achieve the learnings sampled on the test; hence any difference found must be a difference in capacity. This basic assumption has been seriously questioned by a number of psychologists and educators. While we can determine what a child has or has not learned, we have difficulty determining why the learning has or has not occurred.

Educational practice is seldom determined by the causes of an educational disorder; it is usually related to the manifestation of the problem. Understanding causes might help to determine a learning expectation, but not how that expectation will be achieved. Our expectation for a child might be different if we consider him retarded rather than learning disabled. But should it? Expectation is a two-edged sword. To expect too much may lead to disappointment and frustration; to expect too little might limit achievement. Teachers need to balance this sense of expectation for all children—whether retarded, learning disabled, normal, or gifted. A continued reassessment of what the child can do on the basis of each learning experience is helpful.

Severely and profoundly retarded children are often identified early in life, through either physical abnormalities or the failure to develop normally. These children may not walk or talk when expected as a result of general developmental retardation. More mildly retarded children are often detected only when they begin school. Their failure to learn to read or to respond to other academic requirements can lead to a referral to a psychologist and subsequent diagnosis of retardation.

Learning disabled children are a varied group. Many definitions of this category have been proposed, but each is complicated and inadequate in defining the attributes of the total group thus labeled and in separating this group from other categories of exceptionality. This group includes children with neurological impairments as well as those with functional impairments. Children suffering from hyperactivity; perceptual-motor impairment; emotional lability; impulsivity; specific learning disabilities in reading, spelling, arithmetic, or writing; disorders of speech and hearing; and neurological problems have all been included in this category.

In general, the approaches to teaching children with learning disabilities have not differed greatly from those used for retarded children. A popular approach is the use of a clinical model of teaching, one that includes several steps. It begins with (1) the diagnosis of the specific learning problem, then (2) the establishment of goals often stated in behavioral terms to ameliorate the learning problem, (3) the development of a program specifically aimed at the learning problem, and finally (4) an assessment of the changes in the original problem to determine if the program has succeeded. The curriculum strategy is one of simplifying the program and teaching directly to the area of weakness. Task analysis becomes important in generating learning activities, for if the failure is in a complicated area of performance, the teacher is expected to break down that performance into its simpler components, which can then each be taught separately and, hopefully, be reintegrated. This approach assumes that it is easier for these children to learn simpler tasks than complex tasks. There is also an assumption here that learning problems are best attacked directly. Finally, the assumption that learning is behaviorally based also underlies the clinical-model approach. The use of behavior analysis has paralleled this strategy as a way of dealing with retarded and learning disabled children. Using behavior analysis techniques is much like using a diagnostic/prescriptive method of teaching. Goals are determined in behavioral terms and the processes of *shaping*—using successive approximations toward the behavioral goal—and *chaining*—building complex behaviors out of sets of simpler ones—are based upon some task analysis. Also, contingency management—the scheduling and use of reinforcers and punishments to influence the child's behavior—is practiced.

In addition to these general approaches to the education of retarded and disabled children are a number of perceptual-motor approaches. Among the best known of these are the Frostig program,[18] which teaches visual-perceptual skills, the Kephart program,[19] which focuses on perceptual-motor skills, and the Delacato program,[20] which advocates patterning of muscular movements to complete learnings missed at earlier stages of development. Although there are strong advocates of these and other programs, there is still an absence of firm research evidence that would allow the field to unequivocally support any specific approach.

Some educators suggest that rather than focus on the difficulties of these children, we should try to capitalize on their strengths. Such a strategy might increase the child's sense of success, which could be generalized to other areas of accomplishment. Still other educators suggest a broadly based program. They argue that the educational goals for these children should be no different from goals for normal children and that unnecessary narrowing of curriculum, either toward a child's

[18] Marianne Frostig and D. Horne, *The Frostig Program for the Development of Visual Perception* (Chicago: Follett, 1964).

[19] Newelle C. Kephart, *The Slow Learner in the Classroom* (Columbus, Ohio: Charles E. Merrill, 1960).

[20] Carl H. Delacato, *Neurological Organization and Reading Problems* (Springfield, Ill.: Charles C Thomas, 1966).

strengths or toward his weaknesses, is essentially wrong. What might be varied, however, is the pacing of instruction, allowing these children more time for learning when it seems desirable.

Other curriculum options are possible for educating these children. Research by Mary Rowe related to science education (presented in chapter 6) demonstrates that reading achievement is often increased for slow-learning children by increasing their involvement in discovery-oriented science activities. While the logic of teaching directly to the area of deficit seems irrefutable, from a psychological point of view it might very well be that indirect methods of teaching toward deficits might be more effective and, in the long run, more efficient.

Integration of retarded children with normal children would allow a range of strategies that support learning. Peer modeling has been shown to be an effective learning technique. It is quite possible that in mainstreamed classes these children will be able to learn more from other children than directly from their teacher. Some educators suggest that an open classroom—with various goals and paces of learning—might be ideally suited for mainstreaming. It also allows for more activity-based learning than is found in more traditional classes. This form of learning has been shown to be effective with retarded and learning disabled children since before the beginning of the Montessori method (see chapter 2).

THE EMOTIONALLY DISTURBED OR BEHAVIORALLY DISABLED CHILD

A number of emotional disturbances, behavioral disorders, and socio-emotional problems can be identified in young children. These range from some of the most severe, such as infant autism, through more moderate problems of conflict with the environment. A variety of explanations as well as classifications characterize this area of exceptionality. Included are children who withdraw totally from reality, such as the schizophrenic or autistic child, or who withdraw less excessively, such as the child who daydreams or lives in a world of fantasy. There are those who manifest anxiety through developmental regression or phobias, and those who manifest antisocial aggression through acting-out behavior or delinquency, the latter being a legal rather than a psychological or educational construct. The causes for the various emotional problems in children are not definitely known. Some theories suggest that the causes are primarily neurological or physiological; others that they are basically a function of family relations or problems of upbringing; still others that they are situationally determined.

The suggestions for treatment are equally varied: drug therapy, family counseling, psychotherapy for the child and/or his family, behavior modification techniques, and other forms of developmental or psychoeducational treatments. For the teacher, the suggestion of psychotherapy or family counseling is not helpful, for although a school might refer a child and his parents to some outside agency for help, the teacher must still respond to the child's behavior in the classroom. Suggestions for the teacher need to be related to helping the child adjust to the school setting or to modifying the setting to be more responsive to the child's needs. Different theories suggest different teaching strategies.

A teacher adhering to one theoretical viewpoint, for example, might welcome a show of aversive behavior and allow children to act out their conflicts in class as a form of therapeutic catharsis. A teacher with a different viewpoint might wish to change the child's behavior so that incidents of acting out are lessened and more desirable social behaviors manifested in the class.

In recent years, advocacy of behavior modification techniques—using operant conditioning to change children's behavior—has increased. The child might be removed from class and put into a special environment that is more manageable in order to decrease the manifestations of negative behavior. He may then be eased back into the classroom, where the teacher can learn to develop behavior management techniques to sustain the change. If she is not careful to modify those elements in the classroom that set off the negative behavior in the first place, the child may revert to his original condition.

Often the child stays in class and help is provided to the teacher directly in the classroom. The teacher learns to understand the child and the causes of his behavior and to increase her ability to work successfully with him. She might analyze and change the classroom environment to support the more positive aspects of the child's behavior. A crisis-intervention teacher or resource-room teacher could be made available to provide additional help on a long-term basis when the need arises.

CHILDREN WITH SENSORY PROBLEMS

A number of children are considered exceptional because they are handicapped in normal sensory channels. These include children who are deaf or hard of hearing, and blind or partially sighted. Either condition can exist from birth or occur at any point in the child's life due to accident or illness. The educational consequences of these problems differ, depending on when they began. The ability to hear, both himself and others, is important in the child's development of language. Deafness does not limit the language development of those children who become deaf after the establishment of basic language patterns. Although children blind from birth may be unaware of certain basic concepts, such as color, this disability does not seem to have the same profound effects on development as deafness.

Visually impaired children are usually categorized as either blind or partially sighted. A blind child cannot have his vision corrected to better than 20/200; a partially sighted child has his best correction between 20/200 and 20/70. Blind children are generally identified in infancy, but the partially sighted may not be identified until much later. The greater the degree to which the child can respond to visual stimuli, the higher the probability that his problem will not be detected until entrance to school.

In dealing with the blind or partially sighted child, the teacher needs to help him use the sensory channels he has available to gain the maximum information possible from the environment. Much sensory data that can be gained through hearing or touch, less important to the fully sighted child because of its redundancy, becomes of major importance to the visually impaired child. Shapes can be learned by touch, and distance and direction can be determined by sound. A child can use his existing senses to a much greater extent than is normally expected to compensate for a difficulty in one sensory modality. Thinking skills can still be exercised by mentally operating on available sense experiences. Many of the standard materials of the nursery and kindergarten—such as blocks, puzzles, and manipulative materials—are well suited for the visually impaired child. The teacher needs to help him use materials optimally, and she should acquire and develop other appropriate materials as needed.

Visually impaired children have difficulty moving about independently and caring for themselves. Adults are often over-protective and limit their movement learning opportunities for fear of injury. Children can be helped to become independent in self-care skills and to move about their environment. They can learn to use climbing apparatus, ride tricycles and wagons, dig in sand, and move about the classroom and the outdoor play area. Some assistance will be needed, especially in the beginning. The teacher should be careful to orient the child to the physical environment, and not to make changes in the organization of the room without reorienting him. Rails and ropes might be set up in appropriate places to help him move about. He can also be helped to dress, feed, and toilet himself, although extra training might have to be provided in each situation.

As the visually impaired child moves into the primary grades he will, of course, have difficulty in reading. If the impairment is not great, large-print books and magnifiers can enable the child to read normally. If the problem is more profound, Braille reading and writing should be taught. A blind child can continue in a regular classroom for part of the day if Braille instruction is provided by an itinerant teacher or a resource-room teacher. The classroom teacher could probably cope with arithmetic instruction with some modification of the normal program, but reading and writing instruction will require a special teacher.

The educational problems of the hearing impaired child can be profound. He may not only have problems communicating, so important from both a social and educational point of view, but his competence in many language-based activities may be limited. If the child has some residual hearing, he should be fitted with a hearing aid. Even though such a device may distort the quality of sound, it will widen the child's sensory contact with the external world. Care should be taken that he learns how to use the hearing aid, and that the teacher is able to help him if he has problems with it (e.g., she may have to change the battery).

The teacher needs to be aware of the child's problems and modify the room to limit his difficulties with it. Care can be taken to diminish unnecessary and confusing noises. Covering the floor of the block building area with indoor-outdoor carpeting, for example, will lessen the noise generated there without limiting the activities of the other children. In addition, the teacher should speak face-to-face with him, allow him to sit close to her when stories are read, and support his production of speech even when there are difficulties.

If the child is deaf, it is important that he develop some communicating skills. Speechreading or lipreading is advocated by some educators of the deaf; the use of sign language or the manual alphabet is advocated by others. Still others prefer a combination of the two approaches. Whatever the approach used in the school, it will probably require the availability of a resource or consultant teacher in addition to the classroom teacher.

As important as developing language skills is for the hearing impaired child, developing skills in communicating with nonimpaired children and adults is also important. For this reason, even part-time placement in a regular class should be considered as a way of providing the child with skills to live as normal a life as possible.

CHILDREN
WITH COMMUNICATIONS DISORDERS

A survey of the literature suggests that there is considerable incidence of communication disorders in young children. How serious the disorders may be is questionable, however. Among those identified are articulation problems, voice problems, stuttering, and language disorders. The majority of young children's communications problems are related to articulation: sound substitution, sound omission, and sound distortion (including lisping and baby talk). The question of seriousness is related to the prevalence of articulation disorders and the fact that many of them are not evident at later ages. It seems reasonable that many of these are problems of delayed development, which clear themselves up in time. However, some of these disorders will require additional help, and it is difficult to separate the two sets of problems.

Voice problems include excessive nasality or inadequate nasal emission during speech as well as problems of pitch, intensity, and flexibility, leading to monotone or stereotyped speech. Stuttering, or hesitations in speech patterns, may appear in early childhood. Just how serious most stuttering problems are with young children is also questionable. One of the more serious speech problems is delayed speech or aphasia, the partial or total failure of speech to develop. Some speech disorders are the result of other developmental problems, such as cleft palate or cerebral palsy.

While speech and language problems are handled primarily by speech therapists in schools, the classroom teacher can do a number of things to help the child with them. One of the important roles of early childhood education is to enhance language development in children. Activities with this aim provided to children with language disorders can have an equal or greater impact than on normal children. Some of these activities are suggested in chapter 4. The child needs to be allowed the time to produce speech communications and to be rewarded in his efforts, even though his achievements may not seem great. The teacher should keep him from becoming too self-conscious or too defeatist in his attempts to communicate with others. As far as the aphasic child is concerned, there is probably little that a classroom teacher can do in helping him with his problem. She should recommend the help of physicians and speech clinicians.

CHILDREN WITH PHYSICAL
OR MOTOR PROBLEMS

Young children can have many different physical or motor problems. While many of these problems do not create learning difficulties, they often create problems for the child in working within the expectations of the school. The more severe problems are dealt with at home or in hospitals. However, the ambulatory child can often be accommodated in schools, fitting well into regular classes if appropriate accommodations are made.

Included in this category of children with special needs are those with cerebral palsy, who suffer from a complex neuromuscular condition due to brain injury prior to or at birth. Epileptics, and children with other chronic illnesses such as rheumatic fever, congenital heart defects, or cystic fibrosis, and children with congenital malformations of the heart, hip, or spinal column are also included.

Although children with these physical problems represent a small minority of the child population, their numbers are increasing. This is due partly to advances in medical practice and technology, which are saving infants that might formerly have died at birth or shortly thereafter. It is probably also due to the increases in toxic substances in our environment and in drug-related problems among pregnant women.

The key to working with this group of children is to analyze the classroom and modify it as needed to allow them to function as competently and independently as possible. The teacher might also have to design learning experiences and movement activities so that they are within the capabilities of these children.

Each of the exceptionalities discussed in this chapter was presented separately, but they do not always occur in isolation from one another. Often, as noted, physical disabilities are related to speech problems or other problems. Many times teachers are faced with multiply handicapped children. Combined handicaps often complicate diagnosis and create problems in remediation, as well. The fact that children can suffer from a range of exceptionalities underlines the basic problems of classification in the field. For the classroom teacher, a label for a child is less important than a descriptive statement of his educational strengths and weaknesses and of the disabling or strengthening aspects of his development that must be considered in designing an individual program. The major disadvantage of labels is that they easily lead to stereotypes, thus preventing the child from being regarded as a child rather than a "hyphenated child." Stigmas are also associated with certain exceptionalities. Parents are legitimately afraid that once the child is labeled, a low learning expectation will be created that will become a self-fulfilling prophecy. Once a child is placed on an educational track, no matter how informal, it is very hard to switch him to a different track.

TEACHING THE EXCEPTIONAL CHILD

The preparation of teachers of exceptional children is a highly specialized separate field. Programs are specifically designed to train teachers of deaf children, gifted children, emotionally disturbed children, and children with other specific exceptionalities. Each program prepares teachers with special knowledge and skills. The regular classroom teacher is bound to have to deal with children in many of these categories of exceptionality, but she could hardly be expected to complete all these programs.

How, then, can the teacher learn to cope with the many problems that face her? Perhaps it is unfair to ask teachers to be prepared to work with a range of children with exceptionalities while maintaining a full classroom as before. Special help needs to be provided to classroom teachers as exceptional children are integrated into their classes. Resource personnel, crisis intervention teachers, and consultants have been recommended to help classroom teachers better understand and educate the exceptional child, as well as to provide specific techniques as required. The child may also be taken out of the classroom for periods of time for those aspects of his program which are beyond the capability of the regular teacher or beyond the range of regular classroom activities. Additional supplies and equipment might also have to be supplied. Consideration must also be given to reducing the number of children in a classroom when exceptional children are introduced.

In addition, there are some things a regular classroom teacher must learn. A general understanding of the nature of exceptionalities in children as well as a knowledge of the growth and development of normal children is a desirable, even necessary requirement. In addition, she should know some of the basic techniques of education for exceptional children. This should create no problem, for these basic instructional strategies are little different from the strategies suggested for normal children. There are differences in specific content and methods, however. Here the teacher must learn to rely on outside experts, consultants, resource-room teachers, and clinicians who will work jointly with her in designing and implementing programs for these children.

In addition, certain personal characteristics are helpful. The teacher needs concern and caring for children without unnecessary sympathy and pity; flexibility in dealing with educational goals and methods; willingness to try new techniques and remain tentative in her approval of tried and true techniques; willingness to communicate problems and to share concerns with others; ability to function in a cooperating relationship; undying optimism and faith in the utility of education; and ability to accept some degree of failure as well as success. Somehow the requirements for teaching these children are the same as those for teaching all children . . . only more.

SUGGESTED READINGS

BOWLEY, AGATHA H., and LESLIE GARDNER, *The Young Handicapped Child.* London: E. and S. Livingstone, 1969.

DUNN, LLOYD M., ed., *Exceptional Children in the Schools.* New York: Holt, Rinehart and Winston, 1973.

HAWKINS, FRANCES POCKMAN, *The Logic of Action: Young Children at Work.* New York: Pantheon, 1974.

HEEDMANN, MARY ALICE, *The Slow Learners in the Primary Grades.* Columbus, Ohio: Charles E. Merrill, 1973.

HEWETT, FRANK M., *Education of Exceptional Learners.* Boston: Allyn & Bacon, 1974.

SMITH, ROBERT M., and JOHN T. NEISWORTH, *The Exceptional Child: A Functional Approach.* New York: McGraw-Hill, 1975.

James L. Hoot

CHAPTER TWELVE

YOUNG CHILDREN WITH SPECIAL EDUCATIONAL NEEDS: II

Over the years a number of terms have been used to label poor children for whom the school's traditional programs do not seem to be effective, including "disadvantaged," "economically depressed," "children of the inner city," and "culturally deprived." Sometimes these children are identified as being from minority groups, or from subcultural backgrounds: Southern Appalachian whites, residents of urban black ghettoes, Mexican-Americans, Cubans, Puerto Ricans, and Native Americans. We identify in this group children reared in poverty, whether in rural or urban circumstances. Many within this group are from subcultures that have traditionally experienced discrimination and been isolated from the majority culture.

THE CONCEPT OF THE DISADVANTAGED

The concept of cultural deprivation or even of disadvantage has emerged from a view that these children are somehow deficient. A large proportion of them suffer from some degree of school failure. Many live in poverty. A popular belief is that since ours is an egalitarian society, all persons have equal access to its rewards, which include personal success and affluence. Persons not achieving these rewards must suffer from some liability that keeps them from success. Thus a deficit model develops suggesting that since the schools as they exist are naturally good, the fault for group failure rests in the group that is failing. This group comes to school lacking the requisites for success, because of either constitutional or cultural limits.

Given this explanation, one does not consider the school responsible for children's failure to learn, or the instruments of academic evaluation as possibly discriminatory. Rather, some educators and psychologists have indicated that there are limits to the intelligence and school achievement we can expect of disadvantaged populations, because of either basic genetic factors, proposed by Arthur Jensen,[1] or limiting factors in the child's environment, suggested by Martin Whiteman and Martin Deutsch.[2] While both these positions have been adopted by some educators, serious criticism has been raised about each.

Another set of explanations suggests that these persons are not culturally deprived or even disadvantaged, but rather culturally *different*. The cultures of these nonmainstream groups have developed differently from that of white, middle-class America. Not only are their experiences different, but the concepts they acquire, the values they hold, the labels they place on things, their style of behaving, learning, living, and even their languages are different. The schools are not designed to relate to the language or culture of these children. The failure does not come from anything inherent in genetic makeup, or in the child-rearing environment, but rather from the improper match of the children's backgrounds and cultural demands and the schools' instructional demands. Children may be instructed in a language that is alien to them—thus, they do not learn. They may be asked to compete with one another although their valued style of interacting is cooperative—thus, they do not learn. Or they may be demeaned and degraded by the instructional materials used.

In a real sense, these children are *disadvantaged*. But the disadvantage does not come from any inherent deficiencies within the child's culture. Rather, it comes from limits imposed by poverty and from the school culture that conflicts with the children's culture, making little use of the strengths they bring to the setting.

At a recent conference of early childhood educators, one conferee began her presentation by stating that she was disadvantaged in that setting. All the other participants were Americans, fluent in English. She was an Israeli; Hebrew was her native language. Consequently, she found herself linguistically disadvantaged. However, if the rules of the conference had been that all presentations were to made in Hebrew, she would have been at an advantage and all the others would have been disadvantaged. In this sense, the culturally different child is a culturally

---

[1] Arthur R. Jensen, "How Much Can We Boost IQ and Scholastic Achievement?" *Harvard Educational Review*, 39, no. 1 (Winter 1969), pp. 1–123.
[2] Martin Whiteman and Martin Deutsch, "Social Disadvantage as Related to Intellective and Language Development," in *Social Class, Race, and Psychological Development*, eds. Martin Deutsch, Irwin Katz, and Arthur R. Jensen (New York: Holt, Rinehart and Winston, 1968), pp. 86–114.

disadvantaged child in school. Only when his culture is accepted, when his language or dialect is used in school, and when his values are honored does the disadvantage fade. Just as exceptionality needs to be defined within a school situation, disadvantageousness can be understood only within the context of the interactions and expectations of a particular situation. This form of disadvantageousness cannot be erased by any form of compensatory education. A high-quality education is important and necessary, but it must also be meaningful and relevant. The change must come in the school setting, not in the child.

FACTORS AFFECTING CONCERN
FOR POOR AND MINORITY CHILDREN

Multiple factors have led to the concern for the education of these children. Among the social factors are the civil rights movement and the politically voiced concern about the existence of poverty in an affluent country. In addition, changes in psychological theory, especially as related to the development of intelligence, support newer hypotheses about the effects of educational treatment on children. Further, there has been increased concern about the intellectual content offered to children in schools.

The 1954 Supreme Court decision that separate educational facilities for black children could not provide equal educational opportunity heralded a long battle to bring about integration and equality in the schools. This difficult task is still incomplete. In addition to the legal barriers to desegregation, the segregated housing patterns in most communities are barriers, necessitating elaborate changes in organization and transportation in schools aiming to desegregate their facilities.

When minority-group children were grouped with "advantaged" students, they often fell behind in academic work. Some educators attributed the failure to the inadequate schooling previously available, and others suggested that the homes and communities in which these children were reared provided inadequate background for school learning. Programs of compensatory education—designed to make up for early environmental inadequacies—were developed, sometimes as an aid to integrating the schools, other times as an alternative to integration. Some of these programs derived from the field of special education, where research had shown that early experiences could increase measured intelligence in mentally retarded children.[3] This implied that these

---

[3] Samuel A. Kirk, *Early Education of the Mentally Retarded* (Urbana, Ill.: University of Illinois Press, 1958).

children's experiences led to lower intelligence, a circumstance that could be altered by early schooling.

A third factor in the concern for poor and minority children is the recent change in the concept of the school's role. Beginning with the early 1960s, the early childhood years were thought to provide increased opportunities for nurturing intellectual development. New curricula for teaching the sciences, social sciences, mathematics, and languages were developed for lower grade levels. Changes in human development theories added support to the arguments of new curriculum developers; the ideas of Jean Piaget or B. F. Skinner were often invoked in support of the new curriculum proposals. Pioneer programs supported generally enriched preschool education for disadvantaged children and specifically designed learning opportunities to alleviate learning deficits.

In 1965 Project Head Start, under the auspices of the Office of Economic Opportunity, provided the first mass preschool program for poor children. A number of experimental models were established throughout the United States. As it became evident that a single year or a few months of education prior to children's entrance to school was inadequate to meet their needs, Project Follow-Through was conceived to extend these programs through the primary grades. As it exists now, Follow-Through utilizes a number of program models in the hope that some judgment can result from their comparative evaluation.

When we discuss any group of children—whether a class, or a cultural or ethnic group—we necessarily must talk of central tendencies. Descriptions may apply to many, but certainly not all of the group members; individual differences do abound. Thus our statements of what exists in the backgrounds of these children and what should be done for them must serve as working hypotheses to be tested in the reality of the classroom. Such limitations, by the way, are true of any statements made regarding work with any children.

CHARACTERISTICS OF POOR AND MINORITY CHILDREN

The consequences of being poor impact a child from birth; indeed sooner, for the percentage of stillbirths, premature births, obstetrical complications, and infant mortalities is higher for the poor than for the general population. As the poor child matures, his chances of being ill are greater than average and he may suffer from nutritional problems brought about by the lack of food or an improperly balanced diet. Though this is sometimes the result of inadequate dietary knowledge, it is also a direct result of being too poor to buy needed foods. Poor persons must often pay more for food in slum areas, or are offered inferior goods at the same prices charged in middle-class areas for quality goods. These price differences may be the result of both the higher costs of doing business in slum areas and different shopping patterns of slum dwellers (such as buying in smaller quantities), but the slum also provides opportunities for unethical practices by merchants. In addition, the relatively high costs of other necessities—rent, furniture, and so forth—leave a smaller percentage of income available for food.[4]

Children of poverty may be less healthy than affluent children, both suffering from more physical problems and being more susceptible to illness. This results from a general lack of medical services near their homes, their inability to pay for expensive fee-based private medical services, as well as from difficulties in using what services are available, either in clinics or hospital emergency rooms.

Generally speaking, fewer doctors and hospitals locate in slum areas than in middle-class areas. Where clinics exist, people often need to make great expenditures in time and energy to use them. There may be long lines requiring tedious waiting. In addition, the impersonal treatment in clinics and the patients' inability to establish a continuing relationship with a doctor often discourage them from seeking medical attention for minor problems.

Family patterns in poverty areas also affect children. Single-parent families are not limited to the poor, but a large proportion of poor children are reared with the father absent, in part because of policies relating to the administration of welfare and the Aid to Dependent Children programs. Generally, such aid has not been available in homes in which the father is present, often causing the parents' separation in order to qualify for aid. Poor families may have many children. Consequently, living accommodations are generally less than adequate and crowded. Also, distinct differences in child-rearing patterns are found in minority cultures.

The most apparent characteristic of many poor and minority children is their inability to cope with the academic studies of the school. They frequently manifest a lower ability to perform on verbal tasks than on nonverbal tasks. Because many school learning tasks become increasingly verbal in nature, these problems are heightened as the children continue through school.

Some psychologists have suggested that these children's poor showing on academic tasks is the result of lower intelligence, supporting their point with IQ test scores. The previous discussion on intelligence tests indicates that they do not provide a useful basis for comparing in-

[4] David Caplowitz, *The Poor Pay More* (New York: The Free Press, 1963).

telligence across cultures. Even within the same culture, their validity and the validity of their educational application are open to serious question.

Differences in intellectual styles have been identified among children, suggesting that a particular style might be nurtured by a specific culture. The difference in stylistic demands between school tasks and cultural tasks of a minority population could lead to a disadvantage in school success. Manuel Ramírez and Alfredo Castañeda discuss the difference between field-dependent and field-independent cognitive styles. Originally this distinction was made between those who use internal cues and those who use external cues for perceptual tasks. Field-dependent children, according to Ramírez and Castañeda, do best on verbal tasks, learn materials with human and social content more easily, are sensitive to the opinions of others, and perform better when authority figures express confidence in them. Field-independent children do best on analytic tasks, learn materials with inanimate and impersonal content most easily, and are not greatly affected by the opinions of others. Ramírez and Castañeda cite studies to suggest that Mexican-Americans and black Americans are more field-dependent, while Anglo-Americans are more field-independent.[5] Academic tasks requiring analysis, presented in an impersonal context, could put field-dependent thinkers at a disadvantage in school.

Jensen has stated that minority children lack the ability to learn conceptual material—that is, material taught through understanding. He contends, however, that minority children do not lack the ability to learn material associatively, through memorization. He goes on to suggest that schools might do better by teaching minority children primarily through associative means.[6] Although some researchers have found associative learning patterns useful for the education of minority children, many programs have successfully demonstrated the ability of minority children to learn conceptually. Other distinctions in cognitive style that might have implication for education include impulsivity/reflectivity (the speed at which an individual might respond to a cue or act on a problem), and left/right hemispheric brain dominance, which some educators and psychologists associate with work/creativity differences.

Much has been written about the disadvantaged child's language deficits. Basil Bernstein has postulated two different linguistic codes: *restricted* and *elaborated*. The restricted code is characterized by short, grammatically simple sentences. It is limited and condensed, containing symbols of a low order of generality. It is a language of implicit

[5] Manuel Ramírez III and Alfredo Castañeda, *Cultural Democracy, Bicognitive Development and Education* (New York: Academic Press, 1974).
[6] Jensen, "How Much Can We Boost IQ and Scholastic Achievement?" pp. 111–17.

meaning, useful for reinforcing a sense of identity, but not adequate for communicating information. The elaborated code is more accurate and grammatically correct. It is precise and can express a wide range of thought.[7]

It has been suggested that lower-class children use a restricted code, while school work requires an elaborated code. Thus they have difficulty in school. In fact, all social classes use a restricted code on occasion. Although it is possible that lower-class children use a different code than do middle-class children and that their linguistic forms are not supported in the school, their language has the potential for communicating explicit meanings and logical forms. William Labov has demonstrated the logic inherent in the discourse of speakers of the black dialect and even suggests that their language is better suited for dealing with abstract, logically complex, and hypothetical questions than is the middle-class language. He further states that the middle-class person's language seems more precise in the standardized test situation. That same test situation puts black children at a disadvantage. Labov describes a nonthreatening standard test situation that elicited minimal language samples from a black child whose language was fluent when he could speak with another child and when a bag of potato chips was provided.[8] Problems of test settings as well as dialect differences further explain the poor showing of minority children on standardized tests.

Many of the children labeled disadvantaged do differ linguistically from the majority of Americans. Some of them, such as those from Mexican-American backgrounds, may speak a language at home that is different from the school's language. Others speak a different dialect. Both language and dialect differences create problems in school. Generally accepted English speech is Standard English, and the most prevalent other dialect is Black English. Many people speak regional variations of these dialects. Labov and others have demonstrated that although Black English is significantly different from Standard English, it is regular in its form and has all the capabilities of supporting elaborate thought. It is different but not deficient. However, its use creates a conflict with the demands of the school.

Some children have difficulty learning to read because they

---

[7] Basil Bernstein, "Social Structure, Language and Learning," in *Education of the Disadvantaged,* eds. A. Harry Passow, Miriam Goldberg, and Abraham J. Tannenbaum (New York: Holt, Rinehart and Winston, 1967), pp. 225–44.

[8] William Labov, "The Logic of Nonstandard English," in *Language and Cultural Diversity in American Education,* eds. Roger D. Abrahams and Rudolph C. Troika (Englewood Cliffs, N.J.: Prentice-Hall, Inc., 1972), pp. 225–61.

must translate the dialect of the primer into their own dialect to derive meaning. If the children report what they understand, their verbal responses are often classed as errors because of the differences of the two forms. The process is cumbersome and even without the misunderstandings, one dialect can interfere with learning to read in another.[9]

William Stewart reports an incident in which a twelve-year-old problem reader visiting Stewart's apartment came upon a poem written in Black English. The child was able to read the poem without difficulty. As a result of such experiences, Stewart has suggested that one way of dealing with dialect differences in the school is to present beginning reading instruction in the child's native dialect as a transition to reading Standard English. This could be done by providing primers written in Black English or by using the Language Experience Approach based upon chart stories dictated by the children and transcribed by the teacher without correction.[10]

Stewart's proposal was made almost a decade ago, but little has been done to implement it. Mary Ann Somervill, in a review of research relating to reading and dialect, could find few studies of alternative approaches to reading instruction for children using nonstandard English, although some of the studies she did find showed positive effects of using a dialectical language experience approach or a transitional use of Black English.[11]

Jean Harber and Diane Bryen have identified a number of unresolved issues relating to Black English and teaching reading. Some of these issues relate to the limitations in current knowledge. There is no clear-cut evidence that children's use of Black English does, in fact, interfere with the reading process, or that any method of minimizing such interference would be more effective than traditional forms of reading instruction. Certainly more needs to be known about the variables that affect reading performance. There are also issues relating to the practicality of implementation. A suitable orthography for Black English still has to be selected and teachers would have to become familiar with it and how it differs from Standard English. Finally, there are issues related to culture. Not all black children speak Black English and many parents and leaders in the black community, as well as educators, are opposed to its use for reading instruction. Harber and Bryen also suggest that the lag in reading achievement among low socioeconomic status

[9] Ibid.

[10] William A. Stewart, "On the Use of Negro Dialect in the Teaching of Reading," in *Teaching Black Children to Read*, eds. C. Baratz and Roger W. Shuy (Washington, D.C.: Center for Applied Linguistics, 1969), pp. 156–219.

[11] Mary Ann Somervill, "Dialect and Reading: A Review of Alternative Solutions," *Review of Educational Research*, 45, no. 2 (Spring 1975), 247–62.

black children may be related to the fact that society does not afford them opportunities in which to use Standard English.[12]

A large number of children in the United States are not native speakers of English. The Spanish-speaking population is the largest group, although many others exist. The Spanish-speaking population includes Mexican-Americans, Puerto Ricans, Cubans, Spaniards, and persons from Latin American countries.

The majority of persons in the United States do not derive from an English-speaking heritage. The Native Americans spoke a variety of tongues, and the original colonists came not only from England, but also from France, Spain, Germany, Holland, and other European countries. The slave trade brought persons who spoke a host of African languages to our country—languages that were systematically eradicated in the United States. Each ethnic group brought its language and culture to America. Often immigrant groups maintained their own cultural heritage and supported schools and newspapers in their own language, as did Native Americans. The Cherokee Indians were highly literate in the early 1800s and maintained their own newspaper.

Until the beginning of the twentieth century it was considered legitimate for schools to instruct children in a variety of languages. Laws were established about this time to require the use of English as the language of instruction. These laws were universal until after World War II. During this time, children were often scolded and even punished for using their native language in school. They were often forced to learn to read in a language they had not yet mastered orally, and were taught all other subjects in English, thus increasing their chances of failure. This English requirement turned many a community's language advantage into a disadvantage. Bilingualism is highly valued in many cultures; however, in the United States it became a detriment.

In recent years there has been a reversal of this trend. The earlier eradication of ethnic differences within the American culture has been seen as a manifestation of a "melting pot" view of equality: all persons must be the same to be equal. Instead, we are now viewing equality within a framework that allows us to accept, and even value, diversity. Programs for bilingual and bicultural children have been established to support them in diverging development and to teach them not only the dominant but their own language and culture as well.

Earlier programs for bilingual children were essentially transitional. Just as Stewart has suggested that beginning reading for the black child might be initiated in Black English, with a later shift to Standard

---

[12] Jean R. Harber and Diane N. Bryen, "Black English and the Task of Reading," *Review of Educational Research*, 46, no. 3 (Summer 1976), 387–405.

English, so these programs were primarily concerned with making it easier for the bilingual child to make the transition to the English language. The child's native language would be used in the earlier phases of instruction, perhaps including reading. But as the child's educational career progressed, instruction in the native language would cease and English would become the only language of instruction.

More recently, programs of bilingual/bicultural education have been proposed and are being implemented. Instruction in all areas of the curriculum is presented in both English and another language. The aim of these programs is the improvement not just of the child's spoken or written English, but also of his ability to use his primary language. In some cases, "two-way" programs of bilingual/bicultural education are being offered, in which native English speakers are also instructed in a second language and culture. For such programs to be successful, the language content must be accurate and both languages used for instruction in a range of subject areas. Most important, the school must have a climate in which all languages and cultures are valued.

Differences in cognitive abilities and style, and in language abilities and style, have been the prime concerns of those involved in programs for poor and minority children. This parallels the prime concern of the schools for intellectual, or academic, and language learning. However, other differences within various subcultural groups might also cause conflict with a school program. Children whose culture values cooperation may be at a disadvantage in a school that values competition. Children whose culture values open displays of affection may be disadvantaged in schools that expect them to mask their feelings. Often the nonverbal communication of children of one culture may be misunderstood by teachers of another culture—thus, the children will be at a disadvantage. In one culture, a child who is scolded might be expected to show compliance with authority by looking downward; such behavior in another culture might indicate rebelliousness. All this suggests that teachers must know a great deal about their students and the families and communities from which they come, if they are to avoid placing them at an excessive disadvantage.

But the question of what to do with a realization of such differences remains. Should bilingual children be helped to strengthen their English language abilities at the expense of other language skills? Should children who demonstrate a specific cognitive style be taught only those subjects that are consistent with that style? Or should children be broadly educated to function in a range of settings with a broad set of language, intellectual, and social repertoires? It is the values of the culture and the demands of the community that play the major roles in determining educational goals for children. Our knowledge of children's attributes should be helpful, however, in designing successful programs to achieve the aims that the culture and community requirements determine.

Another point that should not be forgotten is that these descriptions of group attributes of children are descriptions of central tendencies of populations. Not all children in any subcultural group are cognitively field-dependent, speak in an elaborated or restrictive code, or have an average IQ. Differences are a function of many elements, including the child's urban or rural background, the family's assimilation into the majority culture, and its socioeconomic class. Within any group of children individual differences can also be found that do not relate to group variables. There is no substitute for the teacher knowing in depth the educational strengths and weaknesses of each child in her class and the cultural background and values of his family.

DEVELOPING INTERVENTION TECHNIQUES

One of the major changes that have taken place in our thinking about poverty and discrimination is the general feeling that they are not normal and natural. One area of intervention that has been identified to deal with the consequences of poverty and discrimination is education.

Several general approaches and basic assumptions are common to a number of different projects providing teachers with useful information in teaching poor and minority children. These approaches include providing for the out-of-class needs of the child, changing the community structure, working with parents, working with infants and toddlers, making schools more responsive to children's needs, and developing new educational programs.

PROVIDING FOR THE OUT-OF-CLASSROOM NEEDS OF CHILDREN

Because the problems of poor children range far beyond their difficulty with school work, many programs for them put great emphasis on the provision of noneducational services. A good example of this approach is found in Head Start programs.

The concept of the Child Development Center used in Head Start grows out of the assumption that to alleviate their difficulties, one must deal with all the developmental problems of children, not simply with their academic problems. Attention is given to physical, social, and medical problems. The nutritional program provides a well-balanced lunch, nutritious snacks, and sometimes breakfast, concentrating on the nature of the food served, the way it is served, and the children's eating habits. A conscious effort is made to extend children's experiences with food while taking into consideration individual and cultural food preferences. In health services, children are given medical and dental examinations and may receive needed immunizations and treatment. Social services are also part of the Child Development Center's program, helping the parent deal with the problems of raising children, and with family personal problems. In some instances counseling can be offered the parent directly, or he may be referred to a community agency for help. The community worker acts as liaison between parent and agency, interpreting when necessary and helping to see that the proper aid is given.

The teacher is informed about what is happening to a child's family, even when others are responsible for the provision of these services. Changes in family status may be mirrored by changes in the child's behavior in school. Thus, knowledge of what is happening to the child outside school is helpful in interpreting his in-school behavior and in making the school setting more relevant to him at particular times.

CHANGING THE COMMUNITY STRUCTURE

Most schools are considered extensions of the community, reflecting its structure and values. In some instances, the way educational services are provided can have a significant impact on the community structure.

In the Child Development Group of Mississippi, the organization of preschools grew out of the need to cope with the reality of serving black children in isolated Mississippi communities, often without the cooperation of the local school systems or other governmental agencies. The organization also developed from the belief that the preschool program should reflect the cultural heritage and values of the population served. In each community, CDGM committees were established to develop and support the preschools. These committees first had to find adequate physical facilities to house the program; they often repaired and altered buildings to make them usable. In the absence of trained teachers, a teacher would be elected from the committee, irrespective of formal educational background. Resource persons provided consulting services so that novice teachers trained on the job were helped to deal with educational problems. The materials for learning often grew out of the children's experiences in their particular environment.

The experience of CDGM, though short-lived, led to a concept of early childhood education as community development. In organizing to establish a preschool center, committee members developed skills and strategies that could be used in other areas of community concern. Tom Levin has summed up the basic concepts of this community approach to educating young children:

> Preconceived concepts of child development cannot be imposed upon communities of the poor. The program content must develop as a dynamic of the growth of community understanding.
>
> Any community program will be experienced as an agent of an external power unless it is run by the communities of the poor themselves. The strengths and talents of the poor must be fully utilized in the planning and execution of a significant Head Start program.
>
> Putting up cupboards and wiping up juice cannot be the major contribution of the parents and members of the communities of the poor. This concept of the use of the nonprofessional perpetuates a second-class vocational citizenship and encourages relating to the poor as second class human beings. The nonprofessional community aides must be afforded fully dignified work and full and realistic educational opportunities to achieve professional status.
>
> Head Start must be an instrument for social change. Preschool education for communities of the poor which prepares the child for a better life without mobilizing the community toward social change is an educational and sociological "fraud." New approaches to the solution of the problems of poverty are growing out of the increased awareness of self-power developing within the poverty communities. Professionals must be prepared to reject traditional donor-donee relationships which perpetuate loss of self-worth and consequent resignation to powerlessness.[13]

Underlying these concepts is the assumption that the children's education must be embedded in the community structure in which they are reared, for when parents are alienated or powerless, education cannot take hold in their children.

WORKING WITH PARENTS

> One of the most valuable ways of enhancing the effect of the child development center is to involve the parents actively in the program. Such involvement promotes a closer, more continuous relationship between young children and their parents.[14]

[13] Tom Levin, "Preschool Education and the Communities of the Poor," in *The Disadvantaged Child,* vol. 1, ed. Jerome Hellmuth (Seattle: Special Child Publications, 1967), p. 398.

[14] *Parents Are Needed* (Washington, D.C.: Office of Economic Opportunity, n.d.), p. 8.

This statement, in one of the handbooks of the Head Start program, typifies the concern for involving parents in programs. One of the major contributions of Head Start to concepts of parent programming has been the involvement of poor, often uneducated parents in the decision-making process of the school. The change this creates often has significant effects in both the classroom and the communities in which the center operates.

Parents may be helped to acquire specific teaching skills to use with their children. Ira Gordon, at the University of Florida, has developed procedures whereby persons from the community work with parents of infants in that community. The parents are taught specific parent-child interactions during weekly visits to the homes, and are then expected to use them regularly in playing with their children each day.[15]

The Early Training Program directed by Susan Gray is concerned with helping parents develop a feeling that they can cope with their environment, as well as with providing them specific techniques to use with their children.[16]

The Karnes program at the University of Illinois, and the Nurseries in Cross-cultural Education (NICE) directed by Mary Lane of San Francisco State College, also developed specific home tasks for parents to use weekly with their children. In the NICE project, materials such as books, toys, or games and instructions for their use were made available to the parents.[17] In the Karnes program, parents met weekly, and in the two-hour seminars mothers made educational materials such as puppets, flannel boards, matching and lotto games, and materials for sorting and classifying activities. They were also taught songs and finger-plays. They were expected to use the games, songs, and material with their children throughout the week. Ways to use these materials and weekly successes and failures were discussed with the parents.[18]

Specific techniques for working with parents may vary, but there are common considerations. First, the program must go beyond the experience of the classroom if results are to accrue. In addition, the parents should be considered able to learn specific skills needed for edu-

[15] Ira Gordon, "Stimulation via Parent Education," *Children,* 16, no. 2 (March–April 1969), 57–58.

[16] Susan W. Gray and others, *Before First Grade: The Early Training Project for Culturally Disadvantaged Children* (New York: Teachers College Press, 1966).

[17] Mary B. Lane, "Nurseries in Cross-cultural Education," *Childhood Education,* 45, no. 6 (February 1969), 333–35.

[18] Merle B. Karnes and others, "An Approach for Working with Mothers of Disadvantaged Preschool Children," *Merrill-Palmer Quarterly of Behavior and Development,* 14 (April 1968), 174–84.

cating their children effectively. Finally, concern for improving the relationship between parent and child must be part of a program.

WORKING WITH INFANTS AND TODDLERS

With the realization that the process of education begins at birth, some programs have attempted to focus on this earliest educational period. Often new institutions were developed to meet the needs of the very young. The Parent-Child Center and proposed 4-C programs are illustrations of these attempts. These projects see the family as an integral unit and attempt to evolve new patterns of service for whole families rather than simply for children.[19]

A number of the programs were designed to reach the children through their parents. In the Florida program, discussed above, parent educators visited the home to present educational tasks in which parents could engage their children. Similar programs have been developed elsewhere, generally on an experimental or demonstration basis.

Although there has been little follow-up on the long-term impact of the several infant intervention studies supported in the late 1960s, the evidence has shown that good infant education and day care have no ill effects on children. Such evidence has been used to support the establishment of infant care programs for all populations.

MAKING SCHOOLS MORE RESPONSIVE
TO THE NEEDS OF CHILDREN

A number of books have been published in recent years illustrating the negative educational effects that are a result of practices in some slum schools. It would be difficult for the children attending such schools not to fail because of the deep schism between school and community. The books suggest that in order to effect change, the schools themselves need to be restructured, and that this can take place only when they become responsive to the local community.

To achieve this end, teachers need to be sensitive not only to the needs of children, but also to the needs and demands of parents and communities. New school structures may need to be provided to open communication with parents, giving them a legitimate degree of control in school matters. Some ways of doing this are discussed in chapter 15.

[19] Alice V. Keliher, "Parent and Child Centers—What are They? Where Are They Going?" and Jule M. Sugarman, "The 4-C Program," *Children*, 16, no. 2 (March–April 1969), 63–66, 76–77.

DEVELOPING NEW EARLY
EDUCATIONAL PROGRAMS

As a result of the concern for the education of disadvantaged children, a range of new forms of early childhood education was developed. These program models have been described in detail elsewhere.[20] Some of these programs have narrowly defined goals developed from a "deficit" model of compensatory education. They proposed that if disadvantaged children are shown to be lacking in particular skills, as evidenced by low scores on standardized tests of intelligence, language, or academic achievement, then programs should focus on strengthening those deficit areas. The Behavior Analysis classroom developed by Don Bushell at the University of Kansas is an example of a program designed with these goals in mind. The social and academic skills needed for success in the primary grades were the goals of this program.

Other program models have used broader statements of goals in an attempt to move away from this deficit model. They are concerned with broadly conceived intellectual language goals as well as goals related to problem-solving techniques, self-expression, and self-concept. The Open Education model, sponsored by the Education Development Center, and the Bank Street model are examples of such programs. All the program models within the Planned Variations of Head Start and Follow-Through include parent involvement as part of their design.

In addition to differences in goals, differences in basic assumptions about learning and development characterize the models. A program based on behavior analysis principles views knowledge as a practiced repertoire of behaviors. Program goals are stated as observable behaviors, specified at the beginning of the program. Activities are designed as discrete steps to teach simple behaviors that can be integrated into more complex behaviors, or as successive approximations toward the observable behavior set as the program's goal. Motivation for learning is identified as being outside the individual and, hopefully, under control of the teacher. The program conceives of education as the process of transmitting knowledge from the adult to the child.

A program based upon Piagetian principles, such as the Open Education model, views knowledge as a personal construction of each

---

[20] For example, see Eleanor E. Maccoby and Miriam Zellner, *Experiments in Primary Education: Aspects of Project Follow-Through* (New York: Harcourt Brace Jovanovich, 1970); Mary Carol Day and Ronald K. Parker, eds., *The Preschool in Action: Exploring Early Childhood Programs,* 2nd ed. (Boston: Allyn & Bacon, 1977); and Bernard Spodek, *Early Childhood Education* (Englewood Cliffs, N.J.: Prentice-Hall, Inc., 1973).

child. Different forms of knowledge are learned and validated in different ways. Children go through stages of development in which their ways of gaining and verifying knowledge undergo a significant metamorphosis. In such a program, the teacher creates situations to help children abstract principles from experience and test them in an appropriate manner. The child maintains some control over the learning situation, although it is heavily influenced by the physical and social environment. Thus direct instruction and predetermined behavioral objectives, which are appropriate for a behavior analysis program, would be inappropriate for a Piagetian program.

Some proposed models combine principles and practices from a number of psychological theories, views of knowledge, and conceptions of education. Eclectic programs often attempted to respond directly to the identifiable problems of their target population, sometimes disregarding the causes or social contexts of the problems. All the programs have evolved over time and made changes based upon new research or feedback from implementation sites.

An example of how individual programs have made major changes in theory and method is found in a report on the work of the Southwest Educational Laboratory, designed to teach English as a second language to Spanish speakers. In teaching English, the laboratory moved from what was characterized as a "naturalistic" teaching approach, to a phonetic approach, to a drill approach based upon the Bereiter-Engelmann Method, and finally to an approach designed to help children internalize the system of rules by which they speak and understand language—one that can also be considered a naturalistic approach.[21] While the goals of the program remained constant, each of the approaches tried was vastly different from the others. The shifts in emphasis and methodology reported are extreme; however, other projects made equally extreme changes from their original assumptions as they moved into program implementation and testing.

SELECTING AN APPROPRIATE PROGRAM

With the range of programs available, it is no easy task to select the best one for a particular group of children. Since some programs have been designed for specific populations of children, it might be assumed that a program could easily be matched to a group. Programs in early childhood education, however, have a tendency to become gen-

---

[21] Shari E. Nedler, "Explorations in Teaching English as a Second Language," *Young Children,* 30, no. 6 (September 1975), 480–88.

eralized from narrow populations of children to much broader populations. Historically, this happened to the Montessori Method and the
original nursery school, both originally designed for slum populations.
The same generalization of programs is presently seen in a program
created just a few years back for "deprived" children and now being
suggested for "all children," thus raising serious questions about the
original deficit concept upon which these programs were built.

One way of selecting a program is to look at the available
information on program outcomes. The Planned Variations program has
long-term evaluation built into it and outcome reports have been released
regularly.

In a study of the two-year effects of the various models on
academic achievement, evaluators found that three of the models showed
positive effects when compared with non–Follow-Through control children. These models included a behavioral, an open education, and a
bilingual program. Three others—a behavioral, a responsive, and a developmental program—showed lesser effects. The four programs showing
little or no effects after two years were a behavioral, an open education,
a developmental, and a Piagetian program. Because programs were implemented as totalities, it was not possible to determine if differences
found were a result of curriculum model dimensions, implementation
dimensions, or other factors. In addition, major site effects suggested
that site dynamics and population characteristics did much to mediate
any program effects.[22] It may be that, when evaluating curriculum constructions in actual operation, we need to look at model implementation
procedures and curriculum components as only sets of variables within
educational interactions.

Other, less extensive comparative program evaluations are
also available. Merle Karnes evaluated a Bereiter-Engelmann program,
an Ameliorative program, a traditional program, a Montessori program,
and a community-based program, assessing outcomes based upon IQ and
achievement tests. In the early data collections, the Bereiter-Engelmann
and Ameliorative programs, both highly structured and consistent with
behavioral principles, produced the greatest gains on standardized test
scores, although these differences lessened over time.[23] David Weikart
compared a Bereiter-Engelmann program, a Piaget-based program, and
a traditional program using disadvantaged children. Assessment of out-

---

[22] Marvin G. Cline and others, *Education as Experimentation: Evaluation of the
Follow-Through Planned Variation Model. Vol. IIA: Two Year Effects
of Follow-Through* (Cambridge: ABT Associates, 1975).

[23] Merle Karnes and others, *Research and Development Program on Preschool Disadvantaged Children,* vol. I (Washington, D.C.: U.S. Office of Education, 1969).

comes in this study also used IQ tests as well as observation and rating. The findings showed that children in each program did well, but no one program was superior to any other. Weikart suggests that it is the staff planning and continued supervision of teachers rather than program models that can make an educational difference.[24]

Louise Miller and Jean Dyer studied four preschool programs and their effects on disadvantaged children in Louisville, Kentucky. The programs studied were Bereiter-Engelmann, DARCEE, Montessori, and a traditional early childhood program. Unlike the previously mentioned studies, long-term follow-up evaluation was made. Miller and Dyer summarize their conclusion as follows:

> With respect to program effects: (a) The prekindergarten programs did have different effects on children, both in terms of immediate impact and over a 4-year period regardless of what programs they had later. (b) For all prekindergarten programs, the immediate impact on cognitive variables was in predictable directions, with higher levels of IQ and achievement resulting from programs which emphasized these goals. (c) Those prekindergarten program effects which were still detectable after a 4-year period were in the "noncognitive" areas. (d) The most consistent and beneficial effects of these prekindergarten programs occurred for males. (e) Children from all programs declined in IQ over the 4-year period, but the children from the prekindergarten program which had the greatest immediate impact on IQ and achievement declined most. (f) There were virtually no main effects on noncognitive variables which could be attributed to the kindergarten, first-grade, or second-grade programs. (g) Differential effects on both cognitive and noncognitive variables did result from various combinations of prekindergarten and kindergarten programs.[25]

Miller and Dyer's study demonstrates that different treatments produce different outcomes, although differences may not be large or hold up over time. Differences in noncognitive effects were also found. In addition, this study again points to the need to look at the compounding effects that education after the preschool period has on the outcomes

[24] David P. Weikart, "Relationship of Curriculum, Teaching and Learning in Preschool Education," in *Preschool Programs for the Disadvantaged,* ed. Julian C. Stanley (Baltimore: The Johns Hopkins Press, 1972), pp. 29–67.

[25] Louise B. Miller and Jean L. Dyer, *Four Preschool Programs: Their Dimensions and Effects,* Monograph of the Society for Research in Child Development, Serial No. 162, vol. 40, no. 5–6 (October 1975), 136–37.

of preschool programs, a consideration often not taken into account in evaluations of outcomes of early childhood programs.

One of the problems in using many of the evaluation reports becoming available as the basis for judging the relative merits of these programs is the limitation of the instruments of evaluation used. The same problems with standardized achievement and intelligence tests that cause some groups to be systematically judged deficient keep them from becoming good evaluative devices in these designs. In addition, many of the programs have goals whose attainment cannot be readily assessed with these instruments.

In addition, we do not have reliable information on the long-term effects of such programs on children. Some of the research suggests that the positive effects of these programs fade one or two years after the programs terminate, and children who have been involved in special programs look no different from those who have not. Some researchers are also suggesting that "sleeper" effects may be found. While differences may indeed fade after one or two years, these differences may reappear later in the children's school careers. Research is being conducted to determine the long-term effects of programs on young children, and educators will need to monitor closely the findings of such studies as they appear.

More important, since different programs have different goals, the decision to select a program is as much a function of the judgment that its objectives are worthwhile as that they are attainable. The same considerations that must be raised for programs of early childhood education in general are applicable to programs designed for children with special educational needs, no matter what the basis for those needs.

SUGGESTED READINGS

ABRAHAMS, ROGER D., and RUDOLPH C. TROIKE, eds., *Language and Cultural Diversity in American Education*. Englewood Cliffs, N.J.: Prentice-Hall, Inc., 1972.

BARATZ, JOAN E., and ROGER W. SHUY, eds., *Teaching Black Children to Read*. Washington, D.C.: Center for Applied Linguistics, 1969.

CASTAÑEDA, ALFREDO, and others, eds., *Mexican-Americans and Educational Change*. New York: ARNO Press, Inc., 1974.

DEUTSCH, MARTIN, and associates, *The Disadvantaged Child*. New York: Basic Books, 1967.

GINSBURG, HERBERT, *The Myth of the Deprived Child*. Englewood Cliffs, N.J.: Prentice-Hall, Inc., 1972.

JOHN, VERA P., and VIVIAN M. HORNER, *Early Childhood Bilingual Education.* New York: Modern Language Association, 1971.

MACCOBY, ELEANOR E., and MIRIAM ZELLNER, *Experiments in Primary Education: Aspects of Project Follow-Through.* New York: Harcourt Brace Jovanovich, 1970.

STANLEY, JULIAN C., ed., *Preschool Programs for the Disadvantaged.* Baltimore: The Johns Hopkins Press, 1972.

Bernard Spodek

CHAPTER THIRTEEN

ORGANIZING
FOR INSTRUCTION

Once a teacher has considered the goals and content of the program she wishes to provide her children, she is ready to move on to the next step: planning and organizing the environment and her interactions with children. The teacher should keep in mind the children's interests, capacities, limitations, and aspirations. Building on this, she can begin to plan, using abstract expectations to help establish the concrete reality of what will happen in the classroom.

In the early years, children's autonomy is a goal rather than an established fact. We wish them to become independent, knowing full well that they will continue to be dependent upon the adults in their surroundings well beyond the primary grades. The development of autonomy is important, and is nurtured by teaching children to assume responsibility while still providing them with the security and needed guidance of a knowledgeable adult.

Teachers should give much thought to the activities they arrange. Long-range planning helps the teacher organize classroom activities so they accumulate in such a way as to help the children achieve their educational goals. Short-range planning is required for anticipating the many details of day-to-day teaching. Objectives of this type of planning relate to outcomes of specific instructional strategies. Some may be defined in terms of observable behavior; others will be framed in more general terms. As a result of her planning, the teacher needs to organize her day into some form of activity schedule, deploy the children into manageable groups, and organize her room so that children can make the best use of space, materials, and equipment.

The teacher begins planning even before the children enter

school, often based on a prediction about them. She must gather supplies, materials, and equipment, ordering some well in advance of their use.

Activities and lessons should be planned to provide children with opportunities to grow in responsibility and autonomy. The teacher should know what specific learning opportunities each child is ready for, and help him learn to use resources for learning both in the school and outside. Finally, she must provide opportunities for every child to become a responsible member of the class, learning to use the group and respond to it without having his wishes submerged by it. To do so, he has to develop greater self-control and ways of dealing appropriately with his needs and feelings.

PLANNING

Although there are extreme differences of opinion as to the most effective type of planning, most educators agree that a certain amount of preliminary activity should take place before the teacher engages the children in a program. This is called the preactive period of teaching, mentioned in chapter 1. We cannot evaluate a program's effectiveness unless we assess the achievement of goals. These goals must be thought out for each class and each child.

Although it is possible to purchase fully completed lesson plans that include all the activities, songs, games, and finger-plays for each day of the school year, this is not the most effective type of long-range planning for early childhood education—it cannot take into consideration the learning needs and styles of individual children.

LONG-RANGE PLANNING

Effective long-range planning is vital to a program. Without it, a teacher is apt to pile experience upon experience with no thought as to how they relate to one another. The only concern becomes "how to interest the children and keep them busy for a morning." Long-range plans attempt to identify threads that will tie the various elements of the program together throughout the year. These can be based on conceptual schemes or sets of specific skills. The teacher must then decide the degree to which she expects each child to achieve these goals.

Long-range plans help give a program flexibility. As the children move through the program, the teacher, with a greater awareness of the children, must modify her plans to insure that the program is continually appropriate. Without prior thought and preparation, day-to-day learning activities are necessarily limited.

Long-range curriculum planning is often conceived as a linear process. The teacher will begin by defining the long-range goal, then the prerequisites needed to achieve that goal; the prerequisites again become a set of more approachable goals. In this way a series of curriculum steps are identified. The assumption is that if the child adheres to these steps without any serious deviation, he will achieve the ultimate goal. Progress toward that goal is readily assessable in this design.

Given this plan, the teacher needs to estimate each child's level in relationship to the steps identified to start him at the proper level. An example of this form of curriculum planning can be found in the design of the *Science—A Process Approach* program discussed in chapter 6. While such a form of planning is attractive in that it helps the teacher see the relationship between current and future activities, and between immediate and long-range goals, it also has disadvantages. The program's linearity creates rigidity in her response to children. The only form of individual difference that can be accounted for here is the pace of learning—differences in learning styles or children's interests are disregarded.

Rebecca Corwin, George Hein, and Diane Levin have suggested the idea of *curriculum webs* as a form of nonlinear curriculum construction. A single interest, experience, or activity may take the child's learning in many different directions, leading to a range of activities in science, mathematics, and the arts as he moves from the original experience.

In a curriculum web various curriculum areas—language arts, math, science, social studies, and art—are woven into the study through the range of activities noted that the children engage in over a period of several weeks.[1]

Using the idea of the web, a teacher can design rather sophisticated learning approaches that integrate the various curriculum areas in special ways for each group of children. Children will often be able to cope with advanced learning in this fashion without ever having achieved the necessary prerequisites. If a teacher is sure where she ultimately wants to go with a group of children, she can be flexible in planning and in responding to their interests and concerns, straying from the path when it seems appropriate. A digression may lead to a new set of goals or may end up as a short-cut to a set of previously established goals. She may find that dallying or retracing old steps serves her and the children's purposes well and still leads to a reasonable pace of achievement.

No matter what the design of the program used, it is the teacher's responsibility to modify it so that it is responsive to the needs and interests of her children. No textbook author or curriculum development specialist has personal knowledge of the clients for whom the program is

[1] Rebecca Corwin, George E. Hein, and Diane Levin, "Weaving Curriculum Webs: The Structure of Nonlinear Curriculum," *Childhood Education*, 52, no. 5 (March 1976), 248–51.

developed. Only the teacher, knowing the children—their strengths and weaknesses, their backgrounds, and the school environment—can modify the program to fit them. She may be aware of divergence in the children's language backgrounds and wish to develop some special language experiences for them or order additional material. She may be aware of places in the neighborhood that would provide fruitful field trips for them in relation to a planned unit.

Program planning needs to be flexible enough to be modified on the basis of children's spontaneous interests. The teacher may wish to use her own developing interests and skills as her ideas change through reading books, listening to lectures, or rethinking her educational approach.

The identification of plans for the year allows the teacher to think through her program in advance and gather the necessary resources to carry it through. Films, filmstrips, new books, and supplies may have to be ordered in advance. Trips need advance planning. It is always easier to cancel a trip, postpone a visit, or decide not to use a film than to want to carry out an activity and find schedules filled or materials not available.

SHORT-RANGE PLANNING

Teachers must organize for classroom work on a daily, weekly, or periodic basis as well as on a yearly basis. This planning helps in determining what resources not already obtained will be necessary and gathering them. It is necessary to think ahead so that the tape recorder is available when needed, so that enough copies of a worksheet are available, or so that a particular parent can visit the class to speak about his hobby at the proper critical moment.

The program's daily balance and the relationships that can be established among diverse subject areas should be considered in short-term planning. The teacher needs to look at the ways in which different curriculum areas can be related to one another. Children can write sentence stories that correspond to number facts or that tell about measuring experiences, thus integrating mathematics with language activities. Stories read in a book can be acted out in pantomime or with puppets. Science experiences often require quantification. The possible ways of relating learning areas to one another are endless. Each allows the teacher to extend the child's experience beyond the obvious.

Many school systems expect teachers to file weekly lesson plans. These are supposed to aid the teacher in organizing her teaching in advance, and in developing a progression of learnings so that what a child is taught on one day is related to and may grow out of the experiences of the previous day.

Some educators suggest that each detail in an instructional

program should be worked out in advance, to give the teacher ample opportunity for gathering information about its impact on the children. Though it may be fashionable to talk about teaching in terms of specific learning objectives, early childhood educators have been more concerned with getting children involved in a broad range of activities. If the activities are varied enough and if children can differentiate their own roles in each activity, they will find areas of the program that are related to their needs and that will help them grow. Self-selection within carefully prepared alternatives is an important part of education. Adequate planning can insure the availability of legitimate learning alternatives. The goals of the program need to be different for each child and cannot always be identified far in advance.

DEVELOPING ACTIVITIES

The unit of instruction in nursery school and kindergarten is the *activity*. Unlike the *lesson,* the unit of instruction in elementary school, the activity need not have a formal beginning, middle, and end. In fact, activities are often open-ended, coming to no neatly packaged conclusion, but possibly beginning again at some later time. The activity is not teacher-dominated. The teacher may plan the activity, make materials available, provide time, and even influence its direction, but it is the children who carry the activity forward and, in the final analysis, determine its content. Each activity may be conceived as a solitary unit having no relationship to any other activity, or, more often, be conceived more broadly with a series of interrelated activities. The teacher can relate block construction, music, and story activities to a single theme on the same day, or have a series of activities that continue from day to day in which each is an elaboration of the previous one. Activities may be organized into units or planned so that basic concepts and ideas recur in some cyclical fashion.

The teacher should plan her program so that children are involved in different areas of the curriculum. She must also organize her room so that each activity has the necessary space, materials, and equipment available when needed, and so that several activities can take place simultaneously without interfering with one another.

ARRANGING THE ROOM

Schools for young children are housed in many kinds of facilities. Some classes are held in buildings designed to serve educational purposes, but other facilities were never designed for a school. Church buildings and community centers, even homes or stores may become schools for young children. Sometimes a dual arrangement develops with a school organized in a space for one part of the day or week and another activity housed there at another time. Each arrangement creates different problems for the classroom teacher.

Yet teachers have been able to modify the physical space in which they teach. Suspended ceilings can be installed at reasonable expense if the ceiling is too high, thus improving lighting and acoustical qualities. A low or high platform can be built to allow for dramatic play or provide some private space. Even painting the wall a brighter shade, hanging curtains on the windows, or developing attractive wall displays changes the nature of the physical space.

What a teacher does with her room or outdoor area needs to be the result of careful thinking about how it can help the program along. If all children are expected to be involved in the same activity at the same time, there should be less concern about room arrangements than if individual and small group activities are to be nurtured in the classroom. In an individualized program, for example, the room should be arranged so that the children can work without constant teacher supervision and not interfere with each other's activities.

ORGANIZING PHYSICAL SPACE

Space requirements for classroom use are often prescribed by law. Many states require a minimum of thirty-five square feet per child of classroom space in a nursery school. The same minimum figure is sometimes suggested for space in a primary classroom. Many experts, however, recommend that as much as one hundred square feet per child be available. In addition, from fifty to two hundred square feet per child of outdoor space should be provided for the program. The indoor space should be well lighted, well ventilated, and well heated. Ideally there should be easy access from the classroom to the outdoor play area and to toilet facilities. If the classroom has a door leading directly to a play yard or terrace, the program can flow easily between indoors and outdoors.

ARRANGING THE PRIMARY CLASSROOM

Not too many years ago, primary classrooms had neat rows of single or double desks securely bolted to the floor. While desks are seldom bolted into floors today, they might as well be in many classes. Not all teachers see the organization of furniture and equipment as an instructional tool that might need periodic modification.

Most classrooms provide more informal seating arrangements, but this may not necessarily be advantageous to children. Unfortunately, as Philip Jackson has pointed out, we may have made life harder for many children by placing them in informal situations.[2] The temptation to speak to a peer is lessened when only the back of his head is visible. Seating children face-to-face at tables or in informal semicircles while denying them verbal interaction is a torture we would seldom inflict on adults.

Many primary classrooms have chairs and desks or tables arranged informally, grouped together in horizontal rows, or in a semicircle. Chairs may be grouped in a corner for reading instruction; an easel or a table for art work may be placed in the back of the room. In addition, there may be shelves and closets for storage of books and materials, and a display area for science or nature study.

This type of room arrangement supports a classroom in which the basic mode of instruction is verbal, and in which children are expected to function in a total-class learning situation or in a small group situation under the teacher's supervision. It will not support other kinds of learning as well. Constructions for social studies and children's experiments require other kinds of space and other materials. A teacher who wishes to individualize instruction and provide for self-pacing will also find such an arrangement restrictive. Just as schedules reflect the kind of program a teacher wishes to develop, so does the arrangement of the room.

[2] Philip Jackson, *Life in Classrooms* (New York: Holt, Rinehart and Winston, 1968), pp. 3–37.

James L. Hoot

An activity-oriented primary classroom in which individuals and small groups engage in different activities simultaneously would benefit from a room arrangement closely resembling that of a nursery school or kindergarten. As in the nursery school, activity centers might be used for arts and crafts activities or dramatic play. A library center is a critical resource in the primary classroom. In addition, centers for activities in mathematics, science, social studies, and language arts could be developed.

Because there is so much variation among school facilities and groups of children, it is difficult to suggest an ideal room arrangement. However, there are criteria that teachers can use to judge the balance provided in the room and the degree to which the physical design supports the educational design. Adequate separation between activities is important so that children's work won't be interfered with—both physical and visual boundaries work. Also, noisy and quiet, and messy and neat activities should be separated.

Dorothy Gross suggests that a school's physical form should offer different experiences in space. These experiences can include opportunities for children to move vertically as well as horizontally, and experience large and small as well as open and closed space. There should also be places for children to move in and out of the physical space. Safe conditions for experimentation are important. Variation should be provided in light, color, and sound, and the physical furnishings characterized by both sameness and variety.[3] These guidelines suggest that both variety and flexibility should contribute to the design of a physical facility.

Elizabeth Jones has identified five dimensions that can be used to analyze a physical setting. They can be used in planning the physical facility, and selecting equipment and furniture. The dimensions are:

> Soft–hard
> Open–closed
> Simple–complex
> Intrusion–seclusion
> High mobility–low mobility[4]

Soft areas are places where children can relax to read, listen, talk, or play quietly. Softness can be created by providing a small area rug, some pillows, a stuffed animal, an upholstered or a rocking chair—

[3] Dorothy Weisman Gross, "Equipping a Classroom for Young Children," *Young Children,* 24, no. 2 (December 1968), 100–103.
[4] Elizabeth Jones, *Dimensions of Teaching-Learning Environments* (Pasadena, Ca.: Pacific Oaks College, n.d.), pp. 1–19.

even curtains. Other areas in the room should be characterized by hardness. Hard floor and table surfaces facilitate the cleanup of messy materials and can take the punishment of children's work. Out-of-doors grassy areas are soft—paved surfaces are hard.

Many areas of the room should allow for easy access to materials through open-shelf arrangements, while other areas should allow teachers to store things in closed areas away from children. A balance of open-ended and closed-ended instructional materials for the children is important as well. Closed materials have constrained goals and modes of relationship (picture puzzles); open materials provide unlimited alternatives in their goals and modes of relations (clay). In addition, both simple and complex learning materials should be provided. Simple units have one obvious use and no subparts; complex units allow for manipulation and improvisation, with many subparts.

Areas of the room should be secluded to allow for cozy spaces as well as for activities that need to be separated from the group bustle. Other areas should encourage the intrusion of the teacher and children. As activities in the classroom encourage both high and low degrees of movement, the arrangement should support high and low mobility. Traffic patterns and the mobility required by different activities need to be analyzed for this purpose.

Ideally, the indoor space should be designed to support flexible educational programs. This requires that surfaces be treated with acoustical materials wherever possible. Floors can be carpeted or covered with resilient tiles. Walls should be pleasantly but unobtrusively colored and there should be adequate display space, including bulletin boards and possibly a small chalkboard on the walls. Shades or blinds that both reduce glare and darken the room completely can be provided for windows. A drinking fountain and a sink for activity and cleaning purposes limit the number of trips the children make down the hallway. Bathrooms should be adjacent or close to the classroom.

An adequate classroom also has enough storage and locker facilities for children's coats, boots, extra clothing, and personal belongings, and for the teacher's needs. In addition, considerable and varied storage space should be provided for materials and equipment. Large wheel toys, paper, and art supplies all need different kinds of storage facilities.

ACTIVITY CENTERS

Many early childhood classrooms are organized into activity centers, each of which supports some portion of the program. Though the centers can expand or contract with the needs of the program, most are available throughout the activity period.

In the nursery-kindergarten, these centers can include

Arts and crafts center
Housekeeping center
Blockbuilding center
Manipulative materials center
Library center
Music center
Display center

Activity centers in the primary grades are often designed according to subject matter, for example, a mathematics center, a language arts center, a social studies center, and a science center.

At all levels, centers can be organized around specific themes that provide a focus for activities that might otherwise be supported by different centers. An environmental studies center, a transportation center, in fact, a center that focuses on any topic could be created in a classroom. Materials and activities would be organized in that center for as long as the theme holds the children's interest.

However a center is organized, it should include materials related to its purpose for individual and small group activity, with boundaries clearly defined for the use of those materials that limit the interference of outsiders. Centers should be designed to be easily supervised, and their contents should support independent study and activity. Often activity cards such as those described in chapter 7 can provide direction to children without the teacher continually being present. Sometimes activities can evolve out of planning conferences.

A science activity center, for example, should be a place that has reasonable access to water. It could have a display area for plants and animals and shelves that hold such materials as magnifying glasses, magnets, containers of various sizes, and a range of measuring devices. These might be grouped and placed in shallow trays for continued orderly arrangement. The materials in the center would be changed from time to time as different areas of science are investigated. Seasonal changes might suggest material changes. Open-ended questions can title displays, such as: "Which materials sink and which float?"

A reading center would have books on shelves or racks and comfortable places to read. A rug, some pillows, a soft chair, and straight chairs and a table complement the library shelves. The books would be of different levels of difficulty, about different topics, and include both fiction and nonfiction. Such a center could be augmented by a listening station, a cassette recorder or phonograph equipped with headsets, and a filmstrip or slide viewer.

A dramatic play center includes the traditional housekeeping equipment or has other areas for dramatic play as suggested in chapter 10. A thematic approach focuses play on various aspects of adult and community life. Judith Bender suggests collecting materials for play themes in "prop boxes," each supporting one theme. A prop box for automobile repair play would contain discarded, cleaned auto parts, tools, and other materials. The teacher can create a camping box, a beautician's box, or various other boxes.[5]

OUTDOOR AREA

The outdoor play area should have both a paved surface and a grassy area if possible. The pavement allows children to use tricycles or other wheel toys. In addition, blockbuilding is more satisfying on a flat surface. A covered terrace or patio is desirable as part of the outdoors area so that children can be outdoors even when it rains. Some shade is necessary under any circumstances. There ought to be an area for digging; a dirt area will suffice, but a sand box or pit large enough for a group of children to play in is desirable. Such a sand pit can be built right into the ground, with provisions for drainage and a cover to keep the sand clean and usable. A garden should be set aside for the children's use. They can plant seeds, care for the flowers and vegetables, and reap the harvest at the appropriate season.

Provisions should be made for large-muscle activities and for dramatic play. Permanently installed equipment of wood, steel, concrete, and fiberglass, as well as portable equipment such as packing crates, boards, and ladders are useful. Very young children may be offered simple equipment, then, as they become more competent, more sophisticated and challenging equipment. Adequate storage space in the outdoor area, such as a shed in the play yard or a locker at the door leading to the play area, should be available.

The prevailing climate will determine what kinds of activities will be offered children outdoors and, in turn, how the outdoor play area should be designed. Other considerations include the problems of vandalism and the uses that will be made of the area when school is not in session. The outdoor area should be considered an extension of the classroom, providing opportunity for exciting learning experiences.

---

[5] Judith Bender, "Have You Ever Thought of a Prop Box?" *Young Children,* 26, no. 3 (January 1971), 164–69.

EQUIPMENT AND SUPPLIES

While educational supply houses have much of the equipment needed in activity centers, some can be purchased locally in hardware stores, supermarkets, and discount stores. This is often less expensive, since there is no cost for packaging and shipping. If a teacher buys locally, she should be aware of school policy regarding purchases and the possibility of not paying a local sales tax. However, local purchases do take time and the teacher must judge whether the hours spent offset the money saved. Many schools maintain a petty cash fund to help the teacher make small purchases, such as buying cake mixes for a cooking experience or nails for the woodwork area.

In recent years, the availability of instructional kits for children in the early years has increased. These kits contain a complete set of materials and a teacher's manual all neatly packaged for classroom use. Kits are available for teaching mathematics, reading, language skills, cognitive skills, human relations skills, as well as many other areas of learning. The entire program of a class could be taught through kits.

Some educators feel that kits are extremely useful to teachers. They make available materials that would be difficult to assemble, and insure proper instruction through the structure of activities and directions to teachers. They are often well conceived and well designed; some are even field-tested to determine their effectiveness. Other educators feel that kits are antithetical to good early childhood education. In their opinion, they often lack imagination, contain closed-ended activities, and impose a structure on the classroom, leading to mindless teaching. Also they are often overpriced for the materials provided, can be stereotyped, and provide little evidence that they will teach what they promise.

In fact, there are all kinds of kits: good and poor ones, closed-ended and open-ended ones, kits that nurture children's learning and those that exploit children and provide too narrow a range of activities. The teacher needs to assess each kit as she would assess each set of materials provided in the classroom. Unfortunately, the necessary information for judging kits is often not available. Only one report is available on some of the more popular kits in the field.[6] More such reports would be helpful.

Some schools find that expensive pieces of equipment—such as easels, lockers, climbing apparatus, or storage facilities—may be contributed or built by parents or members of the community. Power tools

---

[6] Educational Products Report #48, *Evaluation of Kits for Early Learning* (New York: Educational Products Information Exchange Institute, 1972).

needed for their construction may be borrowed or rented locally. A local sewing center will often lend sewing machines to allow mothers to make doll clothes, sheets for resting cots, or curtains. Bringing the parents together for project work has advantages other than saving money on equipment, for as they meet and work together, they will be knit into a group. They will also have an investment in the school, which might bring them closer to school personnel. Care must be taken that parents do not feel exploited by such work sessions, however.

Many useful learning materials do not have to be bought. The teacher can salvage material that would otherwise be thrown away or even involve children and their parents in this process. Beans or pebbles can be used for counting as easily as can carefully designed mathematics material. Castoff clothes make excellent additions to a dramatic play area. The chassis of a discarded radio, a broken alarm clock, castoffs from repair shops, buttons, egg cartons, and numerous other materials are useful in an early childhood classroom.

CRITERIA FOR SELECTING EQUIPMENT AND SUPPLIES

In selecting equipment and supplies, teachers may use a number of criteria.

COST. The amount of money spent for an object is an important consideration. Price alone, however, is often a false yardstick to value. Some less expensive items will not be as satisfactory for their intended purpose as would more expensive items. Often the more expensive item will last longer and in the final analysis cost less. In any event, the cost of an item has to be balanced with the benefits provided.

RELATIONSHIP TO THE SCHOOL PROGRAM. Educational equipment illustrated in catalogues may be more fascinating to the adult than to the child. Items may be interesting but unrelated to the program. Teachers should select materials and equipment that will be interesting to children and help further their educational goals.

QUALITY AND DURABILITY. There are many elements to consider in judging the quality of a piece of equipment. Equipment adequate for home use is often inappropriate for school. While design is important, the way it is executed is equally important. Judgments about the kind and quality of materials used—the care with which the equipment is fabricated, the way pieces are joined, the type of finish applied—go into determining quality. Often equally priced pieces of equipment are available from more than one supplier, but a careful look at the finished product will tell the watchful teacher that one is a better bargain than the other.

SAFETY. Because of the vulnerability of young children, this criterion is of special concern. School equipment should not have sharp edges or protrusions. Finishes should be nontoxic as well as durable. For very young children, materials should be large enough to prevent swallowing. If the equipment is for climbing, it must be strong enough to take the children's weight without collapsing, and have steps close enough together so that they can be managed easily. While most equipment and materials designed for young children meet safety requirements, this is not universally true. In addition, teachers and parents often provide young children with play equipment originally designed for older children—here, caution is important.

FLEXIBILITY OF USE. Since both budget and space are limited in most programs for young children, teachers should consider equipment that can be used in a variety of ways and situations. Such equipment will need to be stored less often and may replace highly specific equipment. In the dramatic play area, equipment that has few details can often be used most flexibly, for the child's imagination turns a simple box into a rocket ship or a covered wagon. Much equipment, of course, is designed for specific purposes and teachers should not overlook these.

Many educational supply houses throughout the United States manufacture and/or sell equipment and supplies for early childhood educational programs. These firms often have regional offices. Their catalogues or displays at conferences can help a teacher select proper equipment and materials for her classroom. Some of the traditional textbook publishers have also developed kits containing materials in addition to books.

Most teachers have difficulty in selecting appropriate materials and equipment and deciding which manufacturer offers the highest quality at the most moderate price. Unfortunately, there are no *Consumer Reports* for this kind of equipment. It is helpful to ask the advice of teachers who have had some experience using specific equipment.

A set of criteria developed by the Educational Products Information Exchange (EPIE) Institute for evaluating educational materials for all levels is useful at the early childhood level as well.

CRITERION CHECK LIST[7]

I. The producer
   A. Credentials

---

[7] Education Product Report #54, *Improving Materials Selection Procedures: A Basic "How To" Handbook* (New York: Education Products Information Exchange Institute, 1973), p. 13.

      1. Author's education and experience

      2. Reputation—public and local

   B. Claims for the material

      1. Backed by trustworthy evidence

      2. Based entirely on "expert opinion"

II. Administrative requirements

   A. Schedule

      1. Fit to school year organization, including possibility for adaptation

      2. Fit to school day organization, including possibility for adaptation

      3. Lead-in time needed for pilot use, training, etc.

   B. Budget

      1. Initial cost, for materials and training

      2. Ongoing costs, for expendables, replacements, additional training, etc.

   C. Personnel

      1. Additional specialized needed

      2. Additional nonspecialized needed

      3. Schedule and budget for training as required

   D. Space

   E. Legal constraints

III. Curricular requirements

   A. Age, grade, ability level

   B. Subject matter content

      1. Selection and arrangement

      2. Scope

      3. Sequence of presentation

      4. Point of view, including treatment of minorities, ideologies, personal and social values, sex roles, etc.

      5. Media of presentation

      6. Necessity for supplementary materials to complete presentation

IV. Pedagogical requirements

   A. Instructional setting

      1. Suitability of socioeconomic, geographic, ethnic orientation

      2. Student interest, achievement, learning style

      3. Teacher characteristics

      4. Suitability of physical space for recommended implementation

      5. Fit of recommended presentation into standard schedule

   B. Teachers

      1. Necessary background

      2. Pedagogical style

      3. Teaching schedule and load and other school responsibilities

      4. Provision for special training

     5. Necessary for supplementary personnel
       a. Professional
       b. Lay
  C. Methodology
     1. Fixed or flexible?
     2. Specified in detail or implied in materials?
     3. Compatible with what view of how learning takes place?
     4. Pupil-centric or teacher-centric?
     5. Individual, small-group, large-group, or some combination?
     6. If individual, programed?
     7. Heuristic or didactic?
     8. etc. . . .
V. Evaluation requirements
  A. Method for assessing outcomes of instruction and learning
     1. Self- or teacher-administered and scored?
     2. Descriptive or objective?
     3. Norm or criterion as reference?
     4. Diagnostic?
     5. Prescriptive?
     6. Frequency of measurement and reporting
  B. Learner verification of effectiveness
     1. Producer's empirical evidence
       a. Developmental testing reports
       b. Reports on field testing of final form of materials
       c. Evidence of collection of feedback on materials in use
     2. Reports from other schools
       a. Statistical
       b. Anecdotal
       c. Direct, or through organization like EPIE
     3. Results of local pilot use
       a. Statistical
       b. Systematically observed
       c. Collected by questionnaire
         i. From teachers
         ii. From students
       d. Anecdotal
         i. From teachers
         ii. From parents
         iii. From students
         iv. From other sources
     4. Results of follow up during operational use
       a. Statistical

   b. Systematically observed
   c. Collected by questionnaire
      i. From teachers
      ii. From students
   d. Anecdotal
      i. From teachers
      ii. From parents
      iii. From students
      iv. From other sources

A number of guides for the selection of equipment for early childhood education are available. These include lists in textbooks and pamphlets. Some useful lists are found in the following material:

Association for Childhood Education International, *Selecting Educational Equipment for School and Home.* Washington, D.C.: The Association for Childhood Education International, 1976.

Evans, Anne Marie, "How to Equip and Supply Your Prekindergarten Classrooms," in *Early Childhood Education Rediscovered,* ed. Joe L. Frost. New York: Holt, Rinehart and Winston, 1968, pp. 567–76.

Foster and Headley, *Education in the Kindergarten,* 3rd ed. New York: American Book Co., 1969, chapter 7.

Heffernan and Todd, *The Kindergarten Teacher.* Boston: D.C. Heath, 1960, pp. 59–65.

Project Headstart, *Equipment and Supplies: Guidelines for Administrators and Teachers in Child Development Centers.* Washington, D.C.: Office of Economic Opportunity, n.d.

Although all classrooms present differing needs for materials and equipment, it is helpful to know generally what would best fit into the classroom.

FURNITURE

Furniture for an early childhood classroom should be movable and durable, scaled to the children's size. Tables and chairs should be of varying heights since children in any age group vary in size. Tables of different shapes might also be included for many purposes. The same tables can be used for both art work and eating. Special tables might be designated for use in the doll corner, the housekeeping area, the library area, and for display purposes. Trapezoidal tables are quite flexible in that they can be grouped and arranged to create many different shapes. If chairs and tables are stackable, they can be stored in a corner of the room when not in use.

A teacher might wish to have some furniture for her own use: a desk, a couple of chairs, and a file cabinet. If she is provided with office space adjacent to her room (possibly part of a cloakroom) she will not have to sacrifice precious classroom space. Or, she can use an unobtrusive portion of the room to keep her planning materials, records, personal supplies, and first-aid kit.

If young children stay in school a full day, they need cots for rest. Lightweight aluminum cots with canvas or plastic covers that stack for easy storage can be purchased. These are not necessary for children in a half-day program. Children of nursery-school age may rest on mats or rugs stretched out on the floor. Although many kindergartens provide a rest period, formal rest is often unnecessary and substituting an informal quiet activity is advantageous. Such a substitute not only improves the children's tempers and lowers the number of disciplinary problems, but also eliminates the need to provide storage space for mats or cots.

SCHEDULING

A schedule allocates time for each day's activities. Children learn to anticipate future events because of the regularity of daily occurrences. In the nursery school and kindergarten, time allotments are made for activities. Classroom learning may be organized into time periods by subject in the primary grades.

Activities are organized in large blocks of time. The range of alternatives available for the children during the activity periods supports a degree of individuality and allows a variety of outcomes to be planned for different children.

Flexibility is necessary in any schedule that is developed by the teacher. On one day conversations with children may stretch to forty-five minutes, although only twenty minutes have been scheduled. On other days, five minutes may seem too long. A teacher might wish to devote a whole day to a craft project and simply not include a story or music activity. Balance over a long time needs to be considered. Children do not have to be involved in every area of the school curriculum on every day.

An alternative to scheduling time into periods would use some variation of the *integrated day.* If a teacher is concerned with individualizing instruction and developing autonomy in the children, she can plan many program strands to operate at the same time so that children can move from one curriculum area to another at their own pace. Such an organization limits the amount of waiting children do in class, because they make optimal use of their school time in individual learning opportunities. Such organization could also be an aid to integrating school subject matter, for artificial time barriers could be lessened considerably or done away with entirely.

 Although teachers who have not organized their class into large blocks of time might be concerned about providing children with unstructured time, much of the success of this type of scheduling rests on preparing the children to function autonomously. This requires helping them develop skills of independent learning. Some teachers may prefer to retain a structured portion of the day in addition to providing some time for independent activity in an unstructured block of time. Such a period might include opportunities for independent reading, project work, craft activities, and individual research, as well as opportunities to complete elective assignments in various interest areas. Teachers should work with children in joint planning before the activities begin and in evaluation sessions at the end of the period.

James L. Hoot

TRANSITIONS

While teachers generally plan carefully for the content of activity periods, the problems that arise in a classroom often occur between these periods. The demands that children clean up, line up, move from one area to another, or wait can create difficulties. Some children finish their cleanup well ahead of others, and some are naturally less patient than others. Often, scheduling must rely on the movement of other classes, which may be late.

Elizabeth Hirsch suggests that a number of factors contribute to difficulties around transition time. These include boredom, the insistence on conformity, the absence of a future orientation in some children, the absence of clearly defined tasks, and a possible fear of failure.[8] Anticipating the problems of transition periods and planning for them can ease potential difficulties. The teacher can quickly learn which children will have problems during transitions and support them particularly. Making a game of cleanup makes it seem less overwhelming. Giving children specific directions, and seeing that the requirements of the transitions are not beyond their capabilities, also help. A store of short games, stories, poems, and finger-plays fills unanticipated periods of waiting. Most important, the teacher's sense of calm and order will help the children overcome problems that do arise.

ORGANIZING PEOPLE

Placing fifteen, twenty, or more children of like age into a single room for many hours each day creates problems. There is a constant conflict between the needs of the individual and the group. That we teach children in groups rather than individually suggests we are concerned with conformity as well as individuality, for to a great extent group pressure when coupled with the teacher's goal-directedness supports conforming behavior.

We expect young children to give up the natural rhythm of their daily activity when they enter school. We demand that they all come to school at the same time, sit in place for the same period of time, take care of bodily functions at prescribed periods, eat and play together at specific periods, and learn at the same pace. We expect all

---

[8] Elizabeth S. Hirsch, *Transition Periods: Stumbling Blocks of Education* (New York: Early Childhood Educational Council of New York City, n.d.), pp. 4–7.

children to "behave properly" irrespective of their earlier patterns of behavior or the particular expectations of the outside world. Some degree of conformity is necessary for a child to get on in the world and is a form of acculturation, but how *much* conformity is really necessary is an open question.

Many educators have been aware of the inherent conflict between the individual and the group in school and have looked for ways to lessen it. Some children learn faster than others and are more competent in certain areas. Children have different styles, different interests, and need different kinds of learning supports. To ignore these differences and to gear all teaching and classroom practices to the average, expecting the other children somehow to accommodate, limits children and punishes them for being different.

Many techniques have been used to cope with this conflict. One way is to provide a broad range of activities for children to choose among. A portion of the day may be assigned to an indoor or outdoor activity period during which children may select from structured or unstructured tasks and may change tasks at will. Only during short periods of the day are they required to be with the group—for "routine" activities, such as snacks or rest, or for large group instructional activities like music, storytelling, or discussion times.

Too few early childhood classes provide an adequate range of choice. Conformity to group activity and a limited range of learning opportunities too often characterize these classes. In many classrooms, there may be no choice. Continual assignment of the child to prescribed activities may heighten the conflict between group and individual.

GROUPING

Some educators have proposed to lessen the conflict by assigning children to classes with a range of differences. Traditionally, the criterion for assigning children has been academic achievement or reading performance. Although such classes might be more comfortable for teachers who work only with the total class, they present certain problems for the children. Narrowing the range of differences in one area of behavior may have no effect on the range of differences in other areas of behavior or performance. The conflict between the group and the individual still exists. In addition, the placement of a child in a homogeneously grouped classroom creates an expectation of performance for him that may become a self-fulfilling prophecy. A child assigned to a slow class (children know which groups are considered slow no matter how teachers camouflage the fact) often performs according to what is expected of that group. This is probably the least satisfactory way of organizing children.

While homogeneous grouping is advocated by some teachers and parents, there is no evidence that it increases children's learning in any appreciable way. The present trend seems to be toward greater heterogeneity in grouping children. With the proposal to mainstream children with special educational needs into regular classes, a broader variety of educational abilities in each class may soon be the norm.

INSTRUCTIONAL GROUPING

One way of dealing with individual differences often used at the primary level is grouping children for instruction. The organization of a classroom into three reading groups, each representing a limited range of performance levels, is typical. The teacher can work with one group at a time, listening to children read, holding phonics lessons, or engaging them in other tasks. While the teacher is working with one group, other children are engaged in seatwork activity. Using a team approach or individualizing instruction may limit the amount of occupational seatwork needed, since more than one instructional group can be dealt with at one time.

INDIVIDUALIZED INSTRUCTION

Individualized instruction tasks keep the goals of education constant but allow children to move through the same tasks at different paces. The Individually Prescribed Instruction (IPI) program fits into this model. Work is broken down into small steps and children are given individual instructional tasks based on diagnostic tests. They complete work sheets, are tested, and upon evidence of successful attainment, move on to the next set of tasks. All children move through the same series of tasks, but at their own pace. Opportunities are provided for children to skip sets of tasks if they evidence competence in the area.

IPI uses the model of programmed instruction in its attempt to individualize instruction. However, only the pace is individualized. An activity-oriented class individualizes other aspects of instruction. The classroom can become a workshop, allowing children to pursue different enterprises. Goals are different for each child, as are the means used to attain the goals. Children can also be given greater opportunities to feed their interests into the classroom situation or to vary the ways in which they could achieve similar goals, thus changing the teacher's program.

Another way of dealing with individual differences in the classroom suggested by many educators is to do away with the age-grade organization of the school. By increasing the differences in any one classroom, the teacher must look for new solutions. She cannot possibly have the same expectations for all children. In addition, less formal methods of instruction are possible and greater individualization may result. Children can help and teach one another, age-grade expectations are lessened, and the children's own performance capabilities become the basis for judgments about programs.

William Schrankler has identified several advantages of family grouping, as multi-aged grouping is sometimes called. The multi-aged class represents a microsociety that provides an enriched intellectual community for young children. It eliminates age-grade lines and thus allows for cross-age tutoring. It also lengthens the time period for teacher-parent and teacher-child interactions beyond a single term or year. In studying children in multi-aged and unit-aged classes, Schrankler found that a positive relationship existed between multi-age grouping and affective factors, including the child's self-esteem and his positive attitude toward school. There were no differences in academic achievement between children in the two types of classes.[9]

Multi-age grouping, like any organizational scheme, presents the possibility for increasing the individualization, partially by breaking down barriers created by tradition. What teachers do with this potential becomes the crucial factor in supporting children's learning. In some cases, nongrading has meant replacing one criterion for grouping (age) with another (possibly reading achievement), with no change in classroom practice. This is an unfortunate distortion of the principle. In the nongraded approach, the individual differences in the classroom are viewed as an asset. If children are considered learning resources, then increasing the range of children in a school unit can increase the range of learning resources available to each child.

Although each method of dealing with individual differences has been described independently, each can be combined with any number of others to improve the match of instruction to children. Each arrangement requires a different way of thinking through the classroom

---

[9] William Schrankler, "Family Grouping and the Affective Domain," *Elementary School Journal,* 76, no. 7 (April 1976), 432–39.

organization. The layout of the physical facilities can enhance or thwart small group activities. The availability of materials and equipment is also a concern. The teacher does not need a full set of textbooks in an individualized program. On the other hand, a greater *variety* of materials and equipment must be available that the children can use independently.

ORGANIZING ADULTS

Adults play many roles in the education of young children. School principals and center directors assume primarily administrative responsibilities, although they may do some teaching. Head teachers, teacher-directors, and classroom teachers assume primary responsibility for classroom planning and teaching. Teacher aides, assistants, and volunteers may also be involved in teaching as well as supportive activities. Volunteers might be resource persons who are invited into the classroom briefly or part of the ongoing teaching staff, as in many cooperative nursery schools. In addition, new roles are being defined for persons in early childhood education, such as the Child Development Associate,[10] and the Early Childhood Educator.[11] While the titles may be new, the responsibilities are those that have traditionally been met by persons working in the field.

Others in the school community also contribute to the education of young children. Each staff member who has contact with the children leaves his imprint. The cook, custodian, bus driver, and others not hired primarily for educational services still influence the education of children. While the teacher cannot be responsible for or supervise all the encounters the child has with school personnel, she needs to be aware of them, utilizing them to integrate learnings from many sources. It is the teacher's responsibility to orchestrate the experiences children have in school, maximizing their learning possibilities. She must coordinate the use of volunteers and spend some time training them and providing an orientation to the school.

Parents participating in a nursery school, for example, must be made aware of the school's philosophy, routines, techniques of teaching, and methods of control. Their particular roles and responsibilities must be delineated. Often parents are expected to do different things in

---

[10] Jennie Klein and C. Ray Williams, "The Development of the Child Development Associate (CDA) Program," *Young Children,* 28, no. 3 (February 1973), 139–44.

[11] Millie Almy, *The Early Childhood Educator at Work* (New York: McGraw-Hill, 1975).

school than they would at home, or do the same things differently. The reasons for expectations should be explained, and practice sessions for parents might help.

Some educators have advocated formal arrangements of adults with different responsibilities for teaching children in school. A differentiated staffing pattern is a way of using and rewarding teachers with different skills and expertise. Such a pattern, according to Clinton Boutwell, Dean Berry, and Robert Lungren, has five characteristics: a formal system of shared decision making, formal provisions for self-renewal, performance-based organizational roles, formal provisions for professional self-regulation, and a flexible use of human and physical resources.[12] Teams created this way lessen teachers' isolation and could lead to flexible teaching arrangements.

Nursery classes that use a head and assistant teacher in each classroom represent one type of team. A team may be created in a kindergarten or primary classroom by adding a teaching aide—this allows two individuals to work together and facilitates splitting the classroom in various ways, so that adults can attend to several individuals or groups at all times.

A more extensive team can be created by merging classes of children into larger instructional units, allowing school resources to be deployed more flexibly. Some activities require little teacher supervision and a teacher might have responsibility for more children than would normally be found in a self-contained classroom during these activities. Other learning situations might be better organized as small group activities, independent activities, or as conferences. Members of a teaching team have greater freedom to work with individuals and small groups, specializing their functions to a certain degree.

A larger instructional unit can also make good use of diversified team members, because all teachers do not have to be equivalent in competency or responsibility. Thus, a master teacher and a fledgling teacher have opportunities to learn from each other. Part-time teachers can be incorporated into the team, adding additional skills—technical or clerical. Teaming eliminates the problem of teacher isolation, for each teacher constantly interacts with others. A team organization requires a different type of physical facility than the "egg carton" school one generally finds if it is to be optimally effective.

[12] Clinton E. Boutwell, Dean R. Berry, and Robert E. Lungren, "Differentiated Staffing: Problems and Prospects," in *Differentiated Staffing,* ed. Mary-Margaret Scoby and A. John Fiorino (Washington, D.C.: Association for Supervision and Curriculum Development, 1973), pp. 13–18.

In creating a large instructional unit, care must be taken that it does not become so large as to overwhelm the child. Especially with young children, there is the danger of creating a mass in which strong relational bonds between adult and child and between child and child are submerged. Large groups also tend to be handled in a more bureaucratic fashion than small groups. Although there are no reliable rules about the optimal size of a group, some school systems and licensing agencies have established guidelines. These judgments should be made in relation to educational goals, facilities available, teacher competency, and basic conceptions of education, in addition to the absolute number and ages of children involved.[13]

A teacher who wishes to support independent learning must provide a classroom that allows children to behave freely and reasonably. In a physical setting with interest centers, children can move into areas that support a particular activity in which they are involved rather than being constrained at a single desk for most of the day. It is important that teachers realize that the test of a good room arrangement is the degree to which it helps children achieve the goals of the program. Teachers should experiment with room settings and modify them regularly so they fit supportively into a dynamic learning situation.

SUGGESTED READING

BAKER, KATHERINE READ, *Ideas that Work with Children*. Washington, D.C.: National Association for the Education of Young Children, 1972.

Bits and Pieces. Washington, D.C.: Association for Childhood Education, 1967.

JONES, ELIZABETH, *Dimensions of Teaching-Learning Environments*. Pasadena, Ca.: Pacific Oaks College, n.d.

KRITCHEVSKY, SYBIL, and ELIZABETH PRESCOTT, with LEE WALLING, *Planning Environments for Young Children: Physical Space*. Washington, D.C.: National Association for the Education of Young Children, 1977.

MATTERSON, E. M., *Play and Playthings for the Preschool Child*. Baltimore, Md.: Penguin, 1967.

---

[13] See Bernard Spodek, "Staffing Patterns in Early Childhood Education," in *Early Childhood Education*, 71st Yearbook of the National Society for the Study of Education, ed. Ira J. Gordon (Chicago: University of Chicago Press, 1972).

Scoby, Mary-Margaret, and A. John Fiorino, *Differentiated Staffing.* Washington, D.C.: Association for Supervision and Curriculum Development, 1973.

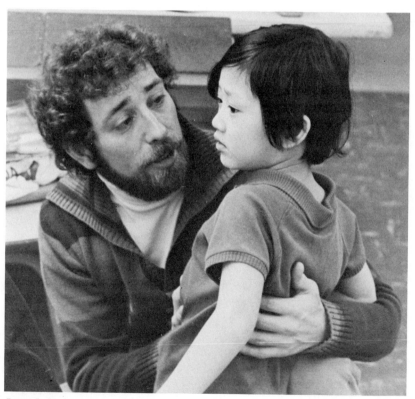

James L. Hoot

CHAPTER FOURTEEN

WORKING
WITH CHILDREN

One of teacher's first concerns is to induct the child into the ways of the school. For many children, entrance into the kindergarten or primary grades is just one of many school beginnings and, since schools are more alike than different, they have experience upon which to base their expectations. For others, the first school day may be the first experience away from home and the teacher may represent the first authority figure other than parents to whom the child has had to relate. In any event, the beginning of school is always fraught with some fear, for the new situation raises a set of questions in the child who does not yet know exactly what to expect. School beginnings, therefore, require special consideration.

BEGINNING SCHOOL:
NURSERY-KINDERGARTEN LEVEL

The child's introduction to school often begins many months prior to the first school day. Many schools provide time in the spring for a visit by children who will be entering that fall. They may be brought into the classroom individually or in small groups, either when the class is in session or after school. They become familiar with the physical layout and are allowed to explore the workable materials and equipment, most of which will be there when they return in September. Most of all, they have a chance to meet the staff with whom they will later interact. The teacher in charge of the class visited will probably be their teacher.

The parents are also given a chance in this orientation to find out about the school's expectations and routines. This allows them to prepare their child for his formal entrance to school.

Figure 14-1   Student Information Form

Name of child _____ Sex _____

Name used at home _____ Date of birth _____

Does your child have any health problems that need special attention in school? _____
_____

Does your child suffer from allergies? (please list) _____
_____

       Is your child toilet trained?   Yes _____ No _____
       Likely to have accidents?   Yes _____ No _____
       Does your child need help in toileting? Yes _____ No _____
       Need help in dressing?   Yes _____ No _____

Does your child have any specific need of which the teacher should be aware? (please specify) _____
_____
_____

Has your child previously attended nursery school? _____

Has he had experience away from parents? _____

Have there been separation problems? (describe) _____
_____

Does your child have any favorite activities? (describe) _____
_____

Are there discipline problems at home? (describe) _____
_____

What methods of behavior control are used at home? _____
_____

Teachers like to gain information about their new children's backgrounds and needs. Conferences with parents are helpful but cannot always be arranged. A student information form, filled out by parents and returned before or when school begins, provides much information. A sample of such a form is presented in figure 14-1. Different schools, however, may need to know different things about their students.

Most children enter school in the fall. Our American tradition requires that they all come to class about the same time, and this mass arrival creates several problems for the teacher. For one thing, they are ignorant of the resources available to them and the procedures they are to follow. In addition, they all have highly individual reactions to this new experience. Some find the new school setting stimulating and exhilarating and, rising to the challenge of a new environment, immediately plunge into exploration, testing every facet of the new situation. Other children find the newness of the situation frightening and withdraw from contact with people or things.

In addition to being aware of the children's reactions to the new school situation, the teacher should be sensitive to the parents' reactions. Some parents wish to leave the child immediately, thus freeing themselves for independent pursuits. Some feel guilt at the sense of freedom and relief they may be experiencing. Others react hesitantly to "giving up" their children. That their children can function independently of them is hard for many parents to take. At times, children's attendance in school is also a sign of the parents' aging, a hard realization to face for many in our society.

If the child has recently moved to the community, an increasing occurrence, adjustment problems may be compounded, because the child must deal with additional uncertainty. And the child who finds himself bused from his neighborhood to a strange, possibly hostile one, has other problems.

This is the situation with which the teacher must deal in her first days. She may add additional problems to the situation herself. A new teacher, unsure of herself and her school, finds the first day more anxiety-provoking than does the experienced teacher who is firmly entrenched in a familiar situation. But to all teachers, the sense of novelty and uncertainty about a new set of children and a new class continues to produce anxiety. Thus, the beginning of each year may generate feelings in the teacher that closely parallel those of the children.

Many teachers find that the transition is eased for them as well as the children if the school term begins with some form of staggered enrollment, in which only a part of the group comes to school for the first week. Teachers often have only one-third of the class attend each day. The three groups may alternate attendance during the first few days, or the children may come cumulatively. The former plan creates a situation in which no one child attends any more days than another child. But children who come to school on the first day and then are kept out for the next two may feel strange when they return.

Starting the school year with a small group each day allows the teacher to give each child the attention he may need, insuring his awareness of school procedures. It also lessens the shock the child would have of working each day within a large group of other children.

Many of the problems of induction are significantly lessened in a nongraded setting. With only a few children beginning school each year, most do not require a formal induction for they are already familiar with the teacher, room, and total school situation. In addition, the more experienced children can help in orienting the younger and newer ones, thus simplifying matters for the teacher. Since she knows many of her children from the previous year, her beginning plans can be more effective; relationships are already established and need only to be extended.

Children do not naturally know how to behave in school nor do they come aware of the rules and regulations. The teacher must make a conscious effort to acquaint them with unfamiliar routines and procedures, and teach them appropriate behavior as if it were a school subject. She can go through a typical schedule, perhaps in simplified form, during these first days. At each transition and before each set of new routines, she talks to the group and tells them what to anticipate next. She demonstrates new routines such as cleaning up after a work period or getting ready for dismissal. One demonstration will not suffice, for the children will need many repetitions before they master routines and feel comfortable with school expectations. Keeping a degree of constancy in the schedule helps them learn an established routine and adds a degree of predictability to the school day. This provides some security for the child; once established, it is a base from which he can operate rather than a system to which he should slavishly adhere.

While teachers are giving attention to the children, they should not forget the parents. In some schools, the parents are expected to leave their children outside the door on the first day and immediately depart. However, it is becoming a standard practice in many nursery schools for parents to bring the new children to school the first day and stay with them if possible. The child need not feel that he is being abandoned or that the school is entirely separate from his home life, for his parent provides a transition. The teacher may begin separation by having the parent leave for a short period of time for a cup of coffee. Usually the child can be weaned from his parent relatively quickly. It may take longer to wean the parent.

BEGINNING SCHOOL:
THE PRIMARY GRADES

The teacher in the primary grades may not have to deal with the problems of separation. Generally, primary children have been to school before and have some idea of what to expect. The primary teacher has many similar concerns, however. As early as possible she should establish classroom routines and organize school life, posting a daily schedule and adhering to it as much as possible. She should also introduce certain procedures of group life. Ways of getting her attention, using materials in the classroom, gaining access to the bathroom, and moving to the outdoor area, lunchroom, or other places in the school need to be presented, explained, discussed, and practiced. In addition, children need to learn what resources are available and how they can be used. Even though they may have had similar experiences in earlier years, each teacher has some different procedures that require them to learn new routines. If operating procedures are clearly communicated to the children, there is a greater chance that they will be followed.

In addition to acquainting children with school procedure, the teacher must get to know them and establish positive relations with each one. Teachers should also become familiar with the children's records, which tell about academic progress and other aspects of school experiences. The meaning of entries in this vital record must be interpreted, for not all teachers have the same expectations of children or the same interpretations of their behavior. A teacher who is aware of the expectations of the child's former teacher can make better use of records in her own assessments.

Academic work can be assessed in a variety of ways. The teacher probably should give informal inventories or tests in the area of reading and mathematics. She may also wish the children to do some writing in class so that writing skill and ability to communicate may be ascertained. Group discussions and short conferences allow her to make judgments about the children's oral language abilities, and gather information about social abilities, interests in school, abilities to handle conflict and deal with frustration, and many other important things. A number of formal and informal evaluation techniques are discussed in chapter 16. At all times the teacher should be aware of the need to make only tentative judgments, for children do change in their relationships as they become familiar with new people and new surroundings. It would be unfortunate to set up a series of expectations based only upon the limited and not too reliable information the teacher can gather in the first few days of school.

During these early days, the teacher and the children often

participate in a series of interactions that allow them to test each other and establish a balanced relationship that may last for the entire school year. Just as the teacher is testing the children in the first few days, they are also testing her. Each child soon finds his place in the classroom social structure, establishing his own identity and set of relationships with the other children and the teacher. Although many friendships and animosities are carried over from earlier years, the fact that most children are in a new class with a new teacher means that a fresh set of balances must be created each fall.

ORGANIZING THE CHILDREN

The teacher can organize the classroom to reflect the children by incorporating their interests into its design and displaying their work. The children, also, can assume much responsibility for their classroom.

Each child needs a place he can call his own. The nursery-kindergarten child is usually provided with a cubby or locker, ostensibly to keep his wraps, but sometimes used as a place of refuge. He has no similarly assigned work space. The primary child may also have a locker for his clothes or simply a hook in a cloakroom or closet. In most classes, he has a desk at which he spends most of the day and does most of his

Bernard Spodek

work. In an activity program, individual desks may be eliminated and the child is expected to work in many areas, moving around the room as he changes his activity. Though a personal desk becomes unnecessary, every child needs a place of his own for his treasures: a drawer in a cabinet, part of a shelf, or even a plastic stacking vegetable bin.

Children need to assume responsibility both for their own space, and for the rest of the room, seeing that things are neat and uncluttered. Early in the year, the teacher should try to instill a sense of responsibility in each child. Every time he uses an area or a piece of equipment, he must clean up and replace the equipment so that others may find and use it.

The room must be properly designed to enable children to operate in this fashion. All equipment and materials should have their own designated spots; shelf areas should be clearly labeled with the names of things. If children cannot read, the teacher can substitute pictures or symbols on these labels. She should also see that shelves are uncluttered and that there is not too much equipment in the room.

Crayons and pencils can be placed in open-topped boxes, paper stacked in neat piles, small jars of paste put on shelves, and small objects like beads or pegs stored in covered containers. There should be racks for drying paintings and a place where clay work can dry undisturbed until it is ready for firing, painting, or taking home.

Finally, the teacher must make sure that the children know how to use and care for the materials. Children may pick up proper habits from the teacher or peers, but unless she makes a conscious effort to teach them, they may never learn some of the skills that lead to individual responsibility.

Children can also assume responsibilities for general care of the room. Every child need not be responsible for every part of the cleanup chore—the group can share responsibility. Sharing, they can set tables and clean up after lunch and snacks, get a room ready for rest, clean scraps of paper from the floor, and care for animals, fish, or plants. A teacher may assign these tasks on a rotating basis, often by setting up a chart and changing jobs weekly. Actually, children enjoy this kind of work, since it allows them to show their developing competencies.

PREPARING FOR SPECIAL ACTIVITIES

It is important that the teacher begin to establish classroom routines early, but children should feel that they are able to depart from routines when appropriate. A special visitor, bringing a pet to class, development of an activity that takes a long time, or a visit to an out-of-school place are all occasions for departing from routines for which teachers can prepare the children. This requires planning that may even involve them.

Although most teachers give lip-service to pupil-teacher planning, there is really only a limited area in which such planning is actually legitimate. If a teacher uses a basal program to teach reading, there can be little effective involvement of the children in planning. Similarly, many other program areas are outside the children's sphere of knowledge so that in any decision making, they would make improper decisions based on ignorance, or be manipulated by the teacher to make the decisions she favored. The key to involvement in planning is the process of decision making.

Legitimate areas for decision making are open to young children. Whether the arithmetic lesson will be held in the morning or the afternoon is not an important decision for the children to make, since the consequences are minor, but decisions about the distribution of resources or preparation for special events have important consequences, yet can be made by children.

The visit of a resource person might be such a special event. Though the teacher might make the arrangements and extend the original invitation, the children can be involved in planning for the visit. This entails helping them to anticipate what may happen and to plan for contingencies.

In planning with the children, the teacher should talk about the purposes of the visit and how they can best use the resources. If the visitor is coming to talk about his occupation, the children may wish to question him about his tasks, equipment, and whatever other aspects of the job interest them. Asking appropriate questions requires that they have a basis for judging the value of questions, and this sometimes requires research prior to the visitor's arrival. Such preparation allows the children to make optimal use of his time.

If the visitor is to perform, the teacher may help the children plan for appropriate room arrangement so they all can see. They might also wish to invite pupils from another class to share the experience. Although few of the problems raised in a preplanning session could be anticipated without the teacher's guidance, it helps them begin to anticipate future contingencies and makes use of their ideas in providing adequately for future events. Children cannot always be involved in these plans, and when involved they may not always make major contributions, but the act of planning and thinking about the future is important.

Children can also contribute ideas to planning for a field trip. Most of the arrangements will have to be made by the teacher, but they will learn by establishing the code of acceptable behavior for the class on trips. The teacher makes arrangements with the school, gets permission from parents and the place to be visited, takes care of transportation, and sets a time schedule. Any field trip, of course, should be related to the school program. Pupil-teacher planning includes helping children anticipate what will be happening on the trip and what uses will be made of it, for it is not simply a time-filling excursion, but is a means of collecting primary source data to be used in school studies. Of course there are occasions when teachers do take children on pleasure excursions, but these are relatively few.

If the children are to make maximum use of the trip, they should be helped in focusing on significant things. Prior knowledge about what they will be seeing is helpful to them, as is more general knowledge about the area of concern. They may do research on the topic by themselves or the teacher may present information from books or films and filmstrips. Children can be helped to formulate questions that the field trip might answer.

Children must learn to behave properly on a field trip. Limitations on behavior are necessary simply because the size of the group and the strangeness of the setting may compound the effects of behavior disorders. Children can be involved in developing an appropriate code of behavior under the teacher's guidance.

What constitutes appropriate behavior on a field trip may vary, for what is appropriate in one setting is not in another. Children walking through a business office or factory where people are working need to behave in quite a different way than in a park or a field. Similarly, traveling on a school bus requires different kinds of behavior than walking through a city street or using public transportation systems. In setting codes of behavior, the teacher should communicate to the children not only the limits of acceptable behavior, but the reason for them. Within these limits, the children should be able to set their own behavior patterns.

DISCIPLINE

Setting rules for appropriate behavior is no different at school than it is at home. The school, as a specialized institution having a particular set of goals and setting, has to establish appropriate kinds of behavior for children. In the old elementary school tradition in which children were to be "seen and not heard," the rules for behaving were simple and understood by all concerned. Children were to speak and move as little as possible, and then only with the express permission of the teacher. The less noise produced, the better the class.

Such an approach for establishing a code of appropriate behavior is no longer desirable, for in the modern school, especially in classes for young children, movement, speaking, and a degree of noise are considered acceptable. In replacing the old code with new standards, though, teachers have often missed the ease of administering the old code. Today, both teachers and children are often not quite sure of the rules; and what might be considered an infraction of rules by one teacher may not be considered so by another teacher in the same school. Relative rather than absolute standards abound.

Children entering school for the first time are not sure what is considered appropriate behavior. In addition, the very young child has often not yet learned to control his desires. If he wants a toy he might simply take it, even though another child is using it. He also often reacts immediately and physically to hurt or frustration. An occasional tantrum by a nursery-age child is not necessarily a sign of emotional disturbance.

Proper behavior in school settings is learned gradually. It should be a goal to be achieved through extended experience rather than an expectation. A teacher should plan for teaching proper behavior as she teaches other things, first becoming aware of her goals. Does she wish to prepare children to be docile and conforming, responsive only to authority? Does she wish to prepare children who have developed many modes and skills of self-expression, but whose concerns are with continually acting out their feelings and desires? Or does she wish to prepare children who are responsive to the needs of others as well as themselves, who are flexible enough to change their behavior in response to a situation, and who behave appropriately because they feel it is right rather than because they have been told to do so?

The type of individual developed is a result of the form of discipline used. If a teacher continually sets limits and tells a child how to behave without explanation, he will become authority-oriented. He will learn that proper behavior is rooted in the commands of authority. On the other hand, a child who is given no limits may learn that his inner desires alone should be responded to continually. Ultimately, we wish to develop autonomous individuals who realize there are reasons for order and limits. We want them to become flexible in their behavior, responding to each situation differently. The development of disciplined behavior requires the use of intellectual abilities. The child must use his intellect to understand the social as well as the physical world, and realize that patterns of behavior have regularity and reason that can ultimately be understood.

John Holt distinguishes among three different types of discipline. According to Holt, a child encounters the discipline of nature—how things work—when he fixes or builds things, learns a skill, or plays a musical instrument. He learns this discipline through feedback from reality. The discipline of society relates to how adults behave within the culture. It is learned through feedback in social settings. The third type of discipline—coercion—is used to protect the child from the consequences of his actions that he cannot anticipate. While some coercive discipline is necessary, coercion for its own sake is improper.[1]

In attempting to develop an approach to discipline based upon reason the teacher may follow several steps:

1. BEHAVIORS EXPECTED OF CHILDREN SHOULD BE KNOWN TO THEM. It is important that the teacher tell the children what is expected of them. All too often children's improper behavior is a result of ignorance. Instructions will have to be repeated many times in many contexts before they truly understand them.

2. CHILDREN NEED TO BE TOLD WHY RULES ARE IN EFFECT. Even if they cannot fully *understand* the reasons for behaving in certain ways, children need to be given the reasons for rules. Their questions should be responded to honestly. Most rules for school behavior are reasonable. Children can begin to see the reason for lining up at a slide that many wish to use, or limiting the amount of time one child can ride on a popular bicycle. Similarly, children can understand why they should be-

---

[1] John Holt and others, "Discipline: The Most Perplexing Subject of All," *Teacher,* 90, no. 1 (September 1972), 54–56.

have differently in a crowded lunchroom than in their own room and why rules are promulgated for behaving certain ways in class, others in the hall, and still others on a school bus.

3.   CHILDREN SHOULD HAVE OPPORTUNITIES TO OBSERVE AND PRACTICE PROPER BEHAVIOR. Simply telling children how to behave may not be enough. They need demonstrations at times, to learn through modeling. They must also have opportunities to *practice* proper behavior, with feedback from the teacher. They may have to go through a series of successive approximations before they learn proper behavior, as in reading and every other curriculum area.

4.   THE BEHAVIOR EXPECTED OF CHILDREN OUGHT TO BE POSSIBLE FOR THEM. A development principle should be applied in this area of performance as in other areas. Children are not miniature adults and should not be expected to behave like adults. Teachers should develop goals of reasonable child-like behavior.

5.   CHILDREN CANNOT ALWAYS BE EXPECTED TO BEHAVE PROPERLY AT ALL TIMES. Nobody is perfect, including adults. We do not expect adults always to be on their best behavior. As a matter of fact, we often feel that it is good for an adult to "let his hair down" on occasion. The same is true for children. They should not be expected to conform to standards of model behavior at all times any more than adults should.

6.   TEACHERS SHOULD BEHAVE WITH CONSISTENCY. The teacher's behavior communicates a message to the children about what is acceptable and appropriate and what is not. If teachers vacillate in their desires or accept certain kinds of behaviors one time and reject or punish the same behavior under similar circumstances another time, they confuse children and blur their goals. Though teachers cannot always behave consistently, this is a goal for which they should aim.

IMPROVING CLASSROOM BEHAVIOR

A number of distinct approaches have been suggested by educators and psychologists to improve children's behavior. These include behavior modification techniques, modeling techniques, psychodynamic approaches, redirecting children's activities, and an ecological approach. Sometimes a teacher can combine several of these approaches in a classroom.

BEHAVIOR MODIFICATION

A number of psychologists have suggested systematic ways, based on the application of behavioral analysis theory, for modifying the behavior of children, including young children, in school settings. These techniques are proposed for all kinds of behavior problems, including academic as well as discipline problems. The overall strategy is that the teacher first studies the problem empirically, then through the systematic application of reinforcers and punishment tied directly to the valued behavior, works on the problem until it is eliminated.

Charles and Clifford Madsen have identified four steps in this process: *pinpoint, record, consequate, and evaluate.* To *pinpoint* is to identify the specific problem behavior and to define the goal of the strategy in terms of observable behavior. The teacher should observe the conditions under which the problem behavior is occurring and the frequency of its occurrence, and *record* these observations directly. Next, she should develop a systematic program in which the target behavior comes under control of external reinforcers. To *consequate,* a system of rewards can be offered contingent upon the child's manifesting the target behavior. If the target is to reduce a negative behavior, manifestations of that behavior may be ignored, and alternative behaviors reinforced. Reinforcers can include social rewards, such as statements of approval or a pat on the back, or material rewards, such as food treats or toys. The opportunity to participate in valued activities can also become contingent upon proper behavior. Sometimes tokens, to be exchanged for rewards later, are used as reinforcers. To *evaluate,* the teacher should allow the program to operate for a reasonable time to determine its success. If unsuccessful, a new program should be developed and tried.[2]

An example of such a program is with a child who does not seem to be willing to clean up after activities. The teacher might observe that at each cleanup time the child takes a piece of equipment into a corner of the room and plays with it. She might then decide to help him clean up, giving him an opportunity to play with a special toy on condition that he help. If he then does help, she gives him the toy. On occasions when he does not help, all toys might be withheld. After a while, the teacher tries to get him to clean up with only an occasional offer of special toys, finally fading the use of the toy completely.

A large number of successful experiences with behavior modification have been reported in laboratory situations, homes, and classrooms.[3] The technique, however, continues to be controversial. Some feel that the focus on behavior leads to a concern for symptoms rather than

---

[2] Charles H. Madsen, Jr., and Clifford K. Madsen, *Teaching/Discipline: Behavioral Principles Towards a Positive Approach* (Boston: Allyn & Bacon, 1970), pp. 23–31.

[3] For example, see Lloyd K. Daniels, ed., *The Management of Childhood Behavior Problems in School and at Home* (Springfield, Ill.: Charles C Thomas, 1974).

causes. Others object to the use of rewards, equating this with bribery. Still others feel that this technique places the control of behavior outside the individual and never helps him deal with the judgment of what is proper behavior, thus limiting his autonomy. While advocates of this approach have countered these arguments, the controversy continues to rage.

MODELING

Another approach to teaching appropriate behavior is the use of modeling techniques, based on social learning theory. This concept was discussed briefly in chapter 3. All of us learn some proper behaviors by watching and emulating others. When we are in a strange social situation, we may look to a person who seems socially accepted to get cues to proper behavior, and then emulate him while trying to abstract rules for the situation.

Modeling is a technique that can be used to learn both positive and negative behavior, depending upon what is modeled. By providing a model of good social behavior a teacher could get the entire class to behave in appropriate ways. The model should be someone who has status in the group so that children wish to emulate his behavior. Some cuing of proper behavior is helpful so that the teacher can point out the behavior that should be modeled. Rewarding the target behavior in children will reinforce it and increase the probability of their maintaining it.[4]

As with reinforcement theory, the focus of this technique is on the behavior rather than on the reasons for behaving. There is less manipulation of the child here, and he ultimately decides whether to model the target behavior, thus increasing autonomy.

PSYCHODYNAMIC APPROACHES

Over the years many early childhood educators have looked to psychodynamic principles to explain children's behavior and provide techniques for improving it. Psychodynamic theorists often view behavior as a manifestation of developmental conflict or needs. Since conflict is seen as a necessary part of growth, they do not value the avoidance of conflict or aversive behavior. Instead, these theorists suggest that teachers need to provide children with the means to work out these conflicts or manifest their feelings in socially acceptable ways. Sometimes catharsis is suggested—children are encouraged to show their feelings, channeling

[4] Albert Bandura and Richard H. Walter, *Social Learning and Personality Development* (New York: Holt, Rinehart and Winston, 1963), pp. 47–108.

hostile feelings into dramatic play, or pounding clay or a punching bag. Serious problems might be handled by a therapist, but day-to-day conflict can be handled by a teacher at school. Theorists also propose that teachers deal with these behavior problems or developmental conflicts in indirect ways, anticipating the problems that might arise.

The human development curricula and the affective curricula discussed in chapter 8 are attempts to help children deal with their feelings and become more sensitive in interpersonal relations. In so doing, these programs are designed to improve classroom behavior by indirect means.

Growing out of the field of psychodynamic theory, the work of Rudolph Dreikurs has attracted its share of advocates in the field of early childhood education. Dreikurs considers that children misbehave for one of four reasons: to gain attention, to display power, to gain revenge, and to display a deficiency in order to seek special service or be exempted from some expectation.[5] Dreikurs proposes that parents and teachers respond to children's misbehavior through the use of *logical consequences* rather than punishment. These consequences, which are set by the authority, are different from punishment in that logical consequences express the reality of the social order, are intrinsically related to the misbehavior, involve no moral judgment on the part of the implementor, and are concerned only with present occurrences.[6]

A logical consequence could have a child miss a valued activity because he has dawdled elsewhere, or require him to clean up an area where he has deliberately created a mess. The key to these actions in changing behavior is that the teacher realize the reasons for a child's misbehavior and, rather than letting him achieve his goal, demonstrate why the behavior is both inappropriate for the situation and ineffective in achieving his desired result. The child is also told, if possible, why the particular consequence has been selected for him.

The use of logical consequences might seem appropriate to what Holt has called social discipline situations; it is not suggested for dangerous physical situations. While its use is suggested in many situations, there seems little evidence of its success or failure.

REDIRECTION

One traditional approach to misbehavior used by teachers of young children is *redirection*. The basic ploy is to take the child's atten-

---

[5] Rudolph Dreikurs, *Psychology in the Classroom,* 2nd ed. (New York: Harper & Row, 1968), pp. 27–45.

[6] Rudolph Dreikurs and Loren Grey, *Logical Consequences: A Handbook of Discipline* (New York: Meredith Press, 1968), pp. 53–82.

tion from the situation creating the difficulty and move him into a situation that will provide immediate satisfactions. A child who is fighting with another over a fire truck, for example, might be steered to the woodworking area. For redirection to be possible, the teacher needs to know her children and which activities have high appeal for them. She must also have alternatives available.

Although redirection is a means to avoid conflict, the suggestion that it be used does not indicate either that conflict can be completely avoided or that conflict is necessarily bad. There are always some situations that will lead to conflict in any classroom. The opposition of individual needs or the clash of strong personalities may cause it. Teachers should help children develop acceptable means of dealing with conflict: compromise, and use of verbal skills, rather than physical coercion, in influencing persons. Teachers continually have to step in to resolve conflicts among children. Unfortunately, they may have to use some forms of arbitrary coercion and even physical restraint; however, this should not mean physical punishment. Ultimately, any system of discipline should move from the teacher controlling the child's behavior to the child becoming autonomous. The success of a teacher's discipline can be judged by the degree of autonomy found in the class.

ECOLOGICAL APPROACH

An intriguing alternative to these approaches to discipline can be extrapolated from an article by Susan Swap dealing with emotionally disturbed children. Swap's thesis is that the disturbance does not reside within the child, but in the interaction between the child and his environment.[7] This argument seems related to that of M. Stephen Lilly discussed in chapter 11. Lilly has suggested that we look at exceptional school situations rather than at exceptional children.[8]

Swap says that many emotionally disturbed children misbehave because they are going through the resolution of conflicts associated with early development stages while most of their peers have successfully resolved these same developmental conflicts earlier. The resolution of these conflicts may be aided or thwarted by environmental conditions

---

[7] Susan M. Swap, "Disturbing Classroom Behaviors: A Developmental and Ecological View," *Exceptional Children,* 41, no. 3 (November 1974), 163–72.

[8] M. Stephen Lilly, "Special Education: A Teapot in a Tempest," *Exceptional Children,* 37, no. 1 (September 1970), 43–45.

in the child's educational setting. Often, because the setting was designed for more emotionally mature children, the conflict is irritated by conflict with the environment. By understanding the child's conflict level and modifying the environment to help him in his task of conflict resolution, the teacher can effectively limit disturbances in the classroom. Elements in the school environment that can be modified include the physical setting, the educational requirements placed upon the child, and the nature of the teacher-child interaction pattern.

We know that children in their early years are rapidly confronted with developmental change, and that this can produce personal conflict. We also know that children develop unevenly; for instance, a child may be more mature in his language development than in motor development at a particular time. In addition, in any one class, even an age-graded one, there will be children representing a range of developmental levels. The teacher needs to become a careful observer of children's behavior and a skillful judge of the developmental levels represented by that behavior. Rather than attempting to modify the child to fit the setting, she should work at modifying the setting to fit the child. By modifying academic requirements, creating varied space in the classroom, and using different kinds of educational materials and degrees of structure in the program she can limit the number of conflicts between the child and the school setting.

Some children require formal structure while others do better in open settings. Some learn mathematics best with manipulative materials, but once they have passed the stage of requiring these materials, their presence may hamper learning. Some children do best in large groups of peers while others prefer seclusion. Some require challenge while others need security. No one program best fits all children; no one set of teacher behaviors leads to the greatest amount of pupil learning. A flexible teacher in a flexible environment can match the demands and requirements of the setting to the needs of the child, and thus lessen discipline problems.

The acceptance of individual differences in children requires that the teacher become aware of the child's developmental level and the environmental conditions that enhance or thwart his learning, whether academic or social. From a behavioral analysis point of view, this means becoming aware of *setting events* that usually lead to particular behaviors, whether good or bad; also, becoming aware of the *natural reinforcers* in the environment, for each environment provides satisfactions as a result of particular kinds of behavior for specific children.

An understanding of where each child is developmentally and

the degree to which environmental conditions will help or hinder him in the development of constructive behavior patterns will help the teacher in the search for improved educational opportunities for all children. Thus, the considerations raised in the previous chapter relating to the factors a teacher must consider in organizing for instruction need to be considered also when she is concerned with discipline in the classroom.

In the final analysis the classroom teacher must realize that "proper behavior in a classroom" is as much a teaching goal as is learning to read or learning to express oneself creatively through art media. The child is not born with a sense of what is considered appropriate behavior; he must learn it. In addition, what might be considered good behavior in one setting is not necessarily considered good behavior in another. A parent might want his child to act in an assertive manner, telling the child to stand up for his rights. The teacher might consider the child aggressive or even combative, rather than assertive. Such differences might stem from differences in values and goals that parents and teachers have for the same child or from a distortion that could arise when a child attempts to overstress a parent's goal. Another child might be lacking in social skills and find that socially inappropriate behavior is the only means available to him to gain the attention of other children or adults. Still another child may simply be unaware of the rules for appropriate behavior in school. Each of these situations would require a different response from the teacher as well as a different approach to teaching the child appropriate behavior.

All classrooms have some children who do not behave appropriately at all times. Teachers also find that they are not as effective with some children as with others. Too often, teachers foolishly feel that their ability to control a class at all times is crucial to their ability to teach, and that any failure in dealing with a child or a group on occasion means failure as a teacher. They need to realize that they are not infallible, and that they, like all other professionals, need the help of others. Sometimes they can call on other teachers. A principal can often provide an additional resource. In some schools, teachers have access to school counselors, psychologists, and social workers. Appropriate use should be made of all these resources.

SUGGESTED READING

Discipline and Learning: An Inquiry into Student-Teacher Relationships. Washington, D.C.: National Education Association, 1975.

GNAGY, WILLIAM J., *Maintaining Discipline in Classroom Instruction.* New York: The Macmillan Company, 1975.

HYMES, JAMES L., *The Child Under Six.* Englewood Cliffs, N.J.: Prentice-Hall, Inc., 1963.

MADSEN, CHARLES H., JR., and CLIFFORD K. MADSEN, *Teaching/Discipline: Behavioral Principles Towards a Positive Approach.* Boston: Allyn & Bacon, 1970.

James L. Hoot

CHAPTER FIFTEEN

WORKING
WITH PARENTS

The close relationship between the education of young children and parent programming has been evident throughout the history of early childhood education. This relationship may have grown out of an understanding of the close bond between parent and young child, a bond causing the parent to become the prime influencer of the child's learning and development. Because this bond may have a greater impact on the life of the child than any educational programs, educators have learned to use it to extend their programs.

The writings of Johann Amos Comenius and Johann Heinrich Pestalozzi, educators who predated the creation of kindergartens and nursery schools and who were concerned with young children, expressed the belief in the importance of the mother's role in the education of the young. Friedrich Froebel, pioneer of the kindergarten, also expressed his belief in the importance of educating mothers for child rearing as well as in the significance of the harmonious education of children in school and at home.

As kindergartens were established in the United States, classes were formed for the mothers as a means of carrying out Froebel's philosophy. In some cases in which kindergartens were organized as philanthropic agencies, the mothers' clubs were concerned with the acculturation of the family, helping to "Americanize" as well as teaching about child-rearing practices. Classes for all kindergarten parents were concerned with teaching about child study and about the theory and practice of kindergarten education.

It is interesting to note that the importance early kindergarten educators placed upon involving mothers significantly affected the total

American education scene. The National Congress of Mothers grew out of a convocation of women connected with these kindergarten mothers' classes. This group eventually became the National Congress of Parents and Teachers, an organization well-known in school circles today.

As nursery schools developed, they were thought of as an important influence in augmenting and improving healthy parent-child relationships. Margaret and Rachel McMillan's emphasis on placing nursery schools close to children's homes, allowing parents to observe nursery-school practices, and establishing a good working relationship between parent and teacher were all meant to support close cooperation between the home and the school. The hope of the pioneers of nursery education was that the parents themselves would ultimately become responsible for the education of their young children.

As the nursery school was transplanted into the United States, this concern for a close relationship between family and school in the early years continued. One of the first established in the United States was a parent-cooperative nursery school started by a group of twelve faculty wives at the University of Chicago in 1916. These parents wanted to secure "social education for their children, parent education for themselves and a little free time for Red Cross work."[1]

The nursery school and kindergarten were often the creation of the parents they were designed to serve. Nursery schools are still organized by groups of parents and concerned community members and even today, one may still find kindergartens sponsored by elementary school parent-teacher associations. Parents who create a school feel a sense of belonging to that school in a way that few parents in established schools can experience.

The relationships between schools and parents at the early childhood level are as diverse as the kinds of schools that exist and the populations of parents they serve. The day care center operates quite differently in its relationship to the families it serves than does the parent-cooperative nursery school. Similarly, the primary grades of an elementary public school may also support a different relationship between home and school than does a private nursery school.

Recently, concerns about parent programs have shifted from viewing the parent as only a client of educational institutions to viewing him as a policy maker. The concern for community control of schools and the parents' demand to have a voice in educational policy making at

---

[1] Katherine Whiteside Taylor, *Parents and Children Learn Together* (New York: Teachers College Press, 1968), p. 294.

all levels must be understood as an extension of their responsibility for the education of their children.

To some extent, this right to determine policy is considered part of every relationship that a client has with a professional, for, in all but a few situations, he may select the professional that best characterizes his concept of treatment. In the area of education, however, neither the client nor the professional has the freedom of selection that characterizes most other client-professional relationships. Public educational institutions hold such a real monopoly over educational services that choice of school or teacher is not usually available to the parent, nor can most teachers determine which children will be included in their class. This lack of choice is one constraint that molds the relationship between parent and teacher.

Just as physicians have resisted public advocacy groups that have attempted to influence the medical profession to be more responsive to its clientele, so teachers' groups have resisted the move to local control and the involvement of parents and community members in the immediate decision-making process. Hannah Hess dramatically describes the conflict between parents and professionals in one school in New York.[2] Although this is a description of a single school, such conflict is not an isolated instance. The fact that a national organization has been established to help the public deal with schools so they will be more responsive to their clientele suggests that these feelings are widely held.[3] The move toward bureaucratic teachers' organizations bargaining collectively with bureaucratic school systems has led to the suggestion that parents be involved in collective bargaining discussions as a third party whose primary concern for the children might otherwise not be considered.[4]

WHO OWNS THE CHILD?

In our culture we believe that parents have the right to rear their children in any way they see fit. Actually, however, the parent's right is significantly abridged as a result of our concern for the safety of the child. No

[2] Hannah S. Hess, *The Third Side of the Desk: How Parents Can Change the Schools* (New York: Scribner's, 1973).

[3] The Institute for Responsive Education (1704 Commonwealth Ave., Boston, Mass. 02215) publishes a regular newsletter, *Citizen Action in Education*.

[4] Charles W. Cheng, "Community Representation in Teacher Collective Bargaining: Problems and Prospects," *Harvard Educational Review*, 46, no. 2 (May 1976), 153–74.

parent has the right to inflict bodily harm on his child. Although the publicity given to battered children in our communities might make this seem a recent concern, Humane Societies have been in existence for many years for the protection of animals and *children.*

The imposition of society on the rights of parents goes far beyond stopping dangerous parental practices, for the states also legislate compulsory education. Every parent *must* send his child to school for a certain period and is held responsible for his attendance. This requirement grows as much from the cultural need to maintain the social order as from personal needs of children and their parents.

As schools begin to offer educational opportunities for the very young, the matter of compulsory attendance becomes even more critical. Schools for the young concern themselves with teaching basic attitudes and concepts that go beyond traditional instruction in the three R's. Although parents are free today to keep a child out of school until age six or seven, it may well be that in the future the compulsory school attendance laws will include requirements for children ages five, four, or even younger. This may present no problem for parents in complete agreement with school authorities as to the goals of education and the means for achieving them, but serious problems may develop when the school authorities and the parents disagree about either goals or means. At this point, the responsiveness of schools to the needs, wishes, and demands of parents may be crucial.

Who does own the child? It becomes evident that the "ownership" of children by parents is far from unencumbered by our society. In many schools, however, teachers feel that they own the child, at least while he is in the classroom, and that their right to determine what experiences will be provided is inviolable. It is a "right" delegated to them by society by virtue of their special knowledge and preparation, authorized in the issuance of a teacher's certificate and evidenced by the signing of a contract with a school board.

The traditional view of the parent as owner of the child has been commented upon by Mary Van Stolk in relation to child abuse. The reluctance of society to interfere with the "ownership rights of parents" allows the child's rights to be violated.[5] Only recently have the rights of children begun to be recognized and child-advocacy groups established to protect these rights from incursion by parent or social institution.

Just as restraints are placed upon what parents can do to children, restraints are placed upon teachers. The curriculum set by the

---

[5] Mary Van Stolk, "Who Owns the Child?" *Childhood Education,* 50, no. 5 (March 1974), 259–65.

school board, the regulations set by administration, and the state laws relating to education all create some restraints. In addition to these, professional restraints are imposed implicitly by the teachers and informally communicated by the colleagues in a school.

One of the larger issues confronting education today relates to the extent to which parents' wishes and demands should also constitute a legitimate set of restraints upon teachers' actions. Parents have traditionally been kept out of decision-making roles in school except at the broadest level, as in school board membership. Aside from this arena, however, teachers have not considered parents an important source of constraint. Parents who came to school to meet with teachers were to be informed, listened to, placated, and counseled. Seldom did the teacher see the parent as a source of decision making about classroom procedure. Parents' limited knowledge about schooling was considered adequate reason to deny their legitimate involvement in the decision-making process, and even when they were considered knowledgeable, such matters were thought to be outside their sphere.

The establishment of policy advisory committees, including many parents in Head Start programs, and the demands of black, native American, and Mexican-American parents for community control of schools, suggest that the relationship between parent and teacher may be changing in many communities. This change is toward more involvement of parents and other community members, as extensions of parents, in important areas of decision making relating to school policy and classroom practice. The teacher in a ghetto elementary school may soon find her relationship to the parents of the children in her class similar to that of the teacher in the parent-cooperative nursery school. Although the parents are the clients of the teacher, they also hire her and constitute the governing board of the school concerned with making decisions about school policy and its implementation.

If this change does come about, teachers will need to view their roles in relationship to schools and children in a somewhat different light, and will need to develop new skills in working with parents and new perceptions of what constitutes a viable parent-teacher relationship.

Such a relationship is further compounded by the demands that teachers are making through their organizations, for increased decision-making power along with improved salaries and working conditions in their contracts. On occasion, parent and teacher groups have clashed in their independent demands for a greater voice in educational policy. In some cases, however, they have joined together in the common pursuit of educational opportunity for all children through shared decision making.

Traditionally the boundary of teacher-parent-community power has been determined by the kinds of decisions that need to be made.

Parent and/or community agents have been responsible for policy decisions, and teachers and administrators for decisions relating to policy implementation. These lines, however, are often blurred, for implementation can affect policies considerably and policy decisions often require professional knowledge of probable consequences.

DIFFERING ROLES IN WORKING WITH PARENTS

The content of a parent-teacher relationship varies greatly with the parent population and with the particular institutional setting. Teachers should be sensitive to the needs of parents and provide a range of programming possibilities. Generally, the teacher's role may consist of communicating pupil progress to parents, sharing information, jointly solving problems, organizing parent meetings, developing parent education programs, supervising classroom participation, and providing professional consultation to policy-making groups. Each element of a parent program is different and requires different skills and techniques of the teacher. Although teachers are not prepared as parent counselors and often lack the preparation to be parent educators, their position allows them to serve the parent population in a unique way. Within the limitations of skills and roles, teachers should accept the challenge in each area, although some areas might be more satisfying.

REPORTING PUPIL PROGRESS

One part of evaluation is the report to parents of the child's progress in school. Report cards, letters, and individual conferences are discussed more fully in chapter 16. It is important in reporting to be sure that the criteria for making judgments are public, and that the parents understand the goals of the program and their child's progress. Avoiding adverse reporting can be dangerous; parents should be informed regularly and frankly.

SHARING INFORMATION

Reporting pupil progress is usually one-way communication, with the only feedback relating to whether the message is received. Parents and teachers both have information about the child that would be useful to exchange—information not necessarily related to pupil progress. Teachers often elicit useful information about children through the applications that many nursery schools and kindergartens require prior to

James L. Hoot

admission. Data on children's health and developmental background is required in this form, an example of which is presented in chapter 14.

Such forms may be supplemented by individual conferences at the beginning of school or during a preschool orientation session. Holding such conferences a few weeks after the child's entrance to school allows the teacher time to collect information about his initial reaction and developing behavior patterns. She may then be able to ask specific questions relating to important areas of behavior. What is significant for one child may be irrelevant to the teacher's understanding of another child.

Such a sharing conference held at any time of the year is useful particularly if the teacher finds that she has problems with a child. The information provided by a parent often helps explain a child's change in behavior. Similarly, parents may wish information from the teacher that will help them deal with the child at home. If the teacher and parent are both concerned primarily with his welfare, information-sharing conferences may provide the beginning of a beneficial mutual relationship in support of him. Such conferences can easily lead to joint problem-solving sessions.

JOINT PROBLEM SOLVING

The child's entrance in school often leads to a new awareness on the part of the parents. In many families, the child may have had few contacts with other children his age up to this time. Sometimes the parents will have made few demands of him, or not had the opportunity to compare him with other children at a similar developmental stage. If, in addition, the family has had few contacts with a pediatrician, the parents may suddenly see problems or abnormalities that have existed but not been evident to them.

The entrance into school, with its new demands on the child, may suddenly bring forth a series of behavior problems. Hearing losses, poor vision, or other problems may also appear as new pressures are placed upon the child. At times, a change in the family situation—divorce, the arrival of a new baby, or moving to a new community—may also cause problems to occur in class. The teacher may be able to handle these problems without outside help, but she must sometimes work out solutions with the parents. Sharing information, pooling ideas for dealing with the problems, and developing a consistent way of handling the child both at home and at school may go a long way in providing solutions to difficult problems. The teacher may play a crucial role in helping parents deal with these problems, for quite often she is the only professional with whom they have regular contact.

The teacher may suddenly find herself in a role for which she is poorly trained, because she has not been prepared as a psychologist, social worker, or guidance counselor and is a child development specialist in only the broadest sense. Yet within her responsibility as teacher she must find ways to help the parent become aware of problems and deal with them. Sometimes this requires a friendly conversation over a cup of coffee; other times it may require a series of conferences leading to referral to an appropriate agency. The teacher must be careful not to overstep the bounds of her role. Often it is best to refer a problem to someone else better qualified. She should become familiar with the agencies that service children and their families in her community and with the procedures used to seek the help of each agency. Many schools have ancillary personnel—guidance workers or family coordinators—that can help the parent and teacher deal with problems.

Although referral is a significant contribution that teachers can make, the importance of the personal support they can provide should not be underestimated.

HOME VISITS

Parent conferences generally take place in the school, the domain of the teacher—a place where she feels comfortable. However, this may be a place in which parents feel less than comfortable. Some parent activities can be transferred into the home.

A home visit has many advantages, among them familiarity and comfort for the parent. A conference in the home may allow the parent to talk more freely than he would at school, where he faces the teacher across a desk. In addition, the teacher can learn about the child's environment, and perhaps understand him better. Home visits may also be more convenient for parents not able to come to the classroom during school hours; often, fathers as well as mothers can be reached by the teacher through home visits.

If a home visit is to be effective, the parents should feel that they are inviting the teacher into their home. Forcing a visit on an unwilling family may cause hostility. The teacher might propose a number of dates and times so the visit can take place at a mutually convenient time. A teacher who visits the home without warning is acting unfairly. Such an action can be disastrous to the hopes of establishing a working relationship.

The purpose of a home visit is similar to that of a conference: sharing information and working on problems. The teacher should be careful that these purposes are achieved while friendly social relations are established.

INFORMAL CONTACTS

Many of the contacts a teacher has with parents are informal. The child's arrival or departure from school, the meetings of the parents' association, and the invitation to a parent to accompany the class on a field trip all provide opportunity for informal contacts. The teacher should convey a feeling of friendliness and mutual concern for the children in these sessions. Holding parents at a distance or talking down to them can destroy the relationship that the rest of the parent program is attempting to build.

These occasions also allow the teacher to hold mini-conferences—short informal sessions in which minor problems can be dealt with or information elicited easily. Such conferences can be extremely fruitful for the amount of time and energy expended. Teachers should encourage them, being careful not to become too involved with the parents when they need to be working with children.

PARENT MEETINGS

There are many occasions when the teacher must deal with parents in groups rather than individually. She may be called upon to plan and direct parent meetings, or looked upon as a resource for meetings planned and executed by the parents themselves.

The first meeting for which the teacher has responsibility is often the orientation meeting that takes place close to the children's entrance to school. This provides an opportunity to communicate to the parents what school will be like for them and for their children. If parents have never had a child in school before, this type of information is an important part of the meeting. They may be full of questions and may feel uncertain about the school. Honest responses to questions and the acceptance of parental anxiety can help build a good relationship. Such a meeting may also be used to provide parents with information about the school's expectations of them and their children.

Although orientation meetings usually require the transmission of a great deal of information, the teacher should be careful to communicate the fact that the school is a friendly place that welcomes parents as well as children (assuming that this is true). Teachers should allow time for informal chatter and opportunities for parents to become acquainted with one another. If information can be printed in a simple brochure or leaflet, more of the meeting time is devoted to establishing relationships and less to lecturing. It is a waste of meeting time to read materials to parents that they could easily read themselves.

During the school year, the teacher may want to call other meetings, to talk about her program, show some of the children's work, and answer parents' questions about what their children are doing. Because such meetings deal directly with their children, parents are usually happy to attend them. Care must be taken to schedule meetings at times when there can be maximum attendance. It may be necessary to provide an informal baby-sitting arrangement for the children of invited parents, or to allow the children to come to the meetings in order to insure attendance. In some communities, however, parents can make their own child-care arrangements.

Most schools have a formal parent or parent-teacher association that attempts to organize all the parents in the school. It plans regular meetings and social events throughout the school year. Though the responsibility for such meetings is often in the hands of the parent officers, teachers may be asked to serve on programs or to act as resource persons.

The attendance of teachers at these meetings is important in building close ties with families. A brief word to a parent on such an occasion can frequently do more in establishing good relationships than can a lengthy conference.

PARENT EDUCATION PROGRAMS

In many schools, formal or informal parent education programs are organized in conjunction with educational programs for young children. These vary from highly organized courses that teach about child growth and development, child-rearing practices, and homemaking skills, to informal club activities whose content is determined by the parents themselves. Still other programs may focus on group process and parent interaction rather than on any substantive content. In some cases, the responsibility for parent education will lie outside the domain of the classroom teacher and a parent educator or group worker may be assigned to it. In other situations, the classroom teacher is responsible.

Many parent-cooperative nursery schools require that parents enroll in a parent education program as a prerequisite for the child's enrollment in the program. Nursery schools in settlement houses, parent-child centers, and Head Start programs often include a strong parent education component in their total service program. In some cases, parents are required to spend many hours in classes. Sometimes the maintenance of a parent library is a strong addition to a program.

More recently, many parent education programs have been concerned with teaching specific parental skills that will support children's intellectual and language learning in the school. A typical program may portray model parental behavior such as including children in discussions, conveying to them the meanings of parental action, reading simple stories aloud, and providing instructional activities and material in the home. The specific techniques needed are often taught directly to parents, who then practice them under supervision. Sometimes kits of materials are lent to parents for their use with children at home. In these programs, working with babies may be stressed as much as with preschoolers. The hope is that ultimately all the children in a family will be affected by what the parent learns.

Many parent education programs are becoming home-based rather than school-based, with parent educators working directly in the homes of their clients. Edith Levitt and Shirley Cohen identified some of the characteristics that many of these programs have in common. They usually make provision for pretraining and orientation of workers as well as orientation of parents. The workers generally provide specific guidance to parents and often demonstrate activities with the child as they observe. Programs for low-income parents rely heavily on the use of paraprofessionals as trainers, while programs for handicapped children use primarily professionals. The parent worker is generally responsible for the evaluation of the children's progress and parents are often consulted in regard to activities for the children.[6]

---

[6] Edith Levitt and Shirley Cohen, "Educating Parents of Children with Special Needs—Approaches and Issues," *Young Children*, 31, no. 4 (May 1976), 263–72.

Bernard Spodek

In addition to these common elements, many differences exist among the programs of parent education. These parallel the differences in approach to the education of young children discussed in chapter 3 and lead to a range of specific treatments for parents.

SUPERVISING PARENT PARTICIPATION

Parent participation in classroom activities is an integral part of the organization of cooperative nursery schools and Head Start programs. Parents can be invited into classes to read stories to children, provide tutoring services for needy children, help with instructional groups, help with classroom routines, and serve as resource persons. They can often participate as teaching assistants as well.

Careful supervision should be provided when parents are invited to participate in the teaching program. A series of orientation meetings with participating parents can help lessen possible confusion. They need to know about the program, including the daily schedule of activities and the rules and patterns of behavior expected of children in different areas of the classroom and the school. Finally, they need to be told their specific responsibilities. The development of a parent manual containing this information is helpful if a number of parents are used in the program.

Teachers should supervise parents who participate in the program, keeping track of their behavior and possibly making notes to be used in evaluative conferences later. At the end of the day, it is useful for the parents and teacher to meet to review the work that both have done. Praise and support should be amply given, as should criticism and advice for improving practice. As parents continue their work with the teacher, their areas of responsibility and amount of freedom can often increase.

WORKING WITH PARENT POLICY BOARDS

The most difficult part of the teacher's relationship with parents often is working with them in developing educational and administrative policy for schools. Sometimes the difficulty stems from the teacher's feeling that she is better prepared to make decisions than are the parents because she has a greater amount of specialized knowledge upon which to base a decision. In addition, she has a vested interest in the decisions the parents might make about school practices. Teachers have their own ideological biases as well, which can affect what they consider proper school policy.

Both parents and teachers may come to board meetings with their own particular difficulties. Minority group members and lower-class parents may view teachers with a certain amount of distrust. Parents' previous experience as victims of discrimination or differences in values and behavior patterns may lead to their feeling suspicion. Teachers, on the other hand, may have difficulty communicating with persons who do not share their personal and professional vocabulary.

The effectiveness of a teacher's relationship with a board is a function of the trust shared by all involved. This takes time, energy, and effort and grows out of a series of encounters in which the teacher demonstrates that she can be trusted; it is facilitated by a show of competence and an honest concern for the children in the program. Keeping lines of communication open, listening to parents, and keeping the sources of decisions public also help the teacher gain trust.

Ultimately, the teacher's role working with a policy board is to help the parents make their decisions. These decisions may be different from those she might make, but this must be accepted. This does not mean the teacher abrogates her professional responsibility, but rather that she must redefine that responsibility. The teacher should use her role in policy board sessions to educate the parents, seeing that they have appropriate information upon which to base their decisions. Further, she must help them anticipate the consequences of their decisions upon the program and people involved. A teacher who can allow parents to move independently beyond her shows a great deal of professional maturity.

DEVELOPING TECHNIQUES
FOR WORKING WITH PARENTS

Working with parents, like working with children, requires the development of long-range plans, interview and guidance skills, and the ability to work with small and large groups. Teachers must also develop skills in evaluating and recording the results of encounters with parents.

PLANNING

A teacher must be clear about the purposes of parent contacts, knowledgeable about the availability and use of resources, and able to think through the consequences of parent activities. Most important is the need to match the parent activity to the specific purposes of parent work.

If a teacher wishes to refer a parent for help to a social agency, she must be able to communicate that need to the parent without becoming too threatening. She ought to have available the names and addresses of social agencies and know how to apply to them. If she wishes to enlist parents in helping with a child's behavior problem in class, she should have observational records of his behavior available so she can be concrete in her descriptions of the problem.

A total parent program should be planned on a full-year basis. This allows the teacher to create a balance of different kinds of parent contacts during the year. Meetings can be spaced so they occur with a degree of frequency without interfering with school operations or family traditions. In addition, teachers can anticipate the needs of the parent programs and prepare for them. If conferences are to be held, she must collect examples of the children's work or behavior as well as records relating to school performance.

In planning meetings with groups of parents, a teacher should think through the proposed content of the program well in advance, make arrangements for speakers or films if they are to be used, and assign responsibility for specific tasks such as hostessing or cleaning up to insure a smooth-running meeting.

She should also plan to have appropriate space available. A large meeting may require a school auditorium or multipurpose room. A class mothers' meeting might be held in the classroom after school but require rearrangement of the furniture. A conference with individual parents might best be held in a special room, or in the classroom if it will be quiet and free of interruptions. A parents' work session, using woodwork tools or sewing machines, requires special facilities and adequate space. Just allocating space for a parent bulletin board or a display of books requires the teacher to plan.

INTERVIEWING

Interviewing techniques include both the means of gathering information from and providing information to parents. A teacher should learn how to put a parent at ease in a conference; providing coffee or speaking first about general school matters of interest to the parent is reassuring. Such simple steps can help the teacher establish rapport. She should not spend too much time in preliminaries, however, for if the parent feels she is "beating around the bush," he can become defensive, thereby creating rather than solving a problem.

Teachers often find it useful to use an interview schedule or outline to make sure they elicit the information they want and cover all points in a conference. An interview schedule should always be flexible, however. The teacher should not read questions directly from the form, because it is only a guide to insure that the purposes of the conference are met.

Counseling techniques are also useful for the teacher. It is vital to learn how to *listen* to parents. This requires that she know something about them and be sensitive to their feelings as well as to the information communicated. It is important to listen responsively, reacting to their messages when appropriate and helping them work toward realistic solutions of problems regarding the children.

Although it is sometimes easy to give advice, within a parent-teacher context the counseling must be particularly meaningful and relevant to each specific situation. If a child should be read to at home, the teacher should help the parents find the source of books, or make books available. She should also help them learn some of the reading techniques that will eventually benefit the child.

WORKING WITH GROUPS

Large groups are not as useful as small ones for the development of discussions and support of interaction processes. Small-group sessions require the teacher to use group leadership techniques. As the leader, she must convene the group and chair the discussion; she must be sensitive to the needs of the group and allow the members to become responsible for its actions. She cannot impose her will on the group unless she wishes discussion to cease and parent involvement to lessen, but neither can she allow the discussion to move aimlessly for long periods of time. She must become a democratic leader, responsive and flexible, while maintaining her authority, if she wishes to best use the group process.

Although group discussion is an effective technique for working with parent groups, sometimes a "hands-on" approach is useful. Engaging parents in workshop activities utilizes nonverbal as well as verbal forms of learning. Teachers can lead parents into activities parallel to the children's to help them understand the learning potential of the activities. "Open science" or "new math" is often not well understood by parents unless they have experienced these forms of learning. Similarly, they might consider play activities or craft activities useless unless they can realize the outcomes of these activities are valuable learnings. Sylvia Newman describes a set of workshops and auxiliary activities that she instituted in a school program to help parents understand its content and to develop ways of extending the children's school learning in the home.[7]

Large group meetings are practical for expository purposes— the same speakers or films used for these can be used for small groups as well.

A group convened by a teacher frequently develops its own independent life. Projects undertaken by parents may develop for the education of the group's members or as a service to the school. Changes in the nature of the group sometimes require more time than a teacher can possibly give if she wishes to remain the group leader; in this event, she may help find another leader, either someone from the group itself or from outside. She may then continue working with the parent group as an adviser. Teachers can feel legitimate pride when groups they have started become autonomous as a result of their leadership.

The group process is a powerful force. Groups can be helpful and supportive, or aggressive and oppressive. It is important to use the group process carefully, ever cautious of any limitations in skills involving working with groups.

USING PUBLIC RELATIONS TECHNIQUES

Most of the ways of working with parents discussed here have dealt with face-to-face relations, but other types of relationships with family and community should also be established. A good school should have a

---

[7] Sylvia Newman, *Guidelines to Parent-Teacher Cooperation in Early Childhood Education* (Brooklyn, N.Y.: Book-Lab, Inc., 1971).

strong, though not necessarily polished program of public relations. Because the school belongs to the parents and the community, it must be responsive to them and communicate what happens in school.

A good public relations program includes maintaining a rapport with the community so that parents and others feel welcome in visiting the school. This should go beyond the annual "Open School Week" that has become an American tradition.

Displays, both in and out of school, are also helpful in telling the community what children are doing. Art work, the results of projects, tapes of children's songs and stories, and so forth can be tastefully organized and used to tell parents about the children's school experiences. Local merchants are often helpful in making space available for such displays and in other kinds of support. The local news media can tell the school's story to the public. Field trips, holiday celebrations, and other special events are often considered newsworthy by local media.

Teachers can carry on their own public relations activities through newsletters, notes sent home, and invitations to parents to participate in special events. All these need to be considered in a good public relations program.

While good public relations are important to a school, teachers need to be careful that their parent programs do not become *just* public relations programs. When parents are invited into school, when their opinions and advice about educational matters are solicited, when they are invited to become members of advisory committees and boards, they expect that their ideas will be considered worthy, that their contributions will be respected, and that they will be heard and responded to. At times, however, schools have established parent boards and advisory committees, often in order to meet requirements of state and federal programs, without making use of the products of these groups. Under these circumstances parents may feel that although they are involved in school activities, they are powerless. What seemed a program of parent involvement can easily be distorted into a public relations program. Such programs of public relations, however, can be counterproductive and lead to frustration and even anger on the part of parents.

WORKING WITH PARENTS: A TWO-WAY STREET

Orville Brim has identified the primary goals of outstanding parent education programs: making the parent more conscious of his role performance, making him more autonomous and creative, improving his inde-

pendent judgment, and increasing the rationality of his role performance.[8]
These goals are little different from those that have been suggested earlier
as appropriate for early childhood education. Just as we wish children to
become more autonomous, more creative, more aware, and more rational
in their judgments and performance, we wish these things also for parents.
The differences in developmental levels of adults and children require
that these general goals be manifest in different ways and in relation to
different social roles. To support parent autonomy, rationality, creativity,
and competence, the teacher must have a helping relationship with the
parent, rather than a prescribing one.

Too often teachers feel that a parent program is an opportunity to do something to the parents—somehow to change them. In reality,
a good parent program works differently, for the parents should also have
an opportunity to influence teachers and possibly to change the school.
A strong parent program can open new avenues of communication. When
there is no information there can be little criticism, but as parents become
more knowledgeable about the school, there will be more—hopefully
constructive to a large degree.

Actually, the judgments of parents can be considered another
source of information about the effectiveness of the program. Parent
grievances should be considered along with other data in making school
decisions, and teachers should always be receptive to parents' ideas and
criticisms. Changes should not be instituted merely as a way of placating
parents, however—teachers should feel strong enough in their professional role to be able to justify their acts in school and to stand by programs they believe to be sound professional practices.

SUGGESTED READING

BAILARD, VIRGINIA, and RUTH STRANG, *Parent-Teacher Conferences.* New
York: McGraw-Hill, 1964.

BEYER, EVELYN, *Sharing—A New Level in Teacher-Parent Relationship.*
Washington, D.C.: National Association for the Education of
Young Children, 1968.

D'EVELYN, KATHERINE E., *Individual Parent-Teacher Conferences.* New
York: Teachers College Press, 1952.

GINOTT, HAIM G., *Between Parent and Child.* New York: Macmillan, 1965.

---

[8] Orville G. Brim, Jr., *Education for Childrearing* (New York: The Free Press,
1965), p. 10.

HEFFERNAN, HELEN, and VIVIAN E. TODD, *Elementary Teacher's Guide to Working with Parents.* West Nyack, N.Y.: Parker Publishing Company, 1969.

HONIG, ALICE S., *Parent Involvement in Early Childhood Education.* Washington, D.C.: National Association for the Education of Young Children, 1975.

HYMES, J. L., *Effective Home-School Relations.* Englewood Cliffs, N.J.: Prentice-Hall, Inc., 1963.

LANE, MARY B., *Education for Parenting.* Washington, D.C.: National Association for the Education of Young Children, 1975.

NEWMAN, SYLVIA, *Guidelines to Parent-Teacher Cooperation in Early Childhood Education.* Brooklyn, N.Y.: Book-Lab, Inc., 1971.

PICKARTS, EVELYN, and JEAN FARGO, *Parent Education: Towards Parental Competence.* New York: Appleton-Century-Crofts, 1971.

James L. Hoot

CHAPTER SIXTEEN

EVALUATING EDUCATION IN THE EARLY YEARS

Teachers are often asked to make decisions about the selection of programs, program elements, or program materials. They are also asked to make judgments about children's ability to profit from educational programs, and the effects of these programs on them. Each of these decisions requires that the teacher be involved in the process of evaluation; that is, collecting information, making judgments based on this information, and developing ways of recording and communicating the results of these evaluations.

The process of evaluation needs to be considered separately from instruction, although the two are interrelated. Evaluation includes both the description and judgment of school programs and children's attainment. Central to this process is a consideration of the goals of education and whether they are achieved.

The achievement of program goals can only be assessed over a period of years. Evaluations of the Head Start and Follow-Through programs, and of similar programs described in chapter 12, often take years. Outcomes apparent at the completion of a program may not be apparent in later years, while other outcomes, not originally apparent, may become obvious later. In addition, the effects of an early childhood program may interact differently with the effects of programs at later levels of schooling.

Long-term evaluation, although complicated and expensive, is necessary, especially as an aid to policy decisions about whether to make early childhood programs available to children who might benefit from them, and selecting specific programs. Not only should the programs' effectiveness in achieving goals be evaluated in these long-term assessments, but the worthiness of the goals must be evaluated as well. As discussed in chapter 3, early childhood programs have a variety of goals, and not all programs agree about their goals.

For the classroom teacher, long-term evaluation has limited use. The teacher needs to act immediately, so she looks to evaluation as the basis for judging immediate past actions in order to plan immediate future actions—short-term goals. She believes the long-term goals will be met if the short-term goals are continually achieved. These short-term goals must, therefore, be related to the long-term goals, either logically or empirically. She may base her evaluation of short-term goals upon observation of children's actions, analysis of their products, or some form of testing.

Many types of goals can be stated for early childhood programs. Sometimes goals are so broadly framed that they are difficult to assess on either a long- or a short-term basis. Programs have as their goals, for example, "supporting the optimal development of the individual," or "developing the ability to live effectively as a contributing member of society." While such goals are worthy, they are often exceedingly difficult, if not impossible, to assess at any but the most subjective or inferential level. The achievement of such a goal as "living effectively as a contributing member of society" is not manifested in school. Nor can the optimal development of the individual be judged during an early childhood program, if ever.

Other programs state their goals in terms of understandings and appreciations that children will gain. Such goals cannot be assessed directly, so an inference must be made as to whether the child has achieved them. The teacher must judge success based upon observable actions that seem to indicate that the child has the understandings or appreciations.

Many programs state goals in specific behavioral terms that are immediately identifiable during the program's operation. Indeed, some psychologists feel that behavioral objectives based upon the requirements of later schooling are the only legitimate goals of education in the early years. The ability to make a specific judgment, categorize an object by a visible attribute, or manifest a particular skill such as reading a prescribed set of words, might constitute such a goal. Behavioral goals are attractive to those concerned with educational evaluation because their attainment is easily judged. Often a criterion level attainment is also stated, thus defining the judgments even more clearly. Information about attainment, which can be immediately supplied to the teacher, can be used to modify the program and improve its effectiveness. The availability of evaluation results is an attractive aspect of the use of behavioral goals.

Behavioral goals are not significant in themselves; they become significant because of their relationship to broader goals of education—often neither behavioral nor observable. In fact, trivial goals may be stated for a program simply because they can be observed directly and hence assessed easily. The relationship between these observable goals and the more significant nonbehavioral ones is inferential. A child may get the right answer to a math problem (a behavior), and we assume from this that he understands the mathematical process involved (an inference). The assumption may not be true, however, and unless we seek additional verification our evaluation can be faulty. The difference between behavioral and nonbehavioral goals may, in the final analysis, be one's conscious use of inference and belief.

The exclusive use of predetermined behavioral objectives to judge educational achievement tends to narrow education, for those activities that do not terminate in stated behavioral objectives may be considered unimportant or as interfering with the achievement of the objectives. Some educational activities terminate in a range of behaviors, some of which cannot be predetermined, rather than single behavioral patterns. Children who do not manifest behaviors predetermined by the evaluators may be incorrectly judged nonlearners. If a teacher wishes to elicit divergent thinking in children, she cannot predetermine acceptable responses. Another danger in the use of behavioral goals is the possibility that the teacher will focus on behaviors that, in the final analysis, may not be related to the program's ultimate goals. Although we wish children to learn to attend to verbal and visual stimuli in the classroom, translating this into an objective such as "the ability to sit still and attend to a story-reading session for a period of ten minutes" may only develop conforming behaviors. Young children can attend without sitting still. A legitimate criterion for attending is what the child gained from the story-reading rather than how little he moved.

Teachers, nevertheless, need to state goals in such a way that some information about the effectiveness of their programs can be collected. The goals of a program should be attainable during its duration, whether this be a day or an academic year. Though behavioral objectives may not be appropriate for all areas of the program, some degree of specificity should be in any statement of goals so that the teacher can determine attainment.[1] Much discussion of evaluation centers totally around pupil achievement, but other forms of evaluation should be the

---

[1] Teachers interested in improving the statement of objectives in behavioral terms might refer to Robert F. Mager, *Preparing Instructional Objectives* (Belmont, Ca.: Fearon Publishers, 1962).

teacher's responsibility as well. These include evaluating program models, program materials, and classroom program implementation.

EVALUATING PROGRAMS

Even at the nursery-school level, different programs exist. Some stress academic achievement, some social relations, and others combinations of goals. Judging and selecting a curriculum is a difficult task; the teacher may have neither the background nor the competence. Ideally, the teacher should participate in the evaluative process even when she does not have final responsibility for accepting or rejecting programs. She implements the programs and her judgment may be based upon sound practical considerations as well as theoretical background. Her intuitive knowledge of what children can use in a classroom is one source of information that can be brought to the evaluative process that the others involved may lack.

One way of preparing to select programs is to determine the program's value base and the values and program preferences of the teachers who must implement it. EPIE Report 42, discussed in chapter 3, presents a set of self-analysis checklists of views of human development and related early childhood program preferences that teachers can use to clarify where they stand and what kinds of programs they prefer.[2] After working through the checklist, they can seek information about available programs to determine if they can match programs and preferences.

Unfortunately, teachers often lack the necessary information to judge programs. Although it is possible to wade through lengthy descriptions of the many programs and materials available to cull the necessary information, few teachers can complete this cumbersome and time-consuming task. Often teachers' decisions about programs relate to selecting a program or textbook series in a single subject area. These decisions might be made by committees for each area independent of selections made in other areas. Too often teachers and curriculum committees are swayed by book salespersons or popular articles, adopting programs without comparing alternatives because they are familiar or have been endorsed by someone. Several sources of information about programs are available to teachers.

[2] EPIE Report 42, *Early Childhood Education: How to Select and Evaluate Materials* (New York: Education Products Information Exchange, Inc., 1972).

Robert Hillerich has suggested ideas for teachers to use in evaluating and selecting a reading program. He feels the teaching staff needs first to determine its philosophy and desired emphasis. They must develop guidelines so they know what to look for in a reading program. The entire staff should be involved in a consensus decision rather than a majority vote. Hillerich presents an evaluation form showing what a group could use to evaluate a kindergarten through second-grade reading program (see figure 16-1).[3]

Arthur Nichols and Anna Ochoa have presented criteria for selecting social studies textbooks for elementary schools that are relevant to the primary grades. They feel one must evaluate both the knowledge and the intellectual components of these books. In looking at the knowledge component, teachers should judge how social issues are handled, whether information is objectively presented, whether an interdisciplinary conceptual base is used, and whether the most recent scholarly findings are reflected in the material. The intellectual component refers to the development of intellectual skills in the book. Teachers need to determine if the book can serve as a base for inquiry, if higher-order questions are asked, if the book could serve as a basis for decision-making, and if the knowledge presented is related to the children's life span.[4]

A system for analyzing social science curricula has been developed by the Social Science Education Consortium. This system describes program attributes using the following categories:

1. *Descriptive characteristics*—The "nuts and bolts" of the curriculum
2. *Rationale and objectives*—Why the program was created and what the anticipated outcomes are
3. *Antecedent conditions*—The particular conditions under which the program might be successful
4. *Content*—The specific changes intended in the knowledge, attitudes, and behavior of the students
5. *Instructional theory and teaching strategies*—The underlying learning theory and teaching strategies, and their relationship in the program
6. *Overall judgments*—Evaluative judgments about the materials

[3] Robert L. Hillerich, "So You're Evaluating Reading Programs," *Elementary School Journal*, 75, no. 3 (December 1974), 172–82.
[4] Arthur S. Nichols and Anna Ochoa, "Evaluating Textbooks for Elementary Social Studies: Criteria for the Seventies," *Social Education*, 35, no. 3 (March 1971), 290–94ff.

Figure 16-1 Evaluation of Reading Program: Kindergarten–Grade 2

Evaluating teacher _____ Grade _____ 3=Very good; 2=Good; 1=Poor; 0=Omitted in program		Name of program			
Teacher edition	Philosophy clear (introduction)				
	Specific direction for skill teaching				
	Ease of use				
	Provision for individual differences				
Content	Interest appeal to children				
	Variety of types of reading				
Format	Physically clear and attractive				
Illustrations	Aesthetic appeal				
ADEQUACY OF SKILL DEVELOPMENT					
Readiness deals with letters and sounds in words, not just with general language development.					
Skills are learned through use, not just through memorizing rules.					
Child is shown how the skill is used in reading.					
Reading includes use of context, emphasis on reading for meaning.					
Suggested questions for discussion cover the inferential and critical as well as literal levels.					
Readiness for comprehension and study skills begins with these skills at the listening level.					
The child is taught a definite system for attacking an unknown word (mark *Yes* or *No* in each column).					
What is the system? (Put a check in proper columns.)					
Guess from context only.					
Remember the word from the introduction.					
Apply a rule or rules.					
Sound out the word.					
Use context and consonant-sound associations.					

From Robert L. Hillerich, "So You're Evaluating Reading Programs," *Elementary School Journal,* 75, no. 3 (December 1974), 179. Reprinted by permission of The University of Chicago Press.

These broad categories are further broken down in subcategories for analysis. The category of *antecedent conditions,* for example, includes subcategories relating to pupil characteristics, teaching capabilities, and community requirements, school requirements, and the articulation of requirements.[5]

An evaluation of social studies projects, programs, and materials, jointly developed by the National Council for Social Studies Curriculum Committee and the Social Science Education Consortium staff, can be found in a 1972 issue of *Social Education.* Each project is analyzed independently and comparisons are made among the programs, a half-dozen of which are appropriate for early childhood education.[6] This information about programs in social studies, along with the analysis of science programs developed by Barbara Waters[7] and discussed in chapter 8, can help provide teachers with a basis for evaluating and selecting programs in these curriculum areas.

Another source of information about educational programs and program components is the Education Products Information Exchange (EPIE). The Exchange evaluates programs and educational products.[8] Some of their reports have been referred to in this chapter and elsewhere in the text.

Information about educational programs can also be requested from the Educational Resources Information Centers. These ERIC Centers, supported by the United States Office of Education, collect information about educational programs in a particular area. Although the information available might not be as systematically developed as the ones provided by SSEC, they still can be a useful resource. Current ERIC clearinghouses are listed below.

ERIC CLEARINGHOUSES

Career Education
Center for Vocational Education
Ohio State University
1960 Kenny Road
Columbus, Ohio 43210

Counseling and Personnel Services
The University of Michigan
School of Education Building,
Room 2108
East University & South
University Streets
Ann Arbor, Mich. 48104

---

[5] W. William Stevens and William Fetsko, "A Curriculum Analysis System," *Social Science Education Consortium Newsletter,* no. 4 (February 1968), 1–4.

[6] "Evaluation of Curriculum Projects, Programs and Materials," *Social Education,* 36, no. 7 (November 1972).

[7] Barbara S. Waters, *Science Can Be Elementary: Action Programs for K–3* (New York: Citation Press, 1973).

[8] EPIE, P.O. Box 2379, Grand Central Station, New York, N.Y. 10017.

Educational Management
University of Oregon
Eugene, Ore. 97403

Handicapped and Gifted
Council on Exceptional Children
1920 Association Drive
Reston, Va. 22091

Higher Education
George Washington University
1 Dupont Circle, Suite 630
Washington, D.C. 20036

Information Resources
School of Education
SCRDT
Stanford University
Stanford, Ca. 94305

Junior Colleges
University of California
96 Powell Library
Los Angeles, Ca. 90024

Language and Linguistics
Center for Applied Linguistics
1611 North Kent Street
Arlington, Va. 22209

Reading and Communication Skills
National Council of Teachers of
English
1111 Kenyon Road
Urbana, Ill. 61801

Rural Education and Small Schools
New Mexico State University
Box 3AP
Las Cruces, N.M. 88003

*Science, Mathematics, and
Environmental Education*
Ohio State University
1800 Cannon Drive
400 Lincoln Tower
Columbus, Ohio 43210

*Social Studies/Social Science
Education*
855 Broadway
Boulder, Colo. 80302

Teacher Education
1 Dupont Circle, N.W.
Suite 616
Washington, D.C. 20036

Tests, Measurement, and Evaluation
Educational Testing Service
Princeton, N.J. 08540

Urban Education
Teachers College
Box 40
Columbia University
525 W. 120th Street
New York, N.Y. 10027

Early Childhood Education
ERIC/ECE
University of Illinois
805 West Pennsylvania Ave.
Urbana, Ill. 61801

Additional information about early childhood education can be sought from the following organizations:

Association for Childhood Education International
3615 Wisconsin Avenue, N.W.
Washington, D.C. 20016
American Montessori Society, Inc.
175 Fifth Avenue
New York, N.Y. 10010

Black Child Development Institute, Inc.
1463 Rhode Island Avenue, N.W.
Washington, D.C. 20005
Council for Exceptional Children
1920 Association Drive
Reston, Va. 22091
Child Welfare League of America, Inc.
67 Irving Place
New York, N.Y. 10010
Day Care and Child Development Council of America, Inc.
622 14th Street, N.W.
Washington, D.C. 20005
National Association for the Education of Young Children
1834 Connecticut Avenue, N.W.
Washington, D.C. 20009
National Council of Organizations for Children and Youth
1910 K Street, N.W.
Washington, D.C. 20006
Parent Cooperative Preschool International
9111 Alton Parkway
Silver Springs, Md. 20910
Southern Association for Children Under Six
Box 5403 Brady Station
Little Rock, Ark. 72205

Teachers might also wish to communicate directly with schools and agencies developing innovative programs as well as with Head Start and Follow-Through programs. Many of these are reported in various education journals and at educational conferences.

EVALUATING CLASSROOMS

The selection of a program represents the beginning of the educational sequence for teachers. It is a promise of learning activities to be. The teacher must see that the promise is fulfilled and that it achieves its desired results. The history of curriculum reform is full of instances where programs in their implementation have differed significantly from the original program intent. By assessing her classroom, the teacher will be able to judge if she is being true to her promise.

A number of observational schemes are available to monitor and assess classroom practices. Most of these are designed for research purposes and require an outside observer—a luxury seldom available to classroom teachers. However, there are some simple techniques that teachers can use to gather information about their own classrooms. They can provide limited but reliable information that can be used to improve educational opportunities for children. Two examples of such techniques follow.

In chapter 13, reference was made to classroom dimensions identified by Elizabeth Jones.[9] Using the dimensions of hard/soft, open/ closed, simple/complex, intrusion/seclusion, and high mobility/low mobility, a teacher can describe the physical dimensions of a classroom and determine if it approximates the setting she desires to create for children. Once she records the dimensions of her classroom, she can modify the room systematically to make it closer to her ideal.

A teacher can also survey the content of the activities she is offering. An activities checklist can be helpful for this form of evaluation.[10] Figure 16-2, for example, contains a checklist of oral language activities that was developed from the topical coverage in chapter 4. A teacher can tally activities that are provided each day in each category and sum these tallies at the end of a week. By comparing the sum for each set of activities, she can determine the breadth of offerings she has provided. Thus she may find that although she has read many stories, she has ignored poetry during one week. She may find that she held many discussions but few conversations with individual children. There is no best balance of activities, but such a checklist can help a teacher decide if her program does contain the balance of activities she intended. Similar checklists can be developed for other content areas and used periodically to provide teachers with implementation feedback.

EVALUATING TEACHING

By evaluating programs and settings the teacher is evaluating the *preactive* aspects of teaching—that is, the planning and preparation activities. It is relatively easy to collect and assess this information. It is more difficult, though, for a teacher to evaluate the *interactive* aspects of teaching—the behavior that takes place in contact with the children. For one thing, it is difficult for a teacher to observe herself, and there is seldom anyone else available for the task. Being objective and honest about one's

---

[9] Elizabeth Jones, *Dimensions of Teaching-Learning Environments* (Pasadena, Ca.: Pacific Oaks College, n.d.), pp. 1–19.
[10] I am indebted to Mary Jensen, graduate teaching assistant at the University of Illinois, for this suggestion.

Figure 16-2 Language Activity Checklist

Teacher _____ Grade ____ Dates _____

Place a tally mark (/) in each category for each activity noted. At the end of the week enter the sum of the tallies in the adjacent box.

Expressive Oral Language Activities

Activity	Tally	Total
Dramatic play		
Conversations		
Discussion sessions		
Creative dramatics		
Puppetry		
Children's storytelling		

Receptive Oral Language Activities

Telling stories		
Reading stories		
Reading poetry		
Allowing book browsing		
Using A-V aids		
Using normal daily occurrences, e.g.,		
1. _____		
2. _____		
3. _____		
Other activities. Specify:		
1. _____		
2. _____		
3. _____		

own behavior is also a problem. And yet teachers need to become aware of their actions and the consequences if they are to improve their teaching.

A number of techniques have been used to analyze and assess teacher behavior. Generally, they require that observations be collected by an observer or through videotaping. The teacher can then analyze the records of these observations.

Probably most practical for the average classroom teacher who wishes to evaluate her own teaching is some nonsystematic way of observing or recalling classroom incidents and analyzing them in relation to pupils' responses. A teacher might be able to sit alone at noon or at the end of the school day and write what she could recall. If, for example, she wishes to focus on a discussion session, she could try to write her questions and comments as accurately as possible. She can then analyze her questions a number of ways. Were they open-ended, requiring divergent responses from children, or closed, demanding a single convergent response? Did the questions elicit answers requiring higher-order thought processes, like analysis or criticism, or lower-order thought processes, like recall? Did her responses to children tease out additional information or did they limit discussion? Was she supportive of their contributions or did she "cut children?" Were her responses personal or stereotyped?

With such an analysis, a teacher is in a better position to determine if her behavior with children is consistent with the way she wishes to be. She knows if she should continue in exactly the same manner or change her performance. She can then plan for changes, and even rehearse them in preparation for the next day.

In such a way, a teacher can begin to become aware of herself in the classroom, and, over time, cover all areas of teaching and analyze her relationships with all the children. With continued self-reflection, she can become more sensitive to their needs and more aware of how to serve them appropriately.

EVALUATING CHILDREN

In evaluating children, we can identify two basic concerns: the *ability* of children to benefit from instructional experiences, and the *degree* to which they benefit. The former leads to a judgment about readiness for learning, the latter about learning outcomes. In either case, the teacher makes a judgment based upon observations of a child's behavior. If we want to judge what children can do, the best way is to observe everything they do. Observational data-gathering expeditions are possible and can yield a great amount of information, but they are cumbersome, time-consuming and expensive, greatly limiting teaching time.[11]

Instead, a teacher can sample children's behavior and products and thus generalize about readiness and achievement. This sampling procedure resembles that used by researchers and public opinion pollsters and, if properly conducted, can provide highly accurate information. To have confidence in this sample, the teacher must be sure that it is representative of the total population of possible products and behaviors; to insure representativeness, she must adopt a systematic procedure.

One systematic procedure is to administer a test with a select number of items to which a child can respond. These items are a sample drawn from a larger number of possible items. The teacher should select widely from all possible learnings to assure representativeness. Tests are useful because the same behaviors are sampled in all the children, and this not only provides information about what each child has learned, but also allows the teacher to make comparisons. Such comparisons can be very dangerous, however, unless they are carefully made.

Classroom tests are not necessarily written examinations. A teacher might administer a test to a group of nursery-school children by taking each child aside and asking a set of standard questions. She can also use standardized procedures, developed and refined through application to a large population of children.

Other ways of sampling behavior do not attempt to elicit comparable samples from each child. Observing classroom behavior and collecting samples of children's products are ways of gathering information. Each technique generates a different kind of information and can reliably provide essentially similar data when used on different occasions or by different persons. These techniques must also be valid; they should collect the kind of information that the teacher purports they collect.

Finally, any method the teacher uses to collect information about the children should be practical. It should not be too time-consuming to use in the classroom, or require equipment not generally available—simple techniques are best. Teachers are busy people who have much more to do than just evaluating children and programs.

Too often teachers consider evaluation the administration of tests at the end of the school year or at the end of a unit of work. The results of such tests may clearly summarize what children have learned during the preceding period, and provide an important source of informa-

---

[11] See Roger B. Barker and Herbert F. Wright, *One Boy's Day* (New York: Harper & Row, 1951).

tion for the next teacher. However, the teacher must use other means of gathering evaluative information as an aid to her instruction.

Primary classroom teachers often use informal inventory techniques to assess a child's ability to read or to perform computational skills; such inventories provide them with a baseline from which to begin instruction. Some teachers also administer readiness or developmental tests at the beginning of kindergarten or first grade to provide a similar baseline for planning.

The educational evaluation of children now often begins prior to their entrance into school. As states have mandated preschool programs for handicapped children, procedures to register and screen them have been established. Since parents are not required to register their children for these programs or to have them screened, simple procedures acceptable to parents have had to be developed. R. Reid Zehrbach describes such a screening procedure that utilizes students, paraprofessionals, and volunteers as well as trained professionals. Parents are invited to bring their children into centers for screening of visual and auditory acuity, speech articulation, and social-emotional, cognitive, and physical levels. As problems are identified, the children are rescreened; then, if necessary, specific evaluation and in-depth studies are made. The results of these procedures are discussed with parents and referred to available services to help those children needing them. The goal of such early identification is to help handicapped children earlier than is normally done and thus improve their chances of being successfully integrated into regular school classes later.[12]

Administering tests to young children has certain inherent pitfalls. They may be unfamiliar with testing procedures and not know appropriate response behavior, making test results invalid. In addition, tests of young children often suffer from low reliability; it may be well to postpone tests until they have been in school long enough to have been acculturated.

A teacher may use ongoing assessment procedures as an aid to planning; she may assess her program at the end of each day in order to plan activities for the following day. Most often, she makes the assessment on a "gut level," evaluating on whether the day went well or poorly. The most outstanding incidents may be recalled and recorded, whether representative or not. Improvement of evaluation techniques and planning are implemented by the use of systematic means of collecting and recording information.

The teacher needs a broad repertoire of techniques for evalu-

---

[12] R. Reid Zehrbach, "Determining a Preschool Handicapped Population," *Exceptional Children*, 42, no. 2 (October 1975), 76–83.

ation. She should understand the uses of each and apply the appropriate ones for each occasion and need. Both standardized and nonstandardized tools should be available to her. A number of standardized tests, some designed to be administered to a group, others to individuals, are frequently used in early childhood:

> *Basic Concept Inventory* (Chicago: Follett, 1968).
>
> *Illinois Test of Psycholinguistic Abilities* (Urbana, Ill.: University of Illinois Press, 1970).
>
> *Metropolitan Readiness Tests* (New York: Harcourt Brace Jovanovich, 1969).
>
> *Peabody Picture Vocabulary Test* (Minneapolis: American Guidance Service, 1970).
>
> *Preschool Inventory* (Princeton, N.J.: Educational Testing Service, 1970).
>
> *Stanford-Binet Intelligence Scale* (Boston: Houghton Mifflin, 1973).
>
> *Wechsler Preschool and Primary Scale of Intelligence* (New York: Psychological Corp., 1967).

Other tests appropriate for young children are described in Oscar Buros, *Tests in Print,* II (Highland Park, N.J.: Gryphon Press, 1974).

These tests become standardized by being administered to a sample population of children in the United States. The results are then analyzed and norms are developed. Judgments can then be made about how a child's score compares to those of the standardizing group. If the children in a particular class are significantly different from the standard population, these judgments can become distorted. This is true of differences in geography, ethnic background, and socioeconomic status, as well as of differences in other attributes. In chapter 13, the discussion of intelligence tests demonstrated how inappropriate use of possibly inappropriate tests can lead to biased identification of children as retarded and improper placement of them in classes for the retarded. In addition, standardized achievement tests may not properly sample the gains of a group of children who are being taught something other than a standard curriculum. Thus, standardized testing can play a role in maintaining existing programs since achievement of novel programs cannot be assessed with these instruments. Other weaknesses of standardized achievement and intelligence tests have led to a range of criticisms in the field.[13] Despite

---

[13] For extensive discussions of these criticisms, see Vito Perrone, Coordinator, *Testing and Evaluation: New Views* (Washington, D.C.: Association for Childhood Education International, 1975); "I.Q.: The Myth of Measurability," *National Elementary Principal,* 54, no. 4 (March/April

this, these tests tend to be heavily used in school districts throughout the nation as well as in research and evaluation projects.

The tests available for use in the early years of schooling can generally be categorized into developmental, intelligence, readiness, and achievement tests. Developmental tests are most often given to very young children. Intelligence tests are usually used to determine the level of general intellectual behavior. Readiness tests are specific to one or more areas of learning for which predictions are made, and items on these tests may be more sensitive to specific instruction. The term readiness is generally conceived as the state in which a child can benefit from instruction—this includes his maturational state, achievement of prior learnings, and motivation for learning. Most tests used to determine readiness assess both maturation and prior learning. The assessment of motivation is made informally by the teacher.

INTELLIGENCE TESTS

Developmental tests are used to determine the degree of maturation. Observation of a child's physical characteristics, such as body proportions or development of the wrist bone, can be used to assess maturation. Most tests, however, consist of items that require children's performance. Frances L. Ilg and Louise Bates Ames's book, *School Readiness,* rev. ed. (New York: Harper & Row, 1972), contains a series of tasks for children to perform. From an analysis of a child's performance on these tasks, a teacher might determine if he is mature enough to profit from school instruction. The tasks described in many of Jean Piaget's reports may also be considered a series of developmental tests: these have been used primarily to determine level of intellectual development.

The information from developmental tests is useful in deciding whether a child is ready for a particular school experience. However, teachers should be careful not to exclude children from formal educational experiences because of lack of maturation. Human development is highly plastic and a child's experiences tend to modify his development. Rather than exclusion, what may be needed are differentiated educational opportunities.

DEVELOPMENTAL TESTS

Intelligence tests contain sets of tasks that require using learned skills for adequate performance at specific levels. The assumption under-

---

1975), entire issue; and "The Scoring of Children: Standardized Testing in America," *National Elementary Principal,* 55, no. 6 (July/August 1975), entire issue.

lying them is that if all children have equal opportunities to learn these skills, the differences in levels of performance are the results of differences in inherent ability. Though it is evident that all children do not have the same inherent abilities, it is equally evident that many do not have the same opportunities to learn the skills sampled in intelligence tests. These tests generally seem to favor children of white, middle-class background and less adequately sample the inherent abilities of minority-group children.

Intelligence tests were originally designed to provide a way of predicting the academic achievement of children. Most intelligence tests can predict academic performance well when there is no significant change in the child's educational circumstances. Evidence suggests that when these circumstances are varied, predictive ability does not hold up as well. Moving children with low IQ levels from an educationally dull to an educationally stimulating environment may not only increase educational performance but also lead to increases in scores on intelligence tests.

Significant decisions about a child's education are often based upon the results of the intelligence tests administered when he is young. For this reason, there are serious dangers in using these tests. Children can be penalized for not being able to score well because they have been denied the opportunity to learn those things sampled in the test. Although intelligence tests do not create discrimination, their careless use can perpetuate unequal educational practices in schools. Improper use can lead to the creation of a cycle of educational disadvantagement from which a child cannot escape, for the opportunity that would allow him to excel in later tests is denied *because* he does not excel in the test.

READINESS TESTS

Readiness tests are used to assess the child's ability to profit from instruction, primarily in making judgments about beginning reading instruction. These tests are actually early achievement tests. They can also be used for diagnostic purposes.

In addition to using formal tests, teachers can also use a range of informal techniques for determining the appropriateness of planned learning experiences for children. Thus, an informal assessment of reading readiness would collect information on the child's language ability and his desire to learn to read, as well as the information on the readiness checklist presented in chapter 5. Observations of children in class, such as those described later, can produce information about readiness as well as achievement. Since these two concepts are so related, any information about a child's present achievement also provides information about his predisposition for further learning.

ASSESSING ACHIEVEMENT

In making judgments about what a child has learned, the teacher uses many techniques and instruments, which include the formal procedures of testing as well as the less formal procedures of observing behavior and collecting products.

ACHIEVEMENT TESTS

Standardized achievement tests are used to assess a child's or class's achievement in the areas of academic learning. Such tests are designed for administration at the primary grades or beyond. They are available for different curricular areas, and teachers may select a full battery of tests or administer only a single subtest.

In interpreting achievement tests, teachers should be aware that they do not sample the total curriculum offerings of the school but are limited to academic skills. Other areas of learning—of equal importance—may not be sampled. Teachers need to insure that inappropriate use of test results does not distort the program offerings.

In interpreting tests, teachers must know the meaning of the concept *grade level*. The achievement test, like the intelligence test, is generally standardized by being administered to a sample group of children representing the total range of children at each level nationally. This population includes children from rural and urban areas, different socioeconomic levels, and all geographic areas. The scores are averaged to create a grade-level norm, with half the test scores falling above the norm and half below. Within the standardizing population, one can often find differences in average test scores of subgroups identifiable by geographic area, degree of urbanization, and socioeconomic status.

Grade-level norms are useful only to the degree that the population tested reflects the standardized population. For any class of children that differs from that population, the norms become less meaningful as a standard. Schools often find that it is useful to establish their own norms rather than use standardized norms.

It is also important to note that norms are descriptive of a population at a particular time. They need not set expectation. It is possible for every group to exceed the norms on almost every achievement test under optimal learning conditions, assuming this achievement is the teacher's goal.

Although standardized tests are useful, many times nonstandardized means are more appropriate. Teachers should develop many formal and informal techniques to sample children's learning systematically. Standardized tests may provide a way of assessing learning and of comparing a single class of children to a large population of children, but nonstandardized methods can provide process data that can be used to improve instruction. A number of children might get the same mathematics item wrong on a particular test. One child's error could result from faulty computation, another's because he did not understand the concept involved, while a third might simply have been careless. A teacher analyzing test errors would recommend different activities for each child. If evaluation is used as a diagnostic tool in planning, this type of data collection becomes invaluable. Nonstandardized means of data collection include teacher-developed tests, observational techniques, checklists, rating scales, sociometric techniques, and collections of children's products.

TEACHER-DEVELOPED TESTS

Teachers can create their own tests when they wish to collect a comparable sample of behavior from all the children in the class. The teacher must carefully construct the test to insure that the desired behavior is being elicited, and be sure that the items are representative of those she wishes to evaluate. Although she may not formally determine the validity and reliability of each test she develops, she should keep the attributes of a good test in mind.

A test may be written and administered to all children at one time, or oral and administered individually. A teacher who wishes to evaluate a field trip may develop a list of questions to ask each child independently, while showing pictures of objects as stimuli to elicit responses. Using the same questions, she will draw a comparable sample of knowledge from each child.

Although similar questions might be asked of a group, the teacher could not be sure if a child's response was the result of the trip experience or of hearing other children's responses. Informal test situations allow her to know about all the children, not just the ones who continually volunteer verbal responses.

OBSERVATIONAL TECHNIQUES

Teachers may take time at the end of a day to record the significant occurrences. They can note what happened to individual children or individual problems that arose. Such anecdotal records are helpful in thinking through a school day and in planning for future activities, but relying on such records alone can be dangerous. Human minds tend to be forgetful, and memory is selective. It is the extraordinary, rather than the normal, that is etched upon teachers' memories, and an unrepresentative picture of a child's behavior may result. The use of running records—on-the-spot observations of occurrences—is far superior in recreating a true picture of the day. Teachers should learn techniques for taking running records.[14]

Direct observation of children's behavior has the advantage of giving teachers clues about the process of their learning. A careful recording of the interactions between a child and other children or between a child and a set of instructional materials can provide the basis for judgments about how a child is thinking or feeling. The results of such observations can be compared over time to judge changes in behavior for individual children.

Observing and recording children's actions is time-consuming, yet this sort of record provides an important source of information upon which to build and evaluate programs. Teachers should develop ways that are practical, take up little time, and still provide an adequate picture of children's behavior.

One way to do this is to systematically sample behavior: select children in some order and keep a running record of each child for a few minutes a day, or observe two or three children engaged in representative activities on any one day. These records should be descriptive. The teacher may then note interpretations and comments on behavior separately. In this way she will always be able to return to the source of her judgments, for she may want to reinterpret a child's behavior as she becomes more familiar with him.

OBSERVATIONAL SCALES AND CHECKLISTS

When teachers are concerned about specific behaviors, they can use less descriptive forms of observation. A teacher who wishes to study aggressive behavior in her classroom may simply use a frequency tally, recording a mark every time an aggressive act is observed. If these are identified by the actual time they occurred or by the activity with which they were related, the teacher has this information in addition to the amount of aggressive behavior occurring. A similar checklist could be used to determine the frequency of other kinds of behavior, such as helping behavior or creative activity.

Teachers might wish to determine the kinds of materials used and the frequency with which children become involved in particular

[14] See Dorothy H. Cohen and Virginia Stern, *Observing and Recording the Behavior of Young Children* (New York: Teachers College Press, 1958).

Figure 16-3 Coded Teacher Observations of Children's Activities

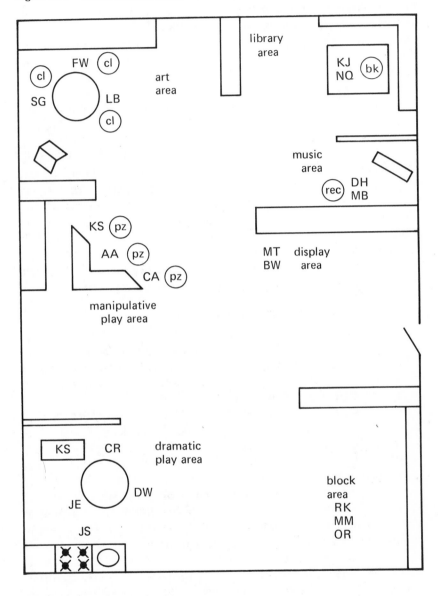

bk   looking at books
cl   clay work
pz   working puzzles
rec   listening to records

learning centers during an activity period. Creating a code with a symbol for each activity and systematically recording each child's placement and activity at intervals (for example, five minutes into the period, halfway through, and five minutes before the period ends) will yield that information (see figure 16-3). Such a chart will also provide the teacher with sociometric information since children in close proximity to one another are often interacting.

The children can assume responsibility for some of the recording, too. If a checklist is available for each activity, they can mark each time they participate.

The teacher can devise a range of simple scales and checklists, depending upon what kind of information she wishes to observe and how she will use it. Teachers can also develop checklists to characterize children's development, social relationships, activity patterns, or any other set of attributes. Chapter 5 contains a useful reading-readiness checklist. Other checklists might involve mathematics learning, self-help skills, and social skills as suggested in figure 16-4. Such information becomes invaluable in planning programs, making decisions about the children, and reporting a child's school experiences to his parent.

SOCIOMETRIC TECHNIQUES

Although teachers are concerned with children's academic achievement, they should also be concerned with social behavior, for social goals are important in education as well. To assess this, teachers can use sociometric techniques.

A simple way of determining the social structure of the class is to ask each child a set of questions to elicit his choice of friends. Such questions as "Whom would you like to play with outside?" "Whom would you like to have sit near you at snack time?" or "Whom would you like to invite home after school?" might be used at the nursery or kindergarten levels. Appropriate questions for older children can be developed as well.

The children's responses to the questions can be plotted on a chart, which will eventually determine the most popular and least popular children and what groupings of friendships exist in the class.

Children's social relationships are not as stable as those of adults. Sociometric techniques, therefore, provide less reliable information about children. Although they may be able to respond to questions about activity mates, best friends can easily change from day to day. Teachers need to collect a number of such observations over a period of time, looking for evidence of stable relationships and shifts that might occur as a result of program changes.

Figure 16-4 Skills Checklist

	Rating	Comments
Name of child _____ Date _____		
Self Care Skills		
Zippers clothes		
Matches shoes to feet		
Ties laces		
Puts on snowsuit alone		
Washes hands properly		
Cleanup Skills		
Washes paint brushes clean		
Sponges tables clean		
Puts materials back in proper order		
Sweeps floor if needed		
Puts apron away properly		
Social Skills		
Shows leadership		
Participates in group activities		
Takes turns		
Follows classroom rules		
Physical Skills		
Is well coordinated		
Can walk a balance beam		
Can hop		
Can skip		
Climbs well		
Can draw a straight line		
Can use scissors well		
Can use a stapler		
Can use a hole puncher		
Can use a paint brush		
Can hammer a nail in straight		
Can saw a straight cut		

Rate each child on a scale from 1 to 5

1 Shows high level of performance consistently
2 Shows good performance, not consistent
3 Shows fair performance, inconsistent
4 Performs poorly and erratically
5 Cannot perform

COLLECTING PUPIL PRODUCTS

Another way of sampling the children's learning in the classroom is to systematically collect the products of their work: drawings and paintings, stories and mathematics work, and reports. Such a cumulative collection allows the teacher to review progress and judge their work at any point in time. The collection of children's products must be systematic; the great temptation is to allow them to carry each product home, leaving the teacher without an important data source. A painting or a story can be periodically selected to keep in school, and if children are told why materials are being collected they will usually not resist. Work with name, date, and circumstance of production helps; if the teacher uses a portfolio for each child, storage problems are minimized.

Some products are hard to collect. A clay bowl will not store in a portfolio, and a child's block construction cannot be saved. A verbal production disappears immediately. Works of this kind can be described or collected on tape or film. These collections are invaluable in assessing children's progress throughout the year and demonstrating it to parents.

JUDGING CHILDREN

The collection of data is only one step in the process of evaluation. The teacher must interpret data and judge them. Finally, plans for action may result from these interpretations.

Teachers use evaluation data to make decisions about children's programs. If the children have achieved the goals of a study unit, the teacher can confidently move on to new work. If they have not, she may wish to plan some special activities or repeat activities. If children do use materials provided, then she may need to modify her program. The constant feedback from the information collected tells the teacher how successful her planning has been and provides clues for the introduction of new program elements.

The information collected on each child can also provide the basis for differentiated educational activities. As the teacher becomes aware of each child's skills, abilities, interests, and behavior patterns, she can plan with this in mind. Programming then becomes more meaningful and closer to the needs of the particular children in a class. Pacing is one dimension of differential programming that can grow out of continued evaluation; other forms can also accrue.

The results of evaluation are often shared with a number of persons. The teacher may be asked to communicate them to future teachers of her students, to ancillary personnel in the school, to the school principal, and to parents. The need for communication and for later reference requires that the teacher use some record-keeping system. Many schools maintain cumulative record folders on children, and teachers may supplement these with their own records. A good record-keeping system is one in which significant information may be found easily.

MAINTAINING CLASSROOM RECORDS

In addition to the cumulative record folder, teachers keep a variety of records on the children that may not necessarily follow them to later classes. Records of daily attendance are generally required, although the form varies among schools. New teachers should become quickly familiar with the procedures in their schools—some schools require that all absences be accounted for, or children may have to submit a release from a physician before entering school after certain illnesses. Even if the child is absent for a short time, it is wise for a teacher to contact the family. Such absences may signal family crisis. At times, families may even move from a community without notifying the school. Brief contact with the family helps the teacher understand the reasons for absence and may provide clues to help her or the child.

As mentioned earlier, the teacher often has the children tally their participation in specific activities. She may wish to transfer the results of the tally to a more compact form later.

The results of teacher's observations are also an important record of the child's activities. Most observations are short and can easily fit on one or two 5″ × 8″ cards. Organizing these in a card file allows the teacher to leaf through quickly to review her understanding of the child.

Regular recording of evaluation results will insure that the teacher has the information available that she will later need. How records are kept is determined by their later use. A review of records may show that a teacher has not attended closely to a child or a group for a period of time. Knowing this, she can focus on these children, thus insuring a continued familiarity with all of the children over the year.

Records are important not only for the teacher's decision making but also as a way of justifying their decisions to others. Because teaching is a public trust, teachers are being called upon more and more to justify their professional acts. Demands may come from supervisors or from the parents and the community the school serves. Although they may feel a need to guard their professional roles, teachers, as all other professionals, are accountable. The ability to document the sources of decisions and judgments is a requirement that the public can make on the professional, and teachers must be prepared to meet this requirement.

REPORTING TO PARENTS

Parents are interested in varying degrees in the progress of their children in school. These contacts represent only one part of the teacher's relationship with parents, but they are important and require the utmost in care and honesty.

An ideal report to a parent should be easy to devise, require a minimum of time and effort to administer, yet be comprehensive. It should communicate clearly and unequivocally the child's behavior and learning in school without being burdensome to read or requiring the parent's comprehension of professional language.

These requirements are easier stated than achieved; it is difficult to communicate clearly when the teacher and the parent may have different referents for the same words. The teacher has a hard time being fully descriptive when she must report on thirty or more children several times during the year. And it is difficult to pinpoint progress without seeming unnecessarily judgmental.

Most reporting systems in practice are the result of compromise. They are systems not to difficult to administer that communicate clearly. Teachers seem unsatisfied with almost all reporting systems, however. Perhaps there is no ideal system. Most schools tend to use report cards, descriptive letters to parents, or parent conferences as ways of reporting; often these are used in some combination.

REPORT CARDS

Many primary classes and kindergartens use report cards as one way of reporting. These cards are relatively simple to complete and communicate fairly well to parents. A report card may contain lines representing various areas of pupil achievement, such as reading and writing. Schools sometimes also include certain behavior characteristics or study habits.

Symbols are often used to report a child's achievement, such as letter grades *A* to *D* or *E,* or *U* for unsatisfactory and *S* for satisfactory achievement. Additional symbols for improvement or high achievement can also be used.

Though it is simple to assign a letter grade, it is often difficult to determine exactly what it communicates. If there are grade-level standards of performance expected of every child in the school, then performance level is fairly well communicated by the report card. It is difficult to know, however, if a child is working at his expected capacity, above it, or below it. If children are graded according to the teacher's estimate of their capability, then the letter or symbol will mean something different for each child and the common base in communication breaks down.

Despite the limitations of report cards, both parents and teachers often report that they like to use them, possibly a result of the security built by years of tradition. However, schools frequently find that they must augment this type of communication. Sometimes supplementary checklists can help elaborate on the content of a report card.

DESCRIPTIVE LETTERS

A report card can communicate a child's level of performance; it cannot communicate the qualitative aspects of school work, however. Teachers may use descriptive letters to tell parents more about the quality and content of the child's work. A letter can often provide a fuller picture for the parent. It might contain information about the child's learning style, about the books he has read, the materials he has used, or the nature of his interactions with others. It can also communicate the nature of the child's experiences in school, something that the parents of uncommunicative children may not know. Teachers may write individual letters about each child. Too often they run out of descriptive phrases for each child, however, and these letters become stereotyped in their descriptions. Some teachers duplicate a single letter telling the parents what the class as a whole has done during the year, supplementing this with individual reports through report cards or conferences.

PARENT CONFERENCES

The most communicative (but also the most time-consuming) means of reporting is the parent conference. In a conference, parent and teacher can sit face-to-face and discuss mutual concerns about the child. Any misunderstandings can be instantly corrected, and the teacher has immediate feedback as to the quality of the communication.

Parent conferences should be planned carefully. The teacher can make a list of concerns as an outline of items to be covered in the conference. Parents bring up their concerns as well. If the teacher has kept careful records, these will prove invaluable in the conference. Observations can be shared, test result ratings and checklists can be referred to, and pupil products can be shown to parents to demonstrate growth over the school year. It is useful to keep a record of a parent conference, noting the topics discussed, the reactions of parents, and any procedures that should follow up the conference, such as additional observation or communication.

Parent conferences are often used at the nursery and kindergarten level because of the lack of grade-level standards upon which to base a grade symbol. This requires that descriptive reporting take place. Conferences can be equally useful at every level of education, however, and in many cases the best communication takes place through a combination of techniques.

Reporting is really only one consequence of a system of evaluation. The major impact of the teacher's evaluation is in the improvement of the educational experience of each child. By knowing her children and the results of classroom activities of each individual, the teacher can return to her planning, continuing activities that have proved successful, replacing unsuccessful ones with new activities, and continuing to extend the learning opportunities of the children in her class. A realistic picture of classroom activities and their consequences can help her provide continually richer educational opportunities to children during their early years in school.

SUGGESTED READING

ALMY, MILLIE, *Ways of Studying Children.* New York: Columbia University Press, 1959.

BUROS, OSCAR K., *Tests in Print II.* Highland Park, N.J.: Gryphon Press, 1974.

COHEN, DOROTHY, and VIRGINIA STERN, *Observing and Recording the Behavior of Young Children.* New York: Teachers College Press, 1958.

DEAN, JOAN, *Recording Children's Progress.* New York: Citation Press, 1972.

GAGE, N. L., ed., *Handbook of Research on Teaching.* Chicago: Rand McNally, 1963.

INDEX